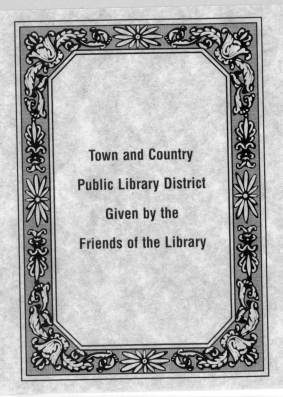

Town and Country

Public Library District

Given by the

Friends of the Library

THE AFRICAN AMERICANS

HENRY LOUIS GATES, JR., AND DONALD YACOVONE

THE AFRICAN AMERICANS

MANY RIVERS TO CROSS

Copyright © 2013 by Henry Louis Gates, Jr., and Donald Yacovone

Published in the United States by: SmileyBooks • www.SmileyBooks.com
Distributed in the United States by: Hay House, Inc.: www.hayhouse.com® • *Published and distributed in Australia by:*
Hay House Australia Pty. Ltd.: www.hayhouse.com.au • *Published and distributed in the United Kingdom by:*
Hay House UK, Ltd.: www.hayhouse.co.uk • *Published and distributed in the Republic of South Africa by:*
Hay House SA (Pty), Ltd.: www.hayhouse.co.za • *Distributed in Canada by:* Raincoast: www.raincoast.com
Published in India by: Hay House Publishers India: www.hayhouse.co.in

Design: Vertigo Design NYC
Indexer: Hazel Abbul
Produced by Stonesong Press, LLC

LIBRARY OF CONGRESS CATALOGING-IN-PUBLICATION DATA

Gates, Henry Louis.
The African Americans : many rivers to cross / Henry Louis Gates, Jr., and Donald Yacovone.
pages cm
Includes bibliographical references and index.
ISBN 978-1-4019-3514-6 (hardcover : alk. paper) 1. African Americans--History. I. Yacovone, Donald. II. Title.
E185.G26 2013
305.896'073--dc23
2013010214

Hardcover ISBN: 978-1-4019-3514-6
Tradepaper ISBN: 978-1-4019-3515-3

16 15 14 13   4 3 2 1
1st edition, October 2013

PRINTED IN CHINA

THIS BOOK IS DEDICATED TO WILLIAM S. McFEELY
and
IN MEMORY OF HENRY HAMPTON

LIST OF ILLUSTRATIONS

INTRODUCTION

BY HENRY LOUIS GATES, JR.

"THE MOST MAGNIFICENT DRAMA IN THE LAST THOUSAND YEARS OF HUMAN HISTORY is the transportation of ten million human beings out of the dark beauty of their mother continent into the new-found El Dorado of the West. They descended into Hell; and in the third century they arose from the dead, in the finest effort to achieve democracy for the working millions which this world had ever seen. It was a tragedy that beggared the Greek; it was an upheaval of humanity like the Reformation and the French Revolution."

— W. E. B. Du Bois, *Black Reconstruction in America, 1860–1880*

The African Americans: Many Rivers to Cross is a companion book to the six-part, six-hour PBS series of the same title, airing for the first time on national, prime-time broadcast in the fall of 2013. This book is the basis of the series and presents in much greater detail the 500-year history of the African American people since the black Spanish conquistador, Juan Garrido, accompanied Ponce de León on his expedition into what is now the state of Florida. It is entirely fitting that the publication of this book and the airing of the television series coincide with this very important 500th anniversary of the presence of persons of African descent in what is today the continental United States.

The African Americans is the first documentary series—since the nine-part History of the Negro People aired on National Educational Television in 1965, and the one-hour documentary, Black History: Lost, Stolen, or Strayed, narrated by Bill Cosby and broadcast in 1968—to chronicle the full sweep of African American history from the origins of the transatlantic slave trade on the west and central coasts of sub-Saharan Africa through five centuries of remarkable historical events right up to today, when our country has a black president yet remains a nation deeply divided by race and class. Indeed, the series and this book end with accounts of the reelection and second inauguration of President Barack Hussein Obama.

One of the central themes of The African Americans is the exploration of the diversity of ethnic origins of the people from Africa and their descendants whose enslavement led to the creation of the African American people, as well as the multiplicity of cultural institutions, political strategies and beliefs, and religious and social institutions that the African American people have created since Juan Garrido and other Africans first explored these shores. All of these elements have defined black society and culture in its extraordinarily rich and compelling diversity over this half millennium: from slavery to freedom, from the plantation to the presidency, from Black Power to the White House. By highlighting the complex internal debates and divisions within the Black Experience historically, The African Americans seeks to show, through fascinating stories about the lives of the people whose sacrifices and dreams made black history, the rich diversity and resilience of the African American community, which the black abolitionist Martin R. Delany perceptively described as early as the 1850s as "a nation within a nation."

Black America, as we will see, has never been a truly uniform entity; in fact, its members have been expressing their differences of opinion from their very first days in this country. Even the road to freedom was not linear; rather, it flowed much like the course of a river, full of loops and eddies, slowing and occasionally reversing current, until ultimately finding its outlet. The African Americans also emphasizes the idea that African American history encompasses multiple continents and venues, and must be viewed through a transnational perspective to be fully understood, even—or especially—in the earliest years of the history of the slave trade and the institution of slavery, revealing the connections among the experiences of black people in the United States, Haiti, Cuba, Jamaica, and Mexico, for example.

This book is composed of stories about black people who were both pioneering and innovative, with the human endeavors of ordinary individuals, unsung heroes whose passions and beliefs changed their world or shaped the worlds that black people made and occupied. In other words, The African Americans is an account of emblematic people, individuals whose stories put a name and a face on a large and complex historical period.

But we also stress material history, especially technological developments and advances, the ways in which trade, industry, and inventions such as the sextant, the slave ship, the cotton gin, the printing press, chromolithography, radio, and the video camera shaped African American history. This is a story, in part, about how a commodity, cotton, was used to turn a group of human beings into commodities, and how those human beings continued to assert their agency, their subjectivity, until finally gaining their freedom. This is a book and a documentary series about how black people, interacting with other human beings in this country and abroad, built their world.

The African Americans foregrounds the marvelous internal worlds of culture and social institutions, both sacred and secular, that black people created in this country within their own spheres of existence, spheres at once self-contained yet reflecting, interacting, and deconstructing with the larger white world that surrounded them. Above all else, this book is concerned with showing that even in the midst of great political adversity and personal vulnerability, even under the harshest conditions, black people for 500 years have explored the fullest range of human emotions and actions, falling in and out of love, inventing novel ways to worship, stressing over the fate and fortunes of their children, and wondering about God's purpose for their lives and their afterlives. In other words, the Black Experience is just one wondrous rendition of the larger experience of being a human being and collectively fashioning a civilization.

✖✖✖

MY OWN FASCINATION WITH AFRICAN AMERICAN HISTORY BEGAN THE DAY IN JUNIOR HIGH SCHOOL WHEN I SAW A PHOTOGRAPH OF W. E. B. DU BOIS. The caption under the picture told me he was the first black man to receive a Ph.D. from Harvard, but I wanted to know more. I wondered who this great man was, how he got there in the first place, and if I, too, might pursue a life of letters. But it would be Lerone Bennett's columns in *Ebony* magazine in the mid-1960s that fired my imagination at the height of the civil rights movement and even more passionately as I grew up with the birth of the Black Power movement. I once wrote in longhand to Mr. Bennett and asked him if he would collect his columns into a book, not realizing that his book *Before the Mayflower: A History of the Negro in America, 1619–1964* was in fact being published. No doubt that helps to explain why when I went to Yale as an undergraduate, I gravitated to the history major. I entered Yale in September 1969, as one of 96 black women and men in the class of 1973, the first fruits of the American academy's adventure in affirmative action. As an undergraduate, I was most interested in American political and cultural history, under the direction of John Morton Blum. But the first course that I took in the history department was called Introduction to Afro-American History. Like just about everybody black at Yale in 1969, I enrolled in this large lecture course taught by William S. McFeely, who counted among his teaching fellows a graduate student named Thomas Holt.

It was already a legendary course; it had been taught previously by Eugene Genovese. And it unfolded week by week in the increasingly volatile atmosphere of escalating protests against the Vietnam War and the simultaneous escalation of the persecution of the Black Panther Party, as well as the trial of Panther leader Bobby Seale, taking place just down the street from Calhoun College, my Yale dormitory, in New Haven. The atmosphere in New Haven and on campus was extraordinarily explosive, and each of Professor McFeely's classes was something of an adventure as we waited for "the Revolution" to come pounding on our classroom door. Nobody missed any of those classes, first because of the quality of Professor McFeely's lectures, and second because the Panthers were likely to show up on any given day, demand "equal time" to espouse their "Ten Point Program" or attempt to intimidate us into giving donations for their meritorious "Free Breakfast Program."

Professor McFeely's lectures were vignettes about the black past that had an uncanny way of serving as allegories for what the black community was experiencing at that time. I well remember his "End of the Second Reconstruction" lecture, delivered just after President Richard M. Nixon, on January 19, 1970, nominated the conservative judge G. Harrold Carswell to replace Justice Abe Fortas on the Supreme Court. The auditorium was packed; you could have heard a pin drop. Threatening clouds of reaction were on the horizon, Professor McFeely warned, and unless we were vigilant, the very policies that had brought all of us black kids to Yale were going to be reversed by a conservative court. It was history teaching designed as an extended metaphor for those who would soon be history makers. Bill McFeely, who would go on to win a Pulitzer Prize in history for his biography of U. S. Grant, was our guide into the wonders of African American history.

But Professor McFeely also taught me something else, and that is, that you don't have to look like the academic subject that you are studying or teaching to be an expert on that subject. No one has a monopoly on academic inquiry simply because of their ethnicity, gender, religion, or sexual preference. And despite the fact that the more militant among us had a most annoying habit of standing up during the question period to ask him what he, a white man, was doing teaching a black history course, he never lost his patience or his composure, never once admonished the student for his or her rudeness. And he did all that he could to ensure that a black historian, John W. Blassingame, would be hired the very next year to replace him as head of that class. I owe so much of my love of African American history to William S. McFeely, and it is for this reason that we have dedicated this book to him.

The documentary series of *The African Americans* is dedicated in memory of Henry Hampton. And so it is fitting that this book be dedicated in his memory as well, along with the dedication to William S. McFeely. Henry was born in 1940 and died all too soon, in 1998. He made 17 documentaries by my count, including the magnificent 14-episode series *Eyes on the Prize*, which was broadcast in two parts, the first covering the crucial years 1954 to 1965 of the civil rights movement, the second exploring its post-1965 afterlife. *Eyes on the Prize* is the gold standard of the historical documentary. Henry won seven Emmys, among a legion of other justly deserved awards and honors.

When I moved to Harvard in 1991, Henry invited me to his offices at Blackside, his film company, in Boston's South End. We hardly knew one another. Patiently, as if he had all the time in the world, he walked me through his stunningly efficient and elegant building, introducing me to his associates and partners,

AFRICANS IN THE AMERICAS

1500–1540

FOR GENERATIONS, WE UNDERSTOOD THE HISTORY OF NEW WORLD EXPLORATION AND COLONIZATION PRIMARILY AS A SET OF EXPERIENCES OF CONQUEST AND PROGRESS, MORE OFTEN THAN NOT WITH the most dire consequences for the "primitive" native populations that the first European explorers and settlers encountered, and "justifiably" conquered or absorbed. And, the standard story continued, these ostensibly one-sided encounters, inevitable acts of human progress and "elevation," laid the foundation for the creation of the modern Western world, the great civilization to which we in the West are heirs.

How can one measure all that was lost in the systematic destruction or dislocation of the civilizations of the peoples whom we know today as the Native Americans?

How can one fully take the toll in human suffering and the irrecoverable losses to world civilization resulting from the four centuries of obliteration of the Native American peoples, beginning with the conquest of the Taino on the island of Hispaniola and the Arawak and the Caribs of the Greater and Lesser Antilles, beginning in the late 15th and early 16th centuries, extending to the domination and subjection of the great Inca and Aztec civilizations in the 16th century, and culminating in the dreadful Trail of Tears in the decade of the 1830s?

But as Aristotle reports Agathon, the Athenian tragic poet, as saying, "Not even God can change the past." And while we certainly cannot change what has already happened, we as scholars, however, are duty bound to preserve the past by recording it in all of its complexity. Part of that process is restoring to the historical record the actions and words of the human beings who, collectively, made that past. Restoring the role that persons of African descent have played in the creation of the saga of Western civilization has been the motivation for our creation of *The African Americans* documentary series, and the writing of this book.

The re-peopling of the Western Hemisphere, through a series of voluntary and involuntary migrations over the past 500 years, was never a one-sided process, and it was never solely a European experience. It may come as a surprise to many Americans to learn that African people played an essential part in this process from the very beginning. According to one source, Alonso Pietro, the pilot of Columbus's ship the *Niña* in 1492, was a mulatto (a person of mixed black and white ancestry), and in 1502 the great Italian explorer was accompanied by a black cabin boy named Diego.

The year after Columbus returned from his final voyage to the Americas in 1504, groups of Africans began arriving in the Caribbean, and several Africans had arrived in 1502, brought to Hispaniola (the island composed of modern Haiti and the Dominican Republic) by the Spanish governor of the island. In 1508, Ponce de León, usually remembered for his explorations of Florida in search of the legendary king of Ethiopia, Prester John, and his fabled fountain of youth, took armed black men with him to conquer Puerto Rico. Diego Velázquez from 1511 to 1512 employed other Africans to help seize Cuba. In fact, Velázquez advised King Ferdinand that "many black slaves" had assisted him in his conquest of the island.

Ultimately, by 1867, according to the Trans-Atlantic Slave Trade Database, approximately 12.5 million Africans had been sold into New World slavery. Of the 11 million or so Africans who survived the Middle Passage, only about 388,000 were shipped directly to what became the United States.[1] The African slave trade to the New World, the largest forced migration in human history, shaped the course of colonization and spawned unique Afro-European societies and cultures stretching from North America to Tierra del Fuego. Without the African presence, the history of the hemisphere—and that of the rest of the modern world—would have been vastly different.

[1]   David Eltis and David Richardson, eds., *Atlas of the Transatlantic Slave Trade* (New Haven: Yale University Press, 2010), 25–27; Matthew Restall, "Black Conquistadors: Armed Africans in Early Spanish America," *The Americas* 57 (October 2000), 173, 176.

✖✖✖

IF NOT ALL OF THE FIRST EXPLORERS AND CONQUERORS OF NEW SPAIN WERE EUROPEAN, IT IS EQUALLY IMPORTANT— and surprising to many of us—to note that not all of the first Africans who assisted the Spanish and Portuguese came as slaves. An untold number of free people of African descent—black conquistadors born in Africa or on the Iberian Peninsula— also accompanied Spanish conquistadors such as Hernán Cortés and Ponce de León, two of the famed explorers of the vast region that would become modern Mexico and the western and southern regions of the United States. And, as we might expect, their exploits were just as heroic and just as problematic as those of their fellow conquistadors. But far more Africans came with the Spanish and the Portuguese as slaves, servants with varying degrees of freedom, attendants, or armed adventurers.

While the number of African explorers is impossible to determine, they participated, in some way, in virtually all of the Spanish expeditions in the New World in the 16th century. These black conquistadors set an example for subsequent racial relations throughout the entire Spanish colonial experience, living their daily lives with degrees of complexity that rarely would be achieved by black men and women in the early English settlements in the Caribbean and in North America. Indeed, wherever Spain set its flag of conquest in the Americas, Africans helped hold the pennant. They participated in the exploration of the lands that would become modern-day Mexico, Costa Rica, Honduras, Panama, Venezuela, Peru, and Chile, as well as Florida, Arizona, New Mexico, and Texas. Men such as Juan Garrido, Esteban, Jan Rodrigues, Gaspar Yanga,

Juan Bardales, Juan García, and Juan Beltrán are just a few of the better-known people of African descent who helped transform the Western Hemisphere.[2]

Perhaps one of the best known and most colorful of the free black conquistadors was Juan Garrido. Born about 1480 in West Africa, Garrido either was sold to Portuguese slave traders or somehow traveled on his own to Lisbon, where about 10 percent of the city was of African descent. In about 1495, he moved to Seville. There, as a free man, perhaps in the employ of a Spaniard named Pedro Garrido, he joined the 1503 expedition of Governor Nicolás de Ovando to Hispaniola—the first of many adventures.[3]

In a 1538 petition to the Spanish Crown asking for financial support for his services and loyalty, Garrido described himself as a free black resident of Mexico City, who for the last 30 years or more had volunteered his services to Spain. "I was present at all the invasions and conquests and pacifications which were carried out . . . all of which I did at my own expense. . . ."[4] Garrido, along with many other free and enslaved blacks, had, in fact, participated in some of the famed expeditions by Spain against Native American populations. For example, in 1508, he and another free black man, Juan González, joined Ponce de León's expedition

---

[2] Restall, "Black Conquistadors," 179–81.

[3] James H. Sweet, "African Identity and Slave Resistance in the Portuguese Atlantic," in *The Atlantic World and Virginia, 1550–1624*, ed. Peter Mancall (Chapel Hill: University of North Carolina Press, 2007), 228.

[4] Restall, "Black Conquistadors," 171; Jane G. Landers, "Juan Garrido," in vol. 3, *African American National Biography*, eds. Henry Louis Gates, Jr., and Evelyn Brooks Higginbotham (New York: Oxford University Press, 2008), 456–57.

Juan Garrido armed with a pike and attending to the horse of Hernán Cortés, who
is receiving an honorific neckband from Aztec officials. Akg-images.

against Puerto Rico. A third black man, a mixed-race conquistador named Francisco Mejías, played a key role in establishing that island's first ranches. At his untimely death at the hands of Carib Indians, Mejías possessed more than 200 pesos in gold.

Immediately after his Puerto Rican adventure, Garrido engaged in gold mining and secured several black slaves to assist him. With native populations decimated by European-induced diseases, labor shortages plagued Spanish efforts to mine, farm, and establish sugar plantations. With a keen eye to the main chance, Garrido joined Spaniards who raided the Caribbean islands of Guadalupe, Dominica, and Santa Cruz in search of Carib slaves, Native Americans with a reputation for fierceness and cannibalism. In 1513 (and again in 1521), Garrido rejoined Ponce de León as he explored and claimed the island of Bimini and all of Florida

for Spain, thereby becoming the first known African to set foot on what was to become the United States. Because we know his name and the date of his landing in Florida, in a sense we can say that Juan Garrido was the first African American, and it is somehow fitting and a bit ironic that this book is being published in the 500th anniversary year of Garrido's arrival in what is now the continental United States.

Later, Garrido made his way to Cuba, where he joined forces with Hernán Cortés and took part, along with other free Africans and slaves, in the 1519 invasion of Mexico and the subjugation of the Aztec empire. In a few extraordinary examples, images of Garrido survive showing him next to Cortés or holding the reins of the Spaniard's horse. In one image published in 1581, Garrido stands in military bearing, shouldering a pike, guarding Cortés as he encounters Aztec emissaries.

Older historical accounts interpreted these images as proof that Garrido was a slave, but in fact he was free. Not only was he free but, despite his pleading of impoverishment to the king of Spain in 1538, he had been handsomely rewarded for his services to Cortés with land and paid positions, especially as the doorman or guard of the Mexico City government and a caretaker of one of the city's aqueducts.

During his time in Mexico City, he engaged in more gold mining and additional expeditions within New Spain, and in 1533 joined again with Cortés in one final journey, which took him all the way to Baja California and the Pacific. He returned to his home in Mexico City in 1536 and died sometime after writing his famed petition, leaving behind a wife, probably a woman of native ethnicity, a family, and an extraordinary legacy.[5]

✦✦✦

GARRIDO'S STORY, THAT OF A FREE BLACK MAN AND A CONQUISTADOR, IS DIFFICULT TO MATCH. However, for sheer drama, none of the recorded experiences of the first Africans in the New World can equal that of the Moroccan-born black explorer known as Esteban. While his early years remain something of a mystery, he began his career in the Americas in 1528 with a journey to Florida in the ill-fated expedition of Pánfilo de Narváez. He would not return to the Spanish colony in Mexico for another eight years, along with only three other survivors of the 300 men who originally began the expedition, and after walking through the virgin American wilderness, across the continent for a total of some 15,000 miles.[6]

In April 1528, five vessels under the command of Narváez, the designated governor of the uncolonized region of Florida, left Havana, Cuba, and arrived in the region of Tampa Bay the next month. Narváez divided his force, sending about 100 or more up the coast while he kept 300 others to march inland in search of legendary cities of gold. By July, having suffered numerous losses, the party reached the area around modern-day Tallahassee. Dogged by oppressive heat and skilled Apalachee archers, the expedition fled west to the Gulf of Mexico in search of their ships. The vessels, however, had long since given up on the mission and returned to Cuba. Stranded, the men constructed rafts and set out to reach Mexico. According to Alvar Nuñez Cabeza de Vaca, the oddly named treasurer of the expedition:

> The work on these was done by the only carpenter we had, and progressed so rapidly that, beginning on the fourth day of August, on the twentieth day of the month of September, five barges of twenty-two elbow lengths each were ready, caulked with palmetto oakum and tarred with pitch, which a Greek called Don Teodoro made from certain pines. Of the husk of palmettos, and of the tails and manes of the horses we made ropes and tackles, of our shirts sails, and of the junipers that grew there we made the oars....[7]

---

5 Jane Landers, *Black Society in Spanish Florida* (Urbana: University of Illinois Press, 1999), 11–12.

6 Perhaps the fullest account is Robert Goodwin, *Crossing the Continent, 1527–1540: The Story of the First African-American Explorer of the American South* (New York: HarperCollins, 2008).

7 A translation of Cabeza de Vaca's narrative can be found at http://www.pbs.org/weta/thewest/resources/archives/one/cabeza.htm.

For a month and a half the survivors drifted along the coast, with men dying from starvation and drowning, others killed by local Native Americans, until they reached a sandbar, near present-day Galveston, Texas. About 16 men, including Esteban, his owner Andrés Dorantes, and Cabeza de Vaca, survived the winter, some resorting to cannibalism, only to be enslaved by Karankawa Indians and remain in bondage until 1534. Twelve of the men died, while the remaining four–Dorantes, Esteban, Cabeza de Vaca, and Alonso del Castillo Maldonado–escaped. They encountered friendlier Indians, and "Estevanico" or "the negro"–as Cabeza de Vaca alternatively referred to Esteban in his narrative–lodged with the tribe's medicine man, where, no doubt, he learned much that proved useful to his survival and subsequent renown.

They encountered other tribes and gained fame in the region as medicine men. While the first Indians had killed their companions and enslaved Esteban and the others, the newer tribes treated them as heroes and, according to Cabeza de Vaca, "They begged us on their knees not to go. But we went and left them in tears at our departure, as it pained them greatly." The men learned several native languages and cultural practices, astounding the inhabitants with stories of their God's powers, claiming themselves to be "Sons of the Sun."[8]

What they did during years of wandering in the Southwest is uncertain. Accounts are conflicting, but sources credit one of the men as laboring successfully as a merchant, brokering trade deals among the various tribes. The strongest evidence points toward Cabeza de Vaca, who claimed as much in his own account of the ordeal:

> I could no longer stand the life I was compelled to lead. Among many other troubles I had to pull the eatable roots out of the water and from among the canes where they were buried in the ground, and from this my fingers had become so tender that the mere touch of a straw caused them to bleed. The reeds would cut me in many places, because many were broken and I had to go in among them with the clothing I had on, of which I have told. This is why I went to work and joined the other Indians. Among these I improved my condition a little by becoming a trader, doing the best in it I could, and they gave me food and treated me well. They entreated me to go about from one part to another to get the things they needed, as on account of constant warfare there is neither travel nor barter in the land.[9]

Other members of their party served as slaves of the Native Americans they encountered–people whom, ironically, they would have enslaved had they had the opportunity. According to one survivor, "We were forced to travel up and down that coast barefoot and without clothing, in the burning summer sun. Our business was to carry loads of wood and drinking water and anything else the Indians wanted and we dragged their canoes through the swamps for them."[10]

---

[8] Dedra McDonald Birzer, "Esteban," *African American National Biography*, ed. Henry Louis Gates, Jr., and Evelyn Brooks Higginbotham (New York: Oxford University Press, 2008), 3: 198.

[9] http://www.pbs.org/weta/thewest/resources/archives/one/cabeza.htm.

[10] Quoted in Goodwin, *Crossing the Continent, 1527–1540*, 235.

After three of their companions were murdered by their Indian captors, Esteban, Dorantes, and Alonso del Castillo conspired to escape–Cabeza de Vaca remained entirely isolated from the others. Esteban and his master Dorantes met up in the Texas backcountry. Esteban, however, decided that life with the Iguace Indians was preferable to his previous life under Spanish slavery. His work as a medicine man gave him a sense of security and importance that he had never known, while Dorantes, a white man, had remained largely enslaved. Although Esteban and Castillo managed to carve out a living among the Indians, in 1533 they began plotting their escape, which was only possible during prickly-pear season since it was the one food available to them on the trail. Esteban led the effort and was informed by friendly Indians that another of their kind was nearby–who turned out to be Cabeza de Vaca. The four, by extraordinary luck, reunited and fled. Esteban, who had great facility with several Indian languages, won the assistance of many Native American tribes as they traveled, who gave the ragged band food without which they surely would have perished. As one historian wrote, "Esteban became the agent of the survivors' constant movement, negotiating with the Indians, choosing the roads they would take, the byways they would explore, and the nations and tribes they would meet."[11]

They were taken in by the Coahuiltecan Indians and quickly earned reputations as wondrous healers, especially the dark-skinned Esteban. Word spread among many different tribes about the powers of these men who seemed to emerge from nowhere and could cure pains and make the lame walk. After

three years, in July 1536, Esteban and one of his companions stumbled upon a Spanish slaving expedition. The Spaniards stared at the two men: one black and the other with long, almost white hair, both adorned with feather headdresses, and deer pelts, carrying the rattles of Indian shamans, and accompanied by about 600 Indian followers. When the white man–Cabeza de Vaca–spoke in perfect Spanish, demanding to be taken to the group's commander, he left them stunned, unable to comprehend the scene before them. The two other survivors soon appeared, putting an end to the eight-year ordeal that saw the men travel about 15,000 miles through modern-day Mexico, New Mexico, Arizona, and Texas. Once back in Mexico City, Cabeza de Vaca and the other Spaniards claimed much credit for their survival, but Esteban's daring resourcefulness was mostly responsible, and his nearly coal-black appearance made him, to the northern tribes, a healer of enormous standing.

⟨✕✕✕⟩

THE REPORTS ESTEBAN AND HIS COMPANIONS PROVIDED regarding the lack of wealth found among those northern tribes did nothing to dampen enthusiasm among the Spanish for the Native Americans' supposed storehouses of gold. In 1539, Spanish Viceroy Antonio de Mendoza purchased Esteban, after the other survivors manifested decidedly little interest in returning north to lead a search for the fabled Seven Cities of Cibola. As a slave, Esteban could not formally head the expedition–although in fact the effort depended entirely upon him–so Mendoza assigned Franciscan friar Marcos de Niza to

---

[11] Goodwin, *Crossing the Continent, 1527–1540*, 254.

lead it. But why would Esteban return to such desolate country? Spanish slavery offered him little, and among the northern Indians he was respected, even worshipped.

By previous arrangement, Esteban set out ahead of the group, leaving crosses behind to mark the trail in New Mexico. He returned to his role as "Son of the Sun" and again gained an extraordinary following. As the Zuñi made preparations to appeal for rain in the windswept high desert, they noted the appearance of a black *katsina*, dressed in animal pelts and adorned with turquoise, bells, and feathers. The Zuñi considered a *katsina* to be a powerful rain spirit who expected reciprocity and stood for honor and respect for ancestors. Esteban had found his calling.

A long train of other Native Americans from various tribes followed him, treating him as a great medicine man, and in turn he spread the word that he could heal them and establish peace. At various stages of his route, Esteban sent Native American runners back to Marcos de Niza with crosses of varying sizes to indicate the significance of his various discoveries. He also set up crosses along his route and instructed his followers to worship them. But at long last, Esteban's luck ran out. He may have become too demanding, intervened too much in local rituals, been too taken with his own power, or simply not have heeded the warnings to leave that he received from Zuñi chiefs.

Ultimately, they saw in him an unwanted harbinger of many more men just like him.[12]

He remained in either Hawikuh or Kiakima in New Mexico, situated beneath a stone outcropping known as Corn Mountain that towers over several Zuñi villages, an area thought by the Spanish to be prosperous. The specifics of Esteban's death are unknown; rumors circulated that the Zuñis murdered him or massacred him with many of his followers. Whatever the case, he was killed, a fact that the Spanish explorer Coronado confirmed the following year.

For the Zuñi, Esteban's story became translated into Chakwaina, a black spirit and iconic doll, who came to symbolize the unfortunate aspects of European impact on native life. For us, Esteban's exploits, like those of his black compatriot, Juan Garrido—a slave and a free man—are emblematic of the complexity of the African presence in the New World, a complicated experience in evidence as early as the very first period of the European exploration and settlement of the lands that would become the United States. In a way, both men can be thought of as "founding fathers," representatives of the experiences of millions of Africans who would become through forced migration, as both slaves and freed persons, a New World, transatlantic African people, the African Americans.

[12] Ramón A. Gutiérrez, *When Jesus Came, the Corn Mothers Went Away: Marriage, Sexuality, and Power in New Mexico, 1500–1846* (Stanford, CA: Stanford University Press, 1991), 10, 39.

THE WORLDS SLAVERY MADE
1526–1763

MANY OTHER AFRICANS BESIDES GARRIDO AND ESTEBAN, BOTH FREE AND ENSLAVED, ASSISTED IN THE COLONIZATION OF NORTH AMERICA IN THE CENTURY OR SO BETWEEN THE LANDING OF COLUMBUS AND THE FOUNDING OF THE ENGLISH SETTLEMENT AT JAMESTOWN IN VIRGINIA IN 1607. And these black people played major, integral roles in an Atlantic world that saw a titanic clash of Spanish, Portuguese, French, Dutch, and English cultures with indigenous Native American cultures, out of which came the United States and all the other countries of the Western Hemisphere.

The development of American history, especially during its earliest period, cannot be understood outside of the context of these rival colonial efforts, and the black role within them. Even as slaves—more accurately, *especially* because of their presence as slaves—people of African descent have profoundly and centrally helped to shape the course of our shared American history for the past 500 years.

Africans would prove essential to Spain's effort to establish hegemony over its claims from the Florida Keys and the Caribbean to the Pacific, and north to the then-unsettled region of Canada. In 1526, two years before the ill-fated expedition of Pánfilo de Narváez and five years after the death of Ponce de León, Lucas Vázquez de Ayllón and a large expedition left Hispaniola for Georgia, probably landing near Sapelo Sound (the heart of Gullah country in the following centuries) on the Atlantic coast. The settlement, known as San Miguel de Gualdape, included about 600 Spanish men, women, and children and an undetermined number of African slaves—the first large group of slaves to arrive in lands that would become the United States. These black slaves may have been Atlantic Creoles or *ladinos*, people of African descent from other Spanish or Portuguese colonies who had become Catholic—either from birth or descent, as were Africans taken to the New World from the kingdom of Kongo in west-central Africa (which willingly converted to Roman Catholicism in the late 15th century), or forcibly converted as a result of their enslavement. These would have been black people who spoke Spanish fluently, were comfortably bicultural, and who served as skilled tradesmen or domestics. Or they simply may have been unacculturated African slaves removed from their initial enslavement in mines or on plantations on the island of Hispaniola and taken to Georgia to perform the most undesirable labor for their owners.

The colony struggled from the start and suffered disease and starvation—as would befall Jamestown in the next century—along with a series of tragedies culminating in Ayllón's untimely death. Chaos ensued, soon followed by a mutiny of the survivors. As winter approached, some of the slaves set fire to the compound of the mutineers—not Ayllón's men—posing interesting questions about the cultural background and political alignment of the slaves the settlers had brought with them. Local Guale Indians took advantage of the colony's disarray and attacked, driving out the surviving Spanish settlers. In a fascinating move, the Africans allied with the Guales and became a Maroon or independent, exiled society, a phenomenon that also took place throughout the Caribbean and Mexico and would become an important feature of New World slavery.

San Lorenzo de los Negros, founded in the 1570s and located near modern Veracruz, Mexico, for instance, became a similar Maroon settlement. Under the military leadership of a former slave named Nyanga (or Gaspar Yanga), it compelled the Spanish Crown to recognize its municipal status and grant it freedom, becoming the first self-governing black entity in the New World shortly after the English settled Jamestown.[1]

Several hundred miles north in the comparatively balmy climate of New York harbor

---

[1] Jane Landers, *Black Society in Spanish Florida* (Urbana: University of Illinois Press, 1999), 12–13; Henry Louis Gates, Jr., *Life Upon These Shores: Looking at African American History, 1513–2008* (New York: Alfred A. Knopf, 2011), 10.

in 1613, a Dutch vessel named the *Jonge Tobias* arrived from the West Indies. The ship anchored off Manhattan Island and deposited a mixed-race adventurer named Jan Rodrigues. Whether the captain, an enterprising merchant named Thije Volckertsz Mossel, set up Rodrigues as his agent or, more likely, simply paid him in supplies and then departed, cannot be fully established. The Dutchman would later claim that Rodrigues was his slave and acted as his agent and guarantor of his monopoly of the trade with the local Indians.

Rodrigues, however, was a free man, probably born on the island of Santo Domingo (facts that a Dutch court fully established), who lived for several months or years on Manhattan Island, trading with the Native Americans there and marrying into at least one tribe. He later received supplies from other Dutch traders and apparently successfully served as an intermediary between Native Americans and the Dutch. While little else is known about him, he may well have been living on the island when the Dutch West Indies Company arrived in 1625. Africans, thus, were bound up in the history of New York from the very first, just as they were the history of Florida and the early Southwest.[2]

Six years after Rodrigues's arrival on Manhattan, in the less hospitable climes of tidewater Virginia, a group of "20. And Odd Negroes" landed at Jamestown, including slaves seized by a Dutch privateer off a Portuguese vessel headed to the slave-trading port of Vera Cruz.[3] While clearly not the first slaves brought to North America, they indeed became the first slaves brought to the region's English settlements. A small and seemingly ordinary event in the history of slavery, it transpired within a harsh and protean Atlantic world. Seen through the lens of what today we call the "Black Atlantic," the arrival of this tiny band of Africans at Jamestown in 1619 symbolizes a complex process that drew every major European power, scores of colonial settlements, and hundreds of ethnic groups on three continents into an economic vortex that enriched both Europeans and African monarchs and merchants, helped spread both Christianity to Africa and Islam to the Western Hemisphere, and made the success of the fragile New World settlements possible. This enormously complex process also created creolized Africans like Jan Rodrigues in New York and, later, Mathias de Sousa, who voted and owned land at St. Mary's settlement in colonial Maryland.

More important, it wrenched 12.5 million people from their African homes and dislocated them throughout the New World, reduced untold millions more over many generations to the status of property, and did not end until Brazil finally outlawed the institution of slavery as late as 1888. The enslavement of the African people and their relocation to the New World, commencing some five centuries ago, created a breathtaking sweep of history that has proven to be one of the most consequential transformations of civilization in world history, one that shaped every country and every people touched by it.

2   Ira Berlin and Leslie M. Harris, eds., *Slavery in New York* (New York: The New Press and the New-York Historical Society, 2005), 34; Graham Russell Hodges, *Root & Branch: African Americans in New York and East Jersey, 1613–1863* (Chapel Hill: University of North Carolina Press, 1999), 6.

3   John Thornton, "The African Experience of the '20. And Odd Negroes' Arriving in Virginia in 1619," *William and Mary Quarterly*, 3d ser., 55 (July 1998): 421-34.

THE ARRIVAL OF THE JAMESTOWN SLAVES IN 1619 OCCURRED AS PART OF AN ENORMOUSLY CONSEQUENTIAL TRADE IN SLAVES, DOMINATED INITIALLY BY PORTUGAL, WHICH HAD THRIVED FOR THE PREVIOUS 100 YEARS. Given the context of the 17th-century Atlantic world, it would have been extraordinary if slaves had failed to make their way to the English colonies. By 1570, historian James Sweet says that in Mexico, black Africans actually outnumbered people born in Europe by 3 to 1, including 20,569 Africans and 6,644 Spaniards; 11,067 criollos (persons of pure Spanish descent born in Spanish America); 2,435 mulattos (of mixed black and white ancestry); and another 2,437 mestizos (of mixed European and Native American ancestry). Of these, about 2,000 were free Maroons (descendants of former slaves). In Peru, "the viceroy's census in 1614 recorded 25,454 people in Lima—10,386 Africans, 9,616 Spaniards, 1,978 Native Andeans, 744 mulattoes, and 192 mestizos. According to Governor Ruiz de Pereda in Havana in 1610: 9,800 whites lived alongside 8,900 blacks, 1,300 Indians. In Brazil in 1620, the ratio of Portuguese to Africans was 1 to 1 (about 50,000 each), but quickly unbalanced with more than 6,200 slaves arriving each year between 1620 and 1625. In fact, between 1501 and 1625 Portugal had shipped 268,000 slaves to Brazil." Even with a high slave-mortality rate, Africans clearly outnumbered those of European descent. And, it is important to emphasize, many of these black people and their mulatto offspring gained their freedom early on.[4]

The great slave-trade historian David Eltis estimates that at least 352,800 slaves had been shipped to the New World by 1625.[5] In the earliest years of their participation in the trade, especially before 1600, the English obtained most of their slaves by preying on ships supplying the Spanish Indies and Mexico, nearly all of which departed from Cape Verde. The slaves involved mostly came from the regions that include modern-day Sierra Leone and Senegal, with the Portuguese traders drawing on the markets of Lower Guinea. For instance, on one 1527 sugar estate on Hispaniola—in what is today the Dominican Republic—most of the slaves came from the Bight of Benin and Upper Guinea, with an even larger number of slaves in Mexico originating from Upper Guinea, the initial name for the region composed today of eastern Guinea, Sierra Leone, Liberia, and northwest Ivory Coast.

In the following years, however, the source of English slaves would shift dramatically to West Central Africa—present-day Angola and

---

[4] Gonzalo Aguirre Beltrán, *Tribal Origins of Slaves in Mexico* (Washington, D.C., 1946?); Jacobo de la Pezuela y Lobo, *Historia de la isla de Cuba* (Madrid: Carlos Bailly-Bailliere, 1868); Malyn Newitt, *A History of Portuguese Overseas Expansion, 1400–1668* (New York: Routledge, 2005), 168; David Eltis and David Richardson, eds., *Atlas of the Transatlantic Slave Trade* (New Haven: Yale University Press, 2010), 23. We are much indebted to Professor Sweet for bringing these figures and sources to our attention.

[5] Eltis and Richardson, eds., *Atlas of the Transatlantic Slave Trade*, 23.

FACING PAGE: *Landing of Slaves at Jamestown, 1619,* by Howard Pyle. Frontispiece for *Harper's Monthly Magazine*, January 1901.

The Slave Trade, by Auguste François Biard, 1840. Oil on canvas. Menil Foundation, Collections of the Image of the Black in Western Art Research Project and Photo Archive. This image was also widely distributed as an engraving by C. E. Wagstaff, London, 1844.

the Democratic Republic of Congo. Portuguese colonization of Angola had much to do with the shift in supply, as did a series of wars between African kingdoms and between the Portuguese and the Africans, as well as the start of direct shipments to Brazil. The trade from this region was largely enabled by agreements made by Angolan kings with Portuguese traders. One, Pedro Gomes Reinel, held an official monopoly (*asiento*) from 1596 to 1601 and sent an astonishing 116 vessels to the Western Hemisphere, shipping 20,478 slaves, at least half of whom were Angolans.[6]

As would so many other Africans who followed, the first slaves that landed at Jamestown originated in the Angolan port of Luanda, probably captured in the Kingdom of Ndongo. They were part of a contract that had been secured to deliver slaves to the Spanish colonies and had been seized on the high seas.

The Portuguese had monopolized the export of slaves from Angola since the early 16th century, working closely with African monarchs, merchants, and intermediaries. Since King Álvaro of Kongo carried on a running dispute with several of his uncles, the slaves that ended up in Virginia probably had been captured as a result of a series of internecine conflicts that had begun in 1616 and ran until 1621, which also included a Portuguese-led war with the Kingdom of Ndongo in which thousands of Kimbundu-speaking people ended up in the slave trade.[7] The rivalry between the Portuguese and Dutch in West Central Africa led to horrific battles as Álvaro's successor, King Pedro II of Kongo, sought alliances to drive out the Portuguese.

Many of the victims of these wars ended up in the transatlantic slave trade. The 1618–1621 campaign, for instance, destroyed Ndongo's capital city and sent thousands of farmers, urban dwellers, craftsmen, and others with the status of serfs into the trade—perhaps as many as 50,000 Africans—many of whom were likely to have Christian names because of the missionary work of the Catholic Church. The wars took a terrible toll. In the three years following the landing of slaves in Virginia, the Portuguese traders sent 15,403 slaves to Brazil and 32 vessels landed another 6,886 slaves in Veracruz, Mexico—all from Angola. And after the conflicts, the trade only increased. From 1624 to 1640, traders sent as many as 5,000 slaves per year just to the Spanish colonies.[8]

Nor did the well-known cargo of slaves that landed in Jamestown represent the first Africans that Englishmen attempted to import. Sir Walter Raleigh's short-lived colony at Roanoke, founded in 1585, was intended to serve as a base for privateering against Spanish commerce, especially raids on the slave trade. Francis Drake had deposited 250 captured slaves there, ones he had seized in raids throughout the Caribbean. Additionally, the English settlement at Wiapoco in 1605 at the mouth of the Amazon had been supplied with African slaves by the Dutch, just as Jamestown would be a few years later.

The same year, Raleigh attempted to establish another colony at Trinidad, this time with several hundred black slaves. While these early English efforts failed, they did so only because an alliance of Spanish and native peoples destroyed them. Equally important, the English modeled their imperial expansion upon Spain and continued to establish similar colonies with slave labor in the Caribbean following

---

[6] Linda M. Heywood and John K. Thornton, *Central Africans, Atlantic Creoles, and the Foundation of the Americas, 1585–1660* (Cambridge: Cambridge University Press, 2007), 38–40.

[7] Thornton, "The African Experience of the '20. And Odd Negroes,'" 421–22; Sweet, "African Identity and Slave Resistance in the Portuguese Atlantic," 225–47.

[8] Heywood and Thornton, *Central Africans, Atlantic Creoles, and the Foundation of the Americas*, 159–61.

the famed landing at Jamestown, firmly establishing a continuity of purpose. Clearly, the English, like their Portuguese and Spanish rivals, considered slavery integral to their colonial ventures. Thus, the introduction of slavery into Virginia was neither accidental nor incidental, but reflected a developing Atlantic-wide effort by England to increase its power and extract wealth from the New World.[9]

✕✕✕

FOR MANY GENERATIONS, HOWEVER, SOME HISTORIANS UNDERSTOOD THE ARRIVAL OF AFRICAN SLAVES IN COLONIAL VIRGINIA AS AN EXCEPTIONAL EVENT in the inevitable growth of human liberty, a kind of unfortunate misstep or afterthought.[10] As Oscar Handlin, a Pulitzer Prize–winning historian, erroneously wrote in a once well-regarded essay, during most of the 17th century few blacks lived in the colonies, and they were not concentrated in any particular region or district. More important, they were not slaves as one would ordinarily define that term: "They came into a society in which a large part of the population was to some degree unfree; indeed in Virginia under the Company almost

everyone, even tenants and laborers, bore some sort of servile obligation. The Negroes' lack of freedom was not unusual. . . . They were certainly not well off. But their ill-fortune was of a sort they shared with men from England, Scotland, and Ireland, and with the unlucky aborigenes [sic] held in captivity." Until the 1660s, this argument goes, black Africans were simply servants, and while some were labeled "slaves," the word more accurately connoted a term of contempt or derogation than it did a permanent status. Historians who subscribed to this interpretation, as in Handlin's case, took pains to disavow assertions of inherent racial inferiority as a determining cause, but the explanation given for slavery's rise placed blame or responsibility squarely upon the shoulders of the enslaved: "The rudeness of the Negroes' manners, the strangeness of their languages, the difficulty of communicating to them English notions of morality and proper behavior occasioned sporadic laws to regulate their conduct."[11] Thus, in this view, slavery as it would be known in the 18th and 19th centuries did not exist in 17th-century Virginia.

It is certainly the case that relatively few slaves existed in the first decades of the Virginia colony, perhaps only 2,000 by 1671. Additionally, during this phase of colonial American history, slaves probably comprised only a quarter of all bound labor, the vast majority of which was white indentured servants.[12] Early Virginia,

---

[9] Eliga H. Gould, "Entangled Histories, Entangled Worlds: The English-Speaking Atlantic as a Spanish Periphery," *American Historical Review* 112 (June 2007): 769; Heywood and Thornton, *Central Africans, Atlantic Creoles, and the Foundation of the Americas*, 20–22, 28–33.

[10] See Edmund S. Morgan, "Slavery and Freedom: The American Paradox," *Journal of American History* 59 (June 1972): 5–29, and Alden T. Vaughan, "A Sense of Their Own Power: Black Virginians, 1619–1989," *Virginia Magazine of History and Biography* 97 (July 1989): 311–54.

[11] Oscar Handlin and Mary F. Handlin, "Origins of the Southern Labor System," *William and Mary Quarterly*, 3d ser., 7, no. 2 (April 1950): 202–04, 208.

[12] John C. Coombs, "Beyond the 'Origins Debate': Rethinking the Rise of Virginia Slavery," in *Early Modern Virginia: Reconsidering the Old Dominion*, eds. Douglas Bradburn and John C. Coombs (Charlottesville: University of Virginia Press, 2011), 248.

for most of its residents, remained a harsh if not brutal environment in which a powerful elite contractually controlled the lives of the majority—many taken from city streets or cast-off second or third sons of the gentry class with no chance of inheritance in England—mostly to cultivate tobacco. And that small elite class did everything in its power to extend the length of the servants' service. The colony, most certainly, was a place in which a few controlled the lives of the many.[13]

Because Virginians did not codify the institution of slavery until the 1660s, and since the expansion of the institution did not occur until the 1680s and 1690s, one school of historians had concluded that early slavery began as a "fluid and permeable" form of "unfree" labor. But African slavery did not exist on an "unfree" continuum in which little distinction could be made between the lives of white indentured servants and black slaves. Revising decades of historical writing about the subject of colonial slavery, an emerging group of historians has recently uncovered a much different story that depicts 17th-century slavery as shockingly similar to that of much later periods.[14] From the very beginning, English settlers understood slavery in all its harsh forms and only codified the practice when it became necessary after 1660, not because of unfamiliarity with the institution, but for economic reasons. The relative scarcity of slaves in the earliest periods can partially be explained by the limitations of available capital, but mostly was because the English obtained their slaves indirectly by

raiding the vessels of Spain and Portugal, having no direct access to African markets.

Moreover, the overwhelming number of Africans that lived in Virginia not only served for life, but their condition was passed on to their children, just as it would be in the 18th and 19th centuries. Tax, court, and probate records show that few Africans gained their freedom during this period, and those that did almost exclusively lived in one area, concentrated on the Eastern Shore.[15]

✕✕✕

HOW AFRICANS BECAME SLAVES AND EUROPEANS MASTERS IS A QUESTION THAT HISTORIANS HAVE DEBATED FOR GENERATIONS. When Europeans became involved in the African slave trade during the 15th century, slavery had been an accepted and acceptable institution since the beginning of civilization, and even was seen as a sign of human progress. Virtually all cultures practiced it, and in Europe beginning with Roman law, societies recognized slaves as both persons and things. In ancient Greece, the hearthstone of democracy, slaves were more widely owned than in antebellum America. Its ubiquity was a primary characteristic of society, with western Europeans enslaving Muslim Albanians, Bosnians, and other Slavs (the origins of the word *slave*), while Russians, Lithuanians, and Poles regularly enslaved one another's war captives well into the 16th century. During

---

[13] Edmund S. Morgan, *American Slavery, American Freedom: The Ordeal of Colonial Virginia* (New York: W. W. Norton, 1975).

[14] Coombs, "Beyond the 'Origins Debate,'" 255.

---

[15] Coombs, "Beyond the 'Origins Debate,'" 243, 258–60; T. H. Breen and Stephen Innes, *"Myne Owne Ground": Race and Freedom on Virginia's Eastern Shore, 1640–1676* (New York: Oxford University Press, 1980, 2005).

the English Civil War, the Earl of Stamford asserted that Royalist soldiers who refused to join the forces of Parliament should be sold as slaves to the Barbary pirates. Even Oliver Cromwell threatened the Scots and the Irish with enslavement if they continued to resist his army. As Seymour Drescher, historian of slavery in the Western Hemisphere, recently wrote, "Judaism, Christianity and Islam viewed slavery as immutable as marriage and human warfare."[16]

In a world accustomed to slavery, anyone could end up in chains, as so many Europeans discovered in their encounter with the Muslim world, especially along the Barbary Coast. Historians John Thornton and Linda Heywood argue that even at the edge of the earth—in a distant frontier town like Jamestown—the English settlers would have shared an understanding (in practice, if not yet in law) of the Portuguese association of "Negro" with "slave," although this association was not inevitable or unalterable in the Spanish world. As we have seen, many black people, such as Juan Garrido and a poet and professor called "el Negro, Juan Latino," functioned as fully free men in Spain and in the Spanish colonies in the New World. The English settlers were well aware of the huge international traffic in black slaves that populated the Spanish and Portuguese colonies in the Caribbean and Latin America.

Equally important, access to and control of labor determined who would gain wealth and power in colonial Virginia. Even in the early colonial period when there were relatively few slaves, the institution of slavery profoundly shaped the colony's developing social structure. Who owned slaves, when they were purchased, and who possessed access to slave markets defined the institution of slavery and its development in colonial Virginia. During the colony's first decades, few "planters" (just about anyone who grew tobacco) possessed sufficient wealth to buy slaves, even if they had been widely available. Those who did, however, overwhelmingly were the richer men who also held some kind of public office, concentrating wealth and political power in the hands of a few.

Although in the first decades of the colony, few settlers could own slaves, it is also clear that even in the 1630s, a *majority* of those who held political office owned black slaves—and in the 1640s, one man owned 40. Additionally, where people lived in the colony and the access they had to London-based tobacco merchants helped decide who could own slaves. Thus, from the very outset, elements of the colony wanted and sought out permanent bound labor. As the number of financially capable men increased along with the availability of slaves, the number of slaves in Virginia increased, and with time the number of non-elite planters able to purchase slaves increased quite dramatically.

What the English thought of "Africans" in 1619 is difficult to say with finality. Prior to colonization, Englishmen—certainly Londoners—were familiar with people of African descent, as was the royal court. At times they used the words *African*, *Moor*, and *Blackamoor* interchangeably, and in other cases appeared to

---

[16] David Brion Davis, *The Problem of Slavery in Western Culture* (Ithaca, NY: Cornell University Press, 1966), 35; Seymour Drescher, *Abolition: A History of Slavery and Antislavery* (Cambridge: Cambridge University Press, 2009), 8 quoted, 10–14.

FACING PAGE: *Young Negress*, by Wenceslaus Hollar, 1645. Etching. Harvard Art Museums/Fogg Museum; bequest of Edwin de T. Bechtel, Harvard University.

W. Hollar fecit
Antverpiæ A° 1645

distinguish between North Africans and those of the sub-Saharan region. Samuel Pepys, for instance, mentions some Africans in his famed diary and recorded a case in which one William Batten left "a handsomely paid guardianship" to a black man. Londoners on any given day could certainly encounter black women and men as laundresses, servants, maids, professional soldiers, pages, entertainers, goldsmiths, needle makers, metalworkers, and even a diver, a royal page, a trumpeter, and a monk. In 1501, a Spanish princess visited London and included black people in her royal retinue.[17]

It is worth noting that there are very few negative visual images of Africans during this early period, whether in English paintings or prints. In English literature, however, we find a range of associations with black people and blackness. For example, in the popular *Geographical History* by Leo Africanus, translated into English in 1600, the Kingdom of Timbuktu emerges as a "well-ordered, prosperous, civilized society in which learning flourished as well as trade...."[18]

Yet given the country's class structure and the kinds of positions that black people largely filled, the English, whatever intrinsic or received understanding they had of sub-Saharan Africans, certainly had been accustomed to seeing them on a daily basis in subordinate roles: as servants, in various other lower-class positions, or even as slaves—however well treated. And inevitably, associations between

black Africans and animals found their way into English literature: a poem by the 15th-century poet William Dunbar described one black woman at court as having "protruding lips like an ape," and even in Shakespeare's depiction of Othello as the "noble Moor," Iago uses animal and sexual associations to turn Othello's father-in-law against him. Additionally, Elizabeth I in 1596 and 1601 (unsuccessfully) ordered the expulsion of "negars and blackamoors" from England. Even in the era of Thomas More, the term *Ethiopian* represented a pejorative to describe people of African descent.[19]

There is certainly ambiguity in the earliest English views of Africa. But by the era of colonization, Englishmen had long been accustomed to living alongside black people. While English colonists might make exceptions for especially learned Africans or those belonging to royalty, anti-black racist views hardened fairly rapidly and all too easily, rendering most blacks an alien people and fit subjects for permanent servitude. Soon—and likely well before the slave codes of the 1660s—the blackness of a person's skin became a signifier of status, a signal that such people should be considered property and inferior by nature, to be held in perpetual bondage, a fact that Morgan Godwyn makes clear in his impassioned defense of the

---

[17] Imtiaz Habib, *Black Lives in the English Archives, 1500–1677* (Burlington, VT: Ashgate, 2008), 2–7, 23, 222.

[18] Eldred Jones, *The Elizabethan Image of Africa* (Charlottesville: University of Virginia Press for the Folger Shakespeare Library, 1971), 29 quoted.

[19] David Bindman, "The Black Presence in British Art: Sixteenth and Seventeenth Centuries," in III, pt. 1, *The Image of the Black in Western Art: From the Age of Discovery to the Age of Abolition*, eds. David Bindman and Henry Louis Gates, Jr. (Cambridge: Belknap Press of Harvard University Press, 2010), 235–36; Habib, *Black Lives*, 7, 24–25. Also see: Mary Floyd-Wilson, "Moors, Race, and the Study of English Renaissance Literature: A Brief Retrospective," *Literature Compass* 3 (2006): 1044–52.

common humanity of Africans and Indians with Europeans, against racist aspersions cast against their "nature" as early as 1680.

The relatively small number of early Africans who managed to become free in colonial Virginia were in all likelihood slaves and never had been indentured servants, since there is no proof that any were given a contract. Nevertheless, a small group of emancipated slaves, against the greatest odds, managed to thrive, at least for a time. John Graweere used his skills keeping hogs to buy his own freedom and, most astonishingly, successfully brought suit in court to win the freedom of his son:

> And whereas the said negro having a young child of a negro woman belonging to Lieut. *Robert Sheppard* which he desired should be made a christian and be taught and exercised in the church of *England*, by reason whereof he the said negro did for his said child purchase its freedom of Lieut. *Sheppard* with the good liking and consent of *Tho: Gooman's* overseer as by the deposition of the said *Sheppard* and *Evans* appeareth, *the court hath therefore ordered* that the child shall be free from the said *Evans* or his assigns and to be and remain at the disposing and education of the said *Graweere* and the child's godfather who undertaketh to see it brought up in the christian religion as aforesaid.[20]

One of the most celebrated instances of a free colonial-era black is that of "Antoney,"

most probably from Angola and perhaps one of the "20. And Odd" Africans who landed in Jamestown in 1619. The muster list of 1625 states that Antoney and his wife had a child together named William, whom they baptized (as they would their future children). They remained together for almost 50 years. By 1635, Antoney; his wife, Mary; and their entire family enjoyed freedom. He changed his name to Anthony Johnson, acquired a large tract of land—250 acres—and a slave of his own, named John Casor. Anthony Johnson became a prosperous man and lived the life of an English colonial planter. One of his sons even acquired 450 acres of land. In 1665, Johnson took his herd of livestock and moved to Somerset County, Maryland. In 1667, his grandson John purchased 44 acres on the east side of Chesapeake Bay and named it "Angola," recognizing his family's African heritage.

Just 40 years after the first "20. And Odd" blacks landed on these shores, however, all Africans arriving in Virginia were legally defined as slaves, to be held in bondage for life. When Anthony Johnson died in 1670, a Virginia court ruled that he was "a negro and by consequence, an alien," and a white Virginian planter was allowed to seize Johnson's land because "as a black man, Anthony Johnson was not a citizen of the colony."[21]

Despite the Johnsons and a few other examples, manumissions, whether through self-purchase or the kindness of masters, rarely

---

20 H. R. McIlwaine, ed., *Minutes of the Council and General Court of Colonial Virginia* (Richmond: Virginia State Library, 1979), 477.

21 Heywood and Thornton, *Central Africans, Atlantic Creoles, and the Foundation of the Americas*, 272, 282–83; Breen and Innes, "*Myne Owne Ground,*" 82–83; James O. Horton and Lois E. Horton, *Hard Road to Freedom: The Story of African America* (New Brunswick, NJ: Rutgers University Press, 2002), 27.

happened during the early years of slavery in Virginia. In an era of intense labor shortages and intensely unequal distribution of wealth, freeing one's working property simply made no economic sense. With great clarity, we can now see that the institution of slavery did not emerge gradually, unthinkingly, or accidentally out of indentured servitude. Instead, it came full born, borne by the sails of wooden ships, learned from the previous century of other Europeans treating black women and men as property. In Virginia, well-connected planters with political power and access to markets developed the institution in phases, based on "wealth, location, and economic need." They sought slaves as white men in the 19th century sought gold and in the 20th century sought oil: with drive, greed, and ambition, fueling an efficient and profitable institution, which grew along with the reach of the British Empire.[22]

From 1501 to 1830, as we have seen, about 388,000 African slaves were shipped directly from Africa to North America. During the same period, about *four million* slaves landed in the Caribbean, with the larger portion going to Haiti and Cuba. Yet by 1830, the black populations of both regions were astonishingly similar: about 2.3 million in North America and 2.4 million in the Caribbean. (Brazil, incredibly, received about five million slaves.) The shocking numbers had as much to do with more favorable living conditions in North America for both whites and blacks (and slightly higher birth rates for both groups) as it did with an exacting Caribbean work regime that required a higher rate of slave importation to replace the deceased. As it turns out, recent migrants suffered higher

death rates than those of African descent born in the Western Hemisphere. Thus, with the near insatiable demand for new slaves in the Caribbean to meet European requirements for agricultural goods—especially sugar—the death rates proved higher among the larger Caribbean population, retarding growth.[23]

Despite the high mortality rates, and perhaps spurred by them, the number of slave imports steadily increased, with a large percentage coming from West Central Africa—from whence hailed approximately 45 percent of all the Africans enslaved and shipped to the Americas before 1866.

⊠⊠⊠

SUCH A TRADE WAS ONLY POSSIBLE BECAUSE AFRICAN LEADERS SAW GREAT ADVANTAGE IN SELLING OTHER AFRICANS TO EUROPEAN TRADERS. One prominent example is that of Queen Nzinga (1583–1663), who ruled the Kingdom of Ndongo in what is now Angola from 1624 until her death in 1663. Converted to Roman Catholicism by the Portuguese, she adopted the Christian name of Ana de Sousa and employed her religious conversion to political advantage throughout her life. She fought wars against the Portuguese and negotiated a series of complex diplomatic alliances with both European and other African states to preserve her power and her

---

[22] Coombs, "Beyond the 'Origins Debate,'" 253–54.

[23] Eltis and Richardson, *Atlas of the Transatlantic Slave Trade*, 196; Herbert S. Klein and Ben Vinson III, *African Slavery in Latin America and the Caribbean* (New York: Oxford University Press, 2007), 119–34. For example, whites and blacks in North America lived longer than Brazilians of any race.

Slave Market of Cairo, by David Roberts, 1846–1849. Lithograph. Library of Congress.

kingdom. Because of her leadership, military prowess (she led troops into battle), and heroic struggle, she is still celebrated in Africa as a symbol of independence and strength.[24]

But slavery was essential to her political and military power, as it was to the region more generally. Slavery thrived in West Africa (and elsewhere) long before contact with Europeans and remained a central institution throughout

the 19th century. Especially in Muslim regions, such as the Sokoto Caliphate of present-day northern Nigeria, slavery became the backbone of the economy. Slaves proved essential to all sectors of society, from local cottage industries and military life to farming and harems. Slaves, as had been the case since the 15th century, were a valuable form of currency, regularly used to pay tribute to political capitals and a far more common medium of exchange than even gold was. As late as the turn of the 20th century, this caliphate very likely possessed as many slaves as existed in the whole of the American South on the eve of the Civil War, about four million. Indeed, the internal trade remained so strong and so integral to the

---

[24] The spelling of her name varies. For a brief biography of Queen Nzinga see: Emmanuel K. Akyeampong and Henry Louis Gates, Jr., eds., *Dictionary of African Biography*, 6 vols. (New York: Oxford University Press, 2012), 4:527–28; John K. Thornton, "Legitimacy and Political Power: Queen Njinga, 1624–1663," *Journal of African History* 32 (1991): 25–40.

region that it constituted a "demographic policy of relocation on a gigantic scale."[25]

From an African perspective, whether as leaders or common people, Europeans were largely irrelevant to the actual enslavement of individuals. While this notion flies in the face of our common assumptions about the history of the enslavement of Africans, the institution of slavery and the trade in slaves to Europeans in West and Central Africa was more a manifestation of local politics and economic structures, resulting primarily from the many wars that plagued central West Africa, especially in the 17th and 18th centuries, than it was an institution forcibly imposed on Africans by Europeans. The transatlantic slave trade resulted from a mutuality of commercial interests between various African elites and European merchants. It surprises many of us today to learn that Europeans *sold guns* to African monarchs, rather than dominated them with arms.

Slavery existed before and long after the European arrival, and the European presence was largely confined to the coast, centered in "factories" or forts that functioned as trading posts. (The Portuguese presence in Angola was an exception to this rule.) Very few Europeans penetrated the African interior for a very long time, which is one of the reasons that the West was riveted by newspaper accounts of Henry Morton Stanley's search for Dr. David Livingstone in 1871. Moreover, the dominance and colonization of Africa and its attendant subdivisions, which resulted in the nation-states created after independence in the late 1950s and early '60s, only occurred after the Congress of Berlin in 1884. In the experience of West Central Africans, as the historian John K. Thornton has emphasized, war brought destruction, murder, rape, injury, loss of property, cannibalism, and even the loss of personal belongings and clothing, but it especially brought slavery. Slavery represented a ubiquitous "solution to problems raised by war."[26]

Queen Nzinga, just as every other African leader of the era, exemplified the integral role slavery played in the social and political life of West Africa. She and her rivals all sought slaves and used them as a common currency with Europeans and with local enemies and allies. Even before the queen assumed leadership, she participated in diplomatic missions to representatives of Portugal—the major European power in the area, along with the Dutch—and used gifts of slaves to facilitate negotiations. During the 1620s, she attempted to court her Portuguese rivals by sending them about 800 slaves as a gift, although the gesture failed to win their cooperation. And in the 1640s, King Garcia II of Kongo did precisely the same thing, sending to the Dutch West India Company a gift of 1,200 slaves, with another 170 going directly to the company director Cornelis Nieulant, hoping to solidify Dutch military assistance.

In 1637, Queen Nzinga sent ivory and slaves to Jesuits in Luanda, hoping to influence Portuguese diplomacy; and when the Portuguese captured her sisters, she paid a

---

[25] Paul E. Lovejoy, *Slavery, Commerce, and Production in the Sokoto Caliphate of West Africa* (Trenton, NJ: Africa World Press, 2005), 1–3, 13–15.

[26] John K. Thornton, "Cannibals, Witches, and Slave Traders in the Atlantic World," *William and Mary Quarterly*, 3d ser., 60 (April 2003): quoted 277, 291.

FACING PAGE: Queen Nzinga, published 1780. Hand-colored engraving. Private Collection/The Stapleton Collection Bridgeman Art Library.

ransom in slaves. When diplomacy turned to war, as it almost always did throughout her reign, she seized as many slaves as possible, and in 1648 turned her capital into a major slave-trading center. When not fighting the Portuguese or seeking alliances with the Dutch, she fought her African political rivals and in the process gained thousands of slaves.[27]

When her fortunes reversed and the Portuguese defeated her army and expelled her from her capital, she allied with the Imbangala—violent bands or cults of local mercenary soldiers with a reputation for murder and cannibalism—and even married an Imbangala leader to strengthen her weakened forces. In doing so, she joined with men who recruited new members through the enslavement of adolescent boys and who represented a major force in the region's slave trade. Equally important, she used the sale of slaves—usually the captured subjects of her rivals—to fund her military campaigns and retain her hold on power. Slavery proved so ubiquitous and so central to political life that some slaves held important political positions within her power structure and that of her clan.[28]

Next to the number and skill of her archers, the ferocity of Queen Nzinga's Imbangala allies, and the guns and cannon of the Dutch, slavery must stand as the single most important element that made possible whatever success she achieved. As the currency of diplomacy and tribute, it brought her the wealth essential to her survival. The numbers are indeed staggering. Before 1640, at least 5,000 slaves went into the international market per year from her territory. But from 1641 to 1660, it is likely that as many as 13,000 slaves per year were shipped to the New World just from the lands she controlled. As one contemporary account maintained, Queen Nzinga's lands were "over flowing with slaves."[29]

⬦⬦⬦

WITHOUT THIS BACKGROUND OF THE AFRICAN ROLE IN THE SLAVE TRADE, WE CANNOT COMPREHEND HOW SLAVERY BECAME TRANSPLANTED TO THE NEW WORLD or how it permeated the Atlantic world during the formative period of North American colonization—and that of all the Americas. How slavery insinuated itself in the cultures bordering the Atlantic is perhaps best illustrated by the case of Ayuba ibn Suleiman Diallo, better known as Job ben Solomon (1702?–1773?).

---

[27] Heywood and Thornton, *Central Africans, Atlantic Creoles, and the Foundation of the Americas, 1585–1660*, 124, 132–33, 134–35, 145, 150–51, 154–55, 163–64.

[28] Thornton, "Legitimacy and Political Power," 31–32, 36; Thornton, "Cannibals, Witches, and Slave Traders," 287; Heywood and Thornton, *Central Africans, Atlantic Creoles, and the Foundation of the Americas*, 132–33, 150–51; Malyn Newitt, ed., *The Portuguese in West Africa, 1415–1670: A Documentary History* (Cambridge: Cambridge University Press, 2010), 143–45, 147.

[29] Heywood and Thornton, *Central Africans, Atlantic Creoles, and the Foundation of the Americas*, 161–62.

FACING PAGE: Job ben Solomon, circa 1750. Etching. Private Collection/ Michael Graham-Stewart, Bridgeman Art Library.

Job, Son of Solliman Dgiallo, High Priest of Bonda in the Country of Foota, Africa.

Solomon's 1734 memoir is the first of a long line of English-language reminiscences by former slaves. The work made Solomon extremely popular on both sides of the Atlantic, and he had his portrait painted, with at least two versions of it widely distributed in engravings.[30]

Born to a wealthy and educated Muslim family in Bondu, West Africa, in what is now Senegal, Job ben Solomon became both a religious leader and a successful merchant trader, which included slave trading. Angering a mysterious Englishman named Captain Pyke during an expedition on the Gambia River in 1730, Mandingo kidnappers captured and sold Solomon and his interpreter, Loumein Yoai, to Pyke. Although Solomon's father attempted to ransom him, he and several other slaves were carried off to Annapolis, Maryland. He was handed over to a trader named Vachell Denton, a well-connected Maryland businessman who worked for a London merchant named William Hunt, who in turn sold Solomon to a planter named Alexander Tolsey. Yoai also ended up in Maryland but went to another owner, near the farm on Kent Island that held the tobacco plantation that became Solomon's unhappy home.[31]

Solomon (whom Tolsey renamed Simon) proved ill suited to the new work and grew sick, so his owner put him to tending cattle. While this task proved easier–it was something he had done in Africa–Solomon nevertheless ran away and made it north to Kent County on the Delaware Bay, where he was captured and imprisoned. His conduct, his strange language, the references to Allah and Mohammed he wrote down (which must have astonished everyone), and his refusal to drink alcohol (the jail that housed him was also a tavern) created quite a local stir.

Word of the strange slave reached Thomas Bluett, a Kent County attorney and a converted member of the Anglican Church who was also a missionary for the Church's Society for the Propagation of the Gospel. Bluett later traveled with Solomon and wrote and published his story in the form of a memoir. A local slave who could communicate with Solomon discovered his owner, who eventually retrieved his property. Rather than punish his slave with a whipping or by severing a foot–an effective means of preventing escape–he gave Solomon a place to pray.

But freedom, rather than kind treatment, was what this Muslim slave trader desired. Astonishingly, he decided to write his father back in Africa to find a way to freedom from American slavery. In a highly unlikely series of events–detailed in his memoir–the letter, written in Arabic, was given to Vachell Denton, who probably believed that Solomon was an African prince who might prove useful in African trade, who sent it to Captain Henry Hunt with instructions to give it, in London,

---

[30] Thomas Bluett, *Some Memoirs of the Life of Job, the Son of Solomon, the High Priest of Boonda in Africa* . . . (London: Richard Ford, 1734). The text can be easily read at http://docsouth.unc.edu/neh/bluett/bluett.html, and one version of the engraving, from *Gentleman's Magazine* in 1750, can be found at http://www.slavevoyages.org/tast/resources/images-detail.faces?image=solomon.

[31] The best source for Solomon's life remains Douglas Grant's *The Fortunate Slave: An Illustration of African Slavery in the Early Eighteenth Century* (London: Oxford University Press, 1968). A biographical sketch of him can be found in *African American National Biography*, eds. Henry Louis Gates, Jr., and Evelyn Brooks Higginbotham (New York: Oxford University Press, 2008), 4:483–85.

to the same Captain Pyke who had started the whole drama.

Pyke, however, had already left for Africa, and the letter remained land-bound. In another improbable series of events, a colleague of Hunt's gave the letter to the famed James Oglethorpe, soldier, philanthropist, founder of the Georgia colony, and member of the Royal African Company (RAC)—the nation's primary trader in slaves. Oglethorpe advised the company director, Sir Bibye Lake, about the strange case of Job ben Solomon. Lake then recruited Professor John Gagnier, who held the Laudian Chair in Arabic at Oxford, to translate the letter.

Oglethorpe read the translation and was so moved by Solomon's plea to his father that the Englishman determined to seek the African's freedom. In a complicated set of negotiations that involved Denton, Hunt, Oglethorpe, Bluett (who traveled with Solomon to England), and Tolsey, the RAC eventually paid for Solomon's freedom, almost £60—perhaps equivalent to $13,000 today. On December 27, 1733, the RAC issued Solomon a certificate of manumission.

Yet Solomon's freedom hardly represents the end of the story. What interest would the Royal African Company, England's primary slave dealer, have in freeing one Muslim slave? The African had met with royalty and took up residence in the RAC's house in London. Enjoying fame and influence, he was able to get the RAC to agree to allow any Muslim enslaved to buy himself out of servitude, "in exchange for two other good slaves." He also used his new-found fame to convince the Duke of Montagu to arrange for the freedom of his servant,

Loumein Yoai, still in Maryland. His relationship with the RAC became very close; he literally depended upon the RAC for his freedom and agreed to return to Africa to help promote the company's interests. Fearing that since the French had established such a large presence in Senegambia he risked re-enslavement without official documents, he obtained a passport assuring him of protection from the French. He sailed in July, under the care of the RAC, which even provided him with a letter of introduction to company officials in Gambia.

Solomon's association with the RAC could not have been stronger. The firm counted on him to increase access to the region's resources and to help resist encroaching French economic interests. The company expanded its reach in the region, seeking to exploit African natural resources, especially gold, gum, cotton, lumber, spices, and the like. The English established an arrangement with the French to gain huge amounts of gum in exchange for slaves and an agreement not to trade in slaves, except in payment for the gum. Solomon did what he could to help promote the company's trade, quite properly feeling deeply indebted to it.

Although he won his own freedom with an astonishing stroke of his pen and was the first to publish a story of enslavement and redemption in English, his extraordinary experiences had no impact whatsoever on his attitude regarding the institution of slavery. One of the first things he did upon returning home was to buy two horses and a female slave. Unlike the many slave narratives that would follow, Solomon's story could not be construed as anti-slavery, only anti-his own enslavement. The world of slavery would not be so easily altered.

✦✦✦

OVER THE COURSE OF THE 18TH CEN-
TURY, THE NUMBERS OF SLAVES SHIPPED
TO THE NEW WORLD BECAME STAG-
GERING AND VERY PROFITABLE TO EV-
ERYONE CONNECTED WITH THE TRADE.
Charleston, South Carolina, alone received
some 187,000, just under half of all of the slaves
imported to the United States. By the close of
Great Britain's official slave trade in 1807, about
3.2 million slaves had been shipped just to the
British Caribbean, and another 1.2 million
to the French West Indies. (Another 193,000
would come to the French West Indies between
1808 and 1867, while 779,000 Africans would
arrive through the Spanish trade, largely to
Cuba, in the same period.) Hundreds of thousands of Africans—more than came to the
United States—endured the Middle Passage to
end their days in Mexico and Peru.[32] And just
over five million Africans would arrive in
Brazil between 1526 and 1867.

Nearly all individuals' stories have been
lost. Job ben Solomon was one of the precious
few who emerged recognizable from the infamous trade and only because of an extraordinary set of circumstances. Most names are
eradicated from the record. Despite remarkable advances in the use of DNA to trace a person's haplogroup and autosomal DNA to their
African regional origins, today only a handful
of African Americans—if that many—can trace
their ancestry to an individual forebear, identified by name, who was first taken out of Africa.

One from that handful began at Bunce (or
Bance) Castle, now a ghostly ruin on the coast
of Sierra Leone. The post, built around 1670
by the British to protect slave merchants of
the Royal African Company, occupied about 14
acres of land on an island in the Sierra Leone
River. Abandoned by the RAC in 1730, the
fortified trading post was taken over by the
London firm Grant, Oswald & Company, then
given over to John and Alexander Anderson,
who operated the slave trading post until the
abolition of the trade in 1807.[33]

While controlled by the English, about
12,300 slaves passed through the island; and
when Richard Oswald and his associates controlled the Bunce facility, most of the slaves
went directly to Charleston, South Carolina,
others to Florida and Virginia. Estimates of the
total number of slaves from Africa's Windward
Coast (stretching from Cape Mount, Liberia, to
the Assini River in the Ivory Coast), plus those
from Bunce Island upstream from Freetown in
Sierra Leone, reached about 5,000 per year by
the mid-18th century.

Even though so many nameless humans
passed through Oswald's hands, he thought of
himself as an enlightened businessman. This was
despite the fact that as many as 80 or 90 of the total number of slaves he shipped each year died in
transit. It's likely that he comforted himself with
the idea that his orders not to brand his property
with a hot iron and to keep slave families together
if possible somehow made the trade more palat-
able. In the end, however, he was a cool businessman with a keen eye for the bottom line.[34]

---

[32] Eltis and Richardson, *Atlas of the Transatlantic Slave Trade*, 26, 216.

[33] Eltis and Richardson, *Atlas of the Transatlantic Slave Trade*, 99.

[34] David Hancock, *Citizens of the World: London Merchants and the Integration of the British Atlantic Community, 1735–1785* (Cambridge: Cambridge University Press, 1995), 175, 203–04; Bunce Island estimate is from http://www.slavevoyages.org/tast/database/search.faces.

write the state's first constitution, served in the Continental Congress, and succeeded John Hancock as its president. He also served on the peace commission, along with John Adams, Benjamin Franklin, and John Jay, that resulted in the Treaty of Paris that formalized American independence from Britain; Oswald, Laurens's business partner, served on the British negotiating team.

Laurens began his merchant career in 1749 and by 1763, when he quit the business, he had achieved enormous wealth, much if it through his slave importation business, Austin & Laurens (later Austin, Laurens & Appleby). In a given shipment he might receive as many as 250 "fine healthy NEGROES," prized for their experience in rice growing. But by 1763, he had grown weary of business and slavery. "I abhor slavery," he once wrote to his son John, although like his contemporary Thomas Jefferson he never manumitted any of them, and two years before his death he still owned 298.[38]

Before the *Hare* even arrived in port, Laurens complained that he was too busy to accept them: "The place is quite clog'd with slaves that God knows what we shall do with them." Upon seeing the cargo, he declared them quite "wretched . . . a most scabby flock." Nevertheless, his advertisement for the cargo described them as "Just imported . . . directly from Sierra Leone, a cargo of likely and healthy slaves to be sold on easy terms."

Elias Ball, Jr. (1709–1786), in need of additional slaves, responded to Laurens's advertisement, wanting to buy several children. Ball owned 1,000 acres of prime land outside of Charleston, making him a man of great wealth and enormous standing, residing at the family's Comingtee plantation. He was reclusive to a surprising degree for the times and married somewhat late. His father, concerned for his bachelor son's mental health, once bought him a talking parrot for company. But Elias Ball in fact longed for Lydia Child, a woman of social standing who had instead married another planter inconveniently named George Chicken.

In 1745, as luck would have it, Mr. Chicken passed from the scene and Ball wed his true love. At the same time, he purchased a new 670-acre plantation, which he dubbed Kensington. At this point, he owned about 75 slaves and with his family estate and lands inherited through his bride, the Ball family lorded over five plantations: Comingtee, Hyde Park, Kensington, St. James, and Strawberry. The Cooper River that runs through Ball family lands and eventually joins with the Ashley at Charleston was generally accepted as part of the Ball domain.[39]

On June 30, 1756, Ball purchased six children from the *Hare's* cargo, four boys and two girls, among them Priscilla, whom he thought to be about ten years old. He could choose from 13 boys and 9 girls—the vessel may have had even more children, as the surviving cargo of 71 also included 8 unaccounted-for slaves who landed but disappeared from surviving records after arriving at Sullivan's Island in Charleston Harbor. Perhaps they died shortly after arriving.

Ball appeared to prefer children over adult slaves—maybe believing that he could more

---

[38] John A. Garrity and Mark C. Carnes, eds., *American National Biography*, 24 vols. (New York: Oxford University Press, 1999), 13:261–63; Henry Louis Gates, Jr., *Life Upon These Shores: Looking at African American History, 1513–2008* (New York: Alfred A. Knopf, 2011), 15; Ball, *Slaves in the Family*, 193.

[39] Ball, *Slaves in the Family*, 142–48.

easily train them—and subsequently bought an additional "13 Gambias Young Negroes," as he recorded in his books, who were about 12 years of age, paying £2,600 (an enormous amount) for this later group. He usually paid cash for his slaves—most planters bought on credit—and gave Oswald's agent £600, about $100,000 in modern value, for the *Hare's* six children. He took them—Sancho, Peter, Brutus, Harry, Belinda, and Priscilla—to his Comingtee plantation. If any of the children had parents on board, they never saw them again.[40]

Because the Ball family preserved its records, we have some idea what happened to Priscilla and the other children purchased on that steamy June day. Belinda disappeared from family records almost immediately, either dying or being resold. Harry and Brutus worked as field hands, with Harry living alone until his death. Brutus disappeared from the records in 1784, either dead or resold at age 35. More is known about Peter, whom Ball renamed Mandingo Peter, who went with Ball to the Comingtee plantation. He lived with a woman named Monemia and with her had several children. In 1777, he and his family moved to the Kensington plantation, where he remained until 1816, apparently dying at age 67. Sancho also worked at Comingtee, married a woman named Affie, and had at least three children, Sancho, Saby, and Belinda, a common slave name perhaps derived from Alexander Pope's narrative 1712 poem *The Rape of the Lock*. Sancho ran away to the British during the Revolution, but was returned to his owner. His story ends tragically, as his wife and children were sold off in 1819—when he was 72—and he lived alone until 1833 when he died at age 86 on Christmas Day.

As for Priscilla, we know that within ten years of her arrival in South Carolina, she married another slave named Primus and had one child, Peter, and by 1763 married another slave named Jeffrey with whom she had nine children, the last born in 1786. Did she do the oppressive work in the rice fields, suffering in the heat, murky water, and endless plagues of insects? Or did she work closer to the plantation house—perhaps washing clothes? We do not know how she spent her days, but we can be sure that she proved extremely hardy or lucky, as a slave in rice country bearing so many children and living until 1811, about age 65. What makes her story so fascinating is that we can not only document her enslavement from the start, but identify some of her descendants that still live in the region today, discovered by Edward Ball while researching his popular book. They represent a tiny handful of American families who can without breaks trace their roots directly back to Africa.[41]

African Americans like Priscilla, as much as anyone, built this country. Between 1700 and 1780, twice as many Africans as Europeans crossed the Atlantic (including the millions who went to Central and South America), and their labor accounted for two-thirds of all colonial exports. Slavery helped transform the 13 colonies from a scattering of vulnerable settlements into a rising economic power. That history, however, also proved harsh, tragic, and violent, inescapable conditions that shaped the course of American history.

---

[40] Ball, *Slaves in the Family*, 193–94; images of the original records are at http://www.choices.edu/resources/documents/SlaveVoyage.pdf.

[41] Ball, *Slaves in the Family*, 450–51.

THE AGE OF REVOLUTIONS
1700–1811

FROM 1701 UNTIL THE CLOSE OF THE LEGAL SLAVE TRADE IN 1808, ABOUT 187,000 SLAVES WERE SHIPPED FROM AFRICA DIRECTLY TO CHARLESTON, SOUTH CAROLINA. Between 1710 and 1740 alone, more than 38,000 slaves were shipped to the Georgia-South Carolina region, creating enormous imbalances between white and black populations and a very large body of slaves with direct memory of African freedom. Additionally, from 1700 to 1740, about 39,000 more slaves were shipped to lands controlled by Spain in North America, which included Florida.

Until Great Britain ended Spanish domination of Florida in 1763, the hundreds of free black people who lived there remained a powerful symbol and a serious threat to the English colonies. The Spanish governor's offer of freedom to any slaves who fled the Carolinas and Georgia for Florida, converted to Roman Catholicism, swore allegiance to the King of Spain, and pledged to serve for four years in the militia destabilized the English settlements and encouraged insurrections. This, effectively, was the first Underground Railroad, and it ran from Charleston to St. Augustine.[1]

In 1693, King Charles II issued a proclamation making it known that runaway slaves could come to Florida and be granted their freedom, in effect ratifying an unofficial policy that the governor of Florida, Diego de Quiroga, had instituted in 1687. Recall that many of the African slaves shipped to the American colonies from the kingdoms of Kongo and Angola were Catholics already. Catholic Spain, an inveterate enemy of Protestant Britain, sought to weaken, if not destroy, the colonies of its British rivals, and both countries were becoming increasingly dependent upon an unobstructed source for African slaves. Between 1720 and 1740, South Carolina rice production grew from 8.2 million pounds a year to 35 million, demanding a commensurate increase in slave labor. By encouraging runaways, the Spanish aimed a dagger at the heart of British power.[2]

From the very beginning of English settlements in the Carolinas, Spain plotted their ruin. The fierce and bloody conflicts that resulted took place within a rivalry that pitted the Spanish, English, various Indian tribes, and Africans against one another for power and survival. As early as 1686, Spanish forces in Florida organized a combined Spanish, Indian, and African raid on Edisto Island, one of the Carolina Sea Islands. They not only killed several Englishmen, but burned a Scots settlement on Port Royal and made off with 13 slaves belonging to the English governor. The Spanish so often attacked English settlements that their African allies and the slaves they seized in the process became extremely familiar with the routes back and forth between St. Augustine and the Carolina coast. When in 1687, eight male and two female slaves escaped by canoe from Carolina and arrived in Florida, the governor had them baptized. They not only entered the Catholic faith, but also the defense forces of the colony and helped construct the grand Castillo de San Marcos, the large, star-shaped coquina fortification that still overlooks St. Augustine and dominates the coast.

English agent William Dunlop visited St. Augustine to protest the Spanish offers of freedom to runaway slaves, but left with only vague promises and no cessation of the flow of fugitives to Florida. In fact, the numbers would only increase as a kind of black-slave grapevine (as crusty John Adams would describe this method of communication in his diary as early as September 1775) spread word among the English slaves about the freedom that awaited

---

[1] The estimates are from the Slave Trade Database: http://www.slavevoyages.org/tast/assessment/estimates .faces; by far and away the best work on blacks in colonial Florida is Jane Landers, *Black Society in Spanish Florida* (Urbana: University of Illinois Press, 1999).

[2] Peter Charles Hoffer, *Cry Liberty: The Great Stono River Slave Rebellion of 1739* (New York: Oxford University Press, 2010), 26.

them in Florida.[3] The number of runaways became so large that the English governor complained to the Spanish that the slaves ran away "dayly to your towns." The flow grew so much that even the Spanish governor sought royal guidance. And this is why Charles II —seeing the value in thereby weakening the English and simultaneously strengthening Spain's Florida settlement—on November 7, 1693, issued his edict proclaiming that Spain would give "liberty to all . . . the men as well as the women . . . so that by their example and by my liberality others will do the same." The astonishing move offered hope to English slaves and also created an unusual multiethnic community in St. Augustine that, while still permitting slavery, also provided freedom and, for a time, a measure of security for African Americans and Native Americans.[4]

From 1702 until 1718, the region saw conflict at unprecedented levels, including two Indian wars, the Tuscarora War of 1711 and the even more catastrophic Yamasee War of 1715, which nearly destroyed the English colony in the Carolinas. All the conflict of this era involved the Spanish at St. Augustine and their African and Indian allies, and took place during Queen Anne's War (known in Europe as the War of the Spanish Secession), which only increased the levels of conflict in the region, along with the competition for slaves. Indeed, one of the prime motives for Native American opposition to the English was their fear of enslavement.

---

[3] "The Negroes have a wonderfull Art of communicating Intelligence among themselves. It will run severall hundreds of Miles in a Week or Fortnight." Adams's diary remarks are at http://www.masshist.org/digitaladams/aea/cfm/doc.cfm?id=D24.

[4] Landers, *Black Society in Spanish Florida*, 23–25.

✦✦✦

SPAIN DID NOT, HOWEVER, MAINTAIN THE UPPER HAND. IN 1702 AND AGAIN IN 1704, AN ENGLISH FORCE INCINERATED MUCH OF ST. AUGUSTINE, but not its invaluable fort, murdering thousands of Christianized Indians and making off with many more as slaves. For Africans in the Carolinas, the conflicts only tightened security measures, increased the number of slave patrols, and made enslavement even harsher in an effort to stem the flow of fugitives to the Spanish. Yet at the same time the English found themselves terrified by the coalition of Indian tribes that had banded together to crush the colony. For instance, in the Tuscarora War, John Lawson, leader of the Bath, North Carolina, settlement, was executed by the Tuscaroras, although they freed one of his slaves–perhaps to further terrorize the whites. The slave reported that Lawson was hanged, but another account revealed that Lawson was impaled with numerous pieces of wood and slowly set on fire.[5]

Facing possible annihilation at the hands of the Indians throughout this era and lacking sufficient manpower, the English took the surprising move of inducting slaves into the colony's militia. While characteristic of Spanish colonies, such a move rarely happened among the English–who outlawed the right of slaves to own firearms–marking a new level of fear and desperation. In 1708, for instance, the Carolina colony awarded freedom to any slave "who in Time of an Invasion, kills an Enemy,"

---

[5] Landers, *Black Society in Spanish Florida*, 25–26; William L. Ramsey, "'Something Cloudy in Their Looks': The Origins of the Yamasee War," *Journal of American History* 90 (June 2003): 44–75; http://www.nchistoricsites.org/bath/tuscarora.htm.

and the colony agreed to compensate the slave's owner for the loss of his property. In 1715, at the start of the Yamasee War, South Carolina voted to provide lances to those blacks "who cannot be supplied with guns in the present expedition." Revealing a level of integration that would rarely, if ever, be duplicated in a military force located in the South until the Korean War, the English reported that at the beginning of the war several "good partyes of Men, White, Indian and Negroes" operated in the field countering Yamasee attacks.

Lacking enough white men, and uncertain of the loyalty of local Indians, the English turned to their slaves for defense, eventually enrolling hundreds in their militia, aiming to have "600 Whites & 400 negroes" under arms. The slaves faced a choice of bearing arms for their masters, and perhaps winning freedom, or running away to the Yamasees, who often proved welcoming hosts but could offer no permanent guarantee of freedom. Peace came to the region by the early 1720s, but the English response was dramatically to increase the number of slaves they imported, creating an even greater racial imbalance in the colony. As one colonial agent lamented, the growing number of African slaves only led "to the great endangering [of] the Province."[6]

The ever-growing body of slaves fresh from Africa and Florida's policy of offering freedom to runaways led to disaster. Slave uprisings occurred in 1720 and 1724, significantly increasing the number of blacks in St. Augustine and of those eager to gain their freedom and take up arms in support of the Spanish Crown. In 1726, a group of escaped English slaves arrived in St. Augustine from the Stono region of South Carolina. Not surprisingly, some of the runaways were combat veterans who had fought with the Yamasee and now volunteered to fight for Spain and against their former masters. According to one account, the following year "Ten Negroes and fourteen Indians Commanded by those of their own colour, without any Spaniards in company with them" attacked the English and seized more slaves, followed up by a combined force of Spanish and former slaves that raided an English plantation on the Edisto River and captured additional slaves.[7]

When the English retaliated against St. Augustine in 1728, they met resistance not only from Spanish troops but also from a black militia unit under the command of Captain Francisco Menéndez (a self-described Mandingo, but also an Atlantic Creole, someone already acculturated to European culture on the African coast, who then enters the Atlantic world either as a slave or free), who served Spain for more than 40 years. He and his troops performed such invaluable service that they earned praise from the king, who in 1733 reissued his 1693 offer of freedom to any slaves who escaped from the English colonies.

In 1738, the runaways and other blacks then living in St. Augustine moved about two miles outside the city to land given by the

[6] Landers, *Black Society in Spanish Florida*, 25–26; Philip D. Morgan and Andrew Jackson O'Shaughnessy, "Arming Slaves in the American Revolution," in *Arming Slaves: From Classical Times to the Modern Age*, eds. Christopher Leslie Brown and Philip D. Morgan (New Haven: Yale University Press, 2006), 181; Peter H. Wood, *Black Majority: Negroes in Colonial South Carolina from 1670 Through the Stono Rebellion* (New York: W. W. Norton, 1974), 125–30.

[7] Landers, *Black Society in Spanish Florida*, 26–28.

Spanish. Their settlement was called Gracia Real de Santa Teresa de Mose, better known as Fort Mose. Not unlike a South American Maroon society, it was commanded by Africans, Captain Menéndez and another black officer, Antonio de la Puente, but functioned as an outer defense for the city. Spanish authorities oversaw construction of the fort and the surrounding homes owned by the black residents, armed the men, and even provided the services of a priest who baptized the converts. Archeologists recovered a St. Christopher medal during recent excavations at the Fort Mose site, which could have been obtained by its original owner in any part of the Spanish empire, or even in the Catholic kingdom of Kongo. A symbol of the patron saint of travelers, the medal is a remarkable symbol of the black diaspora.[8]

THE CREATION OF FORT MOSE, WHICH THE ENGLISH RAZED IN 1739, SPOKE TO A VASTLY DIFFERENT AFRICAN EXPERIENCE IN NORTH AMERICA, one that allowed for measures of freedom and autonomy that would rarely be experienced at the same level until the next century. Because of its success and the freedom it promised to English slaves, the settlement represented an intolerable symbol of black independence and a real threat to the foundations of English slavery. Nothing proved this more dramatically than the events of September 9, 1739, at a branch of the Stono River near Charleston, South Carolina.[9]

Thousands of the slaves shipped to the Carolinas prior to 1740 came from the kingdom of Kongo. So many came from this same African region that South Carolina became known as "the Kongolese center of North America." The fact that a large number of the slaves from this region of Angola were already Catholic made them especially appealing to the Spanish, and ever more threatening to the Protestant English. Some of the English became so fearful of their slaves' religion that they imagined Jesuit priests mingling among them, spreading dissention. But no Jesuits were required to incite Africans laboring under English domination.

On Sunday, September 9, 1739, a day free of labor, about 20 slaves under the leadership of a man named Jemmy provided whites with a painful lesson on the African desire for liberty. Many of the group were experienced soldiers, either from the Yamasee War or their experience in Africa, and had been trained in the use of weapons. They gathered at the Stono River and raided a simple warehouse-like store, Hutchenson's, which supplied the region with manufactured goods from England and continental Europe. They executed the white owners and placed their victims' heads on the store's front steps for all to see. They proceeded to other houses in the area, killing the occupants and burning the structures, swelling their ranks as they marched through the colony toward St. Augustine.

---

[8] Henry Louis Gates, Jr., *Life Upon These Shores: Looking at African American History, 1513-2008* (New York: Alfred A. Knopf, 2011), 22–23.

[9] The best account remains Wood, *Black Majority*, 285–326; also see Hoffer, *Cry Liberty*.

More and more slaves joined the original 20, although others avoided the group or actually helped hide their masters. The insurrectionists soon numbered about 100 and paraded down King's Highway, according to sources, carrying banners and shouting, "Liberty!" In their native Kikongo, they would have thought the word *lukangu*, a term that would have expressed the English ideas embodied in liberty and, perhaps, salvation. They fought off the English for more than a week before the colonists rallied and killed most of the rebels, although some very likely reached Fort Mose.[10]

Even after colonial forces crushed the Stono uprising, additional outbreaks occurred, including the very next year when South Carolina executed at least 50 additional rebel slaves. The appeal of St. Augustine proved too much for the English, and not long after suppression of the Stono rebels, they struck with fury at the city, but especially against Fort Mose. While the English destroyed the fort, Menéndez and his militia retook the outpost the following year, earning acclaim from the Spanish government, which praised "the constancy, valor and glory of the officers . . . the patriotism, courage, and steadiness of the troops." The fort persisted but declined in significance as the Carolina slave regime strengthened, surviving until the 1763 Paris Peace Treaty, when the Spanish abandoned Florida and many of the Fort Mose residents relocated to Cuba.[11]

THE STONO REBELLION, THE LARGEST SLAVE REVOLT EVER STAGED IN THE 13 COLONIES, WAS NOT AN ISOLATED EVENT AND REFLECTED THE TENSIONS OF A SLAVE SOCIETY IN THE MAKING. Uprisings and conspiracies—many inspired by Spanish Florida—took place in Virginia, South Carolina, Georgia, the Caribbean, and even New York City.[12] The New York conspiracy of 1741, while never actually materializing, developed at the end of a series of disturbances—as had been the case in the Carolinas and St. Augustine—that instilled nearly uncontrollable fear in whites and led to devastating consequences for African Americans. In this case, however, the conspiracy came at a time and in a section of the country that few today think of as slave-bound, although New York did not abolish slavery until 1827. And while the region may be fairly characterized as a society with slaves, rather than a slave society, black freedom became every bit as restricted and regulated in the Empire State as in Virginia or South Carolina.[13]

---

[10] John K. Thornton, *The Kongolese Saint Anthony: Dona Beatriz Kimpa Vita and the Antonian Movement, 1684–1706* (Cambridge: Cambridge University Press, 1998), 210–13; Hoffer, *Cry Liberty*, 18–21, 72–74.

[11] Landers, *Black Society in Spanish Florida*, 35, 38.

[12] Herbert Aptheker, *American Negro Slave Revolts* (New York: International Publishers, 1969), 18–20; Christopher Leslie Brown, *Moral Capital: Foundations of British Abolitionism* (Chapel Hill: University of North Carolina Press, 2006), 75–76.

[13] See Jill Lepore, *New York Burning: Liberty, Slavery, and Conspiracy in Eighteenth-Century Manhattan* (New York: Alfred A. Knopf, 2005); Ira Berlin, *Many Thousands Gone: The First Two Centuries of Slavery in North America* (Cambridge: Belknap Press of Harvard University Press, 1998), 47–63, 180, 187, 188, 190.

FACING PAGE: *Fort Mose*, by Jeff Gage. Watercolor. Museum of Florida History.

In 1991, construction workers preparing the foundations for a new federal office building in Lower Manhattan struck wooden boxes containing the remains of several hundred African men, women, and children, all the former slaves of 17th-century Dutch and British householders. Just a few blocks north of City Hall in one of the world's largest financial centers, these remains remind us of the human costs of a nation's formation. Most of the bodies were of children; most of the adults were scarcely out of their 30s when they died, after lives as brutish as they were short. They remind us of both the multinational character of North American slavery during that first century of settlement and how its racial character had hardened by the end of that century.

✕✕✕

THE NEW AMSTERDAM COLONY WAS SETTLED BY THE DUTCH IN THE EARLY 1600S DURING THEIR RISE TO WORLD POWER; it was seized from them in 1664 by the Duke of Albany and York, the future King James II of England. Just two years earlier, James had taken the helm of the newly chartered Royal African Company, which held monopoly rights to the West African slave trade. Although most of those slaves would be consigned to the plantations in the British West Indies, a not insignificant number were redirected to slave auctions in downtown Manhattan, including no doubt many of those laid to rest in the "negro burial grounds." Moreover, the burial site was established because in the 1690s, blacks were barred from interment in the city's churchyards, as had been the practice in decades past.

It surprises many people today to learn that New York City was the leading individual port in the slave trade in the colonies before 1700, receiving 11 shipments direct from Africa, bringing in 1,890 slaves between 1655 and 1698, although the Chesapeake region (where slaves were sold on virtually every river and inlet) took in five times that number of slaves. (In the 18th century, Charleston would receive far more slaves than Virginia, Maryland, and New York combined.)[14]

Thus, we should not be surprised that New York also became a site of rebellion. Despite the ability of a very small group of freed black people to own property, not unlike early colonial Virginia, tensions remained high and the enforcement of enslavement rigorous. In the spring of 1712, slaves—Akan-speaking "Coromantees"—set fire to the house of a white owner, and as the occupants fled the flames, the slaves waited outside to butcher them. One white was stabbed in the back by his own slave. About nine whites died in the revolt and another six were wounded.

Authorities swiftly rounded up about 21 conspirators—many merely on the suspicion of involvement—and began an orgy of executions. Six of the rebels decided to kill themselves rather than be captured and suffer the fate that they knew awaited them. Of those captured,

---

[14] Ira Berlin and Leslie M. Harris, eds., *Slavery in New York* (New York: The New Press and the New-York Historical Society, 2005), 3–10, 31–56.

FACING PAGE: *Slave Sale in New Amsterdam*, by Howard Pyle. *Harper's New Monthly Magazine*, January 1895.

some were broken on the wheel, others hung alive by chains, while others burned at the stake, with one unfortunate captive named Tom slowly roasted for eight hours. One pregnant female slave was allowed to give birth, and was then executed. The remains and several severed heads were displayed along popular roads to show other slaves what lay in store for rebels. The retribution became so fierce that the colony's governor halted the killings and pardoned some of the accused, including some free Spanish black sailors who had been illegally enslaved before the insurrection.

While the governor encouraged citizens to abandon slavery for white indentured servitude, hoping to avoid future incidents, colonists only increased slave imports—as the South Carolinians would do after the Yamasee War—eventually doubling the region's slave population. To exercise increased social control and prevent future threats, the colonial legislature the following year enacted new, harsher regulations designed to rivet the chains of slavery even tighter, virtually eliminating the possibility that a master could ever free a slave.[15]

After the first attempt at rebellion, whites began to imagine insurrections in every whisper of a slave. Rumors of plots surfaced repeatedly in New York and New Jersey, leaving whites keenly attuned to any hint of an effort to burn their city. Hoping to avert another incident, New York outlawed the right of any black to meet with others after sunset. Whites had become so paranoid that in 1731, the words of one drunken slave proved sufficient to ignite a wave of legal killings, whippings, and mutilations. The charge of rape or that a slave had in

any way attacked a white woman would send him to the stake. Additionally, whites blamed the meddling Christianizing efforts of itinerant Great Awakening evangelicals like George Whitefield who had repeatedly warned against the dangers of slave owning. With about 1,700 blacks living in a city of about 7,000 whites determined to grind every person of African descent under their heel, revenge might be inevitable.[16]

In early 1741, Fort George in New York burned to the ground. Fires erupted elsewhere in the city, four in one day, and in New Jersey and on Long Island. Several whites claimed they had heard slaves bragging about setting the fires and threatening worse. They concluded that a revolt had been planned by secret black societies and gangs, inspired by a conspiracy of priests and their Catholic minions—white, black, brown, free, and slave.

Certainly, ethnic groups such as the Papa, from the Slave Coast near Whydah; the Igbo, from the area around the Niger River; and the Malagasy, from Madagascar, constituted coherent groups who may have led a resistance movement. Other identifiable groups were Spanish-American sailors, "negroes and mulattoes," who had been captured in the early spring of 1740, brought to New York from the West Indies, and sold as slaves. The sailors themselves maintained that they were "free subjects of the King of Spain" and hence entitled to treatment as prisoners of war. Known among the conspirators as the "Cuba People," they had probably come from Havana, the greatest port of the Spanish West Indies and a center of a free black population. Having been

---

[15] Berlin and Harris, *Slavery in New York*, 63, 78–80; Gates, *Life Upon These Shores*, 18–19.

[16] Berlin and Harris, *Slavery in New York*, 70; Gates, *Life Upon These Shores*, 20–21.

"free men in their own country," they rightly felt unjustly enslaved in New York.[17]

A 16-year-old Irish indentured servant, arrested in a case of theft and perhaps hoping to convince authorities to go easy on him, claimed knowledge of a plot by the city's slaves—in league with a few whites—to kill white men, seize white women, and incinerate the city. In the investigation that followed, 34 people were executed, including 30 black men, 2 white men, and 2 white women. Seventy people of African descent were exiled to places as various as Newfoundland, Madeira, Saint-Domingue (the French colony on Hispaniola), and Curaçao. Before the end of the summer of 1741, 17 blacks were hanged and 13 more went to the stake, becoming ghastly illuminations of white fears ignited by the institution of slavery they so zealously defended.[18]

The slave revolts threatened in New York City and throughout the early 18th century highlight the centrality of slavery to colonial economic and political development. Despite the threat to their very lives—and ignoring any consideration of justice—the colonists insisted upon the ownership of Africans. The insurrections also shed light on how slaves retained their Atlantic identity, forged in Africa and brought to America. As revealed in religious and burial practices, Africans retained their diverse roots and borrowed ideas and tactics from the Atlantic world. The revolts in the 13 North American colonies also echoed across the other 13 British colonies in the Caribbean, from St. John to Antigua to Jamaica, where an insurrection nearly ended slavery in 1760. Although none succeeded, the rebellions speak resoundingly of the impressive ability of Africans throughout the Americas to forge their own cultures and societies, await a chance for freedom, and strike blows for that liberty, envisioning the scope of their horizons in light of the larger Atlantic world.

◆◆◆

"IF SLAVERY BE THUS FATALLY CONTAGIOUS, HOW IS IT THAT WE HEAR THE LOUDEST YELPS FOR LIBERTY AMONG THE DRIVERS OF NEGROES?" ASKED SAMUEL JOHNSON.[19] Historians are by no means the first to notice the contradiction between colonial assertions of freedom, liberty, and equality and their commitment to slavery. Critics in England, like the great lexicographer and author Samuel Johnson, found little difficulty in rebutting the American colonists' charges that British taxation without representation threatened liberty.

Such critiques, however, were not limited to America's opponents. As early as 1764, colonial statesman James Otis asserted his belief in the right of all, black and white, to freedom. In 1774, the Reverend Jeremy Belknap, founder of the Massachusetts Historical Society, wondered,

---

[17] Berlin and Harris, *Slavery in New York*, 62–89; Eliga H. Gould, "Entangled Histories, Entangled Worlds: The English-Speaking Atlantic as a Spanish Periphery," *American Historical Review* 112 (June 2007): 764–86; Peter Linebaugh and Marcus Rediker, *The Many-headed Hydra: Sailors, Slaves, Commoners, and the Hidden History of the Revolutionary Atlantic* (Boston: Beacon Press, 2000), 174–210.

[18] Berlin and Harris, *Slavery in New York*, 83–89.

[19] Samuel Johnson, *Taxation No Tyranny: An Answer to the Resolution and Address of the American Congress* (London: Printed for T. Cadell, 1775), http://www.samueljohnson.com/tnt.html#top.

"Would it not be astonishing to hear that a people who are contending
so earnestly for liberty are not willing to allow liberty to others?"

"Would it not be astonishing to hear that a peo-ple who are contending so earnestly for liberty are not willing to allow liberty to others?" The next year, Thomas Paine similarly drew atten-tion to his fellow Americans' hypocrisy: "With what consistency, or decency [can] they com-plain so loudly of attempts to enslave them, while they hold so many hundred thousands in slavery; and annually enslave many thousands more, without any pretence of authority, or claim upon them?"[20]

Even the famed Abigail Adams advised her husband that she wished "most sincerely there was not a slave in the province; it al-ways appeared a most iniquitous scheme to me to fight ourselves for what we are daily robbing and plundering from those who have as good a right to freedom as we have." And if they chose to listen, colonists were given re-minders by their own slaves of the contradic-tion they so readily accepted. In 1773 and 1774, Massachusetts slaves petitioned the colonial legislature five times, asserting that "we have in common with all other men a natural right to our freedom." In a famous 1773 petition, four slaves who claimed to be speaking for all the slaves in Massachusetts declared that they ex-pected "great things from men who have made

such a noble stand against the designs of their *fellow-men* to enslave them."[21]

The American Revolution brought un-precedented opportunities for freedom and the possibility to forever alter the institution of slavery. The rhetoric of freedom and liberty that defined the contest between the colonies and Great Britain inspired the slaves. But the message of freedom did not come exclusively from the Patriot side. In fact, in most of the 13 American colonies (it's important to remember that on the eve of the Revolution, Britain had 26 colonies overall, plus two unofficial settle-ments), a slave's best chance of securing his liberty came from Britain rather than the new United States. Struggling in the crosscurrents of many nations and conflicting appeals, most Africans Americans felt no natural allegiance to the Patriot cause—they simply wanted freedom.

HISTORIANS HAVE DONE A RATHER POOR JOB OF ASSESSING THE ROLE OF AFRICAN AMERICANS IN THE REVOLUTION—on either side of the conflict. Until relatively recently, the subject barely ap-peared in histories of the conflict, and to this

[20] Edward Ayers, "Anti-Slavery Sentiment Emerges in Pre-Revolutionary America," http://www.historyisfun .org/antislavery-sentiment.htm; Thomas Paine, "Justice and Humanity" and "To Americans," *Pennsylvania Journal and the Weekly Advertiser* (March 8, 1775), http://www.constitution.org/tp/afri.htm.

[21] Ayers, "Anti-Slavery Sentiment Emerges," http:// www.historyisfun.org/antislavery-sentiment.htm; Herbert Aptheker, ed., *A Documentary History of the Negro People in the United States from Colonial Times Through the Civil War* (New York: Citadel Press, 1962), 7.

day we do not possess anything approaching an accurate count of how many people of African descent fought on either side of the war. Historians still rely on an estimate of the number of black Patriots formulated more than 70 years ago, asserting without any concrete evidence that about 5,000 African Americans fought for the colonists. This number is almost assuredly too low, as at the famed Battle of Bunker Hill, meticulous research has uncovered that there were more than 100 African American participants in that one engagement.[22] Despite the efforts of historians stretching back to the black abolitionist William C. Nell to establish the centrality of blacks to American independence, there is no question that the majority of African Americans–most of whom were slaves–either took no part in the conflict or at the first opportunity fled to the British.[23]

Thomas Jefferson, James Madison, George Mason, Patrick Henry, George Washington, and other slaveholders from New York to South Carolina lost their property to His Majesty's Royal Army during the war. For those slaves who remained on the farm, most owners believed that they were simply waiting for the right opportunity to flee. Richard Henry Lee, Virginia member of the Continental Congress and later a U.S. senator, lamented that all his

neighbors had "lost every slave they had in the world. . . ."[24] Jefferson believed that Virginia alone lost about 30,000 slaves in one year. The number of fugitive slaves encamped, ironically, on Sullivan's Island in Charleston Harbor (the Ellis Island of American slavery) became so threatening that Henry Laurens, the former slave trader and chairman of the city's Committee of Safety, ordered a Patriot raid on the camp.

On December 18, 1775, 54 soldiers disguised as Indians burned the shelters of the fugitives, killed several, and seized four in a raid meant to teach blacks a lesson and embarrass the English, who at the time maintained a small presence in the city but soon left. Earlier, Laurens also had authorized the liquidation of another group of blacks on Tybee Island off the Georgia coast. Again dressed as Indians, about 70 whites slaughtered the entire group.

White Charlestonians lived in dire fear that the tens of thousands of blacks in the region would rise up against them. A few months earlier, in the summer of 1775, jurors condemned to death a free black harbor pilot named Thomas Jeremiah on a rumor that he was planning a slave insurrection with the English. Although Jeremiah was free, successful, and property-owning, and although lacking any concrete evidence against him, city officials ignored the objections of the colonial governor and hanged him, then burned his corpse in the public square. Before he died, someone overheard the condemned man warn

[22] Gary Nash, "Introduction," to *The Negro in the American Revolution*, by Benjamin Quarles (Chapel Hill: University of North Carolina Press, 1966), xiii–xxvi; George Quintal, Jr., comp., *Patriots of Color: A Peculiar Beauty and Merit* (Boston: Boston National Historical Park, 2004), 21.

[23] William C. Nell, *The Colored Patriots of the American Revolution* (Boston: Robert F. Wallcut, 1855); Nash, "Introduction," xviii–xx.

[24] Simon Schama, *Rough Crossings: Britain, the Slaves, and the American Revolution* (New York: HarperCollins, 2006), quoted 118.

that God would one day punish the city for "shedding his innocent blood."[25]

Overwhelming evidence points to the fact that whenever British forces approached, slaves took the opportunity to flee. They did so with good reason. On November 7, 1775, while standing on a captured Patriot vessel, Royal Governor of Virginia Lord Dunmore offered freedom to those slaves who would enlist in the King's army. By proclamation, he announced that he did "hereby further declare all indentured Servants, Negroes, or others (appertaining to Rebels) free that are able and willing to bear Arms, they joining His Majesty's Troops as soon as may be, for the more speedily reducing this Colony to a proper Sense of their Duty." Although Dunmore's "Ethiopian" Regiment proved militarily ineffective, with hundreds dying of a smallpox epidemic, symbolically, it wreaked havoc among Americans.

The Patriots issued no such declaration and, in fact, for a time rejected the recruitment of all black soldiers, terrified by the idea that Dunmore's proclamation would spark a bloodthirsty slave insurrection. Ironically, the ex-slave trader Henry Laurens (who was involved in the sale and purchase of the child Priscilla from Bunce Island) and his son John, an aide-de-camp to Washington, argued for a general recruitment of slaves with an offer of freedom at the close of the war, but South Carolina repudiated the idea. More important and with great portent for the future, George Washington refused to support the recruitment of slaves, although he did approve of allowing free blacks

to serve. He feared dire economic consequences for his own estate from what likely would have turned into a move toward general emancipation; and when the Laurenses pressed their plans on him, Washington contemplated selling off all his slaves.[26]

While the Patriots offered African Americans a mixed message at best, the Crown early and warmly welcomed African Americans into their ranks. Four to five thousand black troops, the total number assumed to have fought in the Patriot cause, were with Lord Cornwallis just before the surrender at Yorktown; many of those who managed to survive the end of the war departed with the British. The same scenario occurred wherever British forces had to evacuate their troops. They withdrew about 30,000 Loyalists and African Americans just from New York, which included at least 3,000 fugitive slaves and likely many more. As many as 8,000 black people left Charleston, South Carolina, in the final evacuation, although most departed as slaves with their Loyalist owners.[27]

Determining with precision the number of slaves who won their freedom as a result of the war is extremely difficult. Some scholars estimate that as many as 100,000 slaves at least made an attempt to reach British lines.

---

[25] Jane G. Landers, *Atlantic Creoles in the Age of Revolutions* (Cambridge: Harvard University Press, 2010), 25, 26–27; Sylvia R. Frey, "Between Slavery and Freedom: Virginia Blacks in the American Revolution," *Journal of Southern History* 49 (August 1983): 376.

[26] http://www.pbs.org/wgbh/aia/part2/2h42t.html; Quarles, *The Negro in the American Revolution*, 16–18, 19–32; Henry Wiencek, *An Imperfect God: George Washington, His Slaves, and the Creation of America* (New York: Farrar, Straus and Giroux, 2003), 224–38; Alan Gilbert, *Black Patriots and Loyalists: Fighting for Emancipation in the War for Independence* (Chicago: University of Chicago Press, 2012), 66–84.

[27] Cassandra Pybus, *Epic Journeys of Freedom: Runaway Slaves of the American Revolution and Their Global Quest for Liberty* (Boston: Beacon Press, 2006), 70–71.

Life of George Washington, The Farmer, by Junius Brutus Stearns, circa 1853, Paris.
Lithograph. Library of Congress.

Whatever the number, the majority who ran away never secured their freedom, and were either returned to their owners, as was stipulated in the terms of the peace treaty with Britain, disappeared without record, or died. But it is likely that at least 10,000 former slaves managed to win their freedom as a result of the war, and the actual figure may even have surpassed 20,000, since British records reveal that about 10,000 more blacks settled in Canada after the conflict ended. In one sense, the American Revolution had turned into the largest slave insurrection in modern history.[28]

---

[28] Pybus, *Epic Journeys of Freedom,* 22–23, 44–45, 48–49, 53, 60, 71; Gilbert, *Black Patriots and Loyalists,* 205–06; Schama, *Rough Crossings,* 8–9.

✖✖✖

MOUNT VERNON, GEORGE WASHINGTON'S ESTATE OVERLOOKING THE POTOMAC RIVER OUTSIDE ALEXANDRIA, VIRGINIA, IS AN AMERICAN ICON. But when the Revolution broke out, more than 200 slaves lived there—all owned by the commander-in-chief of the Continental Army and his wife, Martha. By the time of the president's death in 1799, George and Martha Washington owned 317 African Americans, including 98 children.[29] One Mount Vernon slave was a groomsman named Harry Washington, and his story vividly illustrates the issues at stake for African Americans during the Revolution.

Harry may have been born in Senegambia and brought to Virginia with several shipments of slaves in 1763, but his early years are something of a mystery since Washington owned several slaves named Harry. It is virtually impossible to distinguish one from another in the records that Washington retained, and all we know for certain is that Harry the groomsman began appearing in the records in 1766. Although he claimed to abhor separating slave families, Washington did so when it suited him, and certainly never hesitated to sell off a recalcitrant slave to almost certain death in the Caribbean regardless of family considerations.[30] Harry may have had a wife and perhaps even a son, and if so Washington sent the two to a different plantation and kept Harry at Mount Vernon.

Harry's first confirmed attempt to run away came in 1771, at about age 31, but he was soon captured and returned to the plantation. Was he motivated by the separation of his family or by Revolutionary ideology? We do not know. It is likely, however, that Mount Vernon slaves quickly became cognizant of the growing strife between the colonies and England—perhaps Washington even expressed his anger over Britain's attempt to "enslave" the colonists within the hearing of some of his slaves. It is difficult to imagine that Harry and his fellow slaves did not know that their master was about to become head of the colonists' army.[31]

Without a doubt, Harry also had his own ideas about freedom. Washington, who took the time to get to know many of his slaves, was anything but confident that they would remain loyal if the war came to the region. After all, his slaves had run away before, even in the 1750s, and his cousin Lunt Washington (1737–1796), who managed the estate in the general's absence, expressed both confidence and concern over the state of bonded labor at Mount Vernon. While somewhat ambivalent about the slaves, he felt they would largely remain loyal, but thought that the white indentured servants would run away at the first opportunity. Even so, he knew that like himself, the slaves understood that "liberty is sweet."

Lunt Washington completely misread the slaves he governed. In 1781, 17 escaped from Mount Vernon when a British warship, the *Savage*, appeared in the Potomac near the estate. Earlier, on July 24, 1776, a small fleet of British

---

[29] http://gwpapers.virginia.edu/documents/will/slavelist.html.

[30] Wiencek, *An Imperfect God*, 131–33; e-mail to authors from William M. Ferraro, associate editor, the Papers of George Washington, December 6, 2012.

[31] Pybus, *Epic Journeys of Freedom*, 3–6; Washington owned many slaves named Harry, and Pybus confused a slave that Washington put to work on the Dismal Swamp project with a house slave bearing the same name.

warships sailed up the Potomac and skirmished with some local militia very near to the general's plantation. In the midst of the confusion, three white servants ran away and offered their services to the Crown. Harry might have taken the opportunity to join the runaways, but the British officer who received the servants made no mention of a black slave. Harry later claimed to have run away from Mount Vernon in 1776, but the exact method that he used remains uncertain. By the war's end, at least 17 slaves—and likely many more—owned by the Washingtons and his cousin had followed Harry and fled Mount Vernon. General Washington recovered only two runaways after the surrender at Yorktown and sometime later recovered a few more in Philadelphia, totaling about six or seven. Although he had hired fugitive slave catchers to bring them all back, most got away to live free.[32]

Harry eventually entered a British Pioneer unit as a corporal; the troops, attached to an artillery regiment, did more fatigue work than fighting. He traveled to New York when Lord Dunmore withdrew the remnants of his Ethiopian Regiment and was then transferred to South Carolina. As the war progressed and England's fortunes failed, Harry was evacuated back to New York in 1782, where the following year he and thousands of other freed slaves—including two others from Mount Vernon—were resettled to Nova Scotia.

But the new "freedom" offered by the Crown soured for many American fugitive slaves. The British herded the black refugees into a lonely community they named Birchtown, a windswept, uninviting parcel of land thick with rocks and scrub oak, not a promising location for a farm. But Harry tried his best, marrying a woman named Sara, converting to Methodism, and building a house on 40 acres. When the opportunity arose to resettle in the British colony of Sierra Leone, Harry took his wife and three children there. By 1800, he and many of the settlers had become disenchanted with white domination over the colony, especially their inability to own property, forcing them to live much as the sharecroppers of the post–Civil War era would in the former Confederate states. Ever the rebel, he and several other settlers joined an independence movement, but the colony's government soon crushed the revolt. Harry's freedom, tantalizingly offered by Great Britain, had turned to misfortune. He was exiled to Bullom Shore, an area north of the colony known for malaria, where the groomsman of George Washington died in obscurity.[33]

WHILE THE CROWN AT FIRST APPEARED TO OFFER AFRICAN AMERICANS A MORE PROMISING ROUTE TO FREEDOM, in reality most blacks faced a Hobson's choice: whatever side they chose, the result was fraught with danger—disease, death, discrimination, even possible re-enslavement. Nevertheless, the British kept their word and freed the black Loyalists, resisting the demands of the victorious Patriots that their fugitive slaves be returned. Even if their subsequent lives in Nova

---

[32] Pybus, *Epic Journeys of Freedom*, 71; Wiencek, *An Imperfect God*, 251.

[33] http://gwpapers.virginia.edu/documents/revolution/martha.html; Pybus, *Epic Journeys of Freedom*, 12, 16, 19–20, 218; Wiencek, *An Imperfect God*, 251, 259; A. B. C. Sibthorpe, *The History of Sierra Leone* (New York: Humanities Press, 1971), 47.

Scotia or Sierra Leone proved to be far more difficult than they imagined, these former slaves were able to live as free men and women. Those who sided with the Patriots, at least in the North, stood a chance of enjoying an imperfect freedom in the new Republic, and so did their children.

Many thousands, how many we do not yet know, fought—and many died—at Lexington and Concord, Bunker Hill and Saratoga, Cowpens and Yorktown, and virtually every other major battle of the war. They helped to build a new country and only wanted what every other American expected: a stake in it and the opportunity to fulfill whatever destiny their talents and luck would provide. Jefferson's inspiring words that "all men are created equal" represented a profound challenge to a slave society, ultimately opening a window of hope for some enslaved African Americans.

One such opening for a slave occurred in 1781 in rural Sheffield, Massachusetts, situated in the far western part of the state near the New York and Connecticut borders. The patriarchal-looking and hot-tempered Colonel John Ashley, a wealthy landowner, merchant, justice of the peace, legislator, and head of the local militia, dominated the region. He even had served as a judge on the County Court of Common Pleas before the Revolution and expected the appropriate deference. He married into a slave-owning family across the border in Columbia County, New York, and came into possession of a few slaves, including one named Mum Bett, born about 1744, and her younger sister Lizzie.

Ashley's wife, Annetje Hogeboom, shared her husband's disposition and in a rage against young Lizzie swung a fire shovel at her, but instead hit Mum Bett, who had raised her arm to protect her sister. The scar, which she "bore until the day of her death," launched a legal process that ultimately led to her freedom and helped extinguish slavery in the commonwealth of Massachusetts.[34]

Outraged that her owner felt empowered to beat her "property," Mum Bett left the Ashleys and walked a considerable distance to Stockbridge, where she met with the famed Federalist attorney Theodore Sedgwick, a friend of Ashley's, to lodge a complaint against her owners for the assault and to win her freedom. Very likely, she had heard of the rights the colonists had won as a result of the Revolution. Moreover, given the political roles during the Revolution of her owner and that of Sedgwick, whom Mum Bett may have met as early as 1773, she probably possessed an understanding that the state's new constitution of 1780 (John Adams's handiwork) guaranteed the freedom and equality of the state's citizens:

> Article I. All men are born free and equal, and have certain natural, essential, and unalienable rights; among which may be reckoned the right of enjoying and defending their lives and liberties; that

---

[34] Douglas R. Egerton, *Death or Liberty: African Americans and Revolutionary America* (New York: Oxford University Press, 2009), 104–05; Arthur Zilversmit, "Quok Walker, Mumbet, and the Abolition of Slavery in Massachusetts," *William and Mary Quarterly*, 3d ser., 25 (October 1968): 617–24.

FACING PAGE: Mum Bett, or Elizabeth Freeman, by Susan Anne Sedgwick, 1811. Watercolor miniature on ivory. Massachusetts Historical Society, Bridgeman Art Library.

of acquiring, possessing, and protecting property; in fine, that of seeking and obtaining their safety and happiness."[35]

Despite his friendship with Ashley, and despite the fact that he had once owned a slave himself, Sedgwick and the famed Connecticut lawyer Tapping Reeve took on Mum Bett's case, planning to base it on the idea that Article I of the constitution had effectively ended slavery in the commonwealth. This novel strategy made sense as other legal challenges, especially the Quok Walker series of cases, involved similar issues, developed simultaneously, and in one way or another were inspired by the ideology of the American Revolution that African Americans insisted was their rightful heritage, too. As historian Douglas Egerton has observed, these freedom cases that sprang up in the wake of independence showed that blacks "expected the Revolution to offer not merely new opportunities for freedom but also full participation in the new political order."[36]

These court cases are full of ironies and contradictions. First, as we have mentioned, Sedgwick had been a slave owner and subsequently accepted another case in Rhode Island, but instead served as the attorney for a slave owner. Second, while he hired Mum Bett as a domestic after the close of the case—and she became a virtual family member, even buried in the family plot—Sedgwick never became an antislavery advocate. Third, Tapping Reeve ran an influential law school in Litchfield, Connecticut, where among his many students was John C. Calhoun, who would become one of the United States senators from South Carolina and arguably one of the South's most articulate defenders of the institution of slavery.

The related Quok Walker cases had begun in the spring of 1781, when Walker left the employ of one Nathaniel Jennison, believing that he had an agreement to be freed when he turned 21. But when he abandoned the Jennison farm to work for John and Seth Caldwell, he was about 28 years old. Ironically, the Caldwell brothers were likely the sons of Walker's original owner. Why Walker waited so long to establish his freedom remains a mystery. Jennison found Walker at the Caldwells—whom he later successfully sued for theft of his property's labor—and beat him. Walker, like Mum Bett, had charged his "owner" with assault and asserted his freedom. He also convinced two of the state's best lawyers, Levi Lincoln and Caleb Strong, to take his assault case and win his freedom by challenging the legitimacy of slavery in the commonwealth based on the state constitution. In a final irony, the mercurial Ashley, despite his refusal to accept freedom for Mum Bett and another slave named Zach Mullen, whom he also assaulted for running away, in the end left Mullen and *two other slaves* a legacy in his will.[37]

---

[35] Massachusetts Constitution, http://www.nhinet.org/ccs/docs/ma-1780.htm.

[36] Egerton, *Death or Liberty*, 94; also see Zilversmit, "Quok Walker," 614–24; and Emily Blanck, "Seventeen Eighty-Three: The Turning Point in the Law of Slavery and Freedom in Massachusetts," *New England Quarterly* 75 (March 2002): 24–51. Quok Walker's name was spelled a variety of ways.

---

[37] William O'Brien, "Did the Jennison Case Outlaw Slavery in Massachusetts?" *William and Mary Quarterly*, 3d ser., 17 (April 1960): 223–41; Egerton, *Death or Liberty*, 106–07; Zilversmit, "Quok Walker, Mumbet," 617–18.

More important, however, none of these freedom suits actually outlawed slavery in the commonwealth, despite what historians have written over the years. Judges William Cushing (who owned slaves and resisted freeing them) and Nathaniel Peaslee Sargent are often given credit for instructing their juries to find slavery illegal–based on Article I–but none of the cases recorded any antislavery statements, and the juries decided only the facts in the case, that Mum Bett and Walker had been beaten and, for various reasons, were no longer slaves. In the instance of *Jennison v. Caldwell*, the jury actually found that Jennison (Walker's owner) had been deprived of the labor of his property. Moreover, as one analyst of the cases has asserted, there is "not one shred of evidence to indicate that the *Walker* cases [and Mum Bett's] brought an end to the institution of slavery." In fact, none of the freedom cases brought to trial after 1780 gained any attention beyond their localities, and they failed to be reported in any newspapers of the era.

Additionally, Ashley refused to give up and petitioned the Massachusetts House of Representatives to adopt legislation protecting slave owning. He warned that failure to do so would likely invite huge numbers of black people to Massachusetts seeking their freedom and whom the commonwealth would have to support. Agitated by Ashley's racial rantings, the House passed a bill to end slavery gradually, thus seeking to control manumissions in such a way as to not burden public resources. The Massachusetts Senate rejected the move but kept the idea on its agenda for about three years. Instead, in 1787 the legislature barred any blacks not "citizens" from remaining in the commonwealth for more than two months.

Phillis Wheatley, probably by Scipio Moorhead, 1773. Frontispiece for Wheatley's *Poems on Various Subjects, Religious and Moral* (London: Printed for A Bell, 1773). Library of Congress. Wheatley (1753–1784) published the first book by an African American, wrote against slavery, and played an important role in creating the Black Atlantic literary tradition. Remarkably, she came to Boston from West Africa in 1761, quickly mastered English, and penned her first poem four years later.

Massachusetts finally did outlaw the slave trade in 1788, but upheld any trading contracts made before adoption of the law. While it is true that slavery became economically insignificant in Massachusetts long before 1790, and the first census recorded no slaves in the state, the institution did not die completely. In 1800, 1,339 slaves lived in New England (with probably many missed by the census); and 30 years later, 48 slaves still lived in the region, with at least 1 in Massachusetts.[38]

The significance of the Mum Bett case and the other freedom suits of the 1780s lay more in how they reflected public attitudes in the post-Revolutionary period, rather than in how they shaped opinion or the law. While the various freedom suits did not legally end slavery in the commonwealth, they certainly indicated how juries were likely to decide such cases. As for Ashley and other defenders of slavery of the old order, they simply read public opinion and decided to drop their costly appeals. At least one slave owner made an attempt to sell his human property in the Caribbean before losing them in a suit, but most remaining owners simply released their slaves. Thus, it was not by law or in the courts that slavery died, as the Reverend Jeremy Belknap observed in 1795, but in the court of "publick opinion."

For Mum Bett, the change was profound. She rejected Ashley's belated offers of employment and went to work, happily, for the Sedgwick family, dying in 1829 at 87 years of age. She did not, thankfully, end her days as the slave Mum Bett, but rather as the Massachusetts citizen Elizabeth Freeman, a name that carried with it the aspirations of a people.[39]

---

[38] O'Brien, "Did the Jennison Case Outlaw Slavery in Massachusetts?," 223–25; Edgar J. Bellefontaine, "Chief Justice William Cushing: Stalwart Federalist and Reluctant Abolitionist, The Massachusetts Years, 1772–1789," *Supreme Judicial Court Historical Society Annual Report*, (1993) 20–23, quoted 24; Egerton, *Death or Liberty*, 107–08, 173; Blanck, "Seventeen Eighty-Three," 44–45; 1830 U.S. Census.

[39] For instance, the slave owner in *Tony v. Clapp* dropped his suit after seeing the end of the *Jennison* appeals. Zilversmit, "Quok Walker, Mumbet," 624; Egerton, *Death or Liberty*, 107–09.

FOR A TIME, THE VICTORY OF ELIZABETH FREEMAN AND OTHER NEW ENGLAND SLAVES APPEARED TO BE SETTING THE STAGE FOR SOMETHING MUCH LARGER. The American Revolution had sparked a wave of freedom movements that transformed the Atlantic world. Not coincidentally, northern states, including the commonwealth of Pennsylvania, began adopting gradual emancipation laws.

As early as 1775, Dr. Benjamin Rush and other Philadelphians founded the Quaker-dominated Society for the Relief of Free Negroes Unlawfully Held in Bondage—which before long became the Pennsylvania Abolition Society. Ten years later, in 1785, wealthy patrons organized the New York Manumission Society, which bore primary responsibility for educating black children, but spent most of its resources protecting blacks from kidnapping and providing legal advice. Connecticut and Rhode Island, the great slave-trading center, both adopted gradual emancipation laws, while Vermont, which never possessed any meaningful number of slaves, outlawed the institution in its founding constitution. By 1804, New Hampshire, New York, and New Jersey had followed suit, although in New York slavery did not completely end until 1827.

While one cannot equate abolitionist sentiment with any notion of equalitarianism, the Revolution had, as the Harvard historian Bernard Bailyn once wrote, ignited a "contagion of liberty" that both led many to question the institution of slavery and sparked an unprecedented wave of manumissions, especially in Virginia.[40]

In 1789, the French Revolution followed the American war, and in 1791, just two years later, 100,000 African slaves rose up against their hated French masters in the colony of Saint-Domingue, known because of its astonishing profitability as the "Pearl of the Antilles." Fanned by the crosswinds of the Atlantic, the revolt took cues from the examples of America and France. In time, the slaves executed thousands of whites and burned their plantations. Their rebellion led to the decision to abolish slavery in the colony in 1793, a decision ratified by the French Assembly in 1794 and extended throughout the French Empire.

Despite this, Napoleon Bonaparte sent troops to the island in 1802 under the leadership of his brother-in-law, Charles Leclerc, attempting to rein in the semi-independent colony being led by self-declared "Governor-for-Life" Toussaint Louverture, and then to reinstate slavery. Bonaparte dreamed of making Saint-Domingue into the entrepôt for an empire that would spread out from New Orleans into the Louisiana territory of North America. Over the next two years, however, of the 34,000 unlucky French and allied soldiers sent to restore slavery on Saint-Domingue, 24,000 died and 7,000 lay sick, leaving only 3,000 effective

soldiers in 1803. Before France finally gave up, thousands more would perish.[41]

Jean-Jacques Dessalines (following Louverture's capture and imprisonment in France) turned the revolt into a well-organized revolution and Saint-Domingue into a graveyard for French arrogance and imperialism. Dessalines led his countrymen in the creation of the world's first black republic, renamed the nation of Haiti, officially born on January 1, 1804. It had been the largest and most successful slave revolt in history.

Never before had slaves overthrown their masters and then created their own independent nation. Shock waves could be felt throughout the Atlantic world. Former Saint-Domingue slave owners poured into nearby Cuba and elsewhere in the Americas, including the United States, fleeing the retribution that surely would be visited on any supporter of slavery who remained on the island. Many, along with their African "property," landed in New Orleans, Charleston, Philadelphia, and New York.

Even before the black rebels proved victorious, the revolt and the resulting immigrant influx aroused such fears that in 1802 the governor of South Carolina called out the state militia on a rumor that a shipload of slaves from the island was headed to Charleston. Earlier, in response to the outbreak of violence, Maryland and many southern states temporarily barred the importation of all slaves and even called a halt to the interstate traffic. North Carolina

---

[40] Gates, *Life Upon These Shores*, 36–37; Leon Litwack, *North of Slavery: The Negro in the Free States, 1790–1860* (Chicago: University of Chicago Press, 1961), 3–10; Rhoda Freeman, "The Free Negro in New York City in the Era Before the Civil War" (Ph.D. diss., Columbia University, 1966), 64–67, 319–26; Bernard Bailyn, *The Ideological Origins of the American Revolution* (Cambridge: Belknap Press of Harvard University Press, 1967), 230–46.

[41] Philippe R. Girard, *The Slaves Who Defeated Napoleon: Toussaint Louverture and the Haitian War of Independence, 1801–1804* (Tuscaloosa: University of Alabama Press, 2011), 117–21, 183, 225–26.

barred the presence of any black person from the West Indies; Georgia and Virginia prohibited free blacks from entering their states; and in 1798, Georgia abolished the slave trade by constitutional amendment. A slaveholder's worst fears seemed realized.[42]

✖✖✖

ONE OF THE FIRST AMERICAN ERUPTIONS RELATED TO THE REVOLUTIONARY WAR ON SAINT-DOMINGUE TOOK PLACE IN SLEEPY RICHMOND, VIRGINIA, planned by a slave named for the Bible's divine messenger, Gabriel. Born prophetically in 1776 on the Prosser plantation, just six miles north of Richmond, Gabriel grew up strong and tall, more than six feet in height. He became a skilled blacksmith and learned to read and write, placing him in the 5 percent of southern slaves who were literate. Since Gabriel wore rather fine clothing when not hammering at the forge, and since his owners allowed him to become literate, he was clearly much-favored property. Other slaves looked up to men like him.[43]

Gabriel and his two brothers, Martin and Solomon, grew up in an era of international revolution, intense political confrontations, the rise of evangelical Christianity, and a weakening slave regime in Virginia. In the immediate post-Revolutionary period, Virginia slave owners emancipated about 10,000 slaves, giving real substance to the idea that the Revolution had created a contagion of liberty. In the context of the French Revolution, the rhetoric of Jeffersonian democracy, and evangelicalism, many Virginia African Americans–free and slave–came to know unprecedented levels of liberty and understandably wanted more.

In 1800, Richmond possessed a population of 5,700 people, about half of whom were black. Additionally, about 4,600 slaves and 500 free African Americans lived in the surrounding Henrico County, a region dominated by tobacco and wheat. Whites were the minority. Thomas Prosser, Gabriel's first owner, was both a successful planter and a merchant, a partner in the trading firm of Alexander Front & Company, and a legislator in the Virginia House of Burgesses. With 53 slaves, he was one of the largest slave owners in the county. He was probably typical for the times in the way he treated his slaves, allowing for much time off. As the plantations strove to be self-sufficient, masters had great incentives for their slaves to gain valuable skills–even, as in the case of Gabriel, literacy.

Possession of these skills could give a slave a certain liminal status–what the historian Rebecca J. Scott in another context, using a metaphor from the discipline of statistics, calls "degrees of freedom"–which a later generation of masters would abhor. It was not uncommon for slaves to travel great distances to see family members–with or without the officially required passes–and to hire out their own time when the season permitted it. When Gabriel's owner died in 1798, his son Thomas Henry assumed control of the plantation. He increased the level of economic activity, becoming rather

[42] Jed Handelsman Shugerman, "The Louisiana Purchase and South Carolina's Reopening of the Slave Trade in 1803," *Journal of the Early Republic*, 22 (Summer 2002): 263, 270, 282.

[43] Douglas R. Egerton, *Gabriel's Rebellion: The Virginia Slave Conspiracies of 1800 & 1802* (Chapel Hill: University of North Carolina Press, 1993), 17, 19–22.

more successful than his father, which allowed him to spend much of his time in a townhouse in Richmond, and this left Gabriel even more time to call his own.[44]

Gabriel's road to revolution began prosaically with a scuffle over a stolen pig. Stealing by a slave could bring on severe punishment, depending upon circumstances, but fighting a white man and biting off his ear, as Gabriel did, could lead to execution. One of Gabriel's accomplices in this escapade went unpunished, but another received 39 lashes and narrowly escaped execution by pleading "benefit of clergy." (This holdover from colonial law was grounded in an ancient English law originally applicable to clerics that mitigated capital punishment or the first conviction of a felony. It had expanded to apply to those with literacy in 19th-century Virginia, but by an oversight was only available to African Americans.) Gabriel did not escape punishment, however, and received a brand on one of his hands that meant death if he ever engaged in anything similar again. He came away from the incident with intense resentment. The liberty permitted by his owner allowed Gabriel to visit Richmond often and frequent the many taverns that catered to the working class, white and black. He grumbled to associates over beer and grog and began formulating plans for freedom, inspired by the pig incident and fortified by the heated political controversies between the Jeffersonian Democrats and Federalists.

But even more directly, Gabriel found inspiration in the French and Saint-Domingue revolutions. Coincidentally, he met two French soldiers in the Richmond taverns who had remained behind after the close of the American Revolution and, still fired with Revolutionary fervor, encouraged Gabriel in his desire for freedom, not just for himself but for all slaves and even for oppressed white workingmen. Misunderstanding the context of political debates in the early Republic—or appropriating them for his own ends—Gabriel concluded that Jeffersonian Democratic ideology encompassed the interests of slaves, white mechanics, sailors, and workingmen, who could combine to oppose the Federalist merchant class.

Moreover, the fears that Virginia whites expressed over the impact of the Saint-Domingue Revolution only incited Gabriel further. Conservative whites had spread rumors that the revolutionary government in France had ordered a black rebel from Saint-Domingue to lead an army of former slaves and invade the southern United States. Gabriel could read these reports for himself and overhear the dire stories of whites who had fled the island, and he could speak with the slaves that the French colonial slaveholders had brought to Virginia from Saint-Domingue. In this hothouse of Richmond political life, with stories of the black slave insurrection, the slaves' military victories over their masters, and the granting of their freedom by the French Assembly permeating the air, Gabriel understandably concluded in the spring of the critical political year 1800 that slaves could, in fact, throw off their chains.[45] (Neither he nor Toussaint Louverture could imagine that First Consul Napoleon Bonaparte would seek to reinstate slavery on the island just two years later.)

---

[44] Egerton, *Gabriel's Rebellion*, 17–24.

[45] Egerton, *Gabriel's Rebellion*, 25–29, 31, 34, 38, 43, 46–47; Matthew J. Clavin, *Toussaint Louverture and the American Civil War: The Promise and Peril of a Second Haitian Revolution* (Philadelphia: University of Pennsylvania Press, 2010), 16.

Gabriel believed that he could rally at least 1,000 slaves to his banner of "Death or Liberty," inverting the famed cry of the slaveholding revolutionary Patrick Henry.

Gabriel began his plot in his blacksmith shop, where he convinced his brother Solomon and another servant on the Prosser plantation to join his quest for freedom. The number of his contacts grew, reaching Richmond, other nearby towns and plantations, and well beyond to Petersburg and Norfolk, word spreading through free and enslaved black people who worked the waterways. Aided by his French associates, Gabriel believed that he could rally at least 1,000 slaves to his banner of "Death or Liberty," inverting the famed cry of the slaveholding revolutionary Patrick Henry. With incredible daring—and naïveté—he planned to march to Richmond, seize weapons stored there, and hold Governor James Monroe as a hostage until the merchant class agreed to establish equal rights for all. He did not seek to make war on all white people—far from it. He believed that the interests of the working class, Quakers, Baptists, and French all coincided with African Americans against the merchant class, who, he held, imposed the thralldom under which the oppressed labored.

During the summer, possessing few weapons, Gabriel put his blacksmithing skills to work and began literally making swords out of plowshares and other farm implements. He planned his uprising for the end of August. Word of the day and time had gone out far and wide. But when the time to strike came, one of the worst thunderstorms in recent memory came with it, washing away roads and disrupting travel. Gabriel hesitated, but believed that even a small band could march to Richmond, take the armory, and distribute weapons to slaves and workers who would rally to the cause. Telling so many other black people about his plans represented a necessary gamble to gain supporters, but also exposed him to the possibility of betrayal. Fearing retribution if the plot failed, a slave aptly named Pharoah exposed Gabriel's plans. Others soon talked to save their lives.[46]

Was Gabriel's plot simply naïve? Could it actually have succeeded? Many whites in Richmond thought so. The unpredictable John Randolph believed that the plot had failed only because of the "heavy fall of rain which made the water courses impassable." Outnumbered by African Americans, whites also lacked personal weapons. If Gabriel had managed to rally 100 or more blacks to his standard, he might have been able to seize Governor James Monroe as a hostage as planned and negotiate a settlement, although the chances of such an outcome seem rather slender. Given racial attitudes and white fears of an insurrection in the style of Toussaint Louverture, whites undoubtedly would have crushed any revolt that they believed aimed at taking possession of their

---

[46] Egerton, *Gabriel's Rebellion*, 46–47, 50–53, 58–59, 69–71.

FACING PAGE: *Toussaint L'Ouverture*, by Nicholas Eustache Maurin, one of a series sold in Paris and London in 1832. Hand-colored lithograph. Collection of Henry Louis Gates, Jr.

J. Lith. de Delpech

63

property and their "white women," even if it took time and many lives.[47]

Show trials and prompt executions followed discovery of the plot. Ironically, those free African Americans accused of complicity went unpunished since no Virginia court would recognize the testimony of a slave against a free person, and the only actual witnesses to the conspiracy were other slaves. By October 3, 17 men had been hanged and 30 more languished in jail, with many more death sentences likely to follow. But some white leaders like Thomas Jefferson and even Governor Monroe worried about the impact of a bloodbath of retribution and the costs to the commonwealth as it had to reimburse owners for the loss of their slaves, still considered their property. As the number of executions reached 25, the cost reached the exorbitant amount of $9,000 or so, money that cash-strapped Virginia could ill afford. Thus, authorities began pardoning a few conspirators and transporting others out of state, saving Gabriel for last. Despite his pleas, they hanged him alone on October 10, in front of those who reviled him and imagined a bloodthirsty black Saint-Domingue rapist rather than someone inspired by the liberty and freedom they themselves enjoyed.[48]

The newly formed United States, styling itself as a beacon of freedom and an Empire for Liberty, as Thomas Jefferson termed it, saw only alarm emanating from Saint-Domingue. As president, Jefferson feared that the black republic—formed in 1804 when Dessalines chose the name *Haiti* for the new nation, replacing the French colonial name of Saint-Domingue—would become a base for European adventurism

in the hemisphere. Even worse, the self-freed slaves—whom he called "cannibals of the terrible republic"—might succeed as a nation.

With the Gabriel conspiracy in mind, Jefferson refused to recognize the new Haitian government, fearing the anger of fellow slave owners and the possibility of American slaves emulating their Haitian brothers and sisters, just as Gabriel had done. Although at first he saw benefit in the rebel Louverture checking French aggrandizement in the Caribbean, in fact, lurking behind Jefferson's understandable anti-European diplomacy was racial fear, pure and simple. Since the 1780s, despite whatever nascent antislavery sentiments he harbored, Jefferson anticipated that emancipation, even gradual, would spark a war that could not end "but in the extermination of the one or the other race."[49]

While the American race war that Jefferson anticipated never took place, Haitian independence did—and reverberated through American history straight to the Civil War. In 1862, about a year after the events at Fort Sumter, the great Boston abolitionist Wendell Phillips spoke in the lecture hall of the Smithsonian Institution in Washington, D.C. His stunning lecture "Toussaint L'Ouverture" must have struck that Southern city with all the force of a hurricane. In the midst of our own Civil War, sparked by the terrors of slavery and racial hate, Phillips drew public attention to the earlier war in the Caribbean that was a "war of races and a war of nations," words that must have been painfully familiar to his audience.

He took the opportunity to disabuse Americans of the idea that black men were

---

[47] Egerton, *Gabriel's Rebellion*, 77–78.

[48] Egerton, *Gabriel's Rebellion*, 92–94, 108–09, 110–12.

[49] Tim Matthewson, "Jefferson and Haiti," *Journal of Southern History* 61 (May 1995): 217–18, 225.

incompetent and cowardly. "Some doubt the courage of the negro," he declared, undoubtedly thinking about the federal government's refusal at that time to recruit black soldiers to fight the slaveholders' rebellion. "Go to Hayti, and stand on those fifty thousand graves of the best soldiers France ever had, and ask them what they think of the negro's sword." But when he praised Louverture as a hero, greater than Cromwell, Napoleon, and George Washington, the audience must have heard in those words the metaphorical report of a howitzer.[50] Phillips's remarks testify to the inspiration fired throughout the hemisphere by the Haitian Revolution, and in the hands of African Americans even after Gabriel's ill-fated plan, the results could prove explosive.

In January 1811, about 40 miles north of New Orleans, Charles Deslondes, a mulatto slave driver—and likely a former Haitian slave—on the Andry sugar plantation, took volatile inspiration from the Haitian Revolution. Gabriel's fate probably would have mirrored that of Deslondes if the weather had been different 11 years earlier in Virginia. Deslondes, like Gabriel, had built a network of slaves, including recent arrivals from Africa and Saint-Domingue, and with these forces, he led the German Coast uprising, possibly the largest slave revolt in American history. Although little known, the insurrection involved a small army of at least 100 men and women who sang Creole protest songs while pillaging plantations and murdering whites.

The Haitian Revolution, in fact, hung over the entire episode, encouraging blacks and terrorizing whites.

In many ways, Louisiana was ripe territory for violence. The region experienced enormous growth in slave importations in the period leading up to the revolt, as was the case in South Carolina in the time leading up to the Stono Rebellion in 1739. By 1808, when the legal slave trade ended, somewhere between 20,000 and 29,000 slaves had landed in Louisiana, most after 1803 when the United States took possession of the Louisiana territory from France. In 1809, the number of free black people in New Orleans increased by 3,110, and the number of black slaves there increased by 3,226, because Saint-Domingue exiles who had fled the wrath of the former slaves and found sanctuary in Cuba (where slavery remained legal until 1886) were suddenly forced to vacate the island as a consequence of the Napoleonic wars, when Napoleon imposed his brother as the monarch of Spain. Nothing reveals more marvelously the inextricably intertwined connections within the early-19th-century Black Atlantic world—here specifically defined as the relations among Port-au-Prince, Haiti; Santiago de Cuba, Cuba; and New Orleans, Louisiana—than this migration, which transpired between May 1809 and January 1810. In fact, by the time of Deslondes's revolt, "Saint-Domingue slaves represented almost a third of the 1810 slave population of New Orleans and its precincts (10,824) and 10 percent of the slaves of Orleans Territory (34,660)."[51]

---

[50] Wendell Phillips had also given his address in 1860 at the Cooper Union in New York to cheers and hisses. *New York Times*, February 1, 1860; Wendell Phillips, "Toussaint l'Ouverture," in *Selections from the Works of Wendell Phillips*, ed. A. D. Hall (Boston: H. M. Caldwell Co., 1902), 154 quoted, 121–58; Clavin, *Toussaint Louverture and the American Civil War*, 1–2.

[51] Carl A. Brasseaux and Glenn R. Conrad, eds., *The Road to Louisiana: The Saint-Domingue Refugees, 1792–1809* (Lafayette, LA: Center for Louisiana Studies, University of Southwestern Louisiana, 1992), 25.

This was not the first time Louisiana blacks planned to resist their enslavement. In 1795, when Spain ruled the territory, authorities uncovered a conspiracy near New Orleans. Spanish officials even found a copy of France's Declaration of the Rights of Man in one slave's cabin. What became known as the Pointe Coupée conspiracy ended horrifically for 23 slaves. With no affection for revolutionary ideology from either the United States or France, Spanish authorities quickly hanged the conspirators, severed their heads, and then placed them on poles for all to see.[52]

More than a decade later, Deslondes, sickened by the arrogance of whites and his own role in having to enforce their will, plotted an end to the oppression that he and other people of African descent endured in the insufferable cane fields of Louisiana. After communicating his intentions to slaves on the Andry plantation and in nearby areas, on the rainy evening of January 8, 1811—just seven years after Haiti became independent—Deslondes and about 25 slaves rose up and attacked the plantation's owner and family. They hacked to death one of the owner's sons, but carelessly allowed the master to escape. Deslondes and his men wisely chose the Andry plantation to begin their revolution, because it served as a warehouse for the local militia. The 25 men broke open the stores and seized uniforms, guns, and ammunition. As they moved toward New Orleans, intending to capture the city, their numbers swelled.

Some estimated the force as large as 300, but Deslondes's army probably did not exceed 124.

Alarm coursed through the region as Manuel Andry, Deslondes's owner, managed to arouse whites with his tale of black butchery and warnings about the Haitian-style revolution to come. The territorial governor assigned Wade Hampton, the South Carolina congressman, slave master, and Indian fighter, the task of suppressing the insurrection. Hampton had accepted a military commission in 1808 and the following year took over military command of New Orleans. Hampton quickly threw together a force of militia and about 30 regular U.S. Army soldiers to confront the slaves.

About 20 miles from New Orleans on January 10, 1811, the combined militia and Army force stopped the rebels. They fought a pitched battle that halted only when the slaves ran out of ammunition. The soldiers then charged, led by mounted militia, which sent the slaves into a panic. The rebel line broke and a slaughter commenced. When the slaves surrendered, about 20 lay dead, another 50 became prisoners, and the remainder fled into the swamps. The whites suffered no casualties, which revealed the lack of military skill on the part of the slaves. By the end of the month, whites rounded up 50 more of the insurgents. About 100 survivors were summarily executed, their heads severed and placed along the road that led to New Orleans. As one planter noted, they looked "like crows sitting on long poles."[53]

---

[52] Daniel Rasmussen, *American Uprising: The Untold Story of America's Largest Slave Revolt* (New York: HarperCollins, 2011), 23, 89; Shugerman, "The Louisiana Purchase and South Carolina's Reopening of the Slave Trade," 282.

[53] Rasmussen, *American Uprising*, 105–06, 117, 128–39, 140, 147–48; Junius P. Rodriguez, "Always 'En Garde': The Effects of Slave Insurrection upon the Louisiana Mentality, 1811–1815," *Louisiana History* 33 (Autumn 1992): 400–01.

FOR GENERATIONS, STANDARD AMERICAN HISTORIES DOWNPLAYED THE IMPORTANCE OF THE HAITIAN REVOLUTION AND ITS RELATIONSHIP BOTH TO AFRICAN AMERICANS, slave and free, and to the institution of slavery in the United States. Although once a footnote to the era of revolutions, we now understand its enormous significance much differently. Contemporaries, however, possessed no ambivalence on the subject. For most Americans, it was a cataclysmic event, a foreshadowing of what whites could expect if the slave regime was weakened either from within, by a lapse of rigorous enforcement and supervision, or from without, by the abolitionist "fanatics" of the North. As one commentator remarked, "The scenes of horror which were witnessed in St. Domingo [Saint-Domingue] under the leadership of the ghoul Toussaint long since became by-words for everything that is cruel and infamous." White Louisianans did not doubt the meaning of the Haitian Revolution, and even contended that Deslondes was in Haiti at the time of the revolt and brought his beastly plans back home with him to the north.[54] While the 1811 insurrection was quickly suppressed—and largely ignored even by the popular press at the time—its historical importance can hardly be overlooked today.

The Haitian Revolution rippled through American history, from Gabriel Prosser's Richmond right to Wendell Phillips's stirring evocation of Toussaint Louverture's heroism in the very first year of the Civil War. Even during the Missouri Compromise crisis, which began just eight years after the Deslondes revolt, the fires of the revolution still burned brightly in American slaveholders' imagination. Thomas Cobb of Virginia warned that attempts to stifle the spread of slavery would only encourage America's own "ghoulish" Toussaints and ignite a conflagration that "all the waters of the ocean cannot put out, which seas of blood can only extinguish." When the debates over slavery's extension in Missouri wrenched the country and sparked impassioned speeches in the halls of Congress against slavery as "contrary to the law of nature, which is the law of God," defenders of the "peculiar institution" recoiled in horror. The speaker of Virginia's House of Delegates warned that such rhetoric "would sound the tocsin of freedom to every Negro of the South and we may have to see the tragical events of St. Domingo repeated in our own land."[55]

Thus, for whites and blacks, Haiti became a source of powerful symbolism for revolution. Most whites, however, saw only the savagery of murderous, bloodthirsty, avenging slaves, while African Americans and their white abolitionist allies saw courage and models of resistance that would fire antislavery imaginations for the next six decades. Black sailors transported news about the Haitian Revolution and the fortunes of the new republic from Haiti to ports north, ranging from New Orleans, St. Augustine, Savannah, and Charleston, all the way to New York and Boston. From these cities,

---

[54] Clavin, *Toussaint Louverture and the American Civil War*, 3–4, 16.

[55] Quoted in Robert Pierce Forbes, *The Missouri Compromise and Its Aftermath: Slavery and the Meaning of America* (Chapel Hill: University of North Carolina Press, 2007), 39–40, 145.

word spread to slave communities throughout the South, through books, pamphlets, and newspapers, which were sometimes even sewn into the sailors' clothing (as was the 1829 revolutionary pamphlet of the Boston clothier, Freemason, and black abolitionist David Walker). Slaves and free women and men who detested slavery drew strength from this unprecedented example of freedom born in the Black Atlantic world as they continued to build their lives, their social institutions, their families, and, ultimately, their own cosmopolitan culture and sense of their place in the world.

It would take three-quarters of a century for America to absorb the lessons learned in Saint-Domingue about the fate of the institution of slavery. This culminating moment in the story of slavery in the French part of the Black Atlantic represented a challenge—and an opportunity—that the divided American nation and its conflicted economic interests could not meet. While the American Revolutionary era would, both directly and indirectly, propel some black people to freedom, technological advances in the cultivation and harvesting of cotton—especially the invention of the cotton gin in 1793, ironically the same year in which slavery would first be abolished in Saint-Domingue—would usher in at least 75 years of captivity for the vast majority of African Americans that would turn out to be worse than anything that had come before.

HALF SLAVE,
HALF FREE
1797–1858

FOR FORMER SLAVES AND THEIR CHILDREN FREED AFTER THE AMERICAN REVOLUTION, THE FIRST YEARS OF THE NEW CENTURY OFFERED UNPRECEDENTED OPPORTUNITY. Free black people were able to create new worlds for themselves, North and South, rural and urban. We often think of these years in crude dichotomies: the North free, the South enslaved. The reality proved far more complicated, with surprising pockets of freedom in the South and tragic levels of oppression in the North. In each section of the country, including the Midwest, which saw an even more complex mix of slavery and freedom, a surprisingly large range of responses to the challenges of carving out a life as an African American unfolded.

In the end, the accomplishments of these years—intellectual, political, organizational—played a crucial role in forcing the issue of slavery to the forefront of national politics, creating the momentum that many years later would lead to emancipation. But progress was by no means linear, and many of the era's most fundamental conflicts have never been fully resolved.

The late 18th century saw the beginnings of a democratic ethos that became, for all races and classes, clearly manifest in popular religion. The Second Great Awakening, inauspiciously begun in rural Connecticut, caused "the wilderness to blossom as the rose," as one observer remarked, and "the desert to put on the appearance of the garden of the Lord." Good works and faith, not predestination and faith, now became the hallmarks of American Protestantism. Throughout the eastern states a new evangelicalism arose, an inherently democratic movement that spawned Methodism in the mid-Atlantic region, liberalized orthodox Protestantism in New England, and even encouraged the growth of liberal Quakerism and Unitarianism—the latter group actually sending missionaries from Massachusetts to Connecticut and India. It fueled a reform movement that in one form or another would embrace the North and Midwest and even penetrate into urban areas of the South.[1]

Free black communities emerged from the 18th century with vigor and a sense of possibility. In Boston, Providence, Newport, New York, Baltimore, and Philadelphia, free black people formed schools, Masonic lodges, and self-improvement societies; founded churches; owned homes; and started businesses. Prior to the 1820s, the color line—as W. E. B. Du Bois would famously call it—was a gray area, still permeable and contradictory, rather than the sharp, razorlike edge that it would soon become, wounding those who attempted to cross it. Churches did not yet possess "negro pews"; parades and festivals included African Americans; black military service, while slow to be authorized during the Revolution, had become gratefully appreciated, honored, and respected. By the early 1820s, black community leaders had created a stunning number of institutions; as one historian has written, "by any measure extraordinary, and the painstaking work of ordinary people [made it] all the more so."[2] Before long, successful black communities would begin emerging in Cincinnati and Cleveland, Pittsburgh, Buffalo and Rochester, smaller towns in New England and Ohio—and later in Chicago. For African Americans, some of the most important events of the early republic transpired in Philadelphia.

As a vital commercial center—the nation's first vessel to China, for instance, left from the port of Philadelphia—the city drew immigrants from throughout the Atlantic world. The neighborhoods of Southark and Moyamensing

---

[1]   Joseph Conforti, "The Invention of the Great Awakening, 1795–1844," *Early American Literature* 26:2 (1991): 99–118, 106 quoted; Donald Yacovone, *Samuel Joseph May and the Dilemmas of the Liberal Persuasion, 1797–1871* (Philadelphia: Temple University Press, 1991), 17–42; William Pease and Jane H. Pease, *The Web of Progress: Private Values and Public Styles in Boston and Charleston, 1828–1843* (Athens: University of Georgia Press, 1991).

[2]   James Brewer Stewart, "Modernizing 'Difference': The Political Meanings of Color in the Free States, 1776–1840," *Journal of the Early Republic* 19 (Winter 1999): 696 quoted.

became home to African and Caribbean immigrants arriving from New Jersey, the Chesapeake region, and later, from Virginia. When Toussaint's revolution began in the 1790s, almost 900 Saint-Domingue refugees had settled in the city. By 1800, it had the country's largest urban black population, topping 2,000. Philadelphia, Frederick Douglass would later declare, "holds the destiny of our people."[3]

It also became home to the founder of one of the most important African American religions: Richard Allen—one of the most influential blacks to emerge out of the new republic. Born a slave owned by Benjamin Chew, patriarch of a Philadelphia Quaker family, Allen and his family were sold in about 1768 to Stokely Sturgis, a small farmer in Delaware, a region that possessed about 11,000 slaves. Allen's life was transformed at age 17 by his conversion to the Methodist faith after hearing a preacher in the Delaware woods in 1777. He described the experience as "a shaking of dungeons and a falling of chains."[4] Sturgis, his master, a struggling planter, was similarly affected, although he hadn't been when he purchased Allen and promptly sold off his parents and younger siblings. Characteristic of this unique era, both Sturgis and Allen became caught up in the turbulence and promise of the Age of Revolutions, as well as in the progressive principles of the Methodist faith. In September 1779, Sturgis attended a service by Freeborn Garrettson, himself a former slave owner and one of the most successful early itinerant ministers,

experienced a conversion, and concluded that he could no longer own a slave.[5]

In January 1780, Allen signed an agreement with his master so that he could pay Sturgis $2,000 (an incredibly high figure for the period) over the next five years to earn his freedom. For the next several years, Allen worked tirelessly, hauling salt, laying brick, and chopping wood to buy himself out of slavery. He labored so hard that in August 1783, the year that the new United States formally secured its independence from Great Britain, he paid Sturgis the last installment of his debt—far ahead of schedule. As was the case with Mum Bett and other slaves who gained their freedom, Allen disposed of his slave name—Negro Richard—and chose Allen as a last name, perhaps to honor a Pennsylvania jurist named William Allen who had lived near Allen's first owner, Benjamin Chew.

With his newfound freedom, Allen began traveling and attending many camp meetings and revivals. He then set out to become a minister and spent years as an itinerant preacher, crisscrossing Delaware and Maryland before settling in Philadelphia. Antislavery leaders in Philadelphia spread word of Allen's reputation as a minister and in 1785, the great Methodist evangelist Francis Asbury asked Allen, whom he had known since at least 1779, to travel with him in the South—an idea that understandably repelled the young black Methodist. Although he refused to go, the two bonded in friendship and Allen bought Asbury a horse so that he could continue his travels. When Allen

---

3 Thomas C. Holt, *Children of Fire: A History of African Americans* (New York: Hill and Wang, 2010), 114–17.

4 Holt, *Children of Fire*, 86.

---

5 For Allen's life, see Richard S. Newman, *Freedom's Prophet: Bishop Richard Allen, the AME Church, and the Black Founding Fathers* (New York: New York University Press, 2008).

eventually opened his own church in the 1790s, Asbury conducted the opening service. It was rare for two men of different races at this time to share such a deep and public friendship.

In 1786, Allen was called back to Philadelphia to preach to blacks in St. George's Church; he would remain in the city for the rest of his life. He supported himself by establishing a chimney-sweeping business and, ironically, took on young indentured servants, one white and one a mixed-race Indian. But he put his soul into building a congregation of blacks for St. George's—he began with about 5 black parishioners, but within a year he had gathered together about 42 new African American congregants. He soon began thinking about establishing a separate church just for black parishioners, an idea that white elders of the church denounced. Nevertheless, Allen worked tirelessly to recruit more black members, holding meetings in and out of the church, on street corners, anywhere to gain new adherents. The church grew so much, in fact, that the new funds his labors brought in helped toward construction of a new wing for St. George's.

As so often would happen over the course of the 19th century, black success attracted white resentment and opposition. Church elders tried to restrict Allen's labors and modify his enthusiastic style. Resentment may have been fueled in part by Allen's role in founding the Free African Society, a self-help community uplift group that brought together two of the city's most important black religious leaders, Allen and Absalom Jones (1746–1818). The two worked with surprising success to raise money for a black church and Allen recalled that, in about 1791, they gathered the incredible amount of $390 in one day.

But the defining moment came sometime later in 1792 or 1793 when church elders reversed long-standing policy and attempted to exile black congregants to "negro pews." In an especially humiliating incident, white trustees of the church approached a kneeling Absalom Jones and ordered him to the gallery. When he declined to move, two whites picked up the kneeling man to remove him from the front of the church, thus sparking a mass walkout of the church's entire black membership—led by Richard Allen. Possibly Allen and Jones had planned the confrontation, knowing of the growing white resentment in the church and, like Rosa Parks in the 20th century, had more deliberation in their actions than we have recognized.[6]

Whatever the case, Jones would go on to become the nation's first black Episcopal priest and found St. Thomas's African Episcopal Church, and Allen would work with the great Philadelphia scientist and philanthropist Benjamin Rush to found the Mother Bethel African Methodist Episcopal Church. Allen and 11 other black Methodists met at his home in 1794 and agreed to purchase a former blacksmith shop and move it to a lot Allen had bought at Sixth and Lombard Streets. When the church opened on April 9, 1799, Bishop Asbury ordained Allen as a deacon. By 1803, Allen reported that his congregation had grown to 457 members, and two years later his converted blacksmith shop had been transformed into a respectable brick structure.

His African Methodist Episcopal Church became the first independent black denomination in the United States. It quickly developed

---

6   See Newman, *Freedom's Prophet*, 64–68.

Richard Allen and *Bishops of the A.M.E Church.* Lithograph. Published in Boston by J. H. Daniels, circa 1876. Library of Congress. Clockwise from top: Morris Brown, William Paul Quinn, Daniel A. Payne, Jabez P. Campbell, Thomas M. D. Ward, John M. Brown, James A. Shorter, Alexander W. Wayman, Willis Nazrey, and Edward Waters. Additionally, there are scenes depicting Wilberforce University; the Payne Institute in Cokesbury, Abbeville County, South Carolina; the Bible; early days of African Methodism; missionaries in Haiti; and the A.M.E. Church Book Depository in Philadelphia.

into one of the most important black institutions in the nation, with a publishing house and an astonishingly long-running newspaper and journal, establishing congregations throughout the country, especially in the South after the Civil War. Allen's church also ran a school, ministered to its members' secular as well as religious needs, and became a haven for runaway slaves.[7]

___

7 Albert J. Raboteau, *A Fire in the Bones: Reflections on African-American Religious History* (Boston: Beacon Press, 1995), 79–102.

‹◆›

WHILE PHILADELPHIA TOOK THE LEAD IN THE HISTORY OF BLACK RELIGION, THE CITY BY NO MEANS WAS ALONE IN THE PROCESS OF BLACK COMMUNITY FORMATION. Although Boston possessed a tiny black population, about 761 in 1790, it too exerted leadership and enormous influence.[8] On March 6, 1775, a former slave and leather dresser named Prince Hall and 14 other black Bostonians became Freemasons, inducted into the fraternity by British soldiers stationed in the city to keep watch on the Patriots. In all likelihood, Hall and his companions approached the soldiers because they could find no white American Masons to support their bid to join the fraternity.

Freemasonry had a long and distinguished history in the city, first appearing in June 1739 when a "vast concourse" of people turned out to view a parade of brothers marking the feast day of St. John the Baptist, their patron. Adorned in their iconic aprons and accompanied by a band, they marched through the city and visited the governor's home. In Boston Harbor, a vessel adorned with flags and a Masonic apron fired off its guns every hour in celebration.[9] Hall wisely saw Freemasonry as the most effective avenue for African Americans to gain acceptance and respectability. He could also use Enlightenment ideology of fraternal equality that lay at the core of Freemasonry to attack the institution of slavery, which he knew so intimately.

Little is known about Hall's early years, a mystery made frustratingly complicated by the appearance in surviving city records of several men named Prince Hall, and no documentation exists for his life prior to his emancipation in 1770. While Boston and regional newspapers covered him and the activities of his lodge, we have no idea what he looked like, so typical of early African American history.[10] Hall probably married a Flora Gibbs of Gloucester in 1770 and had one son named Primus Hall, although this may have been the result of an earlier slave marriage that was, of course, unrecognized by law. The son, born in 1756, served in the Revolutionary War, and his father had made drumheads for the Patriots. An enterprising worker, Hall put together a career as a leather dresser and a huckster, or peddler of various goods. His diligence certainly paid off, and by 1800 Hall became one of the few black Bostonians to own real estate.

His hard work, success, and Masonic activities made him a community leader. In 1777, for example, he joined a number of other black petitioners to insist that the Massachusetts legislature abolish slavery. He worked to build a separate black lodge in the city, but found the local white Freemasons hostile and unwelcoming. Through much of its history, white Masons attacked Prince Hall's lodge as illegitimate. In 1787, after years of struggle, Hall

---

[8]   The 1790 U.S. Census actually uses this number to describe "all other free persons," listing whites separately.

[9]   Steven C. Bullock, "The Revolutionary Transformation of American Freemasonry, 1752–1792," *William and Mary Quarterly*, 3d ser., 47 (July 1990): 350.

[10]   While much has been written about Prince Hall, little of it is reliable. One should begin with his capsule biography by Chernoh Sesay, Jr., in *African American National Biography*, eds. Henry Louis Gates, Jr., and Evelyn Brooks Higginbotham (New York: Oxford University Press, 2008): 4:22–24.

received a charter from the Grand Lodge in London, which officially established Lodge No. 459. He then led the way toward establishing black lodges across the North and became recognized by his peers as the country's most important black Masonic leader. In 1797, for instance, the black Philadelphians Richard Allen, Absalom Jones, and James Forten looked to Hall for assistance in getting them recognized as fellow Freemasons.[11]

Also in 1797, Hall delivered a startling address that laid the foundation for the black abolitionist movement. In June, before an audience of Masonic brothers—possibly mixed race, but we do not know for sure—he condemned the slavery that dragged "our friends and brethren . . . from their native country" and kept them under "the iron hand of tyranny and oppression." As a former slave separated from his own family, he knew all too well the pain of "weeping eyes and aching hearts." He mourned those brought to "a strange land and strange people, whose tender mercies are cruel; and there to bear the iron yoke of slavery & cruelty till death as a friend shall relieve them." He also censured the racism that already infected Boston and pointed to Saint-Domingue as a reminder that "God can and will change their conditions, and their hearts too; and let Boston and the world know, that He hath no respect of persons, and that the bulwark of envy, pride, scorn and contempt, which is so visible to be seen in some and felt, shall fall, to rise no more." He predicted (or threatened) that the day would come—as in Saint-Domingue at the very

minute he spoke—that whites would pay for their unwillingness to let the enslaved go free. For one who so earnestly sought acceptance and respectability from whites for himself and his brethren, Hall's astounding address proved remarkably daring.[12]

The fraternity Hall formed is the oldest black institution in North America, and spawned lodges and other allied fraternities across the North—and after the Civil War, throughout the South. It became a driving force in the black antislavery movement and produced many of the nation's most important black leaders and a large percentage of the black antislavery leadership, such as the incendiary David Walker and Lewis Hayden, both of Boston, and both of whom were Masons. Indeed, many local and national black community leaders in the 19th century—such as Booker T. Washington and W. E. B. Du Bois—belonged to the fraternity, which continued to play an important role in the struggle for civil rights in the 20th century.

Prince Hall, among his many activities, had petitioned the Massachusetts legislature to end the institution of slavery, to gain public support for black education, and to support black emigration. He fearlessly condemned the brutality that some whites showered on the city's black citizens and called out for social and political equality, setting the primary goals of the antislavery movement, black and white, that would eventually arise in Boston. Equally important, white political, social, and religious leaders recognized Hall as the spokesman for his community and trusted his opinions. His business

11 Chernoh M. Sesay, Jr., "Freemasons of Color: Prince Hall, Revolutionary Black Boston, and the Origins of Black Freemasonry, 1770–1807" (Ph.D. diss., Northwestern University, 2006), 32.

12 Hall's *A Charge Delivered to the African Lodge, June 24, 1797, at Menotomy, Mass.,* can be read at http://memory.loc.gov.

success and his prominence as a Freemason made his name one of the most recognizable of all African Americans throughout the North, and when he died, in 1807, newspapers around the country registered and lamented the loss.[13]

Events further south, however, would help make discrimination the defining characteristic of the north, thus circumscribing the development of northern black society. By the 1820s, as the Reverend Hosea Easton painfully observed, while the country had been born with a fire for liberty, now a certain "darkness" had crept into the country's soul and its drive for profit had made it insensible to those "allied to you by birth and blood." Instead of enjoying the fruits and promise of liberty, millions of black people faced permanent, racial slavery riveted to their future and that of their descendants. Those supposedly free enjoyed few if any "freedoms" that white men were bound to recognize. The period of fluidity of race relations in early American history was over. As the Massachusetts-born minister Easton would ask:

> Are we eligible to an office? No.–Are we considered subjects of the government? No.–Are we initiated into free schools for mental improvement? No.–Are we patronized as salary men in any public business whatever? No.–Are we taken into social compact with Society at large? No.–Are we patronized in any branch of business which is sufficiently lucrative to raise us to any material state of honour and respectability among men, and thus,

qualify us to demand respect from the higher order of society? No.–But to the contrary. Everything is withheld from us that is calculated to promote the aggrandizement and popularity of that part of the community who are said to be the descendants of Africa.[14]

◆◆◆

NOTHING MARKED THE CHANGE IN RACE RELATIONS MORE DRAMATICALLY THAN THE INVENTION OF THE COTTON GIN IN 1793, and its attendant economic and social transformation. The cotton revolution brought broad and rapid change to America's economy—North and South—and to its very geography, causing immense, often devastating, changes to the lives of millions of black people and Native Americans. This transformation was enabled, like the transatlantic slave trade before it, by new technology. Just as the development of the ship quadrant and sextant had facilitated the seaborne trade in human beings, the introduction of the cotton gin, patented in 1794—a deceptively simple machine that separated cotton seeds from the fibers—exponentially increased the profitability of the crop and created new, unprecedented demands for labor that would only be satisfied by slaves. It would make cotton history's first affordable luxury commodity, speed the growth of the white middle class, and bond the United States to the economics of slavery.

---

[13] Peter P. Hinks and Stephen Kantrowitz, eds., *All Men Free and Brethren: Essays on the History of African American Freemasonry* (Ithaca, NY: Cornell University Press, 2013).

[14] George R. Price and James Brewer Stewart, eds., *To Heal the Scourge of Prejudice: The Life and Writings of Hosea Easton* (Amherst: University of Massachusetts Press, 1999), 54.

The cotton gin was no accidental invention by a Yankee tinkerer with a little time on his hands. Rather, Eli Whitney's invention resulted from sustained and deliberate efforts to create a staple crop that would meet the very specific demands of a large and global industrial machine—the same thing that sugar had done in the Caribbean and Latin America. It was no accident that the gin's introduction coincided with Saint-Domingue's removal from the international sugar market. What made cotton so profitable? It was easily stored and easily shipped, and it came into demand at a time when the prices of older staple crops like tobacco and rice were in decline. Hence, manufacturing and capital resources in the North were ready to exploit it, and a large workforce of slaves in the South was available to harvest it. The gin provided the final, critical missing piece to solve a global economic puzzle. But the gin itself was really just part of a much larger revolution. Cotton's rise led to the creation of a new planter class with immense political power—a class that had access to new markets and new sources of capital (much of it, ironically, in the North)—and, above all, a class that would, in turn, create a new slave labor force.

According to the census of 1790, approximately 650,000 slaves labored in six slave states, mostly picking rice, tobacco, and indigo. Jefferson's Louisiana Purchase in 1803 massively increased the size of the United States—and the amount of land available for farming. It made settlement of Alabama and Mississippi profitable, and gave a cash crop like cotton a vast hinterland with a ready transportation system and an outlet to the sea. This offered by far the greatest profit potential for a world wanting cotton products. The fact that Native Americans populated the lands proved an inconvenience,

but the young nation had a novel solution. White settlers eager to raise cotton pressured the federal government to acquire the Indian land by any means necessary. The result was a relentless and often violent campaign of Indian removal—including the infamous Trail of Tears of the 1830s—and settlement of their lands by whites who replaced virgin forests with cotton plantations worked by black slaves.

One of the most brutal chapters in American history was the forced removal of the so-called Five Civilized Tribes—the Cherokee, Chickasaw, Choctaw, Creek, and Seminole—slaveholders themselves who mistakenly believed that their "civilized" ways would enable them to assimilate into the new American nation and hold onto to their ancestral homelands. By 1850, most Native Americans had vanished from the Deep South, removed to "Indian Territory," which later would become the state of Oklahoma. The United States now consisted of not 6, but 15 slave states, with 3.2 million slaves—of whom 1.8 million were working in cotton, yielding two-thirds of the world's supply and powering the American economy. In 1790, this country produced 1.5 million pounds of cotton; by 1830, that figure grew to 331 million pounds. In 1860, incredibly, production had reached 2,275 million pounds per year.

Cotton, in essence, reshaped the United States, greatly multiplying the profit potential for America's planters—and their demand for slaves. More than ever before, slaves became prized commodities. After the 1808 ban on the international slave trade, American slave masters turned to "growing" their own laborers. Of all the slave societies in the New World, the United States alone succeeded in creating a slave force that reproduced itself. Fewer than 400,000 imported Africans in 1808 had by 1860

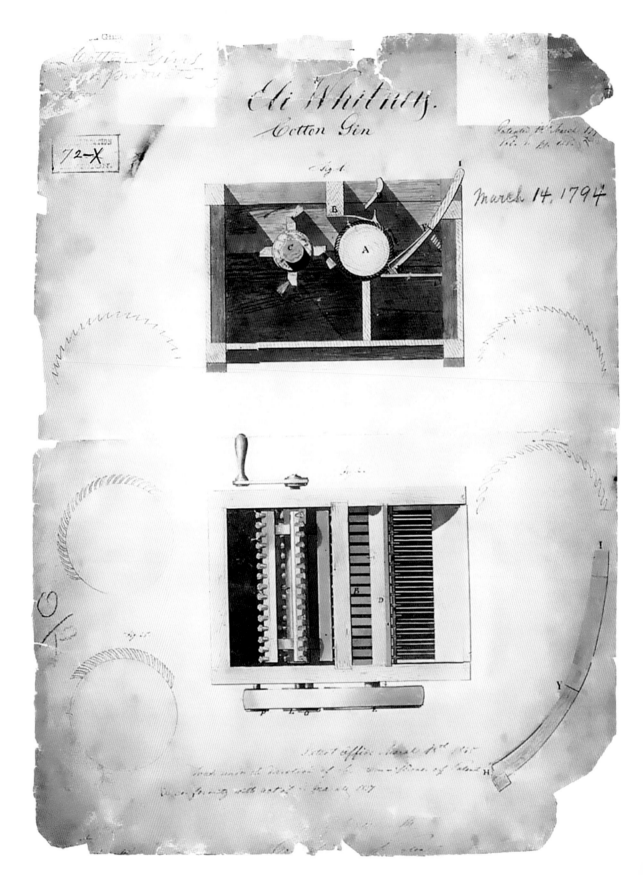

become a population of 4.4 million African Americans, 3.9 million of whom were slaves. According to the scholar of African American studies Ronald Bailey, between 1790 and 1860, the slave population of the United States increased between 25 percent and 33 percent per year, averaging 28.7 percent over the period.[15]

Cotton brought about another demographic change—and for African Americans, a uniquely cruel and destructive one. On the new plantations of the Deep South, cotton meant longer hours for slaves, harder work, and increased brutality. It also meant that slave families in the Upper South had become suddenly and terrifyingly vulnerable. African Americans had spent decades creating these families under slavery, establishing bonds of marriage and kinship as best they could. But cotton's spread into the Deep South created a vast new market for slaves—slaves who could not be imported since the trade had been outlawed by the Constitution and Congress in 1808. Exploiting the natural increase in the slave population, however, made the states of the Upper South a warehouse of exportable human capital, creating an immensely profitable internal slave trade. Slave auctions became large and wrenching daily events in Virginia, Maryland, and the Carolinas, at which wives were separated from husbands, children from parents and siblings. Tens of thousands of uprooted African Americans were put on trains or boats or marched in chains, walking to the plantations of the Deep South. This became the Second Middle Passage, in many ways just as destructive as the first.[16]

As cotton cultivation spread westward from South Carolina and Georgia into Alabama, Mississippi, Louisiana, Arkansas, and Texas, and northward up the Mississippi River Valley, more enslaved people were sent south in the internal trade than came across the Atlantic to North America in the first Middle Passage from Africa. To illuminate this history, we can trace the major routes of the internal trade with stories of individual slaves taken into the Deep South. The routes, along rural roads and small highways, bear little if any trace of their terrible past. But a few lingering signs of their hidden history remain, sites of old slave-trading blocks and abandoned plantations. More intimately, however, we can trace the Second Middle Passage in the words of several of those unfortunate men and women who endured it and later wrote about their experiences, creating a powerful collective portrait of the experience that no single story could encompass.

<hr/>

BORN IN SOUTHAMPTON COUNTY, VIRGINIA, A SLAVE KNOWN AS "FED" OR BENFORD, AND LATER AS JOHN BROWN (1810?–1876), was taken from his home with his mother in about 1820 and sent to

---

[15] Ronald Bailey, "The Other Side of Slavery: Black Labor, Cotton, and Textile Industrialization in Great Britain and the United States," *Agricultural History* 68 (Spring 1994): 35–50.

[16] See Michael Tadman, *Speculators and Slaves: Masters, Traders, and Slaves in the Old South* (Madison: University of Wisconsin Press, 1996) and Walter Johnson, *Soul by Soul: Life Inside the Antebellum Slave Market* (Cambridge: Harvard University Press, 1999).

FACING PAGE: Cotton gin patent, by Eli Whitney, March 14, 1794. National Archives, Digital Vers/Science faction, Corbis UK Ltd.

UNITED STATES SLAVE TRADE.
1830.

United States Slave Trade, 1830, Philadelphia (?). Engraving. Library of Congress. This image shows the Second Middle Passage.

Northampton County, North Carolina.[17] Eighteen months later, he was sold to Georgia and never saw any of his family again. He grew up near Milledgeville on the plantation of the obstreperous Thomas Stevens, an owner known for driving his slaves to the limit and favoring brutal punishments. Stevens then bought lands in Cherokee country; such purchases were one of the motivations for the expulsion of the tribe and the resulting Trail of Tears exodus. Fed moved west with his owner to the area northwest of modern Atlanta.

His master died in 1840, and Fed was inherited by Decatur Stevens, who proved even harsher and more brutal than Fed's first owner. Fed met another slave, a man named John Glasgow, who had been born free in British Guiana and worked as a sailor, but was seized as a slave when he disembarked in Savannah, Georgia. Glasgow never accepted his enslavement and endured brutal beatings on Stevens's plantation. He also told Fed of freedom in England, convincing him to one day seek his own liberation. In his memoir, Fed relates how it felt to be sold to the Deep South as property:

> I really thought my mother would have died of grief at being obliged to leave her two children, her mother, and her relations behind. But it was of no use lamenting, and as we were to start early next morning, the few things we had were put together that night, and we completed our preparations for parting for life by

17 For a brief biography, see Gates and Higginbotham, *African American National Biography,* 1:627–28.

kissing one another over and over again, and saying good bye till some of us little ones fell asleep.... And here I may as well tell what kind of a man our new master was. He was of small stature, and thin, but very strong. He had sandy hair, fierce gray eyes, a very red face, and chewed tobacco. His countenance had a very cruel expression, and his disposition was a match for it. He was, indeed, a very bad man, and used to flog us dreadfully. He would make his slaves work on one meal a day, until quite night, and after supper, set them to burn brush or to spin cotton. We worked from four in the morning till twelve before we broke our fast, and from that time till eleven or twelve at night. I should say that on the average, and taking all the year round, we laboured eighteen hours a day well told. He was a captain of the patrol, which went out every Wednesday and Saturday night, hunting "stray niggers," and to see that none of the neighbours' people were from quarters....

I remained at James Davis's for nearly eighteen months. Once during that period, I remember he took me into the town to a tavern kept by one Captain Jemmy Duprey. There was a negro speculator there, on the look-out for bargains, but he would not have me. I did not know where I was going, when my master took me with him, but when I got back I told my mother, who cried over me, and said she was very glad I had not been sold away from her.

But the time arrived when we were to be finally separated. Owing to a considerable rise in the price of cotton, there came a great demand for slaves in Georgia. One day a negro speculator named Starling Finney arrived at James Davis's place. He left his drove on the highway, in charge of one of his companions, and made his way up to our plantation, prospecting for negroes.... I looked round and saw my poor mother stretching out her hands after me. She ran up, and overtook us, but Finney, who was behind me, and between me and my mother, would not let her approach, though she begged and prayed to be allowed to kiss me for the last time, and bid me good bye. I was so stupified [*sic*] with grief and fright, that I could not shed a tear, though my heart was bursting. At last we got to the gate, and I turned round to see whether I could not get a chance of kissing my mother. She saw me, and made a dart forward to meet me, but Finney gave me a hard push, which sent me spinning through the gate. He then slammed it to and shut it in my mother's face. That was the last time I ever saw her, nor do I know whether she is alive or dead at this hour.[18]

⬥⬥⬥

KATE DRUMGOOLD, BORN IN 1858 NEAR PETERSBURG, VIRGINIA, LIVED WITH HER MOTHER AND SISTERS UNTIL 1861, when her mother was sold south to Georgia. Fortunately for Drumgoold, she was reunited with her mother after the end of the war, but

---

[18] Brown's memoir, *Slave Life in Georgia: A Narrative of the Life, Sufferings, and Escape of John Brown, A Fugitive Slave, Now in England* (London: British and Foreign Anti-Slavery Society, 1855) can be read at http://docsouth.unc.edu/neh/jbrown/jbrown.html.

that rare event was unimaginable at the time.[19] In her own words, she expressed her loss:

> My dear mother was sold at the beginning of the war, from all of her little ones, after the death of the lady that she belonged to, and who was so kind to my dear mother and all of the rest of the negroes of the place; and she never liked the idea of holding us as slaves, and she always said that we were all that she had on the earth to love; and she did love me to the last.
>
> The money that my mother was sold for was to keep the rich man from going to the field of battle, as he sent a poor white man in his stead, and should the war end in his favor, the poor white man should have given to him one negro, and that would fully pay for all of his service in the army. ... And God, in His love for me and to me, never let me know of it, as did some of my own dear sisters, for some of them were hired out after the old home was broken up.
>
> My mother was sold at Richmond, Virginia, and a gentleman bought her who lived in Georgia, and we did not know that she was sold until she was gone; and the saddest thought was to me to know which way she had gone and I used to go outside and look up to see if there was anything that would direct me, and I saw a clear place in the sky, and it seemed to me the way she had gone, and I watched it three and a half years, not knowing what that meant, and it was there the whole time that mother was gone from her little ones.

---

[19] Drumgoold's memoir *A Slave Girl's Story* (Brooklyn: np., 1898) can be read at http://docsouth.unc.edu/neh/drumgoold/drumgoold.html.

✦✦✦

WILLIAM J. ANDERSON'S STORY IS PERHAPS BEST CAPTURED BY THE TITLE OF HIS MEMOIR: *Life and Narrative of William J. Anderson, Twenty-four Years a Slave; Sold Eight Times! In Jail Sixty Times!! Whipped Three Hundred Times!!! or The Dark Deeds of American Slavery Revealed.* Anderson was born in June 1811, in Hanover County, Virginia, to a woman named Susan and to Lewis Anderson, a slave who had served in the military, most likely in the Revolution.[20] Self-taught, Anderson became an invaluable witness to the impact of the Second Middle Passage and relates a story that at times is simply difficult to bear:

> I lived at a place where I could see some of the horrors of slavery exhibited to a great extent; it was a large tavern, situated at the crossing of roads, where hundreds of slaves pass by for the Southern market, chained and handcuffed together by fifties—wives taken from husbands and husbands from wives, never to see each other again—small and large children separated from their parents. They were driven away to Georgia, and Louisiana, and other Southern States, to be disposed of.
>
> O, I have seen them and heard them howl like dogs or wolves, when being under the painful obligation of parting to

---

[20] See William J. Anderson, *Life and Narrative of William J. Anderson, Twenty-four Years a Slave; Sold Eight Times! In Jail Sixty Times!! Whipped Three Hundred Times!!! or The Dark Deeds of American Slavery Revealed.* (Chicago: Daily Tribune Book and Job Printing Office, 1857), http://docsouth.unc.edu/neh/andersonw/andersonw.html.

meet no more. Many of them have to leave their children in the cradle, or ashes, to suffer or die for the want of attentive care or food, or both. . . .

My master was considered one of those cunning, fox-like slaveholders; his craving for gold was almost insatiable; he kidnapped me by night, when all things were as silent as death, handcuffed and chained me securely, while I was ten miles from my mother, and young and in-experienced, helpless and ignorant of the geography of the country. The horrors of leaving my native land I cannot express. I was hurried off, and not permitted to get my clothes or bid my friends farewell.

We arrived early next day in the city of Richmond, the capital of the State. The slave-market space was very much crowded; so he sold me privately, for three hundred and seventy-five dollars. A south-ern trader bought me; he asked me if I ever run, I told him I had. He asked me if I could run fast; I told him I could. He asked once more if I ever ran away; as I always stood much upon truth, I told him I had, once only, and stayed away one day. So he put me in jail, there to remain until he made up his drove of slaves, which was a very few days. But I, a free boy, locked up in jail! It was a bad and horrible feeling.

In a few days he made up his drove, to the number of some sixty-five or seventy. Myself and several men, say twenty or more, were chained together, two and two, with a chain between. In this situation we started, on the 6th of Nov., 1826, for East and West Tennessee. Then we sang the song–

"Farewell, ye children of the Lord, &c."

We traveled a few days, and scenes of sadness occurred; the snow and rain came down in torrents, but we had to rest out in the open air every night; sometimes we would have to scrape away the snow, make our pallets on the cold ground, or in the rain, with a bunch of leaves and a chunk of wood for our pillow, and so we would have to rest the best we could, with our chains on. In that awful situation the reader may imagine how we gained any relief from the suffering consequent upon the cruel infliction we had to endure. We were driven with whip and curses through the cold and rain. . . .

In due time we arrived safely in the slave-pen at Natchez [Mississippi], and here we joined another large crowd of slaves which were already stationed at this place. Here scenes were witnessed which are too wicked to mention. The slaves are made to shave and wash in greasy pot liquor, to make them look sleek and nice; their heads must be combed, and their best clothes put on; and when called out to be examined they are to stand in a row–the women and men apart–then they are picked out and taken into a room, and examined. See a large, rough slaveholder, take a poor female slave into a room, make her strip, then feel of and examine her, as though she were a pig, or a hen, or merchandise. O, how can a poor slave husband or father stand and see his wife, daughters and sons thus treated.

I saw there, after men and women had followed each other, then–too shock-ing to relate–for the sake of money, they are sold separately, sometimes two

Slave pen, Alexandria, Virginia, 1861–1865. Photograph. Library of Congress.

hundred miles apart, although their hopes would be to be sold together. Sometimes their little children are torn from them and sent far away to a distant country, never to see them again. O, such crying and weeping when parting from each other! For this demonstration of natural human affection the slaveholder would apply the lash or paddle upon the naked skin. . . .

We were obliged to work exceedingly hard, and were not permitted to talk or laugh with each other while working in the field. We were not allowed to speak to a neighbor slave who chanced to pass along the road. I have often been whipped for leaving patches of grass, and not working fast, or for even looking at my master. How great my sufferings were the reader cannot conceive. I was frequently knocked down, and then whipped up, and made to work on in the midst of my cries, tears and prayers. It did appear as if the man had no heart at all. My sufferings while obliged to pursue[,] my labor, picking cotton, were too intense for my poor brain to describe, and no one can realize such bodily anguish except one who has passed through the like. I was whipped if I did not pick enough, or if there was trash found in it. The most of slaveholders are very intemperate indeed. My master often went to the house, got drunk, and then came out to the field to whip, cut, slash, curse, swear, beat and knock down several, for the smallest offence, or nothing at all.

He divested a poor female slave of all wearing apparel, tied her down to stakes, and whipped her with a handsaw until he broke it over her naked body. In process of time he ravished her person, and became the father of a child by her. Besides, he always kept a colored Miss in the house with him. This is another curse of Slavery—concubinage and illegitimate connections—which is carried on to an alarming extent in the far South. A poor slave man who lives close by his wife, is permitted to visit her but very seldom, and other men, both white and colored, cohabit with her. It is undoubtedly the worst place of incest and bigamy in the world. A white man thinks nothing of putting a colored man out to carry the fore row, and carry on the same sport with the colored man's wife at the same time.

⬥⬥⬥

SOLOMON NORTHUP'S STORY PROVIDES AN EVEN MORE TRAGIC ELEMENT. BORN FREE IN MINERVA, NEW YORK, THE SON OF MINTUS NORTHUP, a former slave from Rhode Island, Northup worked alongside his father on their farm in Granville, New York. His father owned enough property to become a voter, a significant achievement in a state that in the 1820s restricted the franchise by maintaining property requirements for potential black male voters, but not for whites. Solomon married at the end of 1829 and had a variety of occupations, including working the canal and waterways of western New York. In 1834, he and his wife, Anne, moved their three children to Saratoga, New York, the famed resort city.

In 1841, however, Northup's good luck would take a dramatic turn for the worse when he was tricked into traveling to Washington, D.C., with promises of a lucrative job. Instead, he was drugged, chained, and sold to a slave trader named James H. Burch who transported the helpless Northup to New Orleans and a life of slavery that endured until his rescue in 1853. As the title of his memoir reveals, he spent 12 horrid years in bondage, and the following passage details the process of being sold as property:[21]

---

[21] Solomon Northup, *Twelve Years a Slave: Narrative of Solomon Northup, A Citizen of New-York, Kidnapped in Washington City in 1841* (Auburn, NY: Derby and Miller, London: Sampson Low, Son & Co., 1853), http://docsouth.unc.edu/fpn/northup/northup.html.

James H. Burch was a slave-trader—buying men, women and children at low prices, and selling them at an advance. He was a speculator in human flesh—a disreputable calling—and so considered at the South. For the present he disappears from the scenes recorded in this narrative, but he will appear again before its close, not in the character of a man-whipping tyrant, but as an arrested, cringing criminal in a court of law, that failed to do him justice.

After we were all on board, the brig Orleans proceeded down James River. Passing into Chesapeake Bay, we arrived next day opposite the city of Norfolk. While lying at anchor, a lighter approached us from the town, bringing four more slaves. Frederick, a boy of eighteen, had been born a slave, as also had Henry, who was some years older. They had both been house servants in the city. Maria was a rather genteel looking colored girl, with a faultless form, but ignorant and extremely vain. The idea of going to New-Orleans was pleasing to her. She entertained an extravagantly high opinion of her own attractions. Assuming a haughty mien, she declared to her companions, that immediately on our arrival in New-Orleans, she had no doubt, some wealthy single gentleman of good taste would purchase her at once! . . .

It was but a short time I closed my eyes that night. Thought was busy in my brain. Could it be possible that I was thousands of miles from home—that I had been driven through the streets like a dumb beast— that I had been chained and beaten without mercy—that I was even then herded with a drove of slaves, a slave myself? Were the events of the last few weeks realities indeed?—or was I passing only through the dismal phases of a long, protracted dream? It was no illusion. My cup of sorrow was full to overflowing. Then I lifted up my hands to God, and in the still watches of the night, surrounded by the sleeping forms of my companions, begged for mercy on the poor, forsaken captive. To the Almighty Father of us all— the freeman and the slave—I poured forth the supplications of a broken spirit, imploring strength from on high to bear up against the burden of my troubles, until the morning light aroused the slumberers, ushering in another day of bondage.

The very amiable, pious-hearted Mr. Theophilus Freeman, partner or consignee of James H. Burch, and keeper of the slave pen in New-Orleans, was out among his animals early in the morning. With an occasional kick of the older men and women, and many a sharp crack of the whip about the ears of the younger slaves, it was not long before they were all astir, and wide awake. Mr. Theophilus Freeman bustled about in a very industrious manner, getting his property ready for the sales-room, intending, no doubt, to do that day a rousing business.

In the first place we were required to wash thoroughly, and those with beards, to shave. We were then furnished with a new suit each, cheap, but clean. The men had hat, coat, shirt, pants and shoes; the women frocks of calico, and handkerchiefs to bind about their heads. We were now conducted into a large room in the front part of the building to which the yard was attached, in order to be properly trained, before the admission of customers. The men were arranged on one side of the room, the women on the other. The tallest was placed at the head of the row, then the next tallest, and so on in the order of their respective heights. Emily [a child of seven or eight] was at the foot of the line of women. Freeman charged us to remember our places; exhorted us to appear smart and lively,—sometimes threatening, and again, holding out various inducements. During the day he exercised us in the art of "looking smart," and of moving to our places with exact precision.

After being fed, in the afternoon, we were again paraded and made to dance. Bob, a colored boy, who had some time belonged to Freeman, played on the violin. Standing near him, I made bold to inquire if he could play the "Virginia Reel." He answered he could not, and asked me if I could play. Replying in the affirmative, he handed me the violin. I struck up a tune, and finished it. Freeman ordered me to continue playing, and seemed well pleased, telling Bob that I far excelled him—a remark that seemed to grieve my musical companion very much.

Next day many customers called to examine Freeman's "new lot." The latter gentleman was very loquacious, dwelling at much length upon our several good points and qualities. He would make us hold up our heads, walk briskly back and forth, while customers would feel of our hands and arms and bodies, turn us about, ask us what we could do, make us open our mouths and show our teeth, precisely as a jockey examines a horse which he is about to barter for or purchase. Sometimes a man or woman was taken back to the small house in the yard, stripped, and inspected more minutely. Scars upon a slave's back were considered evidence of a rebellious or unruly spirit, and hurt his sale.

∗∗∗

AS THE SETTLEMENT OF THE DEEP SOUTH WAS REMAKING THE FACE OF THE UNITED STATES, defenders of slavery often went to great lengths to prove that the natural condition of a black person was perpetual enslavement. American independence may have been grounded in the notion that "all men are created equal," but the realities of a burgeoning American economy founded upon cotton and slavery demanded a very different justification. Thus, a powerful movement took hold among the shapers of American popular opinion, North and South, who summoned the most fanciful arguments in defense of slavery, arguments grounded either in questionable interpretations of biblical passages or based on the claims of racial pseudo-science, to argue that Africans and Europeans did not share descent from common ancestors. New and bizarre anthropological ideas, created by scientists including those at Harvard University, measured black people's heads and penises in a search for proof that blacks were inferior, perhaps not fully human. In the 1830s, southern ministers like Virginia's Thornton Stringfellow asserted that slavery was legal and sanctioned

... according to the 1830 federal census, 43 percent of Charleston's free black heads of households *owned* their own slaves.

"by Jesus Christ in his kingdom" and "that it is full of mercy." Southern politicians like South Carolina's John C. Calhoun famously argued that slavery was actually "a positive good," sanctioned by God and suited to the needs and capacities of both blacks and whites.[22]

A kind of national schizophrenia prevailed, with a country asserting its manifest destiny to spread both freedom and slavery throughout the continent. While slavery was either dead or dying in the North and Midwest, a racist ideology sought to shape and justify the treatment of and attitudes toward African Americans both within the institution of slavery and outside of it. In the South, slavery grew unbounded, bringing enormous wealth to a select few, while leaving a large class of whites outside its financial benefits but ensuring a social level below which they could never fall—a social level exclusively occupied by black slaves.

At the same time, however, surprisingly enough, some African Americans in the South experienced levels of financial security and new levels of prosperity that few blacks in the supposedly free North ever could know. Indeed, by 1860, on the eve of the Civil War, more free black people lived in the South than in the North, a fact that strikes us today as counterintuitive. And these free black communities created their own social and cultural institutions, just as Prince Hall and Richard Allen did in Boston and Philadelphia.

In Charleston, South Carolina, for example, the Brown Fellowship Society—an African American fraternal organization—was founded in 1790 and limited to 50 free blacks of "good character." The society provided a strong social network along with a means of burial and widow support for a burgeoning free black society in the urban South. And its story illuminates a class system that emerged in black America long before the end of slavery—a system that underscores the tremendous diversity within the black community even as it violates modern sensibilities: The Brown Fellowship Society excluded dark-skinned blacks from membership. And its members, many of whom came to the states as a result of the Haitian Revolution, felt little in common with the slaves who surrounded them.

In fact, according to the 1830 federal census, 43 percent of Charleston's free black heads of households *owned* their own slaves. Many were family members, bought to keep them close and protect them. But unfortunately, this wasn't the case for all—some were simply slaves, purchased and used for profit by their black owners. Notoriously, one of the society's members, George Logan, was ejected from the association for enslaving another free black man. South Carolina's William Ellison, a free black planter, owned more than 60 slaves and more than 1,000 acres—one of his sons even volunteered to fight for the Confederacy.

[22] See Drew Gilpin Faust, ed., *The Ideology of Slavery: Proslavery Thought in the Antebellum South, 1830–1860* (Baton Rouge: Louisiana State University Press, 1981), 139 quoted.

Furthermore, the Brown Fellowship Society was not the only such organization to spring up in prosperous southern cities as "King Cotton" spread across the land. Free blacks in southern cities like Charleston sometimes actually did better economically than their northern counterparts because they were able to assume a middle position between slaves and whites, profiting from associations with both. Indeed, at the start of the Civil War, free blacks in New Orleans would initially side with the Confederacy, believing that they shared more common interests with white planters than with black slaves.[23]

It's hard to imagine how members of the Brown Fellowship Society must have felt, accruing wealth as black slave owners in a white-run slave society. Their vulnerability must have been palpable. They could not vote, serve on juries, or testify against white people, or (after 1835) operate schools to teach other African Americans. They were not free to marry or move without fear, and if they left the state, laws prohibited them from returning. They had no civil rights. Their business contracts with whites could be extraordinarily fruitful, as in the case of Jehu Jones, Sr., the city's famed hotelier. But even he fell victim to legal restrictions on travel outside the state and could not return after visiting an ill daughter in New York. While these nominally free blacks could have careers as businessmen, innkeepers, skilled craftsmen, tailors, and shoemakers, their tightly restricted lives always kept them on the razor's edge between slavery and freedom.

And they were the lucky ones: They could harbor hopes and dreams. The vast majority of African Americans' lives were swallowed up in despair as the 19th century unfolded. In 1800, Gabriel dreamed of overturning Virginia's "slaveocracy," in accord with the founding principles of American democracy. By 1831, however, a man named Nat Turner had embraced a far narrower goal, one grounded in a bitter history of oppression rather than in the embrace of America's most noble aspirations.

Born on October 2, 1800, in Southampton County, Virginia, the week before Gabriel was hanged, Turner impressed others with an unusual sense of purpose, even as a child.[24]

Driven by prophetic visions and joined by a host of followers—but with no clear goals—on August 22, 1831, Turner and about 70 armed slaves and free blacks set off to slaughter the white neighbors who enslaved them. They began, in the early hours of the morning, by killing Turner's master and his master's wife and children with axes. The story he told in his confession is chilling:

> It was then observed that I must spill the first blood. On which, armed with a hatchet, and accompanied by Will, I entered my master's chamber, it being dark, I could not give a death blow, the hatchet glanced from his head, he sprang from

---

[23] Robert L. Harris, Jr., "Charleston's Free Afro-American Elite: The Brown Fellowship Society and the Humane Brotherhood," *South Carolina Historical Magazine* 82 (October 1981): 289–310; Ira Berlin, *Slaves Without Masters: The Free Negro in the Antebellum South* (New York: Oxford University Press, 1974), 57–58, 312–13; Michael P. Johnson and James L. Roark, *Black Masters: A Free Family of Color in the Old South* (New York: W. W. Norton, 1984).

[24] Stephen B. Oates, *The Fires of Jubilee: Nat Turner's Fierce Rebellion* (New York: Harper & Row, 1975); Scot French, *The Rebellious Slave: Nat Turner in American Memory* (Boston: Houghton Mifflin, 2004).

Nat Turner conspiring with slaves in Northampton, Virginia, 1831. Colored engraving. Private Collection, Bridgeman Art Library.

the bed and called his wife, it was his last word, Will laid him dead, with a blow of his axe, and Mrs. Travis shared the same fate, as she lay in bed. The murder of this family, five in number, was the work of a moment, not one of them awoke; there was a little infant sleeping in a cradle, that was forgotten, until we had left the house and gone some distance, when Henry and Will returned and killed it. . . .[25]

---

[25] Thomas R. Gray, ed., *The Confessions of Nat Turner* (Baltimore: Thomas R. Gray, 1831), which can be read at http://docsouth.unc.edu/neh/turner/turner.html.

By the end of the next day, the rebels had attacked about 15 homes and killed between 55 and 60 whites as they moved, perhaps by design, toward the religiously named county seat of Jerusalem, Virginia. Other slaves who had planned to join the rebellion suddenly turned against the insurrection after white militia began attacking Turner's men, undoubtedly concluding that he would inevitably fail. Most of the rebels were quickly captured, but Turner eluded authorities for more than a month.

On Sunday, October 30, a local white stumbled on Turner's hideout and seized him. A special Virginia court tried him on November 5 and sentenced him to hang six days later. Afterward, enraged whites took his body, skinned it, distributed parts as souvenirs, and rendered his remains into grease. His head was removed and for a time sat in the biology department of Wooster College in Ohio. Of his fellow rebels, 21 also went to the gallows, and another 16 were sold away from the region. As the state reacted with harsher laws controlling black people, many free blacks fled Virginia for good. Turner remains a legendary figure, and it is likely that pieces of his body—including his skull and a purse made from his skin—have been preserved, arousing much controversy.[26]

The difference between Gabriel and Turner is the difference between a man of optimism and a man of despair, one man fueled by ideological fervor and the other inspired by religious visions of vengeance. It's a difference that tells a great deal about how slavery evolved in 19th-century America. Moreover,

---

[26] French, *Rebellious Slave*, 280-81; Andrew Putz, "Skullduggery," *Indianapolis Monthly* (October 2003): 131, 224–25.

the Turner event would be, in the white southern mind, forever linked to the rise of northern abolitionism.

AT RICHARD ALLEN'S MOTHER BETHEL CHURCH IN PHILADELPHIA IN JANUARY 1817, black leaders organized a meeting that showed just how much had changed in the years since the Age of Revolutions. The free black leaders of Philadelphia—the shining star of the free North—wished to discuss the possibility of leaving this country and immigrating to Africa. Back in December 1816, in the halls of Congress, white leaders like James Monroe, James Madison, and Henry Clay founded the American Colonization Society (ACS), formed to return freed slaves and free black people to Africa, their answer to the problem of American slavery and race relations.

Before long, most clergy and reform groups, and 14 state legislatures, endorsed the ACS. Virtually every state in the North possessed auxiliaries of the organization, and the state of Maryland became so enthralled with the idea that it formed its own colonization society (which later merged with the ACS's efforts). Within six years, the ACS began sending settlers to its West African colony in Liberia.

Those who met in Allen's church had good reason to consider leaving the United States. Black life in the North had grown increasingly difficult. Openly discriminated against, generally confined to the lowest levels of society and the least desirable occupations, denied most civil rights, black people struggled amid growing racial intolerance. But more than anything, they lived in fear. The expansion of slavery in the Deep South threatened the very idea of freedom for blacks *anywhere* in America, and rings of kidnappers operated with impunity in major American cities, especially in Philadelphia. With slaves in such great demand, no African American was safe. Richard Allen himself had been temporarily seized in 1806 as a fugitive slave. No free black man in the North—no matter how successful or prominent—could ever be sure of his liberty.

In January 1817, more than 3,000 black men filled Allen's church to hear what their leaders had to say. Richard Allen's close friend James Forten (1766–1842), one of the most successful black businessmen in the United States, took the podium and exhorted them to return to Africa. Forten's story crystallizes the broken dreams of a generation of black Americans. Born free in Philadelphia in 1766, Forten remembered standing in the crowd outside the Pennsylvania State House (now known as Independence Hall) to hear the first reading of the Declaration of Independence. After serving on Steven Decatur's vessel the *Royal Louis* in 1781, he and his fellow crew members were captured by a British warship. The captain, much taken with Forten, offered him opportunities in England. But the young man rejected the offer immediately, declaring, "I have been taken prisoner for the liberties of my country, and never will prove a traitor to her interests." Rather than enjoying a life of leisure, he spent seven months on a British prison ship and only luck saved him from enslavement in the West Indies.[27]

Instead, he became a master sailmaker and eventually bought the business of his white employer. He proved as accomplished a businessman as a sailmaker and acquired great wealth, investing his profits in real estate, banks, a canal, and later in railroad stock. He—and his family—were the cream of Philadelphia's black elite. But his experience with white society proved severely disillusioning. He came to embrace the idea of emigration, initiated and organized by his close friend Paul Cuffee, the wealthiest black man in Boston and along with Forten one of the two richest black men in America. Cuffee was the first African American to sail a ship of returnees back to the African continent, to Sierra Leone in 1815. (He also was the first free black man to visit a sitting president in the White House.)

For free blacks such as Cuffee, Allen, and Forten, removal to Africa was grounded in a conviction that endemic racism and discrimination left African Americans with no future in America. The January 1817 meeting in Philadelphia was to be a referendum on the idea, and Cuffee—Forten's close associate in the emigration scheme—eagerly awaited news from his friend of the results of the vote at the meeting.

Their position seemed well reasoned and grounded in hard experience. But it failed. When Forten called for a vote in favor of going to Africa, not one of the 3,000 men in the room said yes. Their collective decision speaks volumes about the nature of black political priorities during the antebellum era. Although ill-treated because of their skin color and living daily with the possibility of enslavement, they refused to leave. Like Forten during the Revolution, they felt strongly that they had but one country. They were Americans, not Africans.

---

[27] Quoted in Julie Winch, *A Gentleman of Color: The Life of James Forten* (New York: Oxford University Press, 2002), 46.

Paul Cuffee, artist unknown, early 19th century. Oil on canvas. Image courtesy of the New England Historic Genealogical Society, www.AmericanAncestors.org.

This early "Back to Africa" movement was not completely derailed. The idea of colonization was embraced by many prominent whites—most of them racists who saw it as a way to remove troublesome free black people from the United States. In 1821, the American Colonization Society would begin sending the first of more than 13,000 freed slaves to set up a colony in Liberia. And over the coming decades, virtually every African American leader of note would engage—at least briefly—with the notion of voluntary African- or Caribbean-inspired emigration, while almost all would reject enforced, white-directed colonization.

While enslaved African Americans might well see colonization as their only alternative to enslavement, most free black people made a commitment to gain their rights as Americans—no matter how long that might take. A few free blacks like the Reverend Daniel Coker (1780–1846) in 1820, who founded the West African Methodist Episcopal church in Sierra Leone, and John Russwurm (1799–1851), who would help found this country's first black newspaper in 1827, did choose the lure of Liberian freedom over the risks at home (although Coker soon moved from Liberia to the British colony of Sierra Leone). However, support for the ACS among blacks largely evaporated.

In fact, reaction to the American Colonization Society would be the driving force behind something else: a rising abolitionist movement determined to end racism and slavery, not through emigration, but through a fundamental reform of the United States—a reform that would seek to extend full civil rights to all African Americans. Opposition to the colonization movement became a core principle of the black abolitionist movement as it called for equal rights and citizenship for African Americans. James Forten himself became an early convert, and soon emerged as one of the central figures in the antislavery movement. His financial support proved critical to the survival of the most important abolitionist newspaper founded before the Civil War: William Lloyd Garrison's Boston-based *Liberator*.

Over time, Richard Allen also concluded that the destiny of African Americans had to be found in the United States, although in 1824 he saw in the Haitian republic a place where America's "poor and oppressed" could find "an asylum where they will enjoy the blessings of freedom and equality."[28] In August 1824, Allen sent about 50 settlers to the black republic, which grew to about 200; and over the next year anywhere from 6,000 to 12,000 black Americans immigrated to Haiti, at much personal sacrifice to themselves and those blacks who remained behind in Philadelphia. While some thrived, many did not, and 2,000 quickly returned, unable to speak French, dissatisfied with the meager economic opportunities, resentful of the hostility of the Haitian government, and unsympathetic to the Catholic and indigenous religions they found there.[29]

In November 1827, chastened by the Haitian experience, Allen made a compelling argument in *Freedom's Journal*, the nation's first black-owned newspaper, against the plans of the American Colonization Society, writing: "This land which we have watered with our tears and our blood is now our mother country." Then, in 1830, he organized the first National Negro Convention. Forty of the most prominent black Americans gathered in Bethel Church to call for civil rights and oppose African colonization projects—which they now saw as blatantly racist. It was the first concerted effort of black male leaders from across the nation to come together and explore what it meant to be black in America. They debated the most basic aspects of their identity and future, from what they wanted to be called (Africans, Negroes, colored, Afric-Americans) to whether it might be advisable to immigrate to Canada. The convention would meet another dozen times before the Civil War, eventually including such legendary figures as Frederick Douglass, Henry Highland Garnet, William Wells Brown, and Martin R. Delany.

[28] Newman, *Freedom's Prophet*, 247–48, 253, 261–63.

[29] Julie Winch, *Philadelphia's Black Elite: Activism, Accommodation, and the Struggle for Autonomy, 1787–1848* (Philadelphia: Temple University Press, 1988), 49–61.

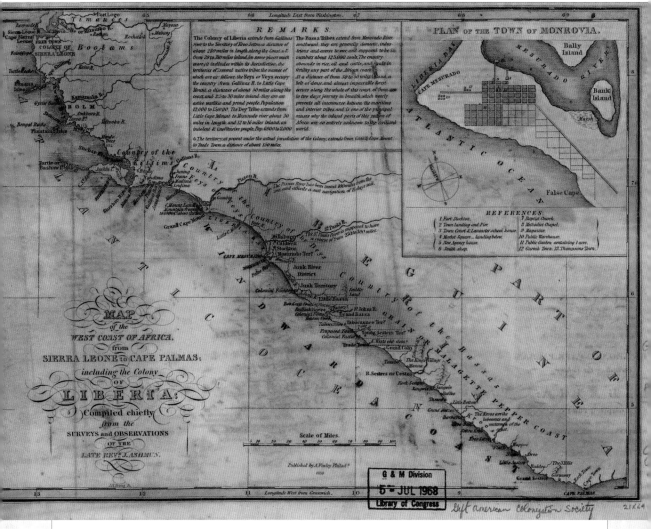

Map of Liberian coast, from Sierra Leone to Cape Palmas, by A. Finley, Philadelphia, 1830. Library of Congress.

American abolitionism is typically portrayed as a movement led and dominated by whites, but black abolitionists played a central and defining role from its inception. Indeed, Allen and Forten were just two of many in a tradition going back to Prince Hall, articulate, committed advocates who first formulated black abolitionism's goals—the destruction of slavery *and* racial prejudice—as early as 1797, and even before, as we have seen in the challenges to slavery, such as Mum Bett's, that were mounted in the courts. And their numbers increased with each passing year, spreading to every state and community in the North, with the centers of action based in Philadelphia, New York, and Boston.

✖✖✖

ONE OF THE MOST IMPORTANT LEAD-
ERS TO EMERGE IN BOSTON DUR-
ING THESE EARLY YEARS WAS DAVID
WALKER (1796?–1830), A FREE BLACK
TAILOR AND CLOTHES MERCHANT FROM
NORTH CAROLINA. He left Charleston,
South Carolina, about the time of the Denmark
Vesey conspiracy in 1822. Vesey, an educated
former slave and successful businessman, led
Charleston's black community and conspired
with other free blacks and slaves to kill whites,
burn the city, and flee to Haiti. After his plot
was exposed by other blacks, city officials
hanged 35 of the accused and executed Vesey
on July 2. By 1825, Walker had settled in Boston.
The following year he joined the Prince Hall
Freemason Lodge No. 459 and became a member of the General Colored Association, placing
him in the leadership of the city's black community. In 1829, he published the pamphlet for
which he is best known, *Appeal to the Colored
Citizens of the World*. Walker's rhetoric rang out
in a call to action as no other African American
had ever dared publicly to proclaim:

> Can our condition be any worse?—Can it
> be more mean and abject? If there are any
> changes, will they not be for the better
> though they may appear for the worst at
> first? Can they get us any lower? Where
> can they get us? They are afraid to treat
> us worse, for they know well, the day
> they do it they are gone. But against all
> accusations which may or can be pre-
> ferred against me, I appeal to Heaven for
> my motive in writing—who knows what
> my object is, if possible, to awaken in
> the breasts of my afflicted, degraded and

> slumbering brethren, a spirit of inquiry
> and investigation respecting our miseries
> and wretchedness in this *Republican Land
> of Liberty!!!!!!*
>
> ...Does the Lord condescend to hear
> their cries and see their tears in conse-
> quence of oppression? Will he let the
> oppressors rest comfortably and happy al-
> ways? Will he not cause the very children
> of the oppressors to rise up against them,
> and oftimes put them to death? "God
> works in many ways his wonders
> to perform."[30]

The book was sewn into the lining of sailors' uniforms so that it could be distributed
surreptitiously by free black sailors traveling
throughout the South—where it had a tremendous impact. Mocking Jefferson's Declaration
of Independence and his racial views, Walker
castigated American hypocrisy on race and
called for militant resistance to slavery. It
would echo through black culture for decades.

Boston would also be home to Maria
Stewart (1803–1879), the first African American
woman to publish a political manifesto. An uncompromising critic of the colonization movement, she readily proclaimed her preference
for death rather than submit to deportation.
She tirelessly urged her brethren to commit to
the antislavery fight and bolstered her call by
rejecting—as David Walker had done—the re-
volting racial ideas of Thomas Jefferson.

> Many think, because your skins are
> tinged with a sable hue, that you are an
> inferior race of beings; but God does not

---

30 David Walker, *Appeal, in Four Articles* . . . (Boston:
D. Walker, 1830).

consider you as such. He hath formed and fashioned you in his own glorious image, and hath bestowed upon you reason and strong powers of intellect. He hath made you to have dominion over the beasts of the field, the fowls of the air, and the fish of the sea [Genesis 1:26]. He hath crowned you with glory and honor; hath made you but a little lower than the angels [Psalms 8:5]; and according to the Constitution of these United States, he hath made all men free and equal.[31]

In perhaps one of the most memorable opening lines in all of American political discourse, on September 21, 1832, Stewart proclaimed to a meeting of the New England Anti-Slavery Society, "Why sit ye here and die?" Don't tell me about southern slavery, she declared, because her condition in the North was little better. She called on her sisters to take charge and help lead their race to freedom, to educate themselves if others would not, to force whites to acknowledge their abilities and, in the end, recognize their right to freedom.

But she assigned special responsibility to black men to speak out, just as she had done. "I would ask," she proclaimed in February 1833, "is it blindness of mind, or stupidity of soul, or want of education that has caused our men who are 60 or 70 years of age, never to let their voices be heard, not their hands be raised in behalf of their color?... If you are men, convince then that you possess the spirit of men.... Have the sons of Africa no souls? Feel they no ambitious desires? Shall the chains of ignorance

forever confine them?" Why have you not spoken out as David Walker did, she asked? As the first black woman to speak out on political issues, Stewart blazed a trail for scores of others.[32]

Stewart would live to see many black men answer her call, one former Maryland slave in particular. Frederick Douglass (1818–1895), who taught himself how to read as a slave, escaped to the North in 1838 and joined the abolitionist movement in 1841. His first autobiography (he would write two more), published in 1845, is one of the most powerful indictments of slavery ever written. It catapulted him into international celebrity and into a leadership in the abolitionist movement—transforming the nation's very concept of democracy. Douglass not only battled slavery and racism, but also whites within the abolitionist movement, one of whom even told him to be less articulate in public and to put a little more of the "plantation" in his speeches. Although widely acknowledged by his fellow African Americans as the movement's leading force, he was sometimes opposed by other black leaders, including Henry Highland Garnet (1815–1882), who was the first to support slave insurrections, and Martin R. Delany (1812–1885), often described by historians as the father of Black Nationalism.

Especially after founding his first newspaper, the *North Star*, in 1848, Douglass transformed himself from a black spokesman for white abolitionists (who sought to reform slavery through moral suasion) to an independent black voice seeking to transform the entire American political system. By the 1850s, Douglass shocked white audiences by telling them that if anyone wanted to make the hated

---

[31] Marilyn Richardson, ed., *Maria W. Stewart, America's First Black Woman Political Writer: Essays and Speeches* (Bloomington: Indiana University Press, 1987), 29.

[32] Richardson, *Maria W. Stewart*, 45, 57.

Fugitive Slave Act a dead letter, they should kill some fugitive slave catchers. Moreover, he expressed his desire to hear that slaves in the South had revolted and "were spreading death and destruction." Douglass was one abolitionist in whom Maria Stewart and all other African American advocates of militant opposition against slavery could take pride.

Fired by the stories of former slaves like Douglass, more and more African Americans were drawn into antislavery and civil rights organizations, vigilance committees, and activist church groups. Inspired by Great Britain's abolition of slavery throughout its colonies in 1834, the movement grew in prominence and scope, expanding the antislavery message to include full citizenship rights and elimination of Jim Crow segregation in marriage, education, and public transportation. Members assisted in countless ways, including boycotting slave-produced goods and organizing fairs and food sales to raise money for the cause. They could also support the informal network known as the Underground Railroad, which helped runaway slaves find their way to freedom and resist the escalating efforts of slave catchers. Indeed, it was through the Underground Railroad system that church groups, women, and ordinary African Americans could exert the most effort to challenge the institution of slavery directly.

Activists like William Still (1821–1902), who ran the Philadelphia Vigilance Committee, the nation's central hub of the Underground Railroad, played crucial roles in resisting slavery and rallying black communities. His book, *The Underground Railroad*, published in 1872, is a dramatic account of the stories of hundreds of former slaves who passed through Philadelphia on their way to other northern cities or to Canada.

One of the most fascinating stories that Still recounted, and which received enormous international attention, began on March 23, 1849, when Henry Brown (1816?–1889) escaped slavery by having himself mailed from Richmond to Philadelphia in a wooden crate. Outraged that his family, including his pregnant wife, had been sold away to North Carolina, Brown had trusted friends seal him up in a wooden crate and ship him by Adams Express to abolitionists in Philadelphia. When Still and his antislavery colleagues pried open the box, out popped Brown, reaching out his hand, saying, "How do you do, gentlemen?" and then singing the hymn "I waited patiently for the Lord, and He heard my prayer."[33] Brown, forever after known as Henry "Box" Brown, then spent about a year traveling across the North lecturing on the evils of slavery. He also published an account of his escape, the *Narrative of Henry Box Brown* (1849), and in 1850 accompanied a moving panorama, *Henry Box Brown's Mirror of Slavery*, which opened in Boston. Fearing for his safety after passage of the new Fugitive Slave Act in 1850, Brown escaped to England.

Perhaps the most ingenious escape recounted by Still was that of William (1824–1900) and Ellen (1826–1891) Craft, who escaped

---

[33] William Still, *The Underground Railroad* (Philadelphia: Porter & Coates, 1872), 70.

FACING PAGE: Frederick Douglass, circa 1840s. Daguerreotype. Collection of Greg French. This is one of the earliest known images of Douglass.

The Resurrection of Henry Box Brown at Philadelphia, by A. Donnelly, New York, circa 1850s. Library of Congress. In this version of Brown's famed escape to freedom, William Still is replaced on the left with a depiction of Frederick Douglass.

enslavement in Macon, Georgia. On December 20, 1848, the two entered a train on the Macon-to-Savannah railroad, a line built by Ellen Craft's owner. They could do so without raising any suspicions as the light-skinned Ellen had cut her hair and dressed as an ill and effete young planter attended by "his" slave, William. Ellen had her faced wrapped in bandages and her right arm in a sling and, feigning lameness, used a cane with her left hand. She wore dark green spectacles and pretended to be "hard of hearing and dependent on his faithful servant (as was no uncommon thing with slaveowners),

to look after all his wants." Thus disguised as master and slave, the two made their way north, stopping in Charleston and staying in a first-class hotel. When questioned, William explained that they were headed to Philadelphia for lifesaving medical treatment for his young master. The deception worked. Upon arriving in Philadelphia, the infirm "master" suddenly became a freed female slave. The two went to Boston, where for the next two years they became celebrated heroes and published an account of their famed escape. After the passage of the Fugitive Slave Act of 1850, however, their former owners sent slave catchers to retrieve them. Fearing for their lives, they too fled to England.[34]

Still also related the riveting account of Jane Johnson (1814?–1872), whose determination to be free shed light on the inner workings of the Underground Railroad. Johnson, born in Washington, D.C., around 1814, had been sold to a civil servant named John H. Wheeler of North Carolina. Wheeler had been assigned as minister to Nicaragua, and on his way to New York in July 1855 with Johnson and two of her children—a third had been sold away—he stopped in Philadelphia. While dining at Bloodgood's Hotel, Johnson alerted some free blacks that she was a slave. They in turn alerted Still, who hurried to the scene, along with a white abolitionist named Passmore Williamson, hoping to assist her in her quest for freedom.

Wheeler and his property, unfortunately, had already left the hotel and boarded a steamer for New York. The two men ran to the docks and found Johnson and her children up on the second deck. Williamson and Still, confronted Wheeler and advised Johnson that she could be free if she desired it. They scuffled with Wheeler, who claimed that Johnson wanted nothing to do with the two men, but she cried out, "*I am not free, but I want my freedom—ALWAYS wanted to be free!! but he holds me.*"[35] The family fled with Still while Williamson debated with Wheeler.

---

34 William Craft and Ellen Craft, *Running a Thousand Miles for Freedom: The Escape of William and Ellen Craft from Slavery*, ed. R. J. M. Blackett (Baton Rouge: Louisiana State University Press, 1999); Still, *Underground Railroad*, 382–91.

35 Still, *Underground Railroad*, 76.

WILLIAM CRAFT.

ELLEN CRAFT.

William and Ellen Craft, from *The Underground Railroad*, by William Still (Philadelphia: Porter & Coates, 1872), 383.

Later that same day Wheeler brought suit against Williamson, claiming that he had kidnapped his property, and the court held him without bail until the end of August, when Williamson's trial took place. With Wheeler sitting in the courtroom—a pistol tucked in his trousers—Johnson (making a surprise appearance in disguise) courageously testified that she alone had decided that she wanted her freedom and that no one had forced her to run away.

With several white female abolitionists at her side—including the famed Lucretia Mott—Johnson testified that "nobody forced me away; nobody pulled me, and nobody led me; I went away of my own free will; I always wished to be free and meant to be free when I came North." But under terms of the Fugitive Slave Act, she could be seized and returned to her owner. When she finished her testimony she fled with Mott and the other women, who then spirited her away to Boston, where she came under the protection of William C. Nell and the Boston Vigilance Committee. She married a local black man, and their home on Beacon Hill became a haven for fugitive slaves.[36]

✕✕✕

BY THE 1850S, AS BLACK VOICES SUCH AS THESE FROM THE FUGITIVE SLAVE NARRATIVES POIGNANTLY AND PASSION-ATELY ARTICULATED THE HORRORS OF SLAVERY AND THE URGE TO BE FREE, the country was coming apart over the question of slavery, especially its status in the western territories. The white South—unalterably committed to slavery and its expansion—conducted

---

[36] Still, *Underground Railroad*, 82.

undisguised war with the black community and its white antislavery allies in the North. In places like Christiana, Pennsylvania, this was no metaphor. The war was real, with gunfights, attempted mass escapes, and murder. Much to the outrage of even moderate northerners, the South—which otherwise insisted on a limited government—had recruited the federal government to take responsibility for retrieving runaway slaves. Congress, through the Fugitive Slave Act of 1850, even set up special courts to hear only fugitive slave cases, "trials" in which the defendants possessed no rights and in which judges received cash incentives to "return" blacks to slavery—even if they had never been slaves.

The notorious Fugitive Slave Act put every free black person in the North at risk of a legally sanctioned kidnapping by suggesting that no person of African ancestry could really be an American citizen, an implication affirmed by the Supreme Court in the *Dred Scott* decision of 1857. The South sent its agents—slave catchers and kidnappers—north to recapture runaways and enslave free people. Among those who responded, one of the most distinctive was Harriet Tubman—or "General Tubman," as John Brown of Harpers Ferry fame admiringly called her—a Moses figure who took enormous personal risks to help slaves gain their freedom.

Born a slave in the border state of Maryland, Harriet Tubman (1820–1913) grew up in a community of mixed free and enslaved African Americans and married a free black man. Fearing she would be sold into the Deep South, as her sisters had been, she fled to Philadelphia in 1849 and became a servant. But she missed her family and began making trips back to Maryland to rescue them. She soon freed her sister

Harriet Tubman, by H. B. Lindsley, circa 1860–1875. Photograph. Library of Congress.

and her sister's two children, and then returned again to rescue her brother and two other men. On her third trip, Tubman went to fetch her husband, only to find he had taken another wife. Undeterred, she found a group of slaves seeking freedom and escorted them north.

Over the next ten years, she made about 19 trips into the South, becoming the most celebrated hero of the Underground Railroad. She proudly claimed that she "never lost a single passenger" and devised a host of clever techniques to facilitate her operation, including using the master's horse and buggy for the first leg of the journey; leaving on a Saturday night, since runaway notices couldn't be placed in newspapers until Monday morning; turning about and heading south if she encountered possible slave hunters; and carrying a sleeping drug to use on a baby if its crying put fugitives in danger. She even carried a gun, which she brandished at the fugitives if they became too tired or decided to turn back, telling them, "You'll be free or die."[37]

Such cases reveal just how extensive, determined, and resourceful the free black community could be in the antebellum years. Despite the heroic sacrifices made by Tubman and others, the Underground Railroad could only help a handful of the enslaved people. The number of blacks who managed to reach freedom was tiny—perhaps 50,000 over the period from 1800 to 1860, although there is no way to ever know the true number.

Whether we speak of Boston, Philadelphia, Washington, D.C., or New York, Detroit, Cleveland, or Chicago—indeed wherever African Americans lived—they remained at the forefront of the freedom struggle, exposing the contradictions of American society. In fact, the broader antislavery movement relied upon black speakers like the Crafts, Henry "Box" Brown, Frederick Douglass, and William Wells Brown to authenticate the abolitionist message and combat the white masters' insistence that their property was content and thrived in slavery. The minister and former slave J. Sella Martin (1832–1876), who was sold eight times, was one of many who put the lie to such claims: "Here a white man says that negroes were contented. Well, I am a negro, and I was not contented.... The white man was not in slavery; I was, and I know where the shoe pinched; and I say I was not contented."[38]

But nothing spoke more profoundly, or more tragically, about the contradictions manifest in a country half slave and half free than the case of Margaret Garner (?–1858). On the frigid morning of January 27, 1856, Garner, her husband, their four children, and her husband's parents escaped from their Kentucky slave owners, along with nine friends from other plantations. They crossed the frozen Ohio River—passing from a slave state to a free state—and split into two groups in Cincinnati. One group made contact with agents of the Underground Railroad and continued on to freedom in Canada. The other group, consisting of eight members of the Garner family, proved not so lucky. They were tracked to the home of a free black man by a force of deputy U.S. marshals, with a warrant for the Garners' arrest under the terms of the Fugitive Slave

---

[37] Quoted in Charles M. Christian, *Black Saga: The African American Experience, A Chronology* (New York: Civitas, 1999), 143.

[38] Quoted in Donald Yacovone, ed., *Freedom's Journey: African American Voices of the Civil War* (Chicago: Lawrence Hill Books, 2004), 26.

The Modern Medea (Margaret Garner). *Harper's Weekly*, May 18, 1867. Wood engraving. Library of Congress.

Act. The Garners barricaded themselves in the home—and decided they would rather die than be captured. This decision led them to do something that is almost impossible to imagine.

By the time the arresting party battered down the door, the family had slashed the throat of their three-year-old daughter Mary, nearly decapitating her. She lay on the floor in a pool of blood. Hiding in the next room were two young boys, bruised and bleeding—one with gashes in his neck, the other with a cut on his face. An infant girl had been struck with a heavy shovel, but was still alive. The gruesome scene was likely a family effort—something that the Garners had done as a group—but blame focused on Margaret, who claimed that she would rather kill every one of her children than have them taken back across the river to slavery.

The Garners were brought to the federal courthouse and abolitionists immediately rallied to their cause. According to the terms of the Fugitive Slave Act, lawyers were ready to argue that the family was free, not slaves, since their slave owners had brought them to Ohio on earlier occasions. If Margaret were free, she would be tried for murder—and surely convicted—but her surviving children would be free. If the court declared her a slave, the whole family would be sent back to bondage in Kentucky.

The case created a sensation in both North and South. It was the longest and costliest fugitive slave trial in American history. The famous abolitionist Lucy Stone rushed to Cincinnati to support Margaret in court. She drew shocked gasps and tears from many listeners when she referred to the fact that some of Margaret's children were "very light, almost white": "The faded faces of the Negro children tell too plainly to what degradation female slaves submit. Rather than give her little daughter to that life, she killed it. If in her deep maternal love she felt the impulse to send her child back to God, to save it from coming woe, who shall say she had no right to do so?"[39]

Steven Weisenburger, who has examined the case, considers it highly probable that Margaret's three younger children were fathered by her owner, Archibald Gaines. At the time of their escape, the Garners faced the imminent threat of being sent to the Deep South, and Margaret's husband had been hired out for many years, forcing the couple to live apart. Their flight was clearly motivated by the powerful desire to keep their family together, and for Margaret to flee the sexual victimization she had suffered repeatedly.

The Ohio court was unmoved. It ruled that the Garners were slaves, and they were sent back to Kentucky. But the steamboat carrying Margaret's family down the Ohio River—this time away from freedom—collided with another vessel. In the ensuing panic, Margaret's nine-month-old baby, Celia, may have drowned, or, in a final, desperate, protective act, her mother may have dropped her baby into the water. We will never know, and her body was never recovered.[40]

By the 1850s, the United States was already at war with itself. The frontier was aflame, and the federal government enforced the Fugitive Slave Act at bayonet point, threatening those who resisted it with charges of treason. Violence would make sense to John Brown in 1859, as it had a few years before—in a different and intensely personal manner—to Margaret Garner, and as it would to Harriet Tubman, Frederick Douglass, Henry Highland Garnet, and to countless others. But it would take more violence than anyone could have possibly imagined before the Civil War to put an end to the the peculiar institution of human slavery in the United States.

---

[39] Mark Reinhardt, *Who Speaks for Margaret Garner?* (Minneapolis: University of Minnesota Press, 2010), 112.

[40] Steven Weisenburger, *Modern Medea: A Family Story of Slavery and Child-Murder from the Old South* (New York: Hill and Wang, 1998).

THE WAR TO END SLAVERY
1859–1865

THE GALLANT CHARGE OF THE FIFTY FOURTH MASSACH... ...S (COLORED) REGIMENT

SITTING IN A COLD JAILHOUSE IN CHARLESTOWN, VIRGINIA, IN LATE NOVEMBER 1859, JOHN A. COPELAND WROTE HIS PARENTS FOR THE LAST TIME.

Dear Parents,

My fate so far as man can seal it, is sealed, but let not this fact occasion you any misery; for remember the <u>cause</u> in which I was engaged; remember it was a holy cause, one in which men in every way better than I am, have suffered & died. Remember that if I must die, I die in trying to liberate a few of my poor & oppressed people from a condition of servitude against which God in his word has hurled his most bitter denunciations. . . . Good-bye Mother & Father, Goodbye brothers & sisters, & by the assistance of God, meet me in heaven. I remain your most affectionate son,

–John A. Copeland

Copeland (1834–1859) had grown up near Raleigh, North Carolina, a free person of color. His parents moved the family to Oberlin, Ohio, in 1843, where he attended Oberlin's famed preparatory school and worked alongside his father as a carpenter. Before long, he became a trusted member of the local antislavery society and helped rescue fugitive slaves. His uncle and co-conspirator Lewis S. Leary (1836–1859) had recruited Copeland for John Brown's army and when he crafted this letter to his parents–John Copeland, Sr., and his mother, Delilah–Copeland was awaiting execution for his role in the attack on the federal arsenal at Harpers Ferry.[1]

Copeland and Leary had combined with Shields Green (1836–1859), Osborn P. Anderson (1830–1872), and Dangerfield Newby (1820?–1859) as the five African Americans who joined John Brown's raiding party of 16 white men intent on striking a blow against the institution of slavery. An audacious plan backed by many prominent African American and New England abolitionists, the venture seems to us today to have had little or no chance of success. The raiding party, few in number, attacked a federal arsenal located in a small, isolated town in a deep gorge, bounded by two boulder-strewn rivers and cut by a rail line. Just before the raid, when Brown revealed his plans to Frederick Douglass–a man not known for timidity–the black abolitionist wished Brown well but wanted no part of what looked like a 19th-century version of a modern terrorist's suicide attack. Harriet Tubman had agreed to join the raid, but was unable to travel at the last minute.

But those who agreed to the raid cared more for destroying slavery than saving their own lives; and Dangerfield Newby still had a wife and children in chains and wished to free them. His wife had written three letters telling him of her white master's financial problems, and of her escalating fears that she and their children would be sold before Newby could rescue them. Those letters were found on Newby's body after he was killed in the attack. Brown shared this same sense of urgency and grounded his scheme in the idea that the slaves represented a combustible mass just waiting for the right spark to catch fire, to rise up and throw off their chains. Had that not happened before, in Stono, South Carolina, New York City, Richmond, Charleston, New Orleans, Southampton, and Haiti?

Indeed, by 1859, the entire nation seemed to be awaiting some terrific explosion. Just about everyone could sense the fear, anger, and hate. After passage of the Fugitive Slave Act in 1850, followed by the *Dred Scott* decision in 1857, tensions between North and South only increased with each passing year. Moderates on both sides of the slavery issue evaporated like water on a hot griddle. The vital center of American politics had disappeared, leaving only the extremes. Northerners, even those who were not especially fond of African Americans, increasingly saw the South as dominated by a narrow set of interests determined to control the federal government and compel it to do its bidding to preserve, protect, and extend the institution of slavery. Major American cities witnessed the forced return of fugitive men and women back into slavery, without a shred of due process and backed by federal bayonets. Those who resisted were arrested for assault, murder, or even treason.

[1] C. Peter Ripley, et al., eds., *The Black Abolitionist Papers, The United States, 1859–1865* (Chapel Hill: University of North Carolina Press, 1991–1992), 5:43–49.

John Brown, by J. W. Dodge, New York, circa 1865. Photograph of original painting, mounted on carte de visite. Library of Congress.

When the Illinois senator Stephen A. Douglas introduced a bill to organize the territories of Kansas and Nebraska in 1854, the national political system snapped under the controversy surrounding the status of slavery in the western lands. The contention not only snuffed out the old two-party system—and the moderate Whig Party of Henry Clay—but gave birth to what is known as the third-party system and the Republican Party, and eventually led to civil war. The controversy also set off an avalanche of violent events: urban and rural riots over fugitive slaves; the assault by South Carolina congressman Preston Brooks on Massachusetts senator Charles Sumner while he sat at his desk in the Capitol; open warfare in Kansas and Missouri between free state and slave state militias; and the infamous *Dred Scott* decision by the United States Supreme Court that not only opened the way for the expansion of slavery, but concluded that all African Americans had "no rights that white men were bound to respect."

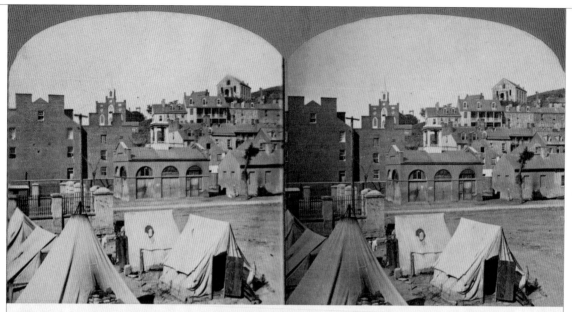

Harpers Ferry Firehouse, by George Stacy, circa 1860. Stereocard photograph. Library of Congress.

Ironically, although it was crushed, John Brown's raid gave African Americans new hope. Especially after the *Dred Scott* decision, many African Americans began giving up on their future in America. While *Dred Scott* did not alter the daily treatment that most African Americans were experiencing in the second half of the decade—anti-black racism had only strengthened since the Fugitive Slave Act—to many, it appeared to place a stamp of finality on their lack of civil rights, now defined as the law of the land by the Supreme Court itself. John C. Bowers, a Philadelphia activist, summed up black sentiment when he lamented that "our friends have even turned against us" and when "Gabriel blows his last trumpet, the negroes will still be in slavery, unless they emigrate."[2]

Emigrationist plans returned to the debate within black abolitionist circles, and even the North's leading black paper, the *Weekly Anglo-African*, early in 1861 closed its doors (temporarily) and sold out to the Haitian Emigration Bureau. Staunch black leaders, seeing little future for the race in the U.S., went to Canada or became seduced by the Haitian appeal. Leaders such as Henry Highland Garnet, William Wells Brown, James T. Holly, William J. Watkins, and—just before the opening of the Civil War—even Frederick Douglass flirted with the idea of black resettlement in Haiti. As James T. Holly wrote in 1859, "to despise the claims of Hayti is to despise the cause of God, by which her promises to bring deliverance to the captives and to those who are bound. . . ."[3]

[2] "Banneker" to Thomas Hamilton, January 22, 1860, in New York *Weekly Anglo-African*, January 28, 1860.

[3] Ripley, *The Black Abolitionist Papers*, 5:9.

John Brown helped change that. While before the raid few blacks fully trusted the promises of white allies like Brown, afterward Brown's loyalty to the holy cause of abolitionism and black freedom was undeniable. "I believe in insurrections," the black Boston lawyer and doctor John S. Rock proclaimed.[4] Even the great American philosopher Ralph Waldo Emerson claimed that Brown had sanctified the gallows as Christ had sanctified the cross. As later generations of African Americans would hang pictures of Lincoln, John F. Kennedy, and Martin Luther King, Jr., in their parlors, 19th-century black Americans saw in John Brown a sainted, Christlike hero who gave up his life so that black men and women might live— in freedom.

For many black people, it now appeared that a clash between North and South was inescapable, and as Frederick Douglass predicted, such a battle would inevitably lead to the emancipation of the slaves. Even if it went against the collective better judgment of Northern whites, Douglass understood from the outset— in ways most Northerners did not—that the Union could not survive a civil war without destroying its root cause: slavery.

Lincoln's election in 1860 convinced most Southerners that their "peculiar institution" was not secure since the government was controlled by those determined to halt the spread of slavery. Although Lincoln and the Republican Party pledged to defend slavery *where it existed*, to enforce the Fugitive Slave Act, and even adopt a constitutional amendment to guarantee slavery in the South,

secessionists brushed such promises aside. From their perspective, all of the North was infected with abolitionist fever and none could be trusted. With the hotspurs of South Carolina, Mississippi, and Alabama leading the way, the other Southern states one after another left the Union after Lincoln's election, setting the stage for a cataclysm.[5]

The very assurances that Lincoln and the Republican Party had given to Southerners throughout the 1860 campaign to convince them that slavery would be secure under a Lincoln administration had precisely the same impact on most African Americans: destroying trust. In hindsight, we readily understand how Lincoln could become a secular saint to African Americans. But looking at history as it unfolded from the perspective of the 1850s, Lincoln only offered more of the same: the preservation of slavery, permanently. While individual Republicans like Charles Sumner or Pennsylvania's great antislavery congressman Thaddeus Stevens proved immensely popular with blacks, in 1860 Lincoln and his party had pledged to suppress black rights and preserve slavery. What in the Lincoln of 1860 could draw black support, or encourage them that change would ever come?

While some accepted Abraham Lincoln as the best that could be hoped for, other blacks refused to compromise on principle. How could an African American support a man who admitted his prejudices against black people, wished that free blacks would leave the country, and pledged himself most vigorously to enforce the Fugitive Slave Act? His

---

[4] Donald Yacovone, ed., *Freedom's Journey: African American Voices of the Civil War* (Chicago: Lawrence Hill Books, 2004), quoted 46.

[5] Henry Louis Gates, Jr., and Donald Yacovone, eds. *Lincoln on Race and Slavery* (Princeton: Princeton University Press, 2009), 113–14, 215–17.

first inaugural address, designed to assure the South that he posed no threat, profoundly disappointed black people, who turned from it, as one of them would put it, "with a more dead despair of our future here" than at any other time. To George E. Stephens, a reporter for the New York *Weekly Anglo-African* and later a sergeant in the famed 54th Massachusetts Regiment, Lincoln's election seemed like merely "the fag end of a series of pro-slavery administrations," embodying the "Godless will of a criminal nation."[6]

According to legend, the fire-eating secessionist from Virginia Edmund Ruffin fired the first and last shots of the Civil War. An ardent defender of slavery, on April 12, 1861, Ruffin pulled the lanyard of one of the many rebel cannons pointing at Fort Sumter isolated out in Charleston Harbor. The last shot he fired came on June 17, 1865, from his silver-barreled musket, which he placed in his mouth, despondent over the destruction of his rebellion. In a sense, both shots marked the beginning of the end of slavery as an American institution. The beginning of the war gave African Americans hope, for the first time, that the government could at long last crush slavery along with the rebellion. The excitement was palpable. Black newspapers cried out: "We want Nat Turner—not speeches; Denmark Vesey—not resolutions; John Brown—not meetings." Black communities across the North began drilling men to ready them for battle. Some Bostonians claimed that a force of 50,000 black men could be quickly assembled to put down the rebellion. In Philadelphia, black leaders instructed their brethren to forget past grievances and help defend the Union.[7]

But that was not to be. From pulpit and press, from state governments and from Congress, blacks were told to "keep out of this; this is a white man's war." The repudiation, perhaps, should have been anticipated. After all, the previous March, John S. Rock had reminded his brethren that the "position of the colored man today is a trying one; trying, because the whole country had entered into a conspiracy to crush him."[8] White men—and their very definition of masculinity—were caught up in racial and nationalist pride. To their mind, no "inferior being" incapable of citizenship could be considered for armed service. The idea was as ludicrous as it was insulting. The Ohio congressman Chilton A. White best summed up the Northern response to black patriotism: "This is a government of white men, made by white men for white men, to be administered, protected, defended and maintained by white men." Stung by such responses, some black leaders counseled patience and advised their brethren to stand ready for the time when "the slave calls." Others, such as A.M.E. Church leaders, advised their parishioners that they simply had no business fighting for a country that oppressed them.[9]

6   Donald Yacovone, ed., *A Voice of Thunder: The Civil War Letters of George E. Stephens* (Urbana: University of Illinois Press, 1997), quoted 12–13.

7   David F. Allmendinger and William Scarborough, "The Days Ruffin Died," *Virginia Magazine of History and Biography* 97 (1997): 75–96; *Weekly Anglo-African* April 27, 1861; Yacovone, *Voice of Thunder*, 14.

8   Yacovone, *Freedom's Journey*, quoted 49.

9   Henry Louis Gates, Jr., *Life Upon These Shores: Looking at African American History* (New York: Alfred A. Knopf, 2011), quoted 123; Yacovone, *Freedom's Journey*, 90.

Stampede among the Negroes in Virginia. Frank Leslie's Illustrated Newspaper, June 8, 1861. Wood engraving. National Portrait Gallery, Smithsonian Institution. Surrounding the crush of "contraband" attempting to enter Fortress Monroe are depictions of Union General Benjamin F. Butler meeting with Confederate Major John B. Cary, fugitive slaves, and employment of contraband by Union forces.

However, almost as soon as the guns thundered across Maryland and eastern Virginia, "the slave" began to call. On May 23, 1861, three slaves belonging to Colonel Charles Mallory of Hampton escaped in the middle of the night by boat to Fortress Monroe. The fort, completed in 1834 and named for President James Monroe, sat on the tip of the Virginia Peninsula at Old Point Comfort near Hampton, at the confluence of the Elizabeth, Nansemond, and James Rivers. It covered 63 acres of land with its walls stretching more than a mile around, and as with the White House and most other federal buildings, the fort had been erected with slave labor.

The three slaves met the fort's commander, General Benjamin F. Butler, a controversial and mercurial Massachusetts lawyer and politician. Butler learned that two of the escaped slaves had wives and families in nearby

Hampton and wondered what he should do with the men; indeed, what could he do? The next day, Confederate Major John B. Cary, who had known Butler before the war, approached the fort under a flag of truce and on behalf of Mallory asked for the return of the man's property under the Fugitive Slave Act. Butler reminded Cary that as Virginia claimed to have left the Union, the colonel could not claim any protection under the Constitution he had repudiated. Butler then declared the men "contraband" of war and put them to work.

Butler's brilliant and seemingly improvised decision resolved the situation with alacrity. But word soon spread that a slave could get free by running to the boys in blue. Within days, other slaves flooded into Fortress Monroe, as recorded in a two-page spread in *Frank Leslie's Illustrated Newspaper*, on June 8, 1861. That November, a reporter for the *Atlantic Monthly* explained that if one slave on the Potomac heard something about emancipation, "in a few days it will be known by his brethren on the Gulf. . . ." As we have seen, and as John Adams had noted as early as 1775, the slaves appeared to have a mysteriously effective "grapevine" that carried messages far and wide. Fugitives began collecting at Fortress Monroe, and by July, about 1,000 former slaves had sought protection there. As the number of runaway slaves would only mount, Butler sought policy clarification from the War Department.

The Lincoln administration had no ready answers and avoided anything that might unsettle the border states, where slavery remained legal even though these states supported the Union. In fact, when General John C. Frémont issued a total emancipation order in Missouri in August 1861, President Lincoln repudiated it as a dangerous policy that

violated the constitutional rights of loyal property (slave) owners. Butler's earlier decision to proclaim the slaves that came into his lines "contraband," however, had given Congress the opportunity to aid the war effort and move more strongly against slavery. While it could not arbitrarily seize slaves, the government could seize the property of anyone who had committed treason. Thus, on August 6, 1861, it passed the first of two Confiscation Acts allowing military commanders to declare "all such property . . . to be lawful subject of prize and capture wherever found."[10]

But such an order did not *require* federal troops to accept all runaways that came into their lines, nor to free any slave they encountered. In fact, early in the war, some Union troops made sport of harassing or killing fugitive slaves, while others participated in an illegal trade in slaves with the enemy. More often, Union soldiers simply ignored the pleas of slaves to protect them from their masters. John V. Givens, an enterprising New York black abolitionist, accompanied the Ninth New York Regiment to Virginia, either as a teamster or servant to an officer, to keep an eye on how the soldiers treated fugitive slaves. In October 1861, he reported that when his regiment neared Charlestown, Virginia—where John Brown had been executed—slaves rushed to greet the troops. Hundreds of black men and women filled the streets, some women carrying their babies, "shouting and thanking God that we had come at last to free them. . . . But what pen can describe the revulsion of their feelings when they were told that we came 'not to free the slaves, but to preserve the Union as it was, with its millions of suffering slaves!'"

---

[10] Gates, *Life Upon These Shores*, 124–25.

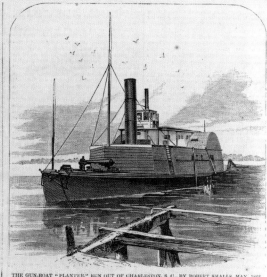

ROBERT SMALLS, CAPTAIN OF THE GUN-BOAT "PLANTER."

THE GUN-BOAT "PLANTER," RUN OUT OF CHARLESTON, S. C., BY ROBERT SMALLS, MAY, 1862.

Robert Smalls and the *Planter*. *Harper's Weekly*, June 14, 1862. Wood engraving. Library of Congress.

Not until two years later did the Emancipation Proclamation put an end to most similar instances.[11]

Some slaves, however, took matters into their own hands. Just before dawn on May 13, 1862, some African Americans quietly set about unmooring the *Planter*, a steam-powered coastal vessel, from its berth in the Charleston, South Carolina, harbor. At the helm was Robert Smalls (1839–1915), a slave just like the rest of the crew. Smalls, a mulatto and the son of his master, relied on the intimate knowledge of local waterways and Confederate defenses he and the crew had accumulated over a year sailing aboard the *Planter*, working for his owners and the rebel navy. But now he would pilot the vessel for himself in a daring break for freedom.

The *Planter* had ferried cotton in and out of Charleston Harbor before the war, and a harbor pilot like Smalls had to know every rock and eddy to perform his job safely. Almost 150 feet in length and about 30 feet wide, the *Planter* could haul 1,400 bales of cotton, the fruit of slave labor, but had been refitted with four cannons, some taken from nearby Fort Sumter. Designed to ply shallow water, the ship could easily navigate the harbor and the many inland waterways of the Carolina coast. After the start of the war, the *Planter*'s owner leased the vessel and its slave crew to the Confederate navy. For more than a year, Smalls piloted the vessel under the command of Captain C. J. Relyea.

When Relyea and the *Planter*'s other white officers violated their orders and left the ship one night to sleep ashore, Smalls saw his opportunity. The *Planter* set out at 3 A.M., with Confederate and South Carolina state flags

---

[11] Yacovone, *Freedom's Journey*, quoted 96.

Contraband crossing the Rappahannock, by Timothy H. O'Sullivan, August 1862. Stereoscope, glass plate photograph. Library of Congress.

snapping in the wind. As they steamed past a Confederate sentry, Smalls stood in the pilot-house in Reylea's coat and trademark straw hat, and in the predawn light no one could detect anything unusual. Smalls then stopped to take on several women and children, including his own family. When the vessel approached the Confederate outpost at Castle Pinckney, Smalls gave the usual signal from the ship's whistle and proceeded past other fortified positions just as on any other day. By the time Confederates realized the ship that had passed Fort Sumter, the third checkpoint, was steaming straight for the Union blockade, nothing could be done. As fast as possible, Smalls lowered the Confederate colors and raised a white flag. The USS Onward, a clipper built in 1852, received the Planter and joined in the rejoicing over the astonishing act of courage and the slaves' freedom.

Smalls and the rest of his crew, following standard military procedure, received compensation for seizure of the Planter. Besides the ship and its armaments, the Union cause had gained an extremely valuable asset in Smalls, who was given command of the vessel—this time under the flag of the United States—and provided Union forces with his extensive knowledge of Confederate coastal defenses.

Equally important, Smalls scored a fabulous propaganda victory over the Confederates and provided newspapers across the North with the opportunity to lampoon slaveholders' arrogance and the opponents of black freedom in the North. One Pennsylvania newspaper used the case to skewer congressmen who had refused to support freedom for the slaves who reached Union lines. What should we do, the paper asked: take the vessel that Smalls heroically seized from under the noses of the rebels and send "the patriot and hero" back to slavery?

Other newspapers took the opportunity to use the "abduction" of the *Planter* as irrefutable evidence of black ability and a powerful argument against the South's pro-slavery propaganda of black inferiority. "What a painful instance we have here of the Negro's inability to take care of himself," another newspaper mocked.[12]

◆◆◆

AS THE WAR PROGRESSED AND FEDERAL TROOPS MOVED DEEPER INTO THE SOUTH, INCREASING NUMBERS OF SLAVES ABANDONED THE PLANTATIONS AND MADE THEIR WAY TO UNION LINES, often arriving in family groups composed of several generations. Many of the new refugees ended up in the growing contraband camps hastily erected by the Union army. By the summer of 1862, what had begun as a trickle of refugees had turned into a flood. The thousands of slaves who abandoned the plantations dramatically helped to transform the aim and meaning of the war. As military success remained elusive, Lincoln's rhetoric about saving the Union broadened to address the pressing issue of slavery in explicit terms. As a generation of historians has asserted, black initiative forced the question of slavery upon a very reluctant administration and pushed President Lincoln down the road toward emancipation. The conduct of the war and the horrific casualty lists also forced the president to rethink the use of black troops, something that previously only black activists and their white allies had insisted upon.

When Lincoln issued the preliminary Emancipation Proclamation after the Battle of Antietam in September 1862, its text threatened the South with the emancipation of the slaves if it did not lay down its arms. But it made no mention of arming black men—even though blacks had served in the Navy since the start of the war. If Lincoln was true to his word (and no one could be sure), the proclamation, Frederick Douglass believed, would sanctify the Union cause and make "justice, liberty, and humanity permanently possible in this country." Yet if the slaves remained a powerful resource to aid the rebellion—and not the Union—then no victory was possible.[13]

The heroism of black men helped change Lincoln's mind—and saved the Union cause. Although the War Department refused to arm black men—despite the fact that they had no trouble giving them picks and shovels—others took the initiative and organized black regiments without explicit federal authority. In August 1862, General James H. Lane, also a United States senator, organized the First Kansas Colored Infantry Regiment. Lane had been battling slave masters since the days of John Brown and bragged about his forays into Missouri to free slaves. He did not hesitate to include the liberated "property" in his regiment, which operated under state, rather than federal, authority. On August 4, 1862, he opened a recruitment office in Leavenworth, Kansas, despite a warning from the War Department that the unit would not be accepted into the regular Union army. Ignoring the administration, Lane recruited free and enslaved blacks,

---

[12] Washington (Penn.) *Reporter*, June 19, 1862; Yacovone, *Voice of Thunder*, 292 quoted.

[13] David W. Blight, *Frederick Douglass's Civil War: Keeping Faith in Jubilee* (Baton Rouge: Louisiana State University Press, 1989), 115 quoted.

Native Americans, and mulattoes and mestizos into the unit. He even made William D. Matthews, a free black of Leavenworth, a first lieutenant—something that the Union army refused to permit until near the end of the war. By September 1862, when Lincoln issued that preliminary Emancipation Proclamation, Lane already was drilling about 600 "colored" recruits, with more coming in every day. The next month, on October 29, 1862, the unit fought its first engagement, at Island Mound, Missouri. Even the Confederates had to confess that the black soldiers "fought like tigers."[14]

But there was more. After Union forces seized New Orleans early in 1862, General Benjamin F. Butler, the architect of the theory of treating fugitive slaves as contraband of war back at Virginia's Fortress Monroe, now commanded the occupation forces there. Shorthanded and facing an enemy organizing to oust him, Butler accepted the offer by local free black men to form segregated units. On September 27, 1862, he organized the First Regiment Louisiana Native Guard, followed later by the Second and Third Guards. After January 1863, the army added additional units and referred to them as the Corps d'Afrique, in recognition of the proud French cultural heritage of the free community of color in New Orleans. Butler permitted the Guards to keep their own black officers, a move that the War Department later reversed. At first they performed mostly garrison duty, but at the Battle of Port Hudson on May 27, 1863, and again at Milliken's Bend on June 7, 1863, the black soldiers of the Louisiana units performed with

such valor and efficiency that their actions went far toward breaking down the army's resistance to a general recruitment of black soldiers.

Perhaps nothing helped change Northern views on the use of black troops more than the First South Carolina Volunteers, under the command of Thomas Wentworth Higginson. Although Higginson was better known for his career as a Unitarian minister and, after the war, as one of the country's most important literary figures, he was an unapologetic champion of John Brown and an uncompromising abolitionist. General David Hunter, the Union commander of the Department of the South, began forming the unit in the occupied South Carolina Sea Islands in the spring of 1862. The War Department rejected his request for official permission to muster the unit, and the House of Representatives even investigated his actions. House members demanded to know if he, in fact, had organized a unit of former slaves in violation of federal law. On June 23, Hunter replied to the inquiry stating that "no regiment of 'fugitive slaves' has been or is being organized in this department. There is, however, a fine regiment of persons whose late masters are 'fugitive rebels.'" Hunter's reply ignited howls of laughter from Republicans, while conservatives growled in disgust. Hunter praised the unit and advised the Congress that by the end of the next fall he could have as many as 50,000 men ready to fight the rebellion.

Hunter was relieved of command, but his replacement, General Rufus Saxton, continued to build the unit with the War Department's grudging consent and mustered in the First South Carolina Volunteers on November 7, 1862. Within six days, Colonel Higginson took the unit into action. Commanded by white officers, but with black noncommissioned officers

---

[14] Dudley Taylor Cornish, *The Sable Arm: Negro Troops in the Union Army, 1861–1865* (New York: W. W. Norton, 1966), 70–76, 79, 92, 96, 98, 103–04; Noah Andre Trudeau, *Like Men of War: Black Troops in the Civil War, 1862–1865* (Boston: Little, Brown & Co., 1998), 6 quoted.

Benjamin F. Butler, by Matthew Brady studio, 1860–1865. Glass plate photograph. Library of Congress.

and comprised entirely of former slaves from the region, the unit performed with exceptional efficiency and daring against the soldiers' former owners. Higginson made sure that the North was well acquainted with the achievements of his unit and wrote a steady stream of letters to newspapers back home describing their conduct under fire. He knew that what his men did and what he said about them would determine the future of black

Emancipation, by Thomas Nast. Engraved by King & Baird and published by S. Bott, Philadelphia, 1865. Library of Congress. Nast depicts the rise of African Americans from the cruelties of slavery—aided by the Freedmen's Bank and public education—to middle-class respectability. The image emphasizes the important role of Abraham Lincoln in establishing black freedom without acknowledging black service in the Civil War.

recruitment—and the course of the war. On February 11, 1863, in the Boston *Daily Evening Traveller,* for instance, Higginson assured Northern readers that his black troops had indeed faced enemy cavalry, infantry, and cannon. In "every instance," he proudly explained, they came "off not only with unblemished honor, but with undisputed triumph."[15]

The Emancipation Proclamation, issued on January 1, 1863, actually freed only a relatively small number of slaves—perhaps 500,000 out of a total of 3.9 million—but its significance far transcended its legal impact. Written by a lawyer to address a specific legal problem—the limits of the president's war powers—the final Emancipation Proclamation wrought a revolution in the aims of the war with all the poetry and eloquence of a real estate transaction. Yet because of it, a war to preserve the Union had become one that aimed to destroy slavery, the central conflict of the war, or as Lincoln's generation phrased it, "the bone of contention." A

[15] Yacovone, *Voice of Thunder,* 27, 49.

moral bombshell, the proclamation also helped prevent European powers from recognizing the South as an independent nation. While limited in scope, having no impact on slavery in the border states or in several areas already occupied by Union forces, it did one additional important thing, without which the South could not have been defeated: It provided for the full-scale recruitment of African American soldiers, a significant fact often overlooked.

By the end of the war, 178,975 black men served in the Army and approximately 20,000 more filled the ranks of the Navy. About 85 percent of African Americans who served in the war were former slaves, but the free black men of the North volunteered for military duty in far higher percentages than whites. For them, service in the war was an extension of the antislavery movement, the final act in a drama that stretched back to the Haitian Revolution, back to the slave petitions during and after the American Revolution, and back even to the slaves who fled from Charleston and Savannah to freedom in Spanish Fort Mose.

Many more black men and women served as laborers, scouts, spies, and stevedores, allowing the Union army to resupply, move, and receive intelligence on rebel troop movements and strength. While Union commanders often relied upon the slaves' knowledge of local terrain, the Lincoln administration actually had a pipeline right into the office of the president of the Confederacy, Jefferson Davis. Mary E. Bowser (1839?–?), a slave, worked in the White House of the Confederacy in Richmond, Virginia, became a Union spy, and worked as part of the espionage ring run by Elizabeth "Bet" Van Lew. Bowser, married to a free black from Philadelphia, took on the identity of "Ellen Bond," a seemingly dull-witted but

reliable servant who won the attention of the president's wife, Varina Davis, and became the Davis family's full-time servant until near the end of the war. She saw everything on the president's desk and, with a photographic memory, could repeat every document she saw. How can one overestimate such a contribution?[16]

When considering the importance of the black role in the Civil War, Colin Powell, our nation's highest-ranking African American army general and statesman, often repeats Frederick Douglass's inspiring words, "Once let the black man get upon his person the brass letters, U.S." and let him "get an eagle on his button and a musket on his shoulder and bullets in his pocket . . . there is no power on the earth . . . which can deny that he has earned the right to citizenship in the United States." For several months after the Emancipation Proclamation was signed—in fact, until July 18, 1863—the recruitment of black troops was considered by the North to be something of an experiment. Despite the heroism of black men under arms in the first years of the war and their documented contribution to the nation's previous wars right back to the American Revolution, many white people, including key members of the Lincoln administration, lacked confidence that black men could be effective soldiers. But most doubts dispersed after the heroic action of the Massachusetts 54th Regiment, a unit of free Northern black men led by white officers, on a hot July night along a sandy beach at the outer edge of Charleston Harbor. Their attack on Fort Wagner, although failing to carry the rebel works, did change Northern public opinion, ending the debate over the advisability of

---

16 Gates and Higginbotham, *African American National Biography*, 1:510–11.

THE GALLANT CHARGE OF THE FIFTY FOURTH MASSACHUSETTS (COLORED) REGIMENT.
On the Rebel works at Fort Wagner, Morris Island near Charleston. July 18ᵗʰ 1863, and death of Colonel Robᵗ G. Shaw.

Fort Wagner and the 54th Massachusetts Regiment, by Currier & Ives, New York, circa 1863. Lithograph. Library of Congress. This print focuses on the death of the regiment's commander, Colonel Robert Gould Shaw.

arming African Americans. Their heroism and the death of their sainted commander, Colonel Robert Gould Shaw, proved black worth to a skeptical Northern public and, as Douglass asserted, laid the basis for the post-war black claims for full citizenship. [17]

Much historical attention has focused on the legacy of the Massachusetts regiment, especially because of the magnificent memorial erected to Shaw and his unit in 1897 on Boston Common, several books, and a 1989 Hollywood film. But the Saint-Gaudens memorial, perhaps the finest example of the art form in the United States, and the iconic attack on Fort Wagner have overshadowed the state's other two black regiments and the equally impressive heroism of the 178,000 men of the United States Colored Troops.

Former slaves wanted the opportunity to fight for their liberation, and Northern blacks wanted to show their patriotism as a basis for

[17] General Colin Powell, Foreword to *Hope & Glory: Essays on the Legacy of the 54th Massachusetts Regiment*, eds. Martin H. Blatt, Thomas J. Brown, and Donald Yacovone (Amherst: University of Massachusetts Press, 2001), xvii.

their postwar claims to full citizenship. Both groups wanted to destroy slavery, and both were treated shabbily by the Lincoln administration. None could be field officers—and those who possessed an officer's rank as a member of the medical corps or as recruiters were either beaten by whites or subjected to withering discrimination. Just as destructive, the highest ranking black officer received less pay than a white private; and black officers had to pay for their own uniforms. (All black troops, in fact, had to pay for their uniforms. They received $10 a month as pay, minus $3 for clothing.) They endured crippling disrespect and insultingly low pay from their own government, and faced an enemy that generally refused to grant them any quarter in combat. Although a few black troops were taken prisoner during the war—and some ended up at the horrid facility at Andersonville in Georgia—most expected to be killed if captured.

The fearsome massacre at Fort Pillow on April 12, 1864, where 64 percent of blacks were killed while only 33 percent of the white Union troops died, tells the story. The battle at the fort, situated about 40 miles north of Memphis on the Mississippi River, was followed by the systematic execution of black soldiers—and black civilians—even after the surrender of the garrison. So loathsome was the incident that Congress investigated the massacre and black soldiers stitched the phrase "Remember Fort Pillow" on their uniforms.

While the war became increasingly savage for all participants with each passing month, for black troops the stakes could not have been higher from the very first. Fighting a war on two fronts—against racism among one's allies at home and against the racism of slavery being defended to the death by a merciless enemy—black soldiers' achievements are all the more astonishing.

✖✖✖

IN AN ATTEMPT TO PENETRATE CONFEDERATE LINES SOUTH OF RICHMOND, VIRGINIA, AND BREAK THE LONG SIEGE OF THE REBEL CAPITAL, General Benjamin F. Butler moved his Army of the James north from Deep Bottom in late September 1864. Butler, who commanded many black troops, believed that if they carried a position that whites had previously failed to seize, it would end any lingering prejudice against them in his army. As he confessed in his memoirs, Butler "deliberately expose[d] my men to the loss of greater numbers than I really believed the capture of the redoubt was worth." Despite Fort Wagner, Port Hudson, Milliken's Bend, and the success of the First South Carolina Volunteers, the white troops of Butler's army lacked confidence in the ability of black soldiers. Thus, Butler concluded that the sacrifice of so many men would prove necessary to create a more effective overall fighting force. After the battle, Butler honored his men with medals and felt duty bound to stand by them after the war because of the great sacrifices they had made to convince their white comrades to trust them in battle.[18]

---

[18] Benjamin F. Butler, *Autobiography and Personal Reminiscences: Butler's Book, A Review of His Legal, Political, and Military Career* (Boston: A. M. Thayer, 1892), 742 quoted.

Thus, soldiers in Butler's command from the 1st, 4th, 5th, 6th, 22nd, 36th, 37th, and 38th United States Colored Troops (USCT) attacked an entrenched position at New Market Heights, Virginia, on September 29, 1864. Waking at 3 A.M. and marching into position, the men received a visit from General Butler an hour later. Facing an enemy on high ground in trenches protected by ditches, felled trees, and a host of other obstacles, the men stared at what must have seemed like an impossible challenge and certain death. Butler fired their spirits and encouraged them to strike fear in their enemies by crying out "Remember Fort Pillow" as they charged the entrenchments. With the sun just breaking over the horizon and fog shrouding the battlefield, the Fourth and Sixth USCT began the assault under orders to use only the bayonet, a standard tactic designed to ensure that attacking troops continued to rush forward.

Christian A. Fleetwood (1840–1914), Alfred B. Hilton (?–1864), and Charles Veal (?–1872) from the Fourth USCT and Thomas Hawkins (1840–1870) and Alexander Kelly (1840–1907) of the Sixth showed such valor that each earned the Medal of Honor, although the initial attack failed. At 7 A.M., the 5th, 36th, and 38th USCT renewed the assault, running over the bodies of their comrades. So many white officers had been killed or wounded that black noncommissioned officers, such as Milton M. Holland (1844–1910), Robert Pinn (1843–1911), and Powhatan Beaty (1839?–1916), took over command of their companies and also won the Medal of Honor. Edward Ratcliff (1835–1915), a sergeant in the 38th from Yorktown, Virginia, was the first enlisted man to enter the rebel trenches, leading Company C of the regiment, for which he too won the Medal of

Christian A. Fleetwood, circa 1900. Photograph. Collection of W. E. B. Du Bois, Library of Congress.

Honor. On September 29, the black units in the assault lost 141 men who were killed and 729 who were wounded.

In two days of fighting, Union forces suffered 391 killed, 2,317 wounded, and 649 either missing or captured. In total, 14 African American soldiers won the Medal of Honor for their valor in the engagement, an unprecedented instance of heroism. Butler's strategy succeeded, but once again black men had to pay the highest and ultimate price to combat the aspersions cast upon their courage by racial prejudice.[19]

---

[19] USCT Casualties of USCT Units at the Battle of New Market Heights, www.nps.gov/rich/historycul ture/casualties.htm.

xxx

WHILE THE "DAY OF JUBILEE" FINALLY CAME WITH THE RATIFICATION OF THE 13TH AMENDMENT IN DECEMBER 1865, ending the enslavement of almost four million people of African descent, some white Americans still wondered about what now to do with the former slaves. In fact, the question loomed over the war from the moment runaway slaves, the "contraband," first began entering Union lines at Fortress Monroe. Indeed, many of the central issues of Reconstruction arose at the start of the war. The flood of former slaves gathering at Fortress Monroe caught the attention of the American Missionary Association—the evangelical organization that would take the lead in freedmen's education. AMA Treasurer Lewis Tappan, an abolitionist for more than 30 years, negotiated an arrangement with General Butler—then in command of Fortress Monroe—to allow the association to teach and care for the many fugitives collecting under the army's protection. In September, the AMA hired Mary S. Peake (1823–1862), a free black from Norfolk, Virginia, to run its first day school for the "contraband."

Peake, born Mary Smith Kelsey in Norfolk, was the daughter of a free black mother and an Englishman, although their names remain unknown. Peake lived with an aunt and uncle in Alexandria, Virginia, for about ten years where she attended school and learned needlework and dressmaking. In 1847, her mother married Thompson Walker and the family moved to Hampton, which possessed a vigorous black community. She joined the First Baptist Church; established the Daughters of Zion, a social welfare organization; and in 1851 married Thomas Peake, a former slave. She also secretly taught slaves to read, against Virginia law. She was teaching in Hampton during the opening months of the war when Confederate raiders burned out the city's black community. The Peakes then moved to a house near Fortress Monroe in which they lived on the second floor and taught school for the AMA on the first.

Her school, focusing on the children of former slaves, emphasized basic elementary education and Bible studies, typical of AMA efforts. Although she began suffering from "consumption"–tuberculosis–she also started an evening school for adult former slaves. She pushed herself, displaying exceptional commitment to her students as her health declined. She became so sick that an AMA agent found her bedridden, but surrounded by her students and still teaching. Her commitment to the work remains a heroic example of religious devotion and dedication to black uplift. The disease overwhelmed her, however; and after suspending her school, she died on September 22, 1862.

The AMA could not be more glowing in its praise of Peake's work. "Even in death," her successor remarked, "the radiance of her life . . . illuminated the society of her race." The organization would not let her contribution come to naught or go unrecognized, so AMA agents established other schools based on her model and formalized her school, renaming it the "Butler School." Then in 1869, the AMA chartered Peake's original school as the Hampton Institute, now Hampton University, which counted Booker T. Washington among its many graduates. Undeservedly obscure, Peake left a fabulous legacy.[20]

---

[20] Joe M. Richardson, *Christian Reconstruction: The American Missionary Association and Southern Blacks, 1861–1890* (Athens: University of Georgia Press, 1986), 3–5; Gates and Higginbotham, *African American National Biography*, 6:292.

✠✠✠

RIGHT AFTER MARY PEAKE ESTAB-LISHED HER SCHOOL AT FORTRESS MONROE, THE UNION NAVY MOVED INTO THE CAROLINA SEA ISLANDS AND SET UP COMMAND AT PORT ROYAL HARBOR. One of their first orders of business was to determine what to do with the 10,000 "contraband" there, the former property of so many runaway masters. Under orders from Secretary of the Treasury Salmon Chase, William W. Pierce, a Boston lawyer, directed efforts and organized a group of missionaries and teachers —they called themselves "Gideon's Band." In March 1862, 53 Northerners arrived to assist the freed slaves in their transition to freedom. Among the many white volunteers was one black teacher from Philadelphia. Her name was Charlotte Forten (1837–1914), a member of the prominent Forten-Purvis families, and she would, fortunately for us, keep a diary of her experiences. Just like her white colleagues, she possessed little if any understanding of local traditions and Southern, rural African American culture and tended to see the former slaves as exotics, lacking rudiments of "civilization." Fortunately, she and her colleagues focused on establishing schools for basic literacy training first, and also inculcating Northern middle-class values among the former slaves.[21]

They pursued literacy with alacrity, but sickened by a lifetime of enforced labor and the imposition upon them of the desires of white people, some of the former slaves showed little desire to meet the occupational or labor

expectations of the missionaries and federal officials. They preferred to raise food crops or no crops at all, instead of the cotton that the government wished them to plant, which only reminded them of their enslavement. (Former slaves in Haiti similarly refused to work on sugar plantations, preferring instead their small subsistence plots.) Many destroyed cotton gins—never wanting to see that cursed machine again—and instead grew corn and potatoes. African Americans knew their own interests and wanted land, which represented the only thing that could safeguard their future, not dollops of cash.

When the federal government sold the abandoned lands seized from the rebel owners in March 1863, African Americans could only purchase 2,000 of the total of 21,000 acres. Obviously, few had any resources to invest. Most of the land went to government officials and speculators. For instance, the Boston abolitionist Edward Philbrick amassed 7,000 acres and transformed the property into a free-labor cotton plantation, believing that marketplace success offered African Americans the best path to independence. Black people, however, insisted on owning their own land and growing their own crops. This tension between the desires of blacks and those of whites pervaded an effort called "the Port Royal Experiment." The beginning of the end of this experiment came, ironically, following a tragically brief period of time during which the former slaves had received just what they requested.

On January 16, 1865, General William Tecumseh Sherman issued Special Field Order No. 15, granting to the local blacks about 400,000 acres of land on the Sea Islands and along the South Carolina coast. The order represented the first systematic attempt to provide

---

[21] The best account of the South Carolina story remains Willy Lee Rose, *Rehearsal for Reconstruction: The Port Royal Experiment* (New York: Random House, 1964).

Contraband working cotton field at the Retreat Plantation, South Carolina, by Hubbard & Mix, Beaufort, South Carolina, 1860s. Photograph on stereocard. Library of Congress.

any form of reparations to newly freed slaves, and it was astonishingly radical for its time. In fact, such a policy—the federal government's massive confiscation of private property formerly owned by Confederates and its methodical redistribution to black former slaves—would be radical at any time.

Although Sherman later said that he had no intention of permanently redistributing these lands, in fact, there was no indication at the time that the confiscation of property belonging to those who had levied war against the United States was anything but legal, and even the moral thing to do. Imagine the history of race relations in the United States had this policy stood—had the former slaves actually had access to the ownership of land,

of property! If the former slaves could have achieved economic self-sufficiency, perhaps the entire history of race relations in this country would have been markedly different. One of the principal promises of America has been the possibility of average people enjoying the right and the opportunity to own land, and all that such ownership entails. Historically, it is the principal means by which one generation passes on *wealth* to subsequent generations in this country.[22]

---

[22] The following account is based on Henry Louis Gates, Jr., "The Truth Behind '40 Acres and a Mule,'" *100 Amazing Facts about the Negro*, *The Root* (January 7, 2013), http://www.theroot.com/views/truth-behind-40-acres-and-mule.

Most accounts of Sherman's Special Field Order No. 15, however, leave out the fact that the idea for massive land redistribution actually resulted from a discussion that Sherman and Secretary of War Edwin M. Stanton held four days before Sherman issued the order. They had met with 20 ministers of the black community in Savannah, Georgia, where Sherman was headquartered following his famous March to the Sea. The meeting was unprecedented in American history. At 8 P.M., January 12, 1865, on the second floor of the transplanted Englishman and cotton merchant Charles Green's mansion on Savannah's Macon Street, the two Union leaders heard what African Americans had to say.

Aware of the great historical significance of the meeting, Stanton presented Henry Ward Beecher (Harriet Beecher Stowe's famous brother) a verbatim transcript of the discussion, which Beecher read to his congregation at New York's Plymouth Church and which the New York *Daily Tribune* printed in full in its February 13, 1865, edition. Stanton told Beecher that "for the first time in the history of this nation, the representatives of the government had gone to these poor debased people to ask them what they wanted for themselves." He had suggested to Sherman that they gather "the leaders of the local Negro community" and ask them something no one else had apparently thought to ask: "What do you want for your own people" following the war? And what they wanted astonishes us even today.

Who were these thoughtful leaders who exhibited such foresight? All were ministers, mostly Baptist and Methodist, and, curiously, 11 of the 20 had been born *free* in the slave states, and all but one had lived as free men in the Confederacy during the course of the Civil War. The remaining man, James Lynch, was a black abolitionist and minister from Baltimore who had attended Dartmouth College and originally came south in July 1863 to become the new chaplain for the renowned 54th Massachusetts Regiment. Although the unit's officers voted to make Lynch their chaplain, the army failed to muster him and at some point he resettled in Georgia.[23] The other nine ministers had been slaves in the South who became "contraband" and hence free when Union forces liberated them.

Their chosen leader and spokesman was a 67-year-old Baptist minister named Garrison Frazier (1798–?), who had been born in Granville, North Carolina, and remained a slave until 1857, "when he purchased freedom for himself and wife for $1,000 in gold and silver," as the New York *Daily Tribune* reported. The Reverend Frazier had been "in the ministry for thirty-five years," and it was he who bore the responsibility of answering the 12 questions that Sherman and Stanton put to the group. Clearly, the stakes for the future of African Americans could not have been higher.

Frazier and his ministerial brothers did not disappoint. What did they tell Sherman and Stanton that the Negro most wanted? Land! "The way we can best take care of ourselves," the Reverend Frazier began his answer to the crucial third question, "is to have land, and turn it and till it by our own labor . . . and we can soon maintain ourselves and have something to spare. . . . We want to be placed on land until we are able to buy it and make it our own." And when asked next where the freed slaves "would rather live—whether scattered among the whites or in colonies by

---

[23] Yacovone, *Voice of Thunder*, 272.

"The way we can best take care of ourselves," the Reverend Frazier began his answer to the crucial third question, "is to have land, and turn it and till it by our own labor . . . and we can soon maintain ourselves and have something to spare. . . . We want to be placed on land until we are able to buy it and make it our own."

themselves," without missing a beat, Brother Frazier (as the transcript calls him) replied that "I would prefer to live by ourselves, for there is a prejudice against us in the South that will take years to get over. . . ." When polled individually around the table, all but one—James Lynch, the Baltimorean—agreed with Frazier.

Four days later, Sherman issued Special Field Order No. 15, after President Lincoln approved it. The response to the order was immediate. When the transcript of the meeting was reprinted in the newspaper of the A.M.E. Church, the *Christian Recorder*, an editorial note intoned that "from this it will be seen that the colored people down South are not so dumb as many suppose them to be," reflecting North-South, slave-free black class tensions that continued well into the modern civil rights movement. The effect throughout the South was electric. The Baptist minister Ulysses L. Houston (1824–?), one of those who had met with Sherman, led 1,000 blacks to Skidaway Island, Georgia, where they established a self-governing community with Houston as the "black governor." By June, 40,000 freedmen had settled on 400,000 acres of "Sherman Land." The general later ordered that the Army could lend the new settlers mules; hence the phrase "40 acres and a mule."

We commonly use that phrase, "40 acres and a mule," but few of us have read the order itself. Section I bears repeating in full: "The islands from Charleston, south, the abandoned rice fields along the rivers for thirty miles back from the sea, and the country bordering the St. Johns river, Florida, are reserved and set apart for the settlement of the negroes now made free by the acts of war and the proclamation of the President of the United States." Section II specifies that these new communities, moreover, would be governed entirely by black people themselves, ". . . on the islands, and in the settlements hereafter to be established, no white person whatever, unless military officers and soldiers detailed for duty, will be permitted to reside; and the sole and exclusive management of affairs will be left to the freed people themselves. . . . By the laws of war, and orders of the President of the United States, the negro is free and must be dealt with as such."[24]

The fifth provision is key, whatever Sherman may have later said—or thought:

In order to carry out this system of settlement, a general officer will be detailed as Inspector of Settlements and Plantations, whose duty it shall be to visit the settlements, to regulate their police and general management, and who will furnish personally to each head of a family,

---

[24] Freedmen and Southern Society Project, http://www.history.umd.edu/Freedmen/sfo15.htm.

subject to the approval of the President of the United States, a possessory title in writing, giving as near as possible the description of boundaries; and who shall adjust all claims or conflicts that may arise under the same, subject to the like approval, treating such titles altogether as possessory.

Despite the obvious promise—in writing—President Andrew Johnson, Lincoln's successor, allowed former slaveholders to take back any land that had gone unsold. The following year, Union soldiers forced black settlers off the land if they did not sign a lease agreement, incredibly, with the original white owners. A largely compliant Congress, worried over the constitutionality of the land seizures, permitted the dispossession of the former slaves. As a result, the majority of blacks lost their claim to "Sherman Land" and any hope for a secure future. And this was an augur of things to come for the former slaves. After a brief decade of hope called Reconstruction, the promise offered by the Port Royal Experiment, Special Field Order No. 15, and three amendments to the Constitution could not withstand the social and political tensions that would undermine attempts to grant full equality to African Americans. Still, as W. E. B. Du Bois would put it, the coming decade of Reconstruction would be America's "finest effort to achieve democracy for the working millions which this world had ever seen."

RECONSTRUCTION AND REDEMPTION
1865–1900

IN JANUARY 1865, THE CHAPLAIN OF THE UNITED STATES HOUSE OF REPRESENTATIVES, WILLIAM H. CHANNING, A BOSTON-BORN ABOLITIONIST AND UNITARIAN MINISTER, INVITED THE REVEREND HENRY HIGHLAND GARNET TO ADDRESS CONGRESS. Prior to him, the only African Americans allowed into the halls of the Capitol carried brooms and dustpans. Channing knew who he was inviting and what Garnet's selection symbolized. Born a slave in Maryland, Garnet rose to become a minister, editor, and intellectual, one of the leading voices of black abolitionism prior to the Civil War.

His best known speech remains his 1843 "Address to the Slaves of the United States" in which he called for slave insurrections. The address proved so disturbing to his fellow abolitionists and white supporters—even John Brown—that the Buffalo National Convention of black leaders where Garnet delivered the address refused to endorse it, and an accurate version of it did not appear in print until March 1863, after the North had declared war on slavery. During the war, Garnet received the call to Washington, D.C.'s 15th Street Presbyterian Church. This had been the pulpit of the Reverend John F. Cook, Sr. (1810?–1855), whose son, John F. Cook, Jr. (1833–1910), had been a member of the delegation that had met with President Lincoln in August 1862 to discuss the president's colonization plans—and the same one later filled by the Reverend Francis J. Grimké (1850–1937), who would in 1909 become one of the founders of the National Association for the Advancement of Colored People (NAACP).[1]

On February 12, 1865, Garnet became the first African American to speak officially in the Capitol building. He urged the nation to ratify Congress's constitutional amendment permanently to end slavery in the United States. In his own words, the black minister asked Congress and the nation to "speedily finish the work he [God] has given you to do." In his *Memorial Discourse*, Garnet drew upon Matthew 23:4 to advise Congress that a heavy responsibility now lay upon its members to act. For too long, others bore the "heavy and grievous burdens

of duties and obligation." Of this, Garnet could speak with authority: "The first sounds that startled my ear, and sent a shudder through my soul, were the cracking of the whip, and the clanking of chains." Congress must act, Garnet explained, and do so until "emancipation shall be followed by enfranchisement, and all men holding allegiance to the government shall enjoy every right of American citizenship." No better encapsulation of black aspirations for the postwar period could have been expressed.[2]

Now that the war had been won, what was to be done with the former slaves? Whites asked this question repeatedly, but it was the wrong question. Formerly enslaved African Americans wanted the same things that white people wanted. The real question centered on what actions whites would take to advance or restrict black freedom—would justice and fairness guide their actions, or would they re-establish slavery but under another name? Frederick Douglass had formulated this very question as early as 1862, in the second year of the Civil War:

> What shall be done with the four million slaves if they are emancipated? This question has been answered, and can be answered in many ways. Primarily, it is a question less for man than for God—less for human intellect than for the laws of nature to solve. It assumes that nature has erred; that the law of liberty is a mistake; that freedom, though a natural want of human soul, can only be enjoyed at the

---

[1] Garnet's 1843 remarks can be read in *Sources of the African-American Past: Primary Sources in American History*, ed. Roy E. Finkenbine (New York: Longman, 1997), 63–66.

[2] Henry Highland Garnet, *Memorial Discourse* (Philadelphia: Joseph M. Wilson, 1865) can be read at http://archive.org/stream/memorialdiscourse00garn#page/n7/mode/2up.

expense of human welfare, and that men are better off in slavery than they would or could be in freedom; that slavery is the natural order of human relations, and that liberty is an experiment. What shall be done with them?

Our answer is, do nothing with them; mind your business, and let them mind theirs. Your *doing* with them is their greatest misfortune. They have been undone by your doings, and all they now ask, and really have need of at your hands, is just to let them alone. They suffer by every interference, and succeed best by being let alone.

Douglass spoke for the race when he advised whites: "Let us stand upon our own legs, work with our own hands, and eat bread in the sweat of our own brows." The path to national reconciliation and justice was clear. "Deal justly with him," Douglass advised. "He is a human being, capable of judging between good and evil, right and wrong, liberty and slavery, and is as much a subject of law as any other man." So simple—but Douglass's sentiments represented as distant a dream as could be imagined for an angry, defiant, defeated South, and even for some Northerners anxious about the economic competition represented by the sudden appearance of nearly four million new workers in the marketplace, hungry for jobs and wages.[3]

With the nation pondering its own future, the former slaves were quick to leave the constraints of the plantation behind. They explored the parameters of their new freedom in countless ways, reorganizing their lives, families, and communities, even taking new names to signify that they were free men and women. Eager to solemnize bonds that had been treated with contempt under slavery, they rushed to marry, sometimes in mass weddings for as many as 70 couples. They established their own churches, which became centers of their communities. Many took to the roads, seeking out the lost family members from whom they'd been forcibly separated. Some former slaves who had succeeded in establishing a life of freedom in the North returned to the South in an attempt to find lost relatives and see what changes the war had wrought. Jermain Loguen's experiences offer a good example of this.

Jermain W. Loguen (1813–1872) had escaped Tennessee slavery in 1835 and eventually became a respected A.M.E. Zion minister and a leader of the Underground Railroad in Syracuse, New York. At the close of the war in July 1865, he returned to Columbia, in central west Tennessee, in search of his past and what had changed. He looked for the familiar whipping post and auction block, but both had disappeared. The slave pens remained, however, places where the "poor, innocent and almost heartbroken slaves" had waited to be chained together and driven to the sugar or cotton fields, places where the "young slave mother begging for her only babe" had "no mercy shown her." Much to his delight, the region's former slave owners and traders had taken up residence in the pens. At last, a measure of justice, he reasoned.

In earshot of those new residents, Loguen preached to both whites and blacks—some of whom had come simply to see what had happened to old "Jarm," the slave who had run away

<hr>

3   Frederick Douglass, "What Shall Be Done with the Slaves If Emancipated?" *Douglass's Monthly* (January 1862), http://www.lib.rochester.edu/index.cfm?PAGE=4386.

so long ago. But even Loguen wasn't ready for one member of the audience. "The Lord was with me and gave me great liberty on that occasion, as we Methodist preachers sometimes say. My old mother, though very feeble, rode ten miles that she might hear her long-lost son." The lucky few, such as Loguen, found parents or lost siblings, but many of the former slaves were left with nothing but their freedom.[4]

Wallace Turnage (1846–1916), a former slave from North Carolina, embodied what "luck" really meant for a slave during the Civil War—and after. Turnage was born in Green County, North Carolina, on a small tobacco and cotton farm that had only seven slaves. His mother was a slave named Courtney and his father turned out to be Sylvester Brown Turnage, the white stepson of Turnage's owner. Since Courtney had given birth to Turnage when she was only about 15 years old, she clearly had been the victim of sexual abuse and intimidation— an all too common fact of slave life. Turnage remained with his mother until 1860, when his owner fell into debt and sent the 14-year-old boy to a Richmond, Virginia, slave dealer. In the late spring, the dealer sold Turnage for $1,000 to a Scottish-born Alabama cotton planter named James Chalmers. Richmond, the nexus of the internal slave trade, was the country's largest market for slaves involved in the Second Middle Passage. Headed to the Deep South, the young Wallace had every reason to believe that he would never see his mother or familiar surroundings again.[5]

His first day at the Alabama plantation proved a shock. A cruel overseer grabbed a poor woman in the field, hauled up her dress and applied the bullwhip. "Then he shook his whip at me and said hurry up young man." The threat was a real one, as later in the year the same overseer expressed his dissatisfaction with the amount of cotton picked by his slaves by making one woman lie down in the field and pull her clothes over her head, then beating her mercilessly. He "gave that woman about two hundred lashes and I thought that was enough except he was going to kill her. I could see the skin fly near about every lick he struck her."[6] By the fall, after seeing enough horrifying abuse and feeling the bullwhip three or four times himself, Turnage decided to flee. But such resistance only enflamed his owners who, in one instance, applied 95 lashes to his back. For as long as Turnage remained in slavery, he plotted his escape. With the Civil War coming to northern Alabama and Mississippi, Turnage tried his best to escape to Union lines. During his third attempt he was caught in Mississippi, ironically turned in by another slave who feared the presence of a fugitive would only cause trouble. Returned to his owner, he received another 25 lashes.

But neither recapture nor the bullwhip would keep Turnage on the farm. His fourth attempt nearly brought him within gunshot of Union lines at Corinth, in far northern Mississippi. Returned to his owner, Turnage fled again in the late summer of 1862 but was recaptured, this time after a mauling by several dogs sent to track him down. Fed up with his chronic runaway, Chalmers sent Turnage to

---

4   Ripley, *The Black Abolitionist Papers*, 5:353–56.

5   Wallace Turnage's memoir and biography are in David W. Blight, *A Slave No More: Two Men Who Escaped to Freedom, Including Their Own Narratives of Emancipation* (Orlando, FL: Harcourt, Inc., 2007).

6   Journal of Wallace Turnage in Blight, *A Slave No More*, 216–17.

"I now dreaded the gun, and handcuffs and pistols no more.
. . . I could now speak my opinion to men of all grades and
colors, and no one to question my right to speak."

Mobile, where he could be sold. He worked in a store—far easier labor than anything he had done previously—until a nephew of former President William Henry Harrison bought the 16-year-old for $2,000 in Confederate money, intent on making the boy a carriage driver and house slave. Turnage proved a disappointment because, once again, he immediately fled. Upon his return, his master had him brutally whipped—his back must have been a cascade of welts and scars—the worst beating of his young life. In response, Turnage again fled, once again unsuccessfully. While he did receive some assistance from other blacks, Turnage's repeated attempts and failures reveal just how hard it was for a slave to escape his chains.

While Turnage had exerted enormous energy and showed astounding courage in his attempt to reach Union lines, in the end the Union lines found him. In August 1864, the Union Navy under Admiral David Farragut famously ran the gauntlet of Confederate forts at the mouth of Mobile Bay, finally closing the last important rebel fort open to commerce. Turnage took advantage of the chaos of the battle and the inattention of rebel soldiers and frightened whites to carefully pick his way through the swamps, avoid the countless snakes, hide in the tall grasses, and eventually use an abandoned rowboat to reach Union forces—at long last seizing his own freedom. "I now dreaded the gun, and handcuffs and pistols no more. . . . I could now speak my opinion

to men of all grades and colors, and no one to question my right to speak."[7]

The story does not stop there, however. It should not surprise us that Turnage—who appeared to have an unfailingly good sense of direction and enormous energy—found his way back to North Carolina, where, astonishingly, he reunited with his mother and his half brothers and sisters. Eventually, he settled in New York City, where he worked a variety of jobs, primarily as a waiter, moved his mother and siblings north, and married in the 1870s.

While Turnage managed to save himself and his family from the retribution visited upon African Americans in the South by their former masters, the North hardly proved to be the promised land. Poverty and limited opportunity relegated the family to tenement squalor. His mother remained in Manhattan, managing to live until age 67, dying in 1898, after a career as a nursemaid, cook, and washerwoman—perhaps the very tasks she had performed in North Carolina. By the 1880s, Turnage had had his fill of Manhattan life and moved his wife and two children across the Hudson River to Jersey City, where he remained until his death in 1916. He still worked in Manhattan, however, and beginning in 1885, took the ferry to work, cruising every day past the Statue of Liberty.

Those African American former slaves who remained in the South, however, confronted formidable obstacles. At the close of the

---

7   Journal of Wallace Turnage in Blight, *A Slave No More*, 257.

war, most faced their freedom without land, money, a home, and in some cases, even without clothes. Congress established the Bureau of Refugees, Freedmen, and Abandoned Lands in an attempt to mitigate the problems facing the former slaves and to negotiate labor contracts that would keep the slaves working, their former owners from bankruptcy, and all from facing ruin. But as General Sherman and Secretary Stanton learned when they asked those Southern black ministers in Savannah in January 1865 what they wanted for themselves, they heard unexpectedly clear and explicit answers. The government appeared to listen at first, as we have seen, and gave them the land they desired and deserved. But before long, the head of the bureau, General O. O. Howard, visited the Sea Islands and advised the former slaves that they would have to give up their land. "Why, General Howard," the assembled freedmen asked, "Why do you take away our lands? You take them from us who are true, always true to the Government! You give them to our all-time enemies! That is not right!"[8]

The disappointment of the Port Royal Experiment did not define the black response to freedom and their hopes for Reconstruction, but it did foretell much. For as long as Radical Republicans could keep Union troops in the South and fight off the determined efforts by President Andrew Johnson to return former Confederates to power and reinstate white racial domination, hope persisted that a new future could be created by African Americans. With new civil rights legislation and three constitutional amendments, and with allies like the

Boston abolitionist Wendell Phillips and Senator Charles Sumner advancing their cause, African Americans achieved unprecedented levels of equality. As W. E. B. Du Bois once remarked, the former slaves "stood a brief moment in the sun."[9]

◆◆◆

THE FORMER SLAVES FLOCKED TO FREEDMEN'S BUREAU SCHOOLS, AND IN PLACES WHERE THESE DIDN'T EXIST, THEY ATTEMPTED TO FORM THEIR OWN. They joined Union Leagues and organized to resist reinstatement of onerous and degrading black codes. Where the Army could enforce the peace, they voted and ran for office. More than half the officeholders in South Carolina between 1867 and 1876 were black men. Some of them, like Stephen Swails (1832–1900), hailed from the North. Swails had served in the 54th Massachusetts Regiment during the war, then decided that his duty still lay in the cause of freedom, so he remained in the South to help in the former slaves' transition to full freedom. Swails served in the South Carolina state constitutional convention of 1868 and in the state senate. He edited a Republican newspaper, practiced law, and was even elected as a trustee of the University of South Carolina. He lasted until 1878, when "Redeemers"–former Confederates determined to restore as best they could the old order and the economic enslavement of the former slaves in all but name– drove him out of office and threatened his life. Others, even the famous fugitive slave narrator

8   Leon F. Litwack, *How Free Is Free?: The Long Death of Jim Crow* (Cambridge: Harvard University Press, 2009), 2 quoted.

9   W. E. B. Du Bois, *Black Reconstruction in America, 1860–1880* (Cleveland, OH: Meridian Books, 1962), 30 quoted.

Harriet Jacobs (1813–1897), returned to the South to help in the work of Reconstruction. Many Northern blacks felt similarly committed and saw their work, whether for the AMA, the Freedmen's Bureau, the Equal Rights League, or any number of other Northern freedmen's aid societies, as integral to their antislavery commitment.[10]

South Carolina proved especially rich and fertile soil for the nurturing of black political leaders. Robert Smalls, who, as we have seen, gained national attention by commandeering a rebel warship, went on to serve in the state constitutional convention of 1868 and in both houses of the state legislature from 1868 to 1874, and in 1872 and 1876 was a delegate to the Republican National Convention. Most significant, the former slave served as a congressman from 1875 to 1878 and from 1881 to 1886. He represented the state's Fifth Congressional District, which included Beaufort, Smalls's home, which is today on the national historic register. In the aftermath of Reconstruction, which ended in 1876, any African American serving in the U.S. Congress faced steep challenges. Intense white resistance limited the chances of sponsoring any important civil rights legislation, eliminating the possibility for real structural change. Nevertheless, the presence of black elected officials such as Smalls, even in the twilight of Reconstruction, gave a public, legislative voice to those who before war's end had none.

When Smalls took his seat in Congress in 1875, the House had become dominated by the Democratic Party, 169 delegates to 109 Republican ones. Of the 107 Southern Democrats, 80 were Confederate veterans, and 35 had been rebel generals. For African Americans and their antislavery allies, the 44th Congress looked more like 1858 than 1868. Nevertheless, Smalls forged ahead with his work, assuming a seat on the House agricultural committee. He also began filing bills, ones that would favorably affect both the white and black constituents in his district. He not only requested funds to erect public buildings like a customhouse and post office, but he also supported the naval presence at Port Royal and presented several private relief bills, even one for Henry McKee, his former master. He became known for his extemporaneous commentary and effective rebuttals to his racist colleagues.

While his political enemies attempted to characterize Smalls as inept and corrupt, in fact he was an effective and astute legislator who properly represented his district. A voice for justice and equal rights at a time when the North was abandoning blacks to the tender mercies of the white South, he bravely co-authored a bill that in effect sought to end segregation in the Army—which would remain segregated until 1948—and make "no distinction whatever . . . on account of race or color."[11]

South Carolina whites, sick of black political power, were determined to seize control and reinstall the Democratic Party in office. On July 4, 1876, just a year after the start of Smalls's congressional career, whites besieged a building in Hamburg, South Carolina (present-day North Augusta), after a black political rally and rolled up a cannon, threatening to use it if those inside

---

[10] Eric Foner, *Freedom's Lawmakers: A Directory of Black Officeholders During Reconstruction* (Baton Rouge: Louisiana State University Press, 1996), 207–08.

[11] Edward A. Miller, Jr., *Gullah Statesman: Robert Smalls from Slavery to Congress, 1839–1915* (Columbia: University of South Carolina Press, 1995), 97.

Robert Smalls as congressman, circa 1870–1880. Glass plate photograph. Library of Congress.

refused to surrender. When they did, many were mowed down. The "Hamburg Massacre" set the tone for the coming months. "Red Shirt" militia and "rifle clubs" roamed the state, intimidating black voters and murdering any black people with the temerity to resist. Such actions, apologists protested, were "excusable, if not justifiable" given the threat posed by black rule.

The next year, South Carolina Democrats "redeemed" the state from Republican rule and declared that the only black voting right they would acknowledge was "permission to vote the all-white leadership of the party into office." Without any federal objection, the party of the former Confederacy reinstituted white domination and virtual slavery with the infamous convict-lease system. Throughout the South, white officials imprisoned thousands of black men on the flimsiest pretexts, then rented their labor to private contractors. The system brought money into state coffers, provided cheap labor to white businessmen, and returned thousands of blacks to servitude. However, despite their efforts, because of 20,000 black votes, Democrats could not unseat Smalls through the ballot box. Instead, they drove him from office with charges of corruption. When he declined a $10,000 bribe from the governor to resign his seat, the state arrested him in October 1877 for taking a bribe from a Republican printer. Found guilty, he was removed from office. But in 1881, his loyal constituents returned him to office. He managed to hang on until 1886, but by then the political landscape of South Carolina had become almost as repressive as in the days before the Civil War.[12]

In 1890, with no hope of returning to office, Smalls published a fascinating account of the political tactics of white Democrats and the state of repression in South Carolina. Reflecting the importance of the author and the significance of his subject, the essay appeared in the *North American Review*, the oldest and most important literary journal in the United States. Smalls put the dilemma blacks faced, as Reconstruction was dying, in the most direct terms:

> In South Carolina there is neither a free ballot nor an honest count, and since the election of 1874 the history of elections in the State is the history of a continued series of murders, outrages, perjury, and fraud. . . . Republicanism was in that year overthrown by murderous gangs called "rifle clubs," who, acting in concert, terrorized nearly the entire State, overawing election officers and defying the courts. The elections in 1878 and 1880 were repetitions of the outrages of 1876. The shotgun and rifle were factors that prevented a thorough canvass, and a false count in those counties where Republicans made contests completed the work. Having perfect immunity from punishment, the encouragement, if not the active participation of the State government, and the protection of the courts of the State, the rifle clubs committed their outrages without restraint, and the election officers their frauds without even the thin veneer of attempted concealment. Elections since then have been carried by perjury and fraud—two things worshipped and adored by the South Carolina Democracy.[13]

---

[12] Miller, *Gullah Statesman*, 93–102, 113–15, 125–31.

[13] Robert Smalls, "Election Methods in the South," *North American Review* 151 (November 1890): 593–600.

HEROES OF THE COLORED RACE.

Heroes of the Colored Race, by J. Hoover, Philadelphia, 1881 and 1883. Chromolithograph. Library of Congress. In contrast to *Emancipation,* by Thomas Nast, *Heroes of the Colored Race* celebrates the emergence of the black political and social leaders Blanche K. Bruce, Frederick Douglass, Hiram Revels, Robert Smalls, Jonathan Lynch, Joseph H. Rainey, and Charles E. Nash. Equally celebrated are Lincoln, U. S. Grant, James A. Garfield, and John Brown—who is given a special place of honor. Moreover, it acknowledges the role of African Americans in securing their own freedom.

SMALLS HARDLY HAD BEEN THE ONLY AFRICAN AMERICAN IN CONGRESS. Hiram Revels (1827–1901) and Blanche K. Bruce (1841–1898) from Mississippi served in the Senate; Benjamin Turner (1825–1894) of Alabama, Josiah Walls (1842–1905) of Florida, Jefferson Long (1836–1901) of Georgia, and Robert DeLarge (1842–1874), Joseph Rainey (1832–1887), and Robert B. Elliott (1842–1884) of South Carolina, all served in the U.S. House. After 1873, several more followed in their footsteps. For a people who only a few short years before were routinely denounced as inferior, fit only for enslavement, the changes since the close of the war seemed almost beyond comprehension. While African Americans had indeed enjoyed a new and warm burst of sunshine, a frightening eclipse, as Smalls's career shows, had begun to cast deep shadows on the future of the black electorate.[14]

The gains of African Americans under Reconstruction were quite significant, but they proved to be all too fragile. Seething over the new assertiveness of African Americans, whites across the South viewed the dramatic results of the war with derision and outrage. Fueled with indignation, many—like those in Hamburg, South Carolina—picked up the guns they had laid down in 1865. In 1866, white mobs in Memphis had attacked the local black neighborhood in a three-day riot of murder, arson, and gang rape; in New Orleans, 34 black people were killed when a police-aided mob attacked a suffrage convention. On Easter Sunday in 1873, whites massacred 150 black members of a local militia in Colfax, Louisiana, an event that helped finally to crush Reconstruction for good.

Faced with an astonishing array of social and political changes following the war, Southern whites resorted to an ever-escalating campaign of racist terror and intimidation. Members of shadowy organizations like the South Carolina rifle clubs and the newly formed Ku Klux Klan terrorized or assassinated black people (and their white allies) who dared to vote or seek an education or otherwise challenge the old order. Whites denounced "carpetbaggers," Northerners who had come

South to aid in the Reconstruction. They were depicted as vultures, greedy Yankees who manipulated their black minions to strip whites of whatever wealth they possessed. Endless, beastly caricatures appeared in the popular press of black politicians as ignorant, apelike, fat, corrupt, and venal, dripping with political patronage all too readily for sale, presiding over legislatures wearing ill-fitting, garish suits.

THE MASKED SENTINEL.

Klan Sentinel, from *A Fool's Errand, By One of the Fools*, by Albion W. Tourgée, enlarged edition (New York: Fords, Howard, & Hulbert; Boston: W. H. Thompson & Co., 1880).

---

[14] *Biographical Directory of the United States Congress, 1774–Present*, http://bioguide.congress.gov/biosearch/biosearch.asp; "Black-American Representatives and Senators by Congress, 1870–Present," *History, Art & Archives: United States House of Representatives*, http://history.house.gov/Exhibitions-and-Publications/BAIC/Historical-Data/Black-American-Representatives-and-Senators-by-Congress/; Gates and Higginbotham, *African American National Biography*, 7:247–49.

◆◇◆

GIVEN THIS UNRELENTING WHITE HOS-
TILITY, ONLY EXTREMELY RESOURCE-
FUL MEN AND WOMEN WHO ENJOYED
RELIABLE CONNECTIONS AND PROTEC-
TIONS from powerful white men could take
advantage of the few opportunities for advancement that existed after the end of slavery.
The "experiment" at Davis Bend, Mississippi—
not far from Vicksburg on the Mississippi
River—represents a startling interlude in the
history of Reconstruction. Not only did one
family of former slaves, led by an exceptionally
enterprising freedman, cooperate closely with
their former owner, but they gained the former master's cooperation to amass a fantastic
level of wealth and property, while establishing a safe and prosperous colony for hundreds
of former slaves. The story's central figures
could not have been more unlikely partners,
and the world they forged still astonishes today,
just as it also reveals the limitations of African
American life in the South after the Civil War.[15]

Back in 1818, Joseph Davis, a wealthy
Mississippi lawyer and brother of Jefferson
Davis, future president of the Confederacy,
purchased 11,000 acres of land to grow cotton in a bend of the Mississippi River near
Natchez and Vicksburg. By 1850, his plantation epitomized southern success, producing
a fine grade of cotton and becoming the home
for 345 slaves. While his brother rose in the
world of national politics, Joseph Davis entered
the top 12 percent of the state's most successful
planters. Each brother owned a plantation in

Davis Bend—Joseph named his Hurricane, and
Jefferson called his Brierfield. While Jefferson
Davis conformed to the archetypal image of
the southern master, never wavering from
his belief in the innate inferiority of African
Americans, brother Joseph proved difficult
to categorize. While striving to embody the
southern ideal of the landed master, he also
read widely in the New England reform tradition and was deeply influenced by the English
social theorist Robert Owen. English utopia-
nism is, perhaps, one of the least likely influ-
ences on an elite member of the slave-owning
aristocracy. Yet Joseph Davis went as far as he
could to adapt it to the seemingly inhospitable
context of slavery.

Key to the success of the scheme—and
the welfare of more than 300 slaves—was one
slave named Benjamin Thornton Montgomery
(1819–1877). Born in Loudoun County, Virginia,
Montgomery was abruptly sold south, making
the Second Middle Passage to Natchez in 1836
and becoming the property of Joseph Davis.
The young slave promptly fled, but was soon
recaptured. Montgomery likely expected a
thorough thrashing at the hands of a dreary
overseer. Instead, Davis asked him why he had
run away and used sympathy and understanding to quell the young slave's fears. He found in
Montgomery much innate ability and encouraged his education. Soon, Montgomery had the
run of Davis's considerable library and began
building his own collection of books.

Davis saw something in the young man
that touched and, perhaps, inspired him.
Before long, Montgomery mastered land surveying, began making architectural plans,
and soon demonstrated considerable skills as
a mechanic. He invented a propeller to replace
a river vessel's paddle wheel, and had he been

---

[15] The following account is based on Janet Sharp
Hermann, *The Pursuit of a Dream* (New York: Oxford
University Press, 1981).

Slave quarters at Jefferson Davis's plantation, circa 1860–1870. Photograph. Library of Congress. Inscribed on the front: "Sent Home by Elizabeth Findley Missionary to the freedmen" and on the back: "Graveyard Joe Davis Plac[e]. Davis Bend, Miss."

free, Montgomery could have obtained a U.S. patent on his invention. Davis also encouraged Montgomery's business acumen, permitting him to open a store on the plantation, a business that would become the foundation for his later success. In short order, Montgomery's store became an important source of supplies for the other slaves and even whites in the region, and he soon was trading up and down the Mississippi River, supplying food and fuel to riverboat captains, maintaining a $2,000 account with a New Orleans wholesaler. His skills proved so invaluable that Davis made him the plantation's business manager. By 1851, Montgomery had married another Virginia-born slave named Mary, had five children, and effectively lived as a free, successful businessman on the Hurricane plantation.

Joseph Davis clearly had the wisdom not to let racism cripple his own economic interests. But the relationship went far beyond that; the two trusted one another implicitly, and Davis encouraged the education of Montgomery's children. He even took the ten-year-old Isaiah Montgomery into his mansion to become his personal valet and private secretary. He hired a slave from his brother's plantation to tutor the Montgomery children, and when they outpaced their teacher, Montgomery hired his own tutor for his children: a white man. One is hard-pressed to think of another similar instance in the entire history of the Deep South.

While it is unlikely that the other 350 or so slaves on the plantation received similar treatment from Davis, life at Hurricane—compared to other plantations in the region—was probably about as good as one could expect under the slave regime. Abundant food for all made life more than bearable, and no record survives of sexual exploitation or severe beatings.

Montgomery, who likely found many opportunities to flee, remained content with his growing authority, his increasing wealth, and the protection he enjoyed as a slave of one of the most powerful men in the state. His remarkable abilities might have become the basis for a highly successful career in the free North, but it was a risk that he found unnecessary to take. Prudence remained the central feature of Montgomery's life and business dealings.

But the war brought changes and revealed much about how the other slaves perceived life at Hurricane. With the approach of Union forces in April 1862, Joseph Davis fled Davis Bend, leaving Montgomery in charge of the entire plantation—clearly an enormous sign of the trust Davis placed in his "property." But the other slaves at Hurricane and at Brierfield, regardless of how well Jefferson Davis and his brother thought they treated the African Americans they owned, fled for the Union blue at the first opportunity. Others broke into their master's home and took furniture and clothing. Of the hundreds of slaves owned by the president of the Confederacy, only 17 remained behind.

Defenders of the Old South like the Davises described slaves as "contented" and slavery as a paternalistic institution that cared for a people who could not care for themselves. African Americans, however, voted with their feet and believed in the benefits of freedom. They also showed Union soldiers where Jefferson Davis had buried his family silver.

While Benjamin cared for the remnants of the plantation, the livestock, and the few other slaves still in Davis Bend, his son Isaiah left with Union Admiral David Dixon Porter, who, for a time, took over as a guarantor of the Montgomery family. He suggested that given the chaos of the war, the family should remove to Cincinnati, where Benjamin worked as a carpenter. Porter, however, found the self-sufficiency of the remaining slaves in Davis Bend to be a great surprise and helped foster it as an independent colony. Montgomery and his family returned after six months and took over leadership of the plantation and the growing number of freedmen who began to collect there. General U. S. Grant also supported the effort, paternalistically believing that the good management of the area proved it could become "a negro paradise."[16]

The local Freedmen's Bureau officer, Chaplain John Eaton, Jr., used his contacts in Philadelphia to promote the colony and make it a model for the rest of the nation. They divided up 1,000 acres among 100 freedmen for their own cultivation, ultimately leasing them the land, rather than granting it to them as was done in the South Carolina Sea Islands or even selling it to them. Nevertheless, at the beginning, the effort worked, and until crops could be planted, the bureau issued rations to the former slaves and protected them with several companies of soldiers from the USCT. For many in the North, there was much poetic justice in seeing the land belonging to the former president of the Confederacy turned over to former slaves.

As the "experiment" continued, much confusion reigned in Washington and within the federal bureaucracy. At first, land was leased to the former slaves and credit lines extended. The land was turned over to whites, who then hired the former slaves, a temporary measure that caused immense frustration and disappointment, just as it had in the

Sea Islands. Many of the freedmen discovered, much to their amazement, that their former masters had proved far more trustworthy than the Yankees.

But the numbers of slaves collecting at Davis Bend had increased dramatically, swelling at one point in early 1864 to more than 10,000. In response, the Army and then the bureau began pouring resources into the colony, setting up a hospital and several schools. By 1865, about a dozen teachers were instructing anywhere from 700 to 1,000 eager students. The work on the Hurricane plantation was an unqualified success, with the freedmen building houses, investing in their lands, and producing crops that brought a profit.

After the Montgomery family returned in the summer of 1865, they organized the black farmers and obtained government leases of the lands for them. Benjamin Montgomery even formed a "Colored Planters" group that sought to take control of the only cotton gin on the plantation and process the cotton at a lower price than the government could obtain. Montgomery continually challenged bureau agents to promote his interests and those of the "Colored Planters" and maintained contact with his former owner, Joseph Davis. As Davis suffered from the Confederate defeat, Montgomery—who had saved his profits from his store—sent his former master writing paper, cigars, and $400. Both cooperated in opposing the Freedmen's Bureau, Montgomery to promote his business and plans for the future of the Hurricane plantation, and Davis to seek restitution of his property and his losses as a result of the Union occupation. The world had surely turned upside down.

For his own part, Montgomery leased more than 200 acres, and as the bureau withdrew

---

[16] Hermann, *Pursuit of a Dream*, quoted 46.

its agents from the Bend, the local African Americans moved in and produced cotton and sufficient crops to feed themselves. Montgomery reopened his store, and under his direction Hurricane became largely self-supporting, with a judicial system and schools that had black teachers chosen by the residents and paid for out of revenue raised through their own assessments. Montgomery was able to keep interlopers at bay by lending up to $20,000 for his fellow ex-slaves to rent the land they had been working.

His store and planting had been so profitable that he could not only guarantee such a sum for the former slaves' rent payments, but he could also buy Hurricane and Brierfield from Joseph Davis. The two men worked out a secret deal in which Montgomery would pay Davis $300,000 over ten years for the lands that had been restored to him. The extent of Davis's commitment is astonishing, given that at the time the state's black codes barred the sale of land to blacks. His intent, however, was to extend his prewar vision well into the future, but this time as a free black colony, owned and run by African Americans.

When Joseph Davis died in the fall of 1870, the Montgomery business interests flourished, and the following year Benjamin's crop produced 2,500 bales of cotton—an outstanding figure. Moreover, the quality of his cotton was superior, winning awards at the 1870 annual St. Louis Agricultural Fair for the best long-staple cotton and in 1876 at the Philadelphia Centenary Exposition for the best short-staple cotton in the world, beating out Egypt, Brazil, and the Fiji Islands. Indeed, Montgomery may have become the third largest planter in all of Mississippi. His company, Montgomery & Sons, became nationally known and in 1873

received R. G. Dun's highest credit ranking, with his business worth valued at $230,000, equal to about $4 million today. The journey from a Virginia slave to a Reconstruction cotton magnate still amazes.

Clearly, Montgomery owed much to his patrons, especially Joseph Davis. Yet his ability to outmaneuver his white competition speaks to his talent, foresight, and discipline. Few people of any background could have accomplished as much as he did. His wife, Mary, and other relatives joined in his various ventures, and all showed remarkable business talent. For several years, Benjamin and Mary lived the life of wealthy planters, actually residing in Jefferson Davis's former home, with its 16-foot ceilings and 10-foot windows. He even received the dubious praise of local whites, who declared him "a sensible darky" who paid $2,447 in taxes and "does not dabble in politics, and does not corrupt himself hunting offices that he is incompetent to fill."[17] His ability to tolerate such praise and ingratiate himself into white racist society proved the key to his success, a strategic talent he passed on to his son Isaiah. Both men followed accommodationist political policies that intended to deflect white opposition away from their efforts. It would be a tactic that Booker T. Washington would turn into an art form and Isaiah Montgomery would later use to protect his own black community at Mound Bayou.

Beginning with the financial depression of 1873 and the expansion of their business into Vicksburg, the fortunes of Montgomery & Sons began to decline. Cotton prices fell and continued to fall over the course of the late 1870s, which caused a corresponding

---

[17] Hermann, *Pursuit of a Dream*, 195.

decline in property values. By 1876, Benjamin Montgomery was facing bankruptcy, and his plantations—the basis for the experiment at Davis Bend—ended up on the auction block, where Jefferson Davis reclaimed them two years later. Nearly broke, Benjamin Montgomery died in 1877, and within two years his firm had gone bankrupt.

And what of the freedmen whom both Joseph Davis and Benjamin Montgomery had hoped to serve and protect? Like so many other blacks across the South, they became entrapped in the cycle of debt inherent in the peonage system. Those who could escaped with the other "Exodusters," the name given to African Americans looking for a new start in Kansas and elsewhere in the West. One son, Thornton, even relocated to Fargo, North Dakota. By 1886, no one from the Montgomery family lived at Davis Bend.

Isaiah Montgomery (1847–1924) also became enamored with the movement west and bought land near Topeka, Kansas, to establish a colony just as his father had done in Mississippi. But he could never bring himself to move there. Instead, he invested his assets in some uncleared land about halfway between Vicksburg and Memphis, Tennessee, where he founded the town of Mound Bayou in 1888. In three extraordinarily difficult years, he managed to clear enough land for the town, establish a lumber business with the trees he cleared, and grow almost 400 bales of cotton, earning almost $9,000. In 20 years, 800 black families—about 4,000 people—had settled in the new colony. The community owned about 30,000 acres, with cotton planted on about 6,000. They built banks, two schools, and six churches, and the AMA even supported an industrial training school there.

Montgomery employed a town-meeting style of government, which gave equal voice to men and women. Learning from his father's experience, Isaiah determined that the key to success lay not only in shrewd business deals but in land ownership, political accommodation, and, ironically, self-imposed racial segregation. Keeping out the controlling interests of whites would, he held, protect black ability to own land, and thus guarantee security and stability.

The price of accommodation, however, proved dear. When Jim Crow society was at its height, Montgomery walked softly and supported the near total disfranchisement of the state's African American population in exchange for peace, an "era of progress." While whites North and South applauded Montgomery's views, black leaders in the North competed to make the most searing indictments of him. Although Frederick Douglass honored the accomplishments of Montgomery and his family, he could not tolerate the abandonment of a central core of his lifelong campaign for black rights. Montgomery's willingness to give up on black suffrage represented "a positive disaster to the race."[18]

In 1909, the centennial year of Lincoln's birth, Montgomery was asked to join President Theodore Roosevelt in ceremonies at Lincoln's birthplace near Hodgenville, Kentucky. There, he placed a copy of the Emancipation Proclamation in the cornerstone of the monument, an act that meant to cast light as much upon his success at Mound Bayou as on the "Great Emancipator." But within five years, his treasured community had crumbled. Northern white investors to whom Montgomery had turned—in violation of his own principles—for the construction

---

[18] Hermann, *Pursuit of a Dream*, 230.

Isaiah Montgomery House, Mound Bayou, Mississippi. Undated photograph. Library of Congress.

of a cottonseed oil–processing plant now demanded payment of their loans. The local bank failed, cotton prices tumbled, and with the onset of the First World War, the Great Migration was in full force, drawing off many black workers with the hope of a better life in the North. "Financial blight" ruined the town, from which it never recovered. For about 25 years, however, the colony at Mound Bayou prospered and fulfilled the expectations of a white slaveholder who had dreamed of this sort of community about 100 years earlier. But at the outset of the new century, the black residents of the daring experiments at Davis Bend and Mound Bayou shared the same fate of other African Americans across the South:

without prospects, without land, and without the political rights that Isaiah Montgomery thought would threaten the economic life of his community.

Other African Americans in the South chose a different path, even as the chasm between the races grew deeper and wider under the harsh regime of Jim Crow. During the 1890s, de jure segregation would become entrenched, sanctified as the law of the land by the Supreme Court in 1896. By 1900, anti-black violence and lynching had reached epidemic proportions, and hard-won political and legal rights had been erased. For example, the last black man in Congress from the 19th century, North Carolina's George Henry White

For African Americans, she remarked, the "lesson this teaches . . . is that a Winchester rifle should have a place of honor in every black home and it should be used for that protection which the law refuses to give."

(1852–1918), would serve from 1897 until 1900. For the next 28 years, no African American would set foot in the U.S. Congress, except as a worker. In 1898, in Wilmington, North Carolina, whites, disgusted by the idea of black men and their white Republican allies holding political office, rampaged through the black community and staged a coup d'état, removing a constitutionally elected administration from office.

Nevertheless, as doors were closing, many African Americans and their allies in the North and South continued to test the limits of repression. Tennessee's Ida B. Wells (1862–1931) is the most famous of the many opponents of lynching and racial oppression, women and men who risked their lives to challenge injustice. Her 1892 anti-lynching tract, *Southern Horrors: Lynch Law in All Its Phases*, was a landmark work that helped create a national resistance movement to lynching. Her work dismissed southern charges that black men represented an inherent threat to the chastity of white womanhood and explained that this fanciful allegation simply masked white desire to reinstitute racial subjugation for economic reasons. For African Americans, she remarked, the "lesson this teaches . . . is that a Winchester rifle should have a place of honor in every black home and it should be used for that protection which the law refuses to give."[19]

In New Orleans on a warm and cloudy June 7, 1892, Homer Adolph Plessy (1863–1925), a little-known activist who had worked as a carpenter, shoemaker, clerk, and insurance collector, took his seat on an East Louisiana Railway train headed to Covington, Louisiana. Plessy, who easily could have passed for white, sat in the car designated for whites only. When the conductor passed to collect tickets, Plessy calmly informed him that he was African American. When advised that he would have to remove to the "colored" car, he refused. Hauled off the train, Plessy landed in jail for violating Louisiana's 1890 law requiring "that all railway companies carrying passengers in their coaches in this state, shall provide equal but separate accommodations for the white, and colored races."

Homer Plessy was freeborn, as was his father; he spoke French, and before the Civil War his relatives had labored as blacksmiths, carpenters, and shoemakers—free men, not slaves. His mother, Rosa Debergue, worked as a seamstress, and his father, Adolphe Plessy, labored as a carpenter who, during the 1870s, had sought to expand black rights in the state. His son would now do the same in the 1890s. Homer Plessy boarded the train on that June day to make a difference, volunteering to assist the New Orleans–based "Citizens' Committee to Test the Constitutionality of the Separate Car Law" (*Comité des Citoyens*), an African American civil rights group that set out to destroy Jim Crow and overturn

---

[19] Gates, *Life Upon These Shores*, 195 quoted.

French Quarter, New Orleans, Louisiana, by William Henry Jackson, circa 1880–1897. Photograph. Library of Congress.

all the destructive civil rights–related decisions of the U.S. Supreme Court of the previous 20 years.[20] Central to the case, however, was the fearless Ohio-born judge, author, and Radical Republican named Albion W. Tourgée (1838–1905).

[20] For the most detailed account of Plessy's life, see Keith Weldon Medley, *We as Freemen*: Plessy v. Ferguson (Gretna, LA: Pelican Publishing, 2003). The text of the 1890 act is at the Center for Digital Research in the Humanities, University of Nebraska–Lincoln, Louisiana Railway Accommodations Act, *Railroads and the Making of America*, http://railroads.unl.edu/documents/view_document.php?id=rail.gen.0060.

Unjustly overlooked today, Tourgée reached near-celebrity status in his own day. He volunteered for military duty in the Civil War, had been severely wounded at the first Battle of Bull Run, and spent time in a Confederate prison. After the war, he moved to North Carolina, seeking a warmer climate for his health. He remained there from 1865 until 1879, most of the time serving as a justice on the state's Supreme Court. His experience, especially with the many cases involving Klan crimes against African Americans, made him a champion of Radical Reconstruction and an uncompromising defender of African American civil rights.

Tourgée is usually remembered for his stunning novel based on his time in the South, *A Fool's Errand by One of the Fools*, which was first published in 1879 and greatly expanded the following year.[21] Tourgée published sequels to his popular first novel and also his own influential newspaper column, "A Bystander's Notes," in the Chicago *Inter Ocean*, a Republican organ that gave voice to African Americans and civil rights issues. In a familiar condemnation, Tourgée's column censured the Republican Party for abandoning its principles and African Americans. "They no longer say 'this is the party of liberty and justice,'" he wrote, "but 'this is the party of self and profit.'"

His unvarnished opinions on racial injustice outraged critics on both sides of the Mason-Dixon line. The Chicago *Times* called upon "decent" white folks to lynch the opinionated reformer, while Joel Chandler Harris, famed for his *Uncle Remus* stories, denounced Tourgée as "a monomaniac" and a "refugee from his own race."[22]

Tourgée became the lead attorney for the *Plessy* case, working with James C. Walker of New Orleans and Samuel F. Phillips, who had been a Tourgée ally in North Carolina and the attorney in the disappointing Supreme Court decision in the *Civil Rights Cases* (1883) that invalidated Congress's Civil Rights Law of 1875. Tourgée had been a consistent critic of the Louisiana law from the moment it passed in 1890 and used his newspaper column to denounce it. He and the New Orleans Creole community that led the attack on the law wanted to use a light-skinned subject like Plessy to show how arbitrary and indeterminate the definition of "race" really was as part of their multipronged attack on the law and the Supreme Court's evisceration of Reconstruction amendments to the Constitution. In the case of a man who to all appearances looked white, they questioned, how could a law mandating "separate and equal" facilities for blacks be reliably and consistently implemented? In his brief, Tourgée coined a phrase—made famous by the dissenting justice John Marshall Harlan—which he contended must serve as the court's guiding principle in all matters regarding race: if "Justice is pictured blind," then "the Law . . . ought at least to be color-blind."[23]

While familiar to us today, this use of the term *color-blind* originated with Tourgée. He meant that it should undermine the constitutionality of the Louisiana law and, thus, the series of court cases that had severely restricted the rights presumably won by black people as a result of the constitutional amendments following the Civil War. Additionally, Tourgée's brief attacked the court's return to a pre–Civil War interpretation of state and federal relations that gave priority to state sovereignty. Reformers and black activists like W. E. B. Du Bois offered the highest praise for Tourgée, placing him in the same category as William Lloyd Garrison and Frederick Douglass. Others, however, like

---

[21] For work on Tourgée see Mark E. Elliott, *Color-Blind Justice: Albion Tourgée and the Quest for Racial Equality from the Civil War to* Plessy v. Ferguson (New York: Oxford University Press, 2006), and Richard N. Current, *Those Terrible Carpetbaggers: A Reinterpretation* (New York: Oxford University Press, 1988).

[22] Mark Elliott, "Race, Color Blindness, and the Democratic Public: Albion W. Tourgée's Radical Principles in *Plessy v. Ferguson*," *Journal of Southern History* 67 (May 2001), quoted 301–03.

[23] Elliott, "Race, Color Blindness, and the Democratic Public," quoted 318.

THE NADIR AND THE RENAISSANCE
1890–1940

ON MARCH 9, 1892, THREE BLACK MEN WOULD DIE AT THE HANDS OF AN ANGRY WHITE MOB IN MEMPHIS, TENNESSEE—SADLY, ONLY ONE OF MANY SUCH INCIDENTS THAT YEAR, PART OF AN EPIDEMIC OF ANTI-BLACK RACIST VIOLENCE THAT SWEPT THE SOUTH AFTER THE END OF RECONSTRUCTION. While lynching had occurred elsewhere in Tennessee, recently Memphis had been spared. But the opening of a black-owned grocery store that drew customers away from the white-owned store, which until then had been the only game in town, fanned the flames of the racism that burned barely beneath the surface, a set of anti-black attitudes and beliefs that had their basis in economic fears and competition.

Founded so close to the end of the Civil War and the end of Reconstruction, the People's Grocery was celebrated by the black community as a grand achievement, especially since it was co-owned by ten black men in the Memphis community. It was located just beyond the city limits in a mostly black area known as the "Curve," which had been largely abandoned by whites, who had begun to set up white-only neighborhoods within Memphis proper. The Curve and other areas like it across the South were part of the larger phenomenon of "the strange career of Jim Crow," as the historian C. Vann Woodward described it in his book of the same name about the implementation of de jure segregation during the decade of the 1890s.[1] Thomas Moss, a postal worker and homeowner, was considered the head of the enterprise by his fellow blacks; his leadership would earn him the distinction of "ringleader" from whites.

The story goes that a fight broke out between three of the owners of the People's Grocery—Moss, Calvin McDowell, and Henry Stewart—and rival white grocers. In the gun battle, the white men were shot. Moss was said to be in the store at the time of the shooting, and rumor had it that he fled when he heard gunshots. True or not, the three black men were locked up in the county jail, where for the next few days they would await trial, guarded by the black militia the Tennessee Rifles. The men inside would never make it to the courthouse.

By the night of March 8, it was clear that there would be no murder charges; all the white men had lived, and the Rifles left their post. Within hours, on March 9, a white lynch mob stormed the unguarded jail and dragged Moss, McDowell, and Stewart from their cells.

The white vigilantes transported the three men north of the city limits, where they killed them in cold blood. In life, Thomas Moss had been a believer in hard work and business as the right route for African Americans to follow; when faced with death, he left a message to his fellow black neighbors, embracing the political stance he had previously eschewed. Eyewitnesses reported that Thomas Moss begged for his life for the sake of his wife, their child, and their unborn baby, but it was in vain. When asked by his murderers if he had anything more to say, Moss said, "Tell my people to go west. There is no justice for them here."[2]

The grisly lynching could have become just another statistic—or not even been recorded. Records of lynching were notoriously inconsistent, fragmentary, and underreported, for obvious reasons. But Moss and the others had a close friend who would not allow their tragic deaths, or Moss's last words, to be forgotten. While their names have been lost to history—at least to the history that is widely taught in classrooms—that friend's has not. Her name was Ida B. Wells, the outspoken anti-lynching activist who was introduced in the previous chapter.

✦✦✦

BORN INTO SLAVERY IN MISSISSIPPI IN 1862, IDA B. WELLS WAS THE CO-OWNER OF THE NEWSPAPER THE *MEMPHIS FREE SPEECH* AT THE TIME OF HER FRIENDS' LYNCHING. Galvanized by that atrocity, the teacher turned journalist used her paper as a platform to crusade against lynching, gathering

---

[1] C. Vann Woodward, *The Strange Career of Jim Crow* (New York: Oxford University Press, 2002).

[2] Paula Giddings, *Ida: A Sword Among Lions: Ida B. Wells and the Campaign Against Lynching* (New York: Amistad Press/Harper Collins, 2008), 183.

statistics and collecting testimony. She published impassioned editorials, urging people to leave the city that had so gravely disappointed them: "There is . . . only one thing left that we can do; save our money and leave a town which will neither protect our lives and property, nor give us a fair trial in the courts, but takes us out and murders us in cold blood when accused by white persons."[3]

So many African Americans took her blunt words to heart and fled Memphis, largely for Oklahoma, that their absence deprived whites of household help and brought some of the city's businesses to a standstill. When white representatives of the City Railway Company came to Wells's office to ask her to use her newspaper's influence to sway black readers positively, she replied, "The colored people feel that every white man in Memphis who consented to [Moss's] death is as guilty as those who fired the guns which took his life, and they want to get away from this town."[4] Shortly thereafter, her business manager was run out of town by a committee of "leading citizens," who left Wells a note saying that anyone trying to publish the paper again would be killed.

After three months of constant agitation following the grocers' lynching, the office of the *Memphis Free Speech* was burned to the ground. Wells bought a pistol to protect herself in the South, then, out of desperation, took her anti-lynching crusade to the North. She settled in Chicago, and it was here where she wrote the pamphlet *Southern Horrors: Lynch Law in All Its Phases*. She later wrote in her autobiography, *Crusade for Justice*, "They had made me

Ida B. Wells, from Irvine Garland Penn, *The Afro-American Press and Its Editors* (Springfield, MA: Willey & Co., 1891). Engraving. Library of Congress.

an exile and threatened my life for hinting at the truth."[5] An uncompromising advocate for civil rights and a gifted speaker, Wells traveled across the country and Europe to draw attention to the issue of white violence against black people in America.

Once in Chicago, Wells's scope widened to include the tensions confronting African Americans in their new urban world, one that included competition for housing and jobs, often with poor white immigrants, in a way they had not experienced before. Her interest was also focused on issues confronting women particularly, and in 1896, she founded the National Association of Colored Women. Wells believed

---

3 Giddings, *Ida: A Sword Among Lions*, 189.

4 Giddings, *Ida: A Sword Among Lions*, 203.

5 Ida B. Wells, *Crusade for Justice: The Autobiography of Ida B. Wells*, ed. Alfreda M. Duster (Chicago: University of Chicago Press, 1970), 62–63.

Lynching of Jesse Washington, May 15, 1916, by Fred A. Gildersleeve. Photograph. Library of Congress. Known as the "Waco Horror," the 17-year-old farmhand was convicted of raping and murdering a Waco, Texas, white woman named Lucy Fryer. Whites seized him from the courtroom, threw a chain around his neck, and dragged him to City Hall. He was hoisted by the chain over a tree limb, doused with coal oil, set over a fire, and roasted. From 1882 to 1930, 492 such lynchings took place in Texas.

the struggle of black women was part of the greater struggle of American women, and in 1914, she formed the Alpha Suffrage Club. Her goal was to show African American women "that we could use our vote for the advantage of ourselves and our race."[6]

Ida B. Wells's influence on turn-of-the-century African American society was powerful. She had forsaken the South for a major northern city and called on others to join her. She was not alone. Beginning in the 1890s, African Americans began to leave the South in large numbers, headed north and west—the start of what we now call the Great Migration.

Economic opportunities beckoned in the northern cities certainly; but for many African Americans, the decision to flee was made in response to the concerted white-supremacist effort to roll back the gains of Reconstruction, an effort that combined the constant threat of violence with economic exploitation to put an end to black political participation in the South.

The flow of African Americans northward that began in the 1890s became a torrent in the first decades of the 20th century. Between 1910 and 1920, northern cities saw an unprecedented explosion of growth in their black populations. In New York, the black population grew by 66 percent; in Chicago, 148 percent. In Philadelphia and Detroit, the number of blacks making new homes for themselves was off the charts, with 500 and 611 percent growth respectively.[7] The Great Migration was one of the largest mass movements of citizens in American history, one that permanently changed not only African American society, but the larger American society as well.

---

[6] Wells, *Crusade for Justice*, 345–46.

[7] "The Western Migration," *In Motion: The African-American Migration Experience*, http://www.inmotion-aame.org/print.cfm:jsessionid=f83023836413530795847 16?migration=6&bhcp=1.

As black people from the South arrived in the North in ever-greater numbers, class and regional tensions flared up within the African American community itself. Perhaps not surprisingly, some of the descendants of the free Negroes in the North were horrified by the arrival of such a large number of their uneducated southern brothers and sisters, whom they saw as English-torturing country Negroes crowding into their black Mecca and embarrassing them in front of the white elite. The sociologist Charles S. Johnson, at the height of the Harlem Renaissance in 1925 (which we will visit again later in this chapter), described them in Alain Locke's anthology, *The New Negro*, as "the slow moving black masses." In the essay, which is included in Locke's section aptly called "The New Negro in a New World," Johnson expressed sympathy for these newcomers leaving the "old strongholds," who, "with their assorted heritages and old loyalties, face[d] the same stern barriers in the new environment."[8] These barriers were erected not only by northern whites, but by the northern blacks long settled there as well.

This class split between the descendants of slaves not freed until the end of the Civil War and the descendants of free northern Negroes had been expressed in print as early as 1865, when a black journalist writing in *The Christian Recorder* said that "the colored people down South are not so dumb as many suppose them to be."[9] And these class tensions only became exacerbated as Jim Crow practices deprived the former slaves

of education and economic opportunities for advancement. By the time the Great Migration began in 1890, there were dramatic differences between the social and economic status of the northern black middle class and the southern working classes, and these differences would come to the surface in various ways as more and more southerners moved north.

One of the most interesting manifestations of this unfortunate phenomenon, as we shall see later in this chapter, was cultural: Ragtime and the classic blues and jazz were art forms sustained in the main by the popular support of "the masses," regular, working-class black people, many of them the recent migrants, while the "higher arts" of literature, painting, sculpture, and so forth were art forms aimed at the black middle class, the group that W. E. B. Du Bois had defined in 1903 as the "Talented Tenth," by which he meant the "college-bred Negro." The Harlem Renaissance artists advocated the creation of these "higher arts" as a way to fight anti-black racism. Popular vernacular forms were often felt to be vulgar and somewhat embarrassing, thereby hampering the goal of using the arts to transform the image of the race among middle-class white Americans.

Some northerners blamed the new migrants for increased racial hostility from whites, while some of the newcomers accused the light-skinned northern elite of being "would-be whites" and "sellouts," harsh opinions that Marcus Garvey—the leader of a massive movement of black working-class people in African American history, including many of the recent migrants—would voice in his speeches over and over, especially in his denunciations of his archrival and nemesis Du Bois, whom he characterized both as an elitist (which he was) and as a mulatto who both wanted to be white and

---

[8]   Charles S. Johnson, "The New Frontage on American Life," *The New Negro*, ed. Alain Locke (New York: Atheneum, 1992), 291.

[9]   Henry Louis Gates, Jr., "The Truth Behind '40 Acres and a Mule,'" *100 Amazing Facts about the Negro, The Root*, January 7, 2013, http://www.theroot.com/views/truth-behind-40-acres-and-mule?page=0,0.

who despised darker-complexioned black people (neither of which were true). The arrival of southern blacks in such large numbers in the North exposed class, cultural, and political differences within the African American community and revealed competing views about how black people could best navigate the era's obstacles.

It was in this agitated environment that the term *Uncle Tom* gained popularity as a damning one. When Harriet Beecher Stowe first published her novel *Uncle Tom's Cabin* in 1852, it was met with near-universal praise, including from black critics. Uncle Tom himself was viewed as noble and brave, certainly not an object of contempt and derision; after all, he died protecting two black female slaves. Frederick Douglass took issue with Stowe's advocacy of returning black people to Africa, and the writer William "Ethiop" Wilson criticized the novel's celebration of "nonresistance" in his book review in the abolitionist newspaper *The Liberator*. But these criticisms were leveled more at Stowe and her novel than at Uncle Tom himself. That would all change, though, around the turn of the 20th century. As early as 1893, the *Indianapolis Freeman* editorialized that "the trouble with the Negro has been, and is to-day, he's got too much 'Uncle Tom,' good 'humble darkey' stock in his rank; and not enough of the Nat Turner blood, without which he need not look to be respected or go forward."[10]

Marcus Garvey brought the term to the fore in 1919, frequently brandishing it at Du Bois in their ever-escalating war of words. (The term retained its power over time, and Malcolm X famously branded Martin Luther King, Jr., an Uncle Tom in 1963.) The Reverend George Alexander McGuire, a follower of Garvey, drew a line sharply in the sand between the "old Negro" and the "new Negro," as Locke would do in *The New Negro* a few years later. And guess which side of the line poor Tom stood on? "The Uncle Tom nigger has got to go," spewed McGuire, "and his place must be taken by the new leader of the Negro race . . . not a black man with a white heart, but a black man with a black heart."[11]

Distinctions were drawn not only between northern and southern, rich and poor, educated and uneducated, but also on perceived personal traits that apparently had everything to do with the aforementioned. And just as the arrival of southern blacks in the North was met with mixed feelings at best by their northern counterparts, their arrival was not cause for celebration among northern whites either. Those northerners who may have once looked upon southern racists with contempt did not exactly welcome the black southerners pouring into their cities. One manifestation of this was the transformation of Harlem from white to black between 1920 and 1930, as its traditional white and often Jewish residents fled to other all-white neighborhoods to escape the onslaught of the African American migrants and West Indian immigrants who were moving to this country willingly. The migrants soon discovered that the racism they were fleeing in the South was present in the North and West as well. It just took different forms.

---

[10] Adena Spingarn, "When 'Uncle Tom' Became an Insult," *The Root*, May 17, 2010, http://www.theroot.com/views/when-uncle-tom-became-insult?page=0,0.

[11] Spingarn, "When 'Uncle Tom' Became an Insult."

✦✦✦

OVER THE COURSE OF THIS BOOK, WE'VE SEEN HOW AFRICAN AMERICAN HISTORY WAS PROFOUNDLY INFLUENCED BY KEY INVENTIONS AND TRANSFORMATIVE TECHNOLOGIES. The sextant, the slave ship, the cotton gin—each shaped history by helping to make slavery possible and profitable. In the Jim Crow era, another influential, albeit overlooked, technology was at work: chromolithography, the new color-printing process that made it possible and inexpensive to create the racist Sambo-style depictions of African Americans that appeared in a wide array of American communications media, from advertising and popular novels to sheet music and postcards. Degrading racist images of blacks could now be distributed to every corner of American society, cheaply and to a degree unimaginable before 1890. They were disseminated to an astonishing degree as the visual, popular-cultural wing of the war to limit black rights in the South, and indeed throughout the North. The onset of Jim Crow laws and cultural practices was a complex effort to erase completely the gains and promise of equality that Reconstruction held out for the black community. And it was devastatingly effective, in part because of the efficacy of the huge proliferation of millions of these Sambo images. Virtually everywhere a white person saw an image of a black person, it was a Sambo figure. The powerful—and lasting—subliminal effects of this veritable campaign of anti-black racist propaganda cannot be underestimated.

In the harsh era defined by *Plessy v. Ferguson*'s doctrine of "separate but equal," these images of deracinated, stupid, lazy, and clownish Negroes played a critical role. The ubiquitous racist caricatures justified Jim Crow by graphically illustrating why the separation of the races was necessary and turned the idea of racial equality into a joke. These images shaped whites' perceptions of black people and sometimes distorted blacks' perceptions of themselves.

"Jim Crow was more than a series of 'Whites Only' signs. It was a way of life that approximated a racial caste system," wrote David Pilgrim, the curator of the Jim Crow Museum of Racist Memorabilia in Big Rapids, Michigan. "The Coon character, for example, depicted black men as lazy, easily frightened, chronically idle, inarticulate, physically ugly idiots. . . . The Coon and other stereotypical images buttressed the view that blacks were unfit to attend racially integrated schools, live in safe neighborhoods, work in responsible jobs, vote, and hold public office." Pilgrim, who refers to himself as a "garbage collector," said these and other similar images were a source of shame to the African Americans who had nothing to do with their production. "With little effort I can hear the voices of my black elders—parents, neighbors, teachers—demanding, almost pleading, 'Don't be Coon, be a man.' Living under Jim Crow meant battling shame."[12]

In segregated turn-of-the-century America, demeaning racial stereotypes were not confined to print media. They had long been an integral part of American popular entertainment, evident in the tradition of blackface performance, which began well before the Civil War. In the Jim Crow era, black entertainers

---

[12] David Pilgrim, "The Garbage Man: Why I Collect Racist Objects," *Jim Crow Museum of Racist Memorabilia*, February 2005, www.ferris.edu/htmls/news/jimcrow/collect/.

had little choice but to bring the popular racial stereotypes onstage, and many made a living by what white performers had done for decades: performing "coon" songs and minstrel acts. Still, some African American performers found ways to subvert the stereotype, turning blackface into a subtle vehicle of social and political commentary, even an expression of shared humanity that the Sambo image was meant to deny.

Bert Williams was one such performer, among the most popular comedians of the vaudeville era, black or white. His star shone, it seemed, in spite of his skin color, at a time when the color line in entertainment was still extremely bold. The historian Fitzhugh Brundage said of the great performer: "Williams humanized blackface by transforming his blackface characters into surrogates for anyone who was down on his luck, who never caught a break, or who shuffled from one mishap to the next. That Williams performed in blackface and turned his character into a forlorn everyman that audiences, white and black, empathized with was a feat of remarkable and subversive artistry."[13]

In the aftermath of Emancipation and Reconstruction, whites intent on restoring the status quo used Sambo as a part of a broad attempt to undermine any legal, cultural, and psychological steps taken toward racial equality and black self-assertion. The production and dissemination of demeaning caricatures of black people, many of which appeared in advertisements, were part of a broad and unprecedented campaign to harness the power of mass communications and mass consumption to stigmatize and marginalize an entire race. Looking back, the concerted effort to dehumanize black people amounted to an American rehearsal for many of the propaganda techniques that the Nazis would use a few decades later as part of their extermination campaign against the Jews.

The assault on blacks in the Jim Crow era was not merely psychological, nor was it merely the province of an extremist fringe, as many today might like to believe. Many leaders of the nation's educational and political establishment accepted the deeply racist assumptions of the day. We need look no further than at the man who occupied the highest office in the nation for proof. President Woodrow Wilson, a respected intellectual and former Princeton professor, segregated his administration and admired the virulently racist D. W. Griffith film *The Birth of a Nation*, which he proudly screened at the White House.

The following section explores these images in greater depth.

[13] W. Fitzhugh Brundage, "Beyoncé, Bert Williams, and the History of Blackface in America," *UNC Press Blog*, March 2, 2011, http://uncpressblog.com/2011/03/02/w-fitzhugh-brundage-beyonce-bert-williams/.

In the aftermath of Emancipation and Reconstruction, whites intent on restoring the status quo used Sambo as a part of a broad attempt to undermine any legal, cultural, and psychological steps taken toward racial equality and black self-assertion.

FROM THE EARLY 19TH CENTURY UNTIL WELL INTO THE 20TH, DEMEANING IMAGES OF AFRICAN AMERICANS PROLIFERATED THROUGHOUT THE ATLANTIC WORLD.

In newspapers and magazines; on music scores; in advertising, handbills, posters, postcards, and trading cards; on boxed and canned foods; on every conceivable kitchen and household item, a flood of belittling and sneering images of black Americans cascaded over the public.

Finding no end of inspiration in the untold number of late-19th-century stage versions of *Uncle Tom's Cabin*—most having almost no connection to Harriet Beecher Stowe's 1852 novel—printers and lithographers manufactured hundreds of posters and playbills depicting gross distortions of the book's title character. But no one was treated more unfairly than Topsy. She, more than anyone, in the late 1800s became the archetype for the foolish, impish, ugly, and ignorant black.

It would be a serious mistake to assume that these depictions were the sole responsibility of white southerners—far from it. Such items were largely created in the North, printed in New York and Chicago and in other northern publishing centers, and could be found throughout the country, advertising everything from stove polish to food to tobacco. The Dixon's Stove Polish advertisement that follows, for instance, promoted a firm in Lynn, Massachusetts, and was printed in Boston on January 24, 1861.

Out of insult grew an industry. One man, however, was responsible for more disparaging images of African Americans than anyone else. Born in 1834 in Greenwich Village, New York, and living until 1917—his long life spanning an era of momentous change for blacks— the then-famous illustrator Thomas Worth sketched hundreds, perhaps thousands, of magazine covers and prints, many for the firm of Currier & Ives. Best known for its nostalgic images of 19th-century folk and pastoral scenes for middle-class Americans—images of Americana still available and treasured— Currier & Ives also bears the responsibility for one of the most damaging print series in American history.

Worth's "Darktown" series can be difficult viewing today. Meant to entertain middle-class whites with what were thought to be harmless lampoons, the series both exercised decisive influence and reflected popular white views of African Americans. By 1884, at least 84 different prints in the series had been published, 30 produced just in one year, and there may have been as many as 200 different versions in the series. Although the number of such Currier & Ives prints declined by 1890, still nearly one half of the firm's entire output was taken up by the "Darktown" series. Worth himself estimated that the firm had printed at least 73,000 copies of his work.

Worth and his many imitators employed humor to segregate people of African descent into a realm of subjugation and buffoonery, and with the advancements in the fields of print technology and photography, distributing such images became easy and ubiquitous. In them, as we can readily see, people of African descent are rendered as half-human caricatures dwelling in a shadow realm intended to prove their inability to live middle-class lives, or indeed *any* life not characterized by ineptitude and ignorance. The myriad depictions reinforced social and political values designed to economically and politically disfranchise an entire race. They systematically attacked every aspect of African Americans' lives, from their political rights to family life, to their business enterprises, even their military prowess— an especially grievous act considering the indispensable contribution of black soldiers in the Civil War. Such caricatures effaced an entire people and their place in American culture.

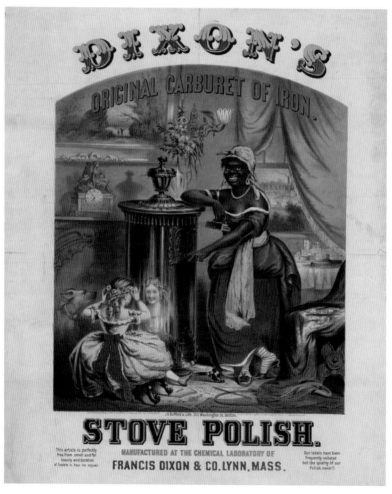

Dixon's Stove Polish, by J. H. Bufford, Boston, November 23, 1860. Lithograph. Library of Congress.

Liberty Frightenin de World, by Currier & Ives, "Darktown" series, New York, 1884. Lithograph. Library of Congress. This disturbing image, actually a mockup of the print that Currier & Ives published, came out two years *before* the erection of the Statue of Liberty and was entitled *Barsqualdi's Statue*, a pun on the sculptor's name and the corruption in the administration of New York Harbor. In the final version of the lithograph, the large volume held by the caricature of an African American was emblazoned with "New York Port Charges." Thomas Worth simultaneously satirized black civil rights and the city's administration.

Additionally, for more than 100 years, minstrelsy served as the nation's dominant form of public entertainment. Virtually every town of any significant size hosted a minstrel show, and usually several at the same time. The advertisements for the performances reprinted here are typical—and similar in intent to the "Darktown" series. They could, however, as in the case of the *George Thatcher's Greatest Minstrels* images, take on an extremely disturbing quality, depicting African Americans as gross, misshapen beings and as the aggregation of society's stereotypes, which they themselves created. Equally important, as the *Coon Hollow* image—printed in New York—affirms, there was only one small step between the demeaning racial humor of the minstrels and lynching in defense of white womanhood.*

---

*Karen Dalton, "Currier & Ives Darktown Comic: Ridicule and Race," unpublished manuscript, W. E. B. Du Bois Institute, 1996.

A Political Debate in the Darktown Club, by Currier & Ives, New York, 1884. Lithograph. Library of Congress.

Cavalry Tactics, by the Darktown Horse Guards, by Currier & Ives, New York, 1887. Lithograph. Library of Congress.

A Darktown Wedding—The Parting Salute, by Currier & Ives, New York, 1892. Lithograph. Library of Congress.

Initiation Ceremonies of the Darktown Lodge—Part First. The Grand Boss Charging the Candidate, by Currier & Ives, New York, 1887. Lithograph. Library of Congress.

A Darktown Tournament—Close Quarters, by Currier & Ives, New York, 1890. Lithograph. Library of Congress.

Tonsorial Art in the Darktown Style, by Currier & Ives, New York, 1890. Lithograph. Library of Congress.

A Fair Start, by Currier & Ives, New York, 1884. Lithograph. Library of Congress.

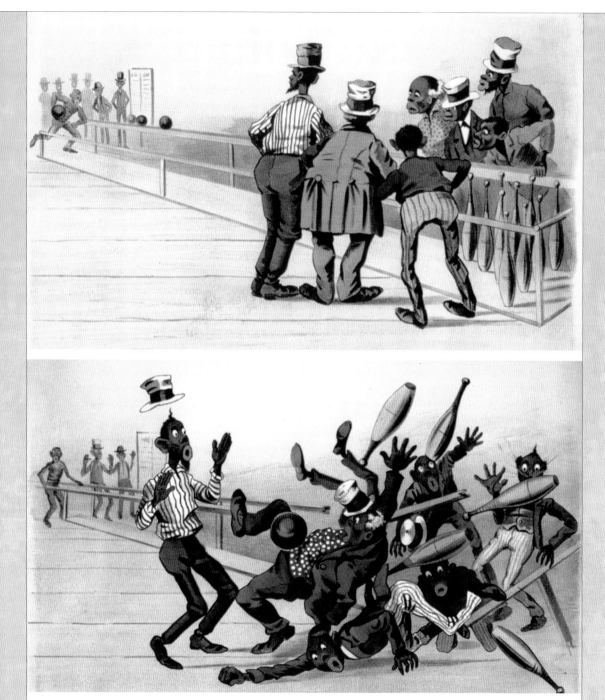

The Darktown Bowling Club. Watching for a Strike and *The Darktown Bowling Club. Bowled Out,* by Currier & Ives, New York, 1888. Lithographs. Library of Congress. These images were also used by the North Carolina Tobacco Company as an advertisement for its loose and plug cut tobacco.

The Golf Crazy Coons, by Strobridge & Co., Cincinnati and New York, 1899. Lithograph. Library of Congress.

Coon Hollow, by Strobridge & Co., Cincinnati and New York, 1894. Lithograph. Library of Congress.

Hello! My Baby, by Strobridge & Co., Cincinnati and New York, 1899. Lithograph. Library of Congress. In one of the many disturbing images to advertise performances of George Thatcher's Greatest Minstrels, stereotypes are fed into a machine to produce pickaninnies. While the image would appear to blame African Americans for the stereotypes that plagued them, upon closer examination, the master of the mill is actually a man in blackface, thus revealing the true author of the images.

George Thatcher's Greatest Minstrels, by Strobridge & Co., Cincinnati and New York, 1899. Lithograph. Library of Congress.

Palmer's Uncle Tom's Cabin, by Courier Co., Buffalo, New York, 1899. Lithograph. Library of Congress.

AS AFRICAN AMERICANS IN BOTH THE NORTH AND SOUTH ARGUED OVER HOW BEST TO REFUTE DEMEANING STEREOTYPES, end white violence, roll back the rising tide of the passage of laws designed to set in stone Jim Crow segregation, and chart a path to racial progress and ultimate social and political equality, the example and message of one prominent African American largely defined the terms of the debate between 1895 and his death in 1915. Booker T. Washington (1856–1915), educator, author, and orator, exhorted African Americans to improve themselves by relying on the American values of thrift and self-help, as he had improved himself. His story of triumph over adversity, which he famously chronicled in his autobiography, *Up from Slavery*, had made him one of the most celebrated and influential black leaders in American history.

Washington, born into slavery, saw himself as a black Horatio Alger—and with good reason: At 16, he walked 500 miles to Virginia's Hampton Normal and Agricultural Institute, the South's first black vocational school, to ask for an education. A brilliant student, he absorbed the educational philosophy of Samuel Chapman Armstrong, the founder of the Hampton Institute, and made it his own, going on to found his own school, the Tuskegee Institute in Alabama. (Both are well-respected universities today.) A gifted writer and speaker, Washington became a national figure and spokesman for the generation of African Americans that confronted the birth of Jim Crow segregation.

He also became the focal point of opposition for all those who thought his strategy of valorizing economic development at the expense of the fight for political rights was deeply flawed and destined to fail. In a way, we can say that Booker T. Washington gave metaphorical birth to the political philosophy of his nemesis, the great scholar W. E. B. Du Bois (1868–1963), a philosophy of engagement and agitation that would manifest itself in the birth of both the Niagara Movement and the NAACP, and in several other forms (including black nationalism, socialism, and communism) over the course of Du Bois's long life. (Du Bois would die in 1963, in exile in Ghana, on the eve of the great March on Washington.)

In September 1895, Booker T. Washington was invited to speak to an integrated audience at the Cotton States and International Exposition in Atlanta. Rejecting an emphasis on politics or achievement in letters as the path to black advancement (as Du Bois and his mentor, Cambridge-educated Alexander Crummell [1819–1898], the founder of the American Negro Academy in 1897, would do), Washington stressed the importance of more prosaic endeavors like agriculture and industrial training. Whereas Du Bois embraced a concept of "race development"—a phrase he used frequently—based on the advancement of his so-called Talented Tenth, you might say that Washington targeted his philosophy to everyone else outside of the educated elite—the undeveloped but no less "talented nine-tenths." He called on white America to provide black southerners with jobs and vocational education and told his people, "Cast down your buckets where you are," essentially urging them to accept discrimination and segregation for the time being, eschew the political realm, and concentrate instead on elevating themselves

Booker T. Washington at his desk in Tuskegee, Alabama, circa 1890–1910. Photograph. Library of Congress.

through hard work.[14] Washington was convinced that once African Americans established themselves as artisans, servants, and laborers, civil rights and social equality would eventually follow. Southern and northern whites alike lavishly praised his speech, which we know today as the "Atlanta Compromise."

While there were many dissenting African American voices, Washington's accommodationist views found many followers within the black community and especially among the white business and political elites, which made him the dominant voice in black politics for almost two decades—so much so that during Theodore Roosevelt's administration, Washington rose to become the president's "race man." Indeed, the legacy of his message of black economic empowerment and his focus on community development can still be felt today.

In fact, had Washington been able to convince the leaders of the American business community to foster black economic mobility, especially in the trades and crafts, thus building a strong and broad middle class, he would be remembered, perhaps, as the father of the African American community. But alas, he was not able to do so, and he is not remembered in the way he most probably hoped he would be. (It may come as no surprise to learn that he had his fair share of "Uncle Tom" insults lobbed at him, and there is even a volume edited by Rebecca Carroll called *Uncle Tom or New Negro?* dedicated to reflections on Washington's ultimate contribution to the African American struggle for civil rights.)

His failure was to assume that American society's economic self-interest—a rising tide to

---

[14] Booker T. Washington, *Up from Slavery* (1901; repr., New York: Tribeca Books, 2012), 106.

lift all boats—would trump anti-black racism. It did not. Black economic advancement was seen as competition for scarce resources; furthermore, white European immigrants were able to step into the role within the economy that Washington envisioned for the freedman. Anti-black racism—in the form of de jure segregation, racial violence, the proliferation of Sambo images, and disenfranchisement—ran rampant during Washington's reign as the dominant voice of black political and educational leadership. The historian Rayford W. Logan named this period of African American history not "the Age of Washington" but "the Nadir." And except for slavery, which is a category of evil and despair all its own, Logan was correct.

Closely related to Washington's call for self-improvement and racial uplift was the Negro clubwomen's movement, which coalesced in Ida B. Wells's founding of the National Association of Colored Women. The middle-class women who led these clubs were firmly rooted in the African American church, long a sustaining force in the black community, and sought to advance their people by upholding moral standards such as cleanliness, thrift, and education. Women like Anna Julia Cooper (1858–1964), Nannie Helen Burroughs (1883–1961), Victoria Earle Matthews (1861–1907), and Mary Church Terrell (1863–1954) pursued a "politics of respectability," as the historian Evelyn Brooks Higginbotham has called it, one intended to provide a role model for lower-class women, while also demonstrating to whites that blacks were good, God-fearing citizens worthy of decent treatment.[15]

---

[15] Evelyn Brooks Higginbotham, *Righteous Discontent: The Women's Movement in the Black Baptist Church, 1880–1920* (Cambridge: Harvard University Press, 1993), 14.

While the clubwomen preached middle-class respectability as the road to uplift, an African American woman entrepreneur with a flair for marketing that very respectability followed Washington's prescription of hard work to phenomenal success. Madam C. J. Walker (1867–1919) started out life as Sarah Breedlove, born in Louisiana to former slaves just two years after the Civil War ended. As Madam C. J. Walker, she became America's first African American female business tycoon and self-made millionaire (one or two others had inherited this amount of wealth or were married to millionaires) and a prominent philanthropist and supporter of civil rights. Her success showed that there were opportunities to be seized, even in segregated America, and that adherence to the gospel of black self-reliance could bear fruit—at least for a fortunate few.

Hers may be the ultimate rags-to-riches story. She started out her life in a cabin in the Deep South and lived her last days in an opulent 34-room mansion overlooking the Hudson River. After moving north to Missouri in 1889 at the age of 20, already a widow, she found work as a laundress, one of the few money-making options open to African American women at the time. For the next several years, she would struggle to support herself and her young daughter. But then her career—and wealth and influence—took off in a most amazing way.

> In 1903 as St. Louis prepared for the 1904 World's Fair, Davis [her second husband's name] supplemented her income by working as a sales agent for Annie Turnbo Pope Malone, whose newly created Poro Company manufactured hair-care products for black women. . . . With $1.50 in savings, the thirty-seven-year-old Davis

moved in July 1905 to Denver, Colorado, where she . . . worked briefly as a Poro agent selling Malone's "Wonderful Hair Grower." In January 1906 she married Charles Joseph Walker, a St. Louis newspaper agent . . . . Adopting a custom practiced by many businesswomen of the era, she added the title "Madam" to her name, then began marketing a line of hair-care products as "Madam C. J. Walker." . . .

In September 1906 when Walker and her husband embarked upon an eighteen-month trip to promote her products and train new sales agents, the American hair-care and cosmetics industry was in its infancy. Settling briefly in Pittsburgh from 1908 to 1910, Walker opened her first Lelia College, where she trained "hair culturists" in the Walker System of hair care. In 1910 the Walkers moved to Indianapolis, then the nation's largest inland manufacturing center, to take advantage of its railways and highway system for their largely mail-order business. . . .

In the midst of Walker's growing success, irreconcilable personal and business differences with her husband resulted in divorce in 1912, though she retained his name until her death. The next year her daughter A'Lelia persuaded Walker to purchase a Harlem townhouse on 136th Street near Lenox Avenue as a residence and East Coast business headquarters. In 1916 Walker joined A'Lelia in New York in order to become more directly involved in Harlem's burgeoning political and cultural activities and entrusted the day-to-day management of her Indianapolis manufacturing operation to her attorney, Freeman B. Ransom, and factory

forewoman, Alice Kelly. From 1912 to 1918 Walker crisscrossed the United States, giving stereopticon slide lectures at black religious, business, fraternal, and civic gatherings. In 1913 she traveled to Jamaica, Cuba, Haiti, Costa Rica, and the Panama Canal Zone to cultivate the lucrative, untapped international market. . . .

By 1916 the Walker Company claimed 20,000 agents in the United States, Central America, and the Caribbean. "Walker," according to historian Davarian Baldwin, "marketed beauty culture as a way out of servitude for black women." . . .

During the spring of 1919 Walker's long battle with hypertension began to exact its final toll. On Easter Sunday while in St. Louis to introduce a new line of products, she became so ill in the home of her friend, Jessie Robinson, that she was rushed back to Villa Lewaro in a private train car. Upon arrival she directed her attorney to donate $5,000 to the NAACP's antilynching campaign. During the last month of her life, Walker revamped her will, bequeathing thousands of dollars to black schools, organizations, individuals, and institutions, including Mary McLeod Bethune's Daytona Normal and Industrial School for Girls, Lucy Laney's Haines Institute, Charlotte Hawkins Brown's Palmer Memorial Institute, Washington's Tuskegee Institute, and numerous orphanages, retirement homes, YWCAs, and YMCAs in cities where she had lived. When Walker died at Villa Lewaro, she was widely considered as the wealthiest black woman in America. . . . At the time of her death, Walker's estate was valued at $600,000 to $700,000, the equivalent of

$6 million to $7 million in 2007 dollars. The estimated value of her company, based on annual gross receipts in 1919, easily could have been set at $1.5 million.[16]

The idea that Walker's hair-care and cosmetic products were designed to allow black women to model themselves after whites by straightening their natural hair dogged her throughout her career, but she balked at the notion. Her own hair loss early in life, she said, came from the substandard living conditions of black homes, which led to substandard hygiene, caused especially by a lack of nourishing shampoos and hair conditioners and ointments. The result was severely dry scalp, which led to hair loss. "Let me correct the erroneous impression that I claim to straighten hair," Walker said. "I deplore such impressions because I have always held myself out as a hair culturist. I grow hair. I have absolute faith in my mission. I want the great masses of my people to take a greater pride in their appearance and to give their hair proper attention."[17]

Booker T. Washington openly criticized Walker's operation, claiming that her products promoted white standards of beauty over black. In fact, although he would ultimately have a change of heart, according to Washington's biographer Louis Harlan, he "first opposed membership in the National Negro Business League for . . . cosmetics manufacturers on the ground that they fostered imitation of white

beauty standards."[18] Ironically, though, the words Walker used to describe her larger goals and aspirations for the social condition of black women were firmly rooted in the beliefs and teachings of Washington himself and of the clubwomen. Walker believed that to gain traction in white society and ultimately achieve economic success and independence, blacks needed to make themselves appealing to white society, and attention to appearance was one means of doing this.[19]

Walker's business acumen enabled other black women to improve their own station in life as well. She herself had been helped and inspired by the National Association of Colored Women, members of which had supported her in her early efforts to sell her hair-care products. Walker in turn lifted up thousands of other African American women—erstwhile farmworkers and domestic help—by hiring them as saleswomen, whom she would eventually call "hair culturists." With what began as peddling scalp treatments and cosmetics such as cold cream and face powder door-to-door across the Midwest, Madam C. J. Walker amassed a fortune and achieved a prominence that defied all expectations of what it was possible for an African American woman to achieve—or, for that matter, what it was possible for African Americans and women in general to achieve—at the turn of the century.

Walker's wealth gave her access to the halls of power denied to the majority of African Americans. She was outspoken against the practice of lynching that had been rampant in the years since Reconstruction, and she was an

---

[16] A'Lelia Bundles, "Walker, Madam C. J." *AANB Online*, African American Studies Center, Oxford University Press, http://www.oxfordaasc.com.

[17] A'Lelia Bundles, *On Her Own Ground: The Life and Times of Madam C. J. Walker* (New York: Scribner, 2001), 122.

[18] Bundles, *On Her Own Ground*, 122.

[19] Bundles, *On Her Own Ground*, 268–69.

ABOVE AND FACING PAGE: Advertisements for Madam C. J. Walker and her hair-care products printed by Alco-Gravure, Inc.; Chicago, New York, Baltimore, Kansas City, Atlanta; undated. Collection of Henry Louis Gates, Jr.

advocate for the rights of black soldiers; that cause took on new meaning for her when the architect of her mansion Villa Lewaro, Vertner Tandy (1885–1949), one of New York's first black architects, became a major in the 15th Regiment, widely known as the Harlem Hellfighters.[20] Her political activism brought her and a handful of other Harlem community leaders all the way to the White House for a meeting with President Woodrow Wilson, in which the group planned to discuss the incongruity of black soldiers' fighting for rights abroad while being denied civil rights at home. The president, who became no-torious for the segregation of his White House after promises in 1912 to the African American community of "absolute fair dealing" with them, canceled the meeting.[21]

Interpreted one way, the aphorism "Beauty is in the eye of the beholder" underscored Madam C. J. Walker's notion that attention to one's appearance could help to elevate one's stature. In 1900 at the *Paris Exposition Universelle*—the World's Fair—a remarkable exhibit of photographs curated by W. E. B. Du Bois opened at the *Exposition des Negrès d'Amerique*, allowing white audiences to see

---

[20] Bundles, *On Her Own Ground*, 220.

[21] Bundles, *On Her Own Ground*, 208.

images of beauty that they would likely never have expected: 363 images of "dignified, well-dressed men and women, living in comfortable and even lavish homes, whose furnishings reflected the occupants' sophisticated tastes and refinement." These were among the earlier images of a "New Negro," a concept or a metaphor—in the words of the time, an ideal "race type"—intentionally created and chosen by black leaders at the turn of the century to counterbalance and implicitly "refute the extremely popular images of blacks as deracinated Sambos, lascivious thieves, and oversexed

'coons.'"[22] It was one of the first, if not *the* first, of a series of definitions—visual and textual—of this so-called New Negro; the first installment, as it were, of a series of redefinitions that would appear next in the pages of the literary journal *The Voice of the Negro* in two articles in 1904 (one on "The New Negro" man, the other on "The New Negro Woman"), and culminate in Alain Locke's complete redefinition of a New Negro as an elite artist, the man or woman of letters as the heart of a racial upper-middle-class vanguard, an implicit leader of the race.

---

[22] Henry Louis Gates, Jr., "W. E. B. Du Bois' Talented Tenth in Pictures," *The Root*, December 2, 2010, http://www.theroot.com/views/web-du-bois-talented-tenth-pictures.

Du Bois's Paris exhibition presented photos of the middle-class, college-bred African Americans who embodied the social and intellectual equality of the race—the revered Talented Tenth, mentioned earlier in this chapter. This was the term that he popularized in a seminal essay published in a September 1903 volume entitled *The Negro Problem* and edited by, of all people, his rival Booker T. Washington.

Although often attributed to Du Bois, the term *Talented Tenth* was first coined by Henry Lyman Morehouse (the man, who happened to be white, for whom Morehouse College was named). He used it in an essay published in 1896, first in *The Independent* magazine and reprinted under the same title only two months later in *The American Missionary*. Morehouse's definition shaped Du Bois's use of the term; according to Morehouse, "An ordinary education may answer for the nine men of mediocrity; but if this is all we offer the talented tenth man, we make a prodigious mistake. The tenth man, with superior natural endowments, symmetrically trained and highly developed, may become a mightier influence, a greater inspiration to others than all the other nine, or nine times nine like them."[23]

Morehouse's unapologetic elitism was mediated somewhat in Du Bois's famous redefinition of the concept as applying to the "college-bred" African Americans, but it could never escape its elitist origins, no matter how

much Du Bois would later try, including in a masterful reconsideration of his own essay nearly 50 years later, "Talented Tenth Memorial Address," delivered at the Nineteenth Grand Boulé Conclave of the Sigma Pi Phi fraternity, and reprinted in *The Boulé Journal* in October 1948.

Du Bois's own family was not wealthy or distinguished, but they had been free from the shackles of slavery for more than 100 years. William Edward Burghardt Du Bois was born in 1868 in Great Barrington, Massachusetts. He ventured south for school, studying at Fisk University in Tennessee, then matriculating at Harvard, where he earned an A.B. degree and an A.M. degree in history in 1890 and 1891, respectively. In 1895, he became the first African American to earn a Ph.D., also in history, from the university. Initially a supporter of Booker T. Washington's Atlanta Exposition speech (Du Bois even sought employment at Tuskegee), he would soon decide that Washington's philosophy was accommodationist, and that political and economic rights were not only inextricably linked, but that, in fact, political rights might even precede the promise of economic mobility for African Americans. Du Bois's critique, titled "Of Mr. Booker T. Washington and Others" and published in *The Souls of Black Folk*, was devastatingly searching, and it set in motion a war of words and actions that pitted the two as leaders of rival factions within the race.

Du Bois charged that Washington's emphasis on vocational education and his call to tolerate racism in the short term would consign black people to menial labor forever. In its place, Du Bois argued for a radical agenda of political action that would be achieved by mobilizing

---

[23] Henry Lyman Morehouse, "The Talented Tenth," *The American Missionary* 50, no. 6 (June 1896; Project Gutenberg, November 21, 2006), http://www.gutenberg.org/files/19890/19890-h/19890-h.html.

FACING PAGE: W. E. B. Du Bois, by Carl Van Vechten, July 18, 1946. Photograph. Library of Congress.

an elite vanguard of race leaders. In 1905, he convened a seminal gathering of black intellectuals, predominantly northern, urban, college-educated black men—representatives of Du Bois's Talented Tenth of African American society and the leaders of what became known as the Niagara Movement. This group believed that political agitation, not accommodation, offered African Americans the key to achieving true rights of citizenship. The Niagara Movement defined what would become the modern civil rights agenda: unrestricted suffrage, freedom of speech, and equality before the law.

As the champion of the Talented Tenth, Du Bois's philosophy was proudly elitist—though again, not in the naked and unapologetic form that Morehouse's definition took. The Harvard-educated scholar saw himself and his peers not so much as distinct from the mass of African Americans—especially the seven million black people who lived in the rural South, often working the same land as their slave ancestors, who made up 90 percent of the nation's turn-of-the-century African American population—but as the natural leaders of the race, the "vanguard," as Alain Locke called it. But after the 1906 Atlanta race riot, when Du Bois and his family lived through four days of terrifying racial violence, Du Bois changed course, convinced now that the fates of all black people, educated and uneducated, were inextricably linked.

In 1909, the year after another bloody race riot in Springfield, Illinois—the hometown of Abraham Lincoln—Du Bois and Ida B. Wells joined a group of white activists and philanthropists to create a new biracial association dedicated to the fighting for the rights of black Americans, the National Association for the Advancement of Colored People. The NAACP's emphasis on political action drew heavily on the goals of the Niagara Movement and represented another public and defiant rejection of Booker T. Washington's policy of accommodation and political quietism.

WHILE DU BOIS AND WASHINGTON AND THEIR SUPPORTERS ARGUED ABOUT THE RIGHT PATH TO RACIAL UPLIFT, the most famous African American of the era paid little heed to either side. Battering white men in the ring and bedding white women out of it, Jack Johnson made it clear that he cared little about elite opinion, black or white.

The son of former slaves, Jack Johnson (1878–1946) became the world heavyweight boxing champion in 1908, at the height of the Jim Crow era. It isn't an exaggeration to say that just about everything about Johnson drove most white Americans to distraction: He was strong, athletic, virile, independent, audacious, exhibitionist, and a gadfly. And he was black. Johnson's flamboyant persona aggravated white anxieties about black male sexuality and economic competition—the twin roots of anti-black racism, oppression, and discrimination, from slavery to the present. His victories triggered race riots and brought widespread calls for a "Great White Hope" to strip him of his title. His interracial marriages and affairs produced a national outcry from whites that ultimately resulted in a stunning 21 bills

FACING PAGE: Jack Johnson, Bain News Service, undated. Glass plate photograph. Library of Congress.

Black officers of the 367th Infantry Regiment, 92nd Buffalo Division, circa 1917–1918. Photograph. W. E. B. Du Bois Collection, Special Collections and University Archives, University of Massachusetts, Amherst. The unit arrived in France on July 18, 1918, and went into battle in the Meuse-Argonne.

banning interracial marriage being introduced in Congress. Johnson was arrested twice and convicted once for "transporting women across state lines for immoral purposes," in alleged violation of the Mann Act, the commonly used name for the White-Slave Traffic Act.

It wasn't only whites who feared Jack Johnson. "With his unfettered hedonism, contempt for race taboos, and lack of patriotism," the Oxford University American history lecturer Stephen Tuck observed, "Jack Johnson was Booker T. Washington's worst nightmare

come to life–in pink pajama shorts."[24] He confounded the clubwomen, who saw his dalliances with white women instead of black women as an affront against them. Yet he hardly lacked for black admirers. His victories had thrilled both the people in growing black urban neighborhoods, far outside the parlors and studies of the Talented Tenth, and the no-

[24] Stephen Tuck, *We Ain't What We Ought to Be: The Black Freedom Struggle from Emancipation to Obama* (Cambridge: Harvard University Press, 2010), 131.

ble, hardworking souls who figured so prominently in the speeches of Washington, in areas Tuck described as "places . . . that reformers couldn't reach, and where [the NAACP journal] *The Crisis* wasn't read."[25]

Even Du Bois, no fan of Johnson, would be moved to write editorials defending him, first in a *Crisis* editorial called "Intermarriage," in which he argued in favor of the practice (which was distasteful to the majority of both blacks and whites) on "physical, social, and moral" grounds, most notably that "to prohibit such intermarriage would be publicly to acknowledge that black blood is a physical taint. . . ."[26] Du Bois wrote about Johnson again 18 months later, this time lashing out at the white press for suddenly smearing the sport of boxing as immoral and brutish. Why now, when boxing had been wildly popular for more than a century? The supposed disdain for the sport, Du Bois stated plainly, was thinly veiled disgust for its preeminent athlete:

> The cause is clear: Jack Johnson . . . has out-sparred an Irishman. He did it with little brutality, the utmost fairness and great good nature. He did not "knock" his opponent senseless. Apparently he did not even try. . . . Why then this thrill of national disgust? Because Johnson is black. Of course, some pretend to object to Mr. Johnson's character. But we have yet to hear, in the case of white America, that marital troubles have disqualified prize fighters or ball players or even statesmen.

It comes down, then, after all to this unforgivable blackness.[27]

No amount of black support or boxing prowess could prevent Johnson's fall. After his conviction, he jumped bail and fled the country by way of Canada, making his way first to Europe, then to South America, and ultimately to Mexico, where his seven-year exile finally came to an end. He publicly promoted the idea of an exile community for African Americans. Advertisements for Johnson's Land Company appeared in black newspapers: "COLORED PEOPLE: You who are lynched, tortured, mobbed, persecuted and discriminated against in the boasted 'Land of Liberty,' the United States . . . BUY A HOME IN MEXICO where one man is good as another and it is not your nationality that counts, but simply you."[28]

◇◆◇

THIS WAS A TUMULTUOUS TIME FOR ALL OF AMERICA. With the outbreak of World War I, black Americans wrestled with the question of whether to join the military and fight overseas in the name of freedom when the United States had done so little to protect their freedom at home.

For some African American leaders, including the socialist and labor activist A. Philip Randolph (1889–1979), the answer was a definitive "No!" A promising actor who was brilliant,

---

25 Tuck, *We Ain't What We Ought to Be*, 132.

26 W. E. B. Du Bois, "Intermarriage" editorial, *The Crisis* 5, no. 4 (February 1913), 180.

27 W. E. B. Du Bois, "The Prize Fighter" editorial, *The Crisis* 8, no. 4 (August 1914), 181.

28 Theresa Runstedtler, *Jack Johnson, Rebel Sojourner: Boxing in the Shadow of the Global Color Line* (Berkeley: University of California Press, 2012), 227.

handsome, commanding, entrepreneurial, and something of an organizational genius, and whose interest in social equality was ignited by reading Du Bois's *The Souls of Black Folk*, Randolph had abandoned what he saw as the too-moderate reform agenda of the growing civil rights movement, electing instead the more radical path of craft unionism and socialism. By near the end of the Great War, Randolph had split completely and publicly from the man who had once inspired him, editorializing in his journal *The Messenger* that African Americans were better off fighting on the battlefield at home instead of on the European one, to "make Georgia safe for the Negro."[29]

In a controversial editorial in *The Crisis*, which he would regret ever publishing, printed four months before the war ended, Du Bois had reached the opposite conclusion. He urged African Americans to fight for their country for reasons not grounded in patriotism, but in Du Bois's analysis of what he saw as a global struggle against colonialism and racial oppression. Convinced that the war would shatter the European colonial system and thereby liberate the oppressed people of color of the world, Du Bois called on African Americans to "forget our special grievances and close our ranks . . . with our own white fellow citizens and the allied nations that are fighting for democracy."[30] In the

end, 375,000 African American men served in the United States Army during World War I.

When the African American soldiers came home from Europe, any hopes that their patriotic service would earn them better treatment were quickly dashed. There was a fierce and violent backlash to put black World War I veterans "back in their place." The so-called Red Summer of 1919 brought some of the worst racial violence the country had seen since slavery, with 25 race riots and 70 reported lynchings. One horrifying statistic makes the point: In Europe, during wartime, 773 black American soldiers had been killed by German troops; back home, during the war and in the five years that followed, more than 1,000 black Americans were killed by white mobs.

Into this furious whirlwind came the charismatic Jamaican publisher and orator Marcus Garvey (1887–1940), with a bracing but divisive message of separatism, hope, and Pan-African racial pride. Garvey arrived in Harlem during the war. He was an ardent admirer of Booker T. Washington, although Washington died before they had a chance to meet. Following Washington's death in 1915, Garvey anointed himself to fill the gap that the controversial leader's death left. Appealing to the increasingly militant feelings of African Americans in the wake of the war, Garvey called on black soldiers who had fought for democracy in Europe to join his fight for equal rights at home.

Garvey's Universal Negro Improvement Association (UNIA) campaigned against Jim Crow laws, lynching, the denial of black voting rights, and racial discrimination. Unlike mainline civil rights organizations such as the NAACP, however, Garvey argued for

---

[29] Jervis Anderson, *A. Philip Randolph: A Biographical Portrait* (Berkeley: University of California Press, 1973), 101.

[30] W. E. B. Du Bois, "Close Ranks" editorial, in *W. E. B. Du Bois: A Reader*, ed. David Levering Lewis (New York: Henry Holt and Company, 1995), 697.

FACING PAGE: Marcus Garvey, August 5, 1924. Photograph. Library of Congress.

The Negro Exodus from North Carolina—Scene at the Railway Station. Frank Leslie's Illustrated Newspaper, February 15, 1890. Library of Congress.

segregation rather than integration, because he doubted that white America would ever treat African Americans as equals. The UNIA grew quickly after the war and boasted large chapters in southern states and Cuba; at its height, it claimed six million members around the globe, a figure no doubt heavily inflated. Nevertheless, the UNIA was the largest mass movement of African Americans up to that time and for years to come. In speeches and publications, including his popular newspaper *Negro World,* Garvey preached a gospel of black pride and self-sufficiency and called on African Americans to return to Africa.

Garvey was hugely popular—and hugely controversial. With the slogan "One Aim, One

God, One Destiny" and his emphasis on black solidarity, the UNIA appealed to millions of poor and working-class people. At the same time, his separatist views and belief that Africa was the black man's destiny sharply divided the African American community. Garvey's many detractors felt that he was undoing decades of progress toward integration. Virtually every other black leader of the day opposed him, and almost all publicly excoriated Garvey's overture to the Ku Klux Klan in 1922. The following year, in the September issue of *The Negro World*, Garvey went so far as to proclaim that openly racist and separatist organizations such as the Klan were "better friends of the race than all other hypocritical whites put together."[31]

As shocking as his statements were, there was, sadly, more than an element of truth in Garvey's inflammatory words—not specifically about the Klan, of course, but in their general meaning. With racial segregation an unwelcome fact of American life, African Americans built separate institutions that allowed their communities not only to survive, but to thrive. To do this, they could not stay where they were, and many looked west.

As we learned earlier, the Great Migration began in about 1890 and assumed several forms: First, many black people moved from rural areas to urban areas within the South; second, migrants from the South began moving to urban areas in the North; and third, many set out for cities in the American West, such as Los Angeles and Denver. But the Great Migration was foreshadowed by the Exoduster movement, during which tens of thousands of

black migrants fled the South, searching for economic opportunity in Oklahoma, Kansas, and Colorado in the late 1870s and throughout the 1880s. Then, between 1890 and 1910, along with tens of thousands of white settlers, African Americans took advantage of the U.S. government's division and selling off of the land that is now the state of Oklahoma. Just as the western frontier called to white Americans, the apparent freedom it afforded spoke loudly to African Americans as well. In 1890, a preeminent African American citizen of Oklahoma heaped the loftiest praise on the territory, calling it a "paradise of Eden and the garden of the Gods."[32]

For a time, the Greenwood district of Tulsa, Oklahoma, seemed just such a place; it was the country's richest African American community. And so it still seemed to be in 1921. Black dentists, doctors, lawyers, and businesses catered to the prosperous, segregated enclave, popularly known as the "Negro Wall Street." Black self-sufficiency, the residents of Greenwood understood, was no guarantee against the risk of racial violence; indeed, to many whites, black prosperity—a violation of the racial order that placed blacks at the bottom —was itself a provocation.

The trouble in Tulsa started, as it did in so many other cities, with an unsubstantiated accusation that a black man had sexually assaulted a white woman. The result was the Tulsa race riot, one of the worst in American history. Over two horrific days, May 31 and June 1, 1921, rampaging mobs destroyed block after block of black middle-class homes, with property damage running into the millions of dollars. As many as 68 African Americans were killed, while

---

[31] Neil A. Hamilton, "Garvey, Marcus," *American Social Leaders and Activists, American Biographies* (New York: Facts on File, 2002), 159.

[32] "The Western Migration," *In Motion.*

Tulsa, Oklahoma, race riot, June 1, 1921. Photograph. Associated Press, Press Association Images. White National Guard members rounded up African American citizens of Tulsa and held them in a fairground, convention hall, and baseball stadium, while their 35-block neighborhood was incinerated.

thousands of black residents were rounded up, interned, and tried for inciting the riot. While violent reactions against black economic prosperity were common in this era, such as the riots in Atlanta, Georgia, in 1906, the riots in Tulsa were particularly damaging and deadly.

Despite the dangers still inherent to black life, as was so cruelly evinced by the events in Tulsa, all-black enclaves continued to provide many African Americans a welcome chance to live and create beyond the reach of white control. The scholar Darlene Clark Hine described the black and white world as "parallel universes." "During Jim Crow," she explained, "blacks built an internal, self-sufficient world that existed as if in a parallel universe to the white world. Blacks founded hospitals, nurse training schools, medical schools, pharmacy schools, drug stores, agricultural businesses, banks, private schools, nursery schools, dressmaking, culinary shops, newspapers, music

schools, theaters, night clubs. There were places where the majority of black people were able to live reasonable lives that included minimum contact with the larger white community."[33]

One artist emerged from a similarly insular, seemingly unlikely world: South Dakota. From his vantage point on the black side of the color line, he explored a robust and complicated world that few white people knew existed.

Oscar Micheaux (1884–1951) plumbed his experience as a black homesteader in South Dakota for the subject matter for his early novels. From farming and writing, Micheaux turned to filmmaking, and in 1919, despite a total lack of experience, he launched the Micheaux Book and Film Company with his first silent film, *The Homesteader.* Micheaux, with an outsize talent for promotion, stressed

[33] Darlene Hine Clark, personal communication to Sabin Streeter, February 6, 2012.

to potential white investors that the novelty of his film would make it a goldmine: "... [T]welve million Negro people will have their first opportunity to see their race in stellar role. Their patronage, which can be expected in immense numbers, will mean in [itself] alone a fortune."[34] Micheaux did indeed draw this new audience, and he went on to have a prolific career, producing an average of two "race movies" a year, telling stories about black characters from a black perspective, for a black audience. His films were low budget and often controversial, focusing on taboo subjects like rape, church corruption, and miscegenation. While he came under sharp criticism for his poor production values and his "intraracial color fetishism"–a term used in 1930 in the New York *Amsterdam News* by reviewer Theophilus Lewis, who complained, "All of the noble characters are high yellows; all the ignoble ones are black"–Micheaux offered black audiences complex portrayals of their lives, on film, at a time when they were not available anywhere else.[35]

◆◆◆

IT IS ONE OF THE ABIDING CONTRADICTIONS OF THE JIM CROW ERA THAT IT FEATURED BOTH BRUTAL RACIAL OPPRESSION AND AN UNPRECEDENTED FLOWERING OF AFRICAN AMERICAN CULTURAL CREATIVITY. Some of that creativity blossomed overseas in Paris in the early 1920s, where Josephine Baker's *Le Revue Nègre*

cabaret show was a continental sensation. While Paris would continue to be the destination of many black artists and intellectuals, who felt they enjoyed greater respect and creative freedom abroad, the epicenter of African American culture was here at home, in the capital of black urban life, Harlem.

The Harlem, or New Negro, Renaissance (the names were used interchangeably) was a uniquely rich and vibrant cultural movement in the 1920s, when talented black artists came together and produced an unmatched outpouring of creative work in literature, art, theater, and music. And although metaphorically centered in Harlem, similar artistic movements emerged simultaneously in Washington and Chicago. Black leaders believed that this national ascendance of black culture could redefine how white Americans and the world thought of African Americans, and how African Americans saw themselves. Instead of being seen as a racial underclass, inferior to other races and cultures, they could now be viewed as genuine cultural innovators–members of a community of artistic and intellectual achievers, with a strong identity and sense of pride. The poet Langston Hughes (1902–1967) coined the phrase that came to describe the movement: "The Negro," he wrote in his autobiography, *The Big Sea*, "was in vogue."[36]

It can be said that the Harlem Renaissance had its roots in some unlikely places: in the music of a Czech composer and in the visual innovation of a legendary Spanish painter. Antonín Dvořák is the musician at the heart of this discussion. One of the greatest composers of classical music at the turn of the century, Dvořák

34 Jane M. Gaines, *Fire and Desire: Mixed-Race Movies in the Silent Era* (Chicago: University of Chicago Press, 2001), 121.

35 Gaines, *Fire and Desire*, 148.

36 Langston Hughes, *The Big Sea: An Autobiography* (New York: Macmillan, 1993), 223.

used the folk music of his native culture in Bohemia as the basis for symphonic music and chamber music. While serving as the director of the National Conservatory of Music in New York City, from 1892 to 1895, he met the early African American composer Harry Burleigh (1866–1949). Through Burleigh, Dvořák was introduced to the spirituals, the body of music created by the slaves, which Du Bois called "The Sorrow Songs" in *The Souls of Black Folk*.

In 1893, in the midst of the very decade in which Jim Crow became the law of the land, Dvořák composed his most famous piece of music, Symphony no. 9: *From the New World*—and it was inspired by those very spirituals that had been composed anonymously in the cotton fields of the American South by African slaves. In 1895, the trailblazing black feminist journalist Victoria Earle Matthews penned a groundbreaking essay, "The Value of Race Literature." Just two years after Dvořák created Symphony no. 9, Matthews used the composer's words to support her own call for a new "race literature." "'I am now confident that the future music of this continent must be founded upon what are the called the Negro melodies,'" she quoted Dvořák as saying. "'In the Negro melodies of America I discover all that is needed for a great and noble school of music. . . . There is nothing in the whole range of composition that cannot find a thematic source there.'"[37]

From this, Matthews concluded, "What is bright, hopeful and encouraging is in reality the source of an original school of race literature, of racial psychology, of potent possibilities, an amalgam needed for this great American race of the future." Matthews's words laid the foundation for the coming Harlem Renaissance, which would happen 30 years after she published this article. But there was a problem, one that would not be solved by art or literature or music, no matter how grand. Matthews called for this new, elevated race literature to "drive out the traditional Negro in dialect,—the subordinate, the servant as the type representing a race whose numbers are now far into the millions."[38] So, nearly a decade before Du Bois made famous the term *Talented Tenth*, and a year before it first appeared in print in Morehouse's essay, Victoria Earle Matthews was advocating that the elite must be the representatives of the race. Once again, we see that divide between the Old Negro and the New Negro. At times it seemed that the New Negroes themselves thought there was something wrong with the Old Negroes, and that some of those stereotypical, racist depictions of them were in some way true.

But in 1907, 14 years after Dvořák's discovery of the spirituals, another European made a discovery that would allow the world—not just the white world, but African Americans themselves—to see Africans and their art as beautiful and worthwhile, something to be celebrated and praised alongside all other art. Pablo Picasso, on a visit to the old Trocadero in Paris, found his way into a room (essentially tucked away behind a closet) full of African sculpture and masks. From this chance discovery, Picasso invented an entirely new way of representing the human form in the visual arts. Called Cubism or Modernism today, it was manifested in Picasso's 1907 painting *Les Demoiselles d'Avignon*. The

---

[37] Victoria Earle Matthews, "The Value of Race Literature," in *The New Negro: Readings on Race, Representation, and African American Culture, 1892–1938*, eds. Henry Louis Gates, Jr., and Gene Andrew Jarrett (Princeton: Princeton University Press, 2007), 288.

[38] Matthews, "The Value of Race Literature," 289.

Of all the art forms, however, it was literature
that launched the Harlem Renaissance.

impact of the masks on the faces of the female figures was unmistakable. African masks, until then thought to be ugly and primitive, of anthropological value only and not the least bit artistic, now formed the structuring principle for new ways of seeing and representing the human figure within European art. With the stroke of a brush, the supposedly ugliest and most devalued thing in the world—black Africans and their art—had become beautiful and worthy. This revaluation of African art produced an electric effect on African American writers, critics, and artists, who in the New Negro movement would call for a genuine artistic renaissance, one that would remove the stigmas connoted by the words *Negro* and *African* that had corrupted the words for as long as they were in use. Black, they would announce to the world, was indeed beautiful.

Of all the art forms, however, it was literature that launched the Harlem Renaissance. Its place was paramount, with Langston Hughes the most famous name to emerge from the period, although artists such as Aaron Douglas (1899–1979) and Augusta Savage (1892–1962), singers like Roland Hayes (1887–1977), and actors such as Paul Robeson (1898–1976) were also hailed as exemplars of this emerging genius of the race. The manifesto of the movement, which we've already touched on briefly, was published in 1925, when the scholar and philosopher Alain Locke (1886–1954) celebrated New York's up-and-coming African American writers in his magnificently edited anthology, *The New Negro*. Yet for all their undeniable talents, the Harlem writers were not the transformative force that

their champions claimed. Many of these representatives of the cultured and upper-class portion of the African American community—which they insisted stood for the potential of the community as a whole—adapted white cultural forms while claiming to have realized an unprecedented form of Negro self-expression.

In fact, it was not Harlem's elite writers but rather its popular musicians—men and women who were not likely to be invited to Harlem's New Negro salons—who made the era's most lasting cultural contributions. Jazz and blues, fortified not by the Talented Tenth but by the black working class, transformed Western music and became an international sensation. Locke either underestimated or simply misunderstood the importance of jazz: In the 400-some pages of *The New Negro*, only one essay, J. A. Rogers's "Jazz at Home," addressed the new phenomenon, a telling omission and one reflecting the class tensions dividing the black community. To be fair, Jean Toomer (1894–1967), Langston Hughes, Sterling A. Brown (1901–1989), Zora Neale Hurston (1891–1960), and a few of the younger writers embraced the emerging vernacular cultural forms, both theoretically and in their own works, while James Weldon Johnson (1871–1938) sought to recuperate older vernacular forms such as the spirituals in his magnificent poetry collection *God's Trombones*, but they were against the tide.

One could argue, in retrospect, that the aesthetics of a "New Negro Renaissance" in the 1920s should well have been constructed upon a foundation of the blues and jazz, if that cultural movement were to have the lasting,

Zora Neale Hurston, by Carl Van Vechten, April 3, 1938. Photograph. Library of Congress.

transformative impact that it so urgently sought to have. But the Renaissance did not fashion itself in this way, at least officially. And that was unfortunate. It's true that classics such as the novel *Cane*, by Jean Toomer, and books of poetry such as *The Weary Blues* and *Fine Clothes to the Jew*, by Langston Hughes, and *Southern Road*, by Sterling Brown, along with *God's Trombones*, remain hallmarks of the best of the black tradition. (Hurston's stunningly brilliant novel *Their Eyes Were Watching God* would not be published until 1937, long after the Harlem Renaissance had ended.) The works of art that most brilliantly characterize the spirit of the black 1920s, however, were those by musical geniuses such as the trumpeter Louis Armstrong (1901–1971), the pianist and composer Duke Ellington (1899–1974), and the singers Mamie Smith (1883–1946), Bessie Smith (1894–1937), and Ethel Waters (1896–1977). This fissure in taste was based in class differences, rooted in the history of slavery and Jim Crow. Armstrong and Ellington were inarguably the most influential African American musical artists of this period, but Waters and the Smiths were right alongside them in their remarkable ability to

Langston Hughes, by Jack Delano for the Office of War Information, 1942. Photograph. Library of Congress.

Bessie Smith, by Carl Van Vechten, February 3, 1936. Photograph. Library of Congress.

transcend the seemingly unbridgeable gap between high and low culture.

In the 1930s, as the Depression hit Harlem and the rest of black America especially hard, African Americans remained divided about the way forward in a deeply segregated and sometimes violently repressive America. Some black leaders urged patience, while others organized to push back against Jim Crow. Many argued that the African American community should turn inward and focus on black self-sufficiency during hard times.

Confronted with a new round of troubles, many African Americans turned to their religious leaders, as they had for generations before. In response, some members of the black clergy combined spiritual guidance with political activism. In 1934, as the breadlines in Harlem grew longer, the Reverend John H. Johnson (1897–1995), pastor of the Protestant Episcopal St. Martin's Church, launched a "Don't Buy Where You Can't Work" campaign, aimed at the Harlem department store Blumstein's, which did not hire black people as clerks or cashiers. (Some years earlier, the store

Louis Armstrong, by William P. Gottlieb, New York, summer 1946. Photograph. Library of Congress.

had hired African American porters and elevator operators.) With African American customers accounting for an estimated 75 percent of sales, according to the *New York Age*, the boycott of the store was financially crippling—and ultimately successful. The store owner William Blumstein softened his stance and agreed to hire some blacks to fill these positions, which would have African Americans dealing with customers and money and essentially acting as the public face of a store that until then had hired blacks only in jobs traditionally thought to be acceptable for African Americans. Less than a decade later, Blumstein's department

store would have the country's first black Santa Claus and would pioneer the use of black models and mannequins.[39]

Across town at the Abyssinian Baptist Church, a charismatic preacher would stand to inherit the largest Protestant congregation in the country from his father. The Reverend

---

[39] Christopher Gray, "Streetscapes/Blumstein's Department Store; How a Black Boycott Opened the Employment Door," *New York Times*, November 20, 1994, http://www.nytimes.com/1994/11/20/realestate/streetscapes-blumstein-s-department-store-black-boycott-opened-employment-door.html.

Adam Clayton Powell, Jr. (1908–1972), would turn his religious flock into the basis of a political constituency and would go on to serve in the U.S. Congress from 1945 to 1971.

In the end, the separation of the races demanded by Jim Crow would help to create the means of its destruction: the black civic and religious organizations created by segregation would play a critical role in bringing down the whole rotten edifice. But that day of reckoning was still to come. In the 1930s, "separate but equal" was still the rule, in fact if not in law, and black folks needed some help finding their way through the segregated maze, literally and figuratively.

In 1936, the postal employee and civic leader Victor Hugo Green (1892–1964?) began publishing a travel guide listing hotels, restaurants, and other establishments willing to do business with African Americans. In places where no hotels accepted black guests, Green's guidebook listed "tourist homes," private individuals who would accommodate black visitors. In the years to come, *The Negro Motorist Green Book* would expand in popularity, covering an ever-larger geographical area and offering African American travelers safe routes through their segregated country. "There will be a day some time in the near future," reads a portion of the introduction, "when this guide will not have to be published. That is when we as a race will have equal rights and privileges in the United States."[40]

The Green Book would be published until 1964.

[40] Victor Hugo Green, *The Negro Motorist Green Book: An International Travel Guide* (New York: Victor H. Green & Co., Publishers, 1949). Downloaded as a PDF at www.miroundtable.org.

❖❖❖

THE DEPRESSION HIT AT THE VERY FABRIC OF THE BLACK COMMUNITY, AT ALL OF ITS LEVELS. WITHOUT PATRONAGE, THE HARLEM RENAISSANCE FLOUNDERED. The lyrical modernism of Jean Toomer and Langston Hughes would give way in the '30s to the harsh social realism of Richard Wright's (1908–1960) novels of naturalism, culminating in his masterpiece, *Native Son* (1940). With the community in economic crisis, left-wing political movements such as the American Communist Party became more attractive to black intellectuals and many black workers. But the most important political shift in the 1930s was the dramatic shift of political allegiances of black voters, who had voted consistently for the Republicans, "the party of Lincoln," since receiving the franchise just after the Civil War and until Franklin Roosevelt's second election in 1936, when they embraced Roosevelt's policies of economic amelioration as well as his overtures to the black community through his wife, Eleanor, and his body of informal black advisers. This Negro "kitchen cabinet," as it was called, was headed by the great activist and educator Mary McLeod Bethune (1875–1955). The African American community remains strongly Democratic to this day, as we shall see in Chapter 9.

But it was only the onset of World War II that ended the Great Depression and the attendant extraordinary economic deprivation that afflicted the African American community. The war would bring change in ways that no one could have predicted. Liberal antidiscrimination executive orders from the president would open up economic opportunities in the private sector, and the necessity of black participation in the war effort would eventually lead to the steady but inevitable dismantling of segregation within the armed services (although this would not happen fully until after the war). And, as in every war since the American Revolution, black men would argue that their heroic and selfless service for their country warranted equal treatment at home.

World War II would turn out to be a crucial period of transition in American race relations.

This time, returning veterans would demand their rights. Civil rights leaders would turn to the courts to end the legacy of the Jim Crow laws, the de jure segregation from the 1890s. And both leaders and ordinary African Americans would, in ways that would have surprised even themselves before the war, engage in forms of direct action and protest that over the next two decades would ultimately strike out legal segregation in every aspect of American life.

Mary McLeod Bethune at her desk at Bethune-Cookman College, by Gordon Parks, January 1943, Daytona Beach, Florida. Photograph. Library of Congress. Among the images on her office walls are those of President Franklin Delano Roosevelt, whom Bethune served in the National Youth Administration, and Madam C. J. Walker.

RISE! A PEOPLE EMERGENT
1940–1968

AFTER TURNING MUCH OF ITS AUTO INDUSTRY OVER TO THE WAR EFFORT, DETROIT BECAME A CENTER FOR THE DEFENSE INDUSTRY DURING WORLD WAR II, DRAWING MORE THAN 100,000 AFRICAN AMERICANS FROM THE RURAL SOUTH IN SEARCH OF JOBS. Ultimately, this wave of "defense migration" would surpass even the Great Migration in scope. From 1933 to 1943, the number of blacks in Detroit doubled, from 100,000 to 200,000—but the Motor City was hardly welcoming. Newly arriving African Americans were excluded from all but one of the city's public housing projects.

Many were forced to live in homes without indoor plumbing, with rents two to three times higher than those paid by families in white districts. Factory discrimination inflamed an already tense racial situation caused by the housing shortage. White defense workers, angered by the recent factory integration policy and promotion of black workers, engaged in hate strikes across the city. By the end of 1942, executives at the Ford Motor Company exacerbated racial tensions throughout the Detroit area when the company reversed its traditionally progressive hiring policies and virtually ceased bringing on African American males.

On June 20, 1943, tensions between black and white defense industry workers over housing and jobs exploded into a devastating race riot that spread across the city. More than 200 individuals were swept up in what became known as the Belle Isle Riots, named for the bridge that stretches across the Detroit River. As was so often the case, unfounded rumors of murder and rape were at the heart of this tragedy.

The false rumor that white sailors had thrown a black woman and her baby into the Detroit River ignited a full-scale riot. By 11:30 p.m. that Sunday, 5,000 people were fighting in the middle of East Jefferson, at the Belle Isle bridge entrance. Police restored order around 2 a.m.

But around midnight, an employee of Wilson's Forest Club had jumped on the stage to spread the rumor about the alleged drownings.

The club was packed with about 700 black people, many of whom poured into the streets and began attacking whites. Around the same time, another false rumor spread to a white neighborhood near the Roxy Theatre on Woodward at Temple that a black man had raped a white woman on Belle Isle.

Whites leaving the theater gathered on Woodward, which separated the white neighborhood from Paradise Valley. They dragged blacks from automobiles and streetcars. At one point, the crowd on Woodward was estimated at 10,000. As daylight approached, the fighting continued.[1]

By the time the two-day riot ended, 34 people were dead, including 25 African Americans, most of whom were killed by Detroit police. The rest of the tally was just as dire. Nearly 700 people were wounded, three-quarters of whom were black. More than 1,800 people had been arrested, more than 85 percent of them African American. Detroit suffered an estimated $2 million in property damage. "Hitler won a battle in Detroit today," wrote the *Chicago Sun*, with good reason: U.S. troops about to ship out to fight the Nazis in North Africa were ordered to stay in Detroit instead, to keep Americans from killing Americans.[2]

The Detroit riot was not an isolated event. Incredibly, it was one of more than 240 racial clashes in the United States in 1943 alone. It came at a time of heightened racial tensions across the country, caused in part by

---

[1]   Brenda J. Gilchrist, "Detroit's 1943 Race Riot, 50 Years Ago Today, Still Seems Too Near," *Detroit Free Press*, June 20, 1993, http://crimeindetroit.com/Documents/Detroit's%201943%20Race%20Riot,%20 50%20Years%20Ago.pdf.

[2]   Stephen Tuck, *We Ain't What We Ought to Be: The Black Freedom Struggle from Emancipation to Obama* (Cambridge: Harvard University Press, 2010), 210.

Detroit riot, Detroit, Michigan, June 20–22, 1943. Bettmann, Corbis UK Ltd.

simmering black anger at white American hypocrisy: While the United States waged what the country officially portrayed as a righteous war in Europe against Hitler's hateful racial ideology, virulent racism ran rampant and unchecked at home. President Franklin Roosevelt had called for a world founded on "four essential human freedoms"–freedom of speech and worship, and freedom from fear and want. Yet those basic freedoms remained far out of the reach of many African Americans, whose lives were constrained by the fear of racist

violence and the reality of crippling poverty and segregation.

In response, the black press mounted a campaign they called "Double V," which stood for victory over fascism abroad and racism at home. The black elite, among them leaders of the NAACP, lobbied hard for the end of segregation in the military, along with increased combat participation for black soldiers (including active service for the Tuskegee Airmen), seeing each as an essential and important step toward demonstrating the merits of wider civil

rights throughout American society following the war. This was the same case that Frederick Douglass had made about black military combat during the Civil War. Douglass's argument proved to be in vain; would history repeat itself following World War II?

As the war raged, segregation and discrimination persisted, even on the battlefield. While FDR issued Executive Order 8802, which desegregated defense industries that contributed to the war effort, the U.S. military itself would remain segregated through the entire course of the war. Nearly 1 million of the 16 million Americans who served in the armed forces during World War II were African American, yet most black soldiers remained confined to the lowest military ranks, relegated to dangerous and undesirable jobs as bomb loaders or service positions known as quartermasters.

The Marine Corps was the last branch of the contemporary military to refuse enlistment by black men (although, according to Marine records, 13 blacks served in the Marines during the American Revolution), but by the Second World War, an executive order issued by the president left them with no choice but to abandon their policy.[3] As in the other branches, the internal command was sharply divided, and the officer corps remained entirely white. A black command structure rose alongside its white counterpart, but it was always subordinate to and under the dominion of white officers. A black officer, for instance, never crossed paths with a white enlisted man, thus removing the possibility that a white man would have to acknowledge the superior status of a black man, even in the military. This is how bizarrely racial segregation manifested itself in America at that time. Black Marine recruits received training in a completely separate facility, Montford Point, which was located in Onslow County, North Carolina, a coastal outpost where soldiers were subject to vicious racial discrimination both off base and on, and whether they were in uniform or not made no difference in how they were treated.

In many ways the world was changing, and with it, so was the military. But extreme prejudice persisted. In a crowning indignity born out of a toxic combination of bureaucracy, scientific ignorance, and racial hatred, the United States Army even insisted that the blood of its soldiers be kept segregated. The African American physician and surgeon Dr. Charles Drew (1904–1950) did not mince words when it came to sharing his opinion of the Army's decision. Calling it "a stupid error" in a 1944 letter to Jacob Billikopf, the director of the Labor Standards Association, Drew wrote: "It was a bad mistake for three reasons: (1) No official department of the Federal Government should willfully humiliate its citizens; (2) There is no scientific basis for the order; (3) They need the blood."[4]

---

3   Michael T. Knight, "Recognizing 233 Years of Black Marines," Marine Corps Base Camp Pendleton, *Marines: The Official Website of the United States Marine Corps,* February 10, 2010, http://www.pendleton.marines .mil/NewsPhotos/NewsArticleDisplay/tabid/5440/ Article/95455/recognizing-233-years-of-black-marines .aspx.

4   Charles R. Drew to Jacob Billikopf, April 15, 1944, in The Charles R. Drew Papers, *Profiles in Science: National Library of Medicine,* http://profiles.nlm. nih.gov/ps/retrieve/ResourceMetadata/BGBBGW.

FACING PAGE: *Wartime Conference for Total Peace* (Double V Campaign), by Elton C. Fax for the National Association for the Advancement of Colored People, 1944. Poster. Library of Congress.

Howard P. Perry, first black Marine, by Roger Smith at Camp Lejeune, North Carolina, March 1943. Photograph. Library of Congress.

Drew was in a position to know. In 1938, with impeccable timing, he pioneered blood-preservation techniques just as the war created an unprecedented worldwide demand for blood transfusions. Through his research at Columbia University, he discovered a method for storing and preserving plasma that would allow it to be shipped overseas and reconstituted for blood transfusions. At the time, Great Britain was desperate for blood for its wounded. As the leading authority in the field, Drew was put in charge of the "Blood for Britain" campaign launched in 1940 by the American Red Cross, the Blood Transfusion Association, and the National Research Council to provide vital plasma to troops fighting Nazi Germany. Nonetheless, the Army continued to keep the blood of African Americans separate from that of whites. Dr. Drew was appalled. A former student quoted him as saying: "'There's only one blood. There is no black blood, no white blood. There is blood.'"[5]

---

[5]   Dr. LaSalle D. Leffall, Jr., interview by Jason Gart, November 19, 2010, The Charles R. Drew Papers, *Profiles in Science: National Library of Medicine*, http://profiles. nlm.nih.gov/ps/retrieve/ResourceMetadata/BGBBJV.

Nine years later, on April 1, 1950, Drew and three other doctors from Howard University were driving to a medical conference in segregated Alamance County, North Carolina. When it was Drew's turn to drive, he fell asleep behind the wheel and crashed the car. The men were taken to Alamance General Hospital, which generally served whites only but did make it a practice to treat blacks in its emergency room. When one of the white doctors on Drew's case recognized his accomplished patient, he ordered that "emergency measures" be taken to save him. But those measures were for naught, and Drew died from brain injury, internal bleeding in the lungs, and multiple injuries.[6] The rumor spread that Drew bled to death after he was denied treatment in a whites-only hospital. The supposed circumstances of his death became the stuff of urban legend—but the legend is simply not true. Although Dr. Drew himself was not turned away, the story was derived from the all-too-real experiences of African Americans struggling to survive in a segregated society.

While segregation remained a regrettable fact of American military life during the Second World War, many African Americans still managed to distinguish themselves on the battlefield and in the air, thanks to the efforts of three women. Mary McLeod Bethune lobbied President Roosevelt successfully to open training programs at several notable historically black universities and colleges. Willa Beatrice Brown (1906–1992), one of only about 100 licensed black pilots in the nation, the overwhelming majority of whom were male, organized Chicago's National Airmen's Association in 1937 to promote interest in black aviation (already sparked by the black aviators who had gone to battle against Italy in Ethiopia in 1935). Eleanor Roosevelt also became involved at the urging of both Bethune and Brown and secured funding from the Rosenwald Fund, long a supporter of projects designed to improve race relations, to expand Tuskegee Institute's pilot-training program.[7] The black pilots of the 99th Pursuit Squadron—known as the Tuskegee Airmen—and Benjamin O. Davis, Sr. (1877–1970), who became the U.S. Army's first African American general in 1940, a year before the United States entered the war, were among those who broke barriers and achieved notable military success. Despite the persistence of segregation, black men and women served with distinction.

Overseas, among the general populace, black soldiers were treated with the respect traditionally bestowed upon men (and today, women) in uniform. Race relations in Europe simply weren't as fraught with tension as they were at home in America, for the simple reason that a much smaller percentage of black people lived in England and France than in the United States, and because neither country had a system of plantation slavery within its borders, although both had extensive colonial holdings whose economies were defined through plantation slavery, such as Jamaica and Saint-Domingue (Haiti), among many others. Once the war ended, however, black veterans returned home to a hostile and unwelcoming nation, despite the proud service record of

6 Spencie Love, *One Blood: The Death and Resurrection of Charles R. Drew* (Chapel Hill: University of North Carolina Press, 1996), 23.

7 Henry Louis Gates, Jr., "3 Women 'Red Tails' Left Out," *The Root*, January 25, 2012, http://www.theroot.com/views/three-women-red-tails-left-out?page=0,0.

"When I came back from Europe . . . we were riding in the back of the buses while German soldiers in the southern states were riding on buses [up front] and going into eating places and movies and things like that."

many African American soldiers and airmen. Seven of these black men would be awarded the Medal of Honor, but only by President Bill Clinton in 1997 after an investigation conducted by scholars at Shaw University in Raleigh, North Carolina, into patterns of racial discrimination in the issuance of the award—another sign of the anti-black racism that persisted during the war.

One soldier who was determined to change things was Damon Keith (b. 1922), a native Detroiter who lived through the Belle Isle Riots and went on to become a leader of the Civil Rights Commission in Detroit and eventually a federal judge. He was inspired to go to law school by his experience in World War II, both as a soldier and as a veteran. Born on July 4, 1922, Keith was the grandson of slaves and the first of his five siblings to attend college. This had been his autoworker father's dream: to see a child of his receive a higher education. Drafted after he completed his undergraduate years at the historically black West Virginia State College, Keith served in the Army, where, like nearly every other African American soldier, he was relegated to the lowest ranks. His commanding officer, a white Alabamian, was brutal, seizing every opportunity to belittle and demean the black soldiers under his command.

Keith had experienced his share of racism in Detroit, and now he faced it in the Army as well. This was not exactly a surprise. It was his return from the war, however, that strengthened his resolve to take an active role in the fight for civil rights. "When I came back from Europe, and we were riding in the back of the buses while German soldiers in the southern states were riding on buses [up front] and going into eating places and movies and things like that," Keith recalled, "Tommie [Newsome, a friend and law student] said, 'Can you imagine us just coming back from Europe fighting for democracy, and the people we were fighting against, whom we've captured, are now enjoying all the benefits of a democracy only because they are white?'"[8]

Keith left the Army as a staff sergeant in 1946 and enrolled in Howard Law School, convinced that the law was the best way to effect social change. And indeed, it would be through a brilliant legal strategy, designed by the Howard Law School dean Charles Hamilton Houston (1895–1950) and executed by his best student and chief lieutenant, Thurgood Marshall (1908–1993), that this strategy would prove to be effective in dismantling de jure segregation, culminating in the famous *Brown v. Board of Education* Supreme Court decision of 1954, the decision that reversed the infamous *Plessy v. Ferguson* decision, after a string of other victories in the courts.

---

8   Trevor W. Coleman, *Crusader for Justice: Federal Judge Damon J. Keith* (Detroit: Wayne State University Press, forthcoming).

In the postwar era, the law was still most certainly not on the side of African Americans, and this was painfully evident on southern buses. During the war, historian Glenda Gilmore noted, gas rationing and consequent overcrowding had turned southern buses into battlefields themselves, as many black soldiers refused to be "Jim Crowed." After the war, that conflict became even more volatile and sometimes erupted into shocking violence.

On February 12, 1946, Army veteran Sergeant Isaac Woodard (1919–1992) was returning home to his family on a Greyhound bus after being honorably discharged and winning an Asiatic-Pacific Campaign Medal with One Star, which he wore on his uniform. In South Carolina, local law enforcement officials pulled him off the bus for asking the bus driver to make an unscheduled rest stop. He was beaten so severely by a policeman with a nightstick that he was left blind for the rest of his life. He was only 27 years old.

Woodard's sacrifice proved to be a necessary catalyst, leading to a profound change. The NAACP seized on the incident, and it garnered national attention, especially in the wake of other lynchings of black veterans that same year. Whites and blacks reacted with outrage to Woodard's abuse. National protests and the emerging Cold War increased pressure on President Truman to address race discrimination, particularly with an upcoming presidential campaign. Hearing about the Woodard incident, Truman spoke plainly and directly: "This shit has to stop."[9] Later that year, Truman appointed a commission on civil rights. In its report, *To Secure These Rights*, the commission recommended the desegregation of the armed forces at long last, anti-lynching legislation (for which Du Bois and the NAACP had been fighting since 1910), and the abolition of poll taxes. Truman would sign Executive Order 9981, issued in 1948. More than a century of agitation to desegregate the military had finally paid off.

The noted radio personality, actor, and filmmaker Orson Welles even dedicated some of his national ABC Radio broadcasts to the Woodard case and to the condemnation of the policeman, whom he called "Officer X," after his acquittal by a local jury. "What does it cost to be a Negro?" Welles asked. "In Aiken, South Carolina, it cost a man his eyes. What does it cost to wear over your skeleton the pinkish tint officially described as white? In Aiken, South Carolina, it cost a man his soul.... Your eyes, Officer X, your eyes, remember, were not gouged away. Only the lids are closed. You might raise the lids, you might just try the wild adventure of looking, and you might see something. It might be a simple truth, one of those truths held to be self-evident by our Founding Fathers and by most of us...."[10]

The crime against Isaac Woodard was shocking. But so, too, was the fact that the blinding of a black soldier by a white policeman could spark national outrage. Lynchings and brutality against blacks had gone on relatively unchecked—and certainly unchallenged—for decades prior to World War II, as we saw in the case of Ida B. Wells's friends in Memphis (described in Chapter 7). The war, however, unleashed powerful forces that helped to mobilize unprecedented pressure for equal rights for African Americans. Northern migration, increased competition for jobs and housing,

---

[9] Tuck, *We Ain't What We Ought to Be*, 40.

[10] "1946-7-28-ABC Lear Radio Show," http://archive.org/details/1946RadioNews.

White-only cabs, by Warren K. Leffler, Albany, Georgia; August 18, 1962. Photograph. Library of Congress.

limited integration of defense industry plants, increased black electoral power (a result of migration), the desegregation of the military in 1948—all of these forces combined to strengthen a movement that had been slowly gathering momentum for years, largely unnoticed by the American public. In the North, African American protests against school segregation, unfair housing, and job discrimination had been building in intensity since the 1920s. In the segregated South, church groups, black women's clubs, civil rights activists, and progressives had been fighting against the lynching and beating of black men and the rape of black women. Now, the wartime changes in aspects of race relations emboldened not just activists, but ordinary individuals, too.

Two years before the Woodard beating, in 1944, a Virginia housewife named Irene Morgan (1917–2007) had been thrown off a bus and arrested for refusing to give her seat to a white rider when ordered to do so by the bus driver. Sitting in the area designated for black passengers, she did not believe she should have to surrender her seat. She is said to have resisted by tearing up the summons she was issued and kicking the arresting officer in the groin. Morgan's action landed her in jail, and while she pleaded guilty to resisting arrest, she did not accept the charges that she had violated the state's law of mandatory segregation on public transportation. The NAACP took her case all the way to the Supreme Court—and won. In the 1946 decision *Morgan v. Commonwealth of Virginia*, the court declared that segregated seating in interstate public transportation was unconstitutional because it violated the Commerce Clause, lending momentum to the NAACP's long, patient, and profoundly brilliant strategy of challenging Jim Crow in the courts.

The NAACP's legal team, led by the Howard Law School dean Charles Hamilton Houston, had been seeking for years to dismantle the legal foundations of de jure segregation, brick by legal brick. But this strategy demanded immense patience and perseverance. Some activists argued that the gradualist legal strategy should be complemented by direct action to test the rulings and press for more immediate change. Hers was not a coordinated effort, but Irene Morgan, a housewife recovering from a miscarriage, had independently carried out one of the first direct actions in the nascent civil rights movement.

Ella Baker (1903–1986) was an early and influential proponent of direct action. A tireless community organizer committed to economic and racial justice, Baker constructed a national foundation for local activism that would manifest itself from the ground up, in contrast to the NAACP's legal strategy, which was a top-down approach. In addition, Baker was a female in a movement totally dominated by male leadership with its fair share of male chauvinism and misogyny, neither of which was a stranger to her.

Baker had been an outspoken crusader for fairness even as a student at Shaw University, which she attended from 1918 to 1927. (One of the country's first historically black colleges, the North Carolina institution was at the time a high school and a university.) Her protests against the dress code, which forbade women from wearing silk stockings, and the rule prohibiting male and female students from walking

Ella Baker, for the NAACP, circa 1942–1946. WGBH Stock sales/Photo Scala, Florence.

across campus together, brought no change in the school's rules but earned her a reputation as a "troublemaker."[11] She continued to speak out, her voice fortunately having more effect in the formative years of the civil rights movement.

As a teacher in worker education with the Works Progress Administration during the 1930s, with roots in the John Dewey philosophy of learning by doing, Baker sowed the seeds of direct action as a form of protest before it was fashionable. Starting out as an NAACP field director and then gaining the title director of branches in the mid-1940s, Baker went from town to town, city to city, throughout the

---

11   Joanne Grant, *Ella Baker: Freedom Bound* (New York: Wiley, 1998), 21.

Rabbi Marc Tanenbaum and Bayard Rustin at the National Interreligious Task Force, Tenth Anniversary Conference, 1982. Photograph. American Jewish Committee Archives. Rabbi Tanenbaum was a founder and program chair of the National Conference on Religion and Race in 1963, marking the 100th anniversary of the Emancipation Proclamation; the Reverend Dr. Martin Luther King, Jr., delivered the closing address. It was here that Tanenbaum introduced his mentor, Rabbi Abraham Joshua Heschel, to King, and the two would go on to march side by side in the 1965 march on Selma. Tanenbaum himself worked closely with civil rights leaders such as Andrew Young, the Reverend Jesse Jackson, Sr., and the Journey of Reconciliation and March on Washington organizer Rustin.

North and South, conducting what were called Leadership Conferences. Her main purpose was to equip regional, grassroots people to organize and defend their own rights as citizens. Baker's philosophy was captured by the title of her favorite hymn, which she borrowed for her organizing workshop, "Give People Light and They Will Find a Way."[12]

In 1947, in response to *Morgan v. Virginia*, the conscientious objector and activist Bayard Rustin (1912–1987) proposed a nonviolent direct action to test compliance with the Supreme

Court's decision desegregating interstate travel. A founding member of the Congress for Racial Equality (CORE)—an interracial group formed in 1942 dedicated to nonviolence as the best means of combating and defeating Jim Crow—Rustin enlisted veteran organizers to assist him, including Ella Baker. It was a most fortuitous alliance. The plan they devised was for a team of black and white activists to ride together in buses from Washington, D.C., through Virginia, North Carolina, and Kentucky. It would be known as the Journey of Reconciliation.

In challenging Jim Crow, the organizers of the Journey of Reconciliation were simultaneously daring and cautious. They deliberately

---

[12] Barbara Ransby, *Ella Baker and the Black Freedom Movement: A Radical Democratic Vision* (Chapel Hill: University of North Carolina Press, 2003), 142.

avoided the dangers of Alabama and Mississippi, where white resistance was violent and unwavering, confining their route to the Upper South. Furthermore, only men would be allowed to make the journey, concerned "that mixing the races and sexes would possibly exacerbate an already volatile situation," which meant that Baker herself could not participate. (It was not the first time that Baker's leadership role in the movement would be limited because of her sex, nor would it be the last. Nor could she have been pleased about it.)[13]

Despite their caution, four of the riders—Rustin himself and another African American, Andrew Johnson, plus CORE members Igal Roodenko and Joseph Felmet, who lived in the North—were arrested during the trip and convicted of violating state law, which still enforced intrastate segregation on buses. First Rustin and Roodenko were sentenced, in May, then a month later Johnson and Felmet. In both cases, the judge handed down a much harsher penalty to the white riders.

> Judge Henry Whitfield, a hard-line segregationist . . . approvingly issued a guilty verdict, assessing Rustin court costs and sentencing Roodenko to thirty days on a road gang. Explaining the differential treatment, he termed Rustin "a poor misled Nigra from the North" who bore less responsibility that white agitators who should know better, and later added a dash of anti-Semitism to his admonition. "I presume you're Jewish, Mr. Rodenky," drawled the judge. "Well, it's about time you Jews

from New York learned that you can't come down here bringing your nigras with you to upset the customs of the South."[14]

Except for the arrests, the Journey of Reconciliation rides were largely peaceful and uneventful. For the most part, no one disputed the men's right to ride the southern buses with whites, but neither did blacks and whites suddenly mix freely on the buses. In the end, the Journey of Reconciliation received considerable publicity and proved that nonviolent direct action could be a viable means of protest. It was a lesson that would be followed later in the civil rights movement of the 1960s, with far-reaching consequences for African Americans and the nation.

⬥⬥⬥

WHILE RACIAL DISCRIMINATION WAS PERCEIVED TO BE A SPECIFICALLY "AMERICAN DILEMMA," as Gunnar Myrdal's best-selling study of the history of American race relations put it in 1944, some leading civil rights activists focused their efforts on internationalizing the freedom struggle. Inspired by leftist politics, and especially by the growing struggle against colonialism in India, Africa, Asia, and around the globe, they attempted to mobilize international public opinion against America's treatment of its African American citizens.

The first black actor to play Othello since the 1800s and the singer who immortalized "Ol' Man River" now spoke words that struck a far too dissonant chord with American audiences. In the late 1940s, the popular singer, actor, and left-wing activist Paul Robeson

---

[13] Raymond Arsenault, *Freedom Riders: 1961 and the Struggle for Racial Justice* (New York: Oxford University Press, 2006), 35.

[14] Arsenault, *Freedom Riders*, 53.

Paul Robeson with W. E. B. Du Bois at the Paris World Peace Conference, 1949. Photograph. W. E. B. Du Bois Collection, Special Collections and University Archives, University of Massachusetts, Amherst.

castigated the hypocrisy of an American government that congratulated itself for victory over fascism abroad while tolerating racial oppression at home. His inflammatory words comparing the U. S. government's treatment of African Americans to Nazi Germany's treatment of Jews brought him before the House Un-American Activities Committee. Asked whether he knew why he was called before the committee, Robeson replied: "My ancestors in the time of Washington baked bread for George Washington's troops when they crossed the Delaware, and my own father was a slave. I stand here struggling for the rights of my people to be full citizens in this country. And they are not. They are not in Mississippi, and they are not in Montgomery, Alabama, and they are not in Washington, and they are nowhere, and that is why I am here today."[15]

Intent on bringing international attention to America's treatment of its black citizens, Robeson took his case to the United Nations in 1951. Following in the tradition of his predecessor, fellow traveler, and mentor W. E. B.

[15] Eric Bentley, ed., *Thirty Years of Treason: Excerpts from Hearings Before the House Committee on Un-American Activities, 1938–1968* (New York: Viking Press, 1971), 770.

Du Bois, Robeson addressed a petition to the new international body titled "We Charge Genocide–The Crime of Government Against the Negro People." The petition referred to thousands of wrongful executions and lynchings, and charged that the United States was engaged in a conspiracy against its black citizens by restricting their right to vote with poll taxes and literacy tests. While Du Bois and other prominent activists endorsed the petition, the charge of genocide was considered too extreme by many white liberals–and by much of the black establishment as well.

Robeson's efforts to mobilize international condemnation of American racism turned him into a pariah, as did his sympathy with Soviet communism and Stalinism during the heyday of McCarthyism. Lionized across Europe, he was repeatedly investigated in his homeland and finally ostracized. The U.S. government revoked Robeson's passport (as it did Du Bois's and many other Americans' accused of being "un-American"), effectively sidelining him and for all intents and purposes ending his career as a stage performer. In 1958, the year the Supreme Court ordered the reinstatement of Robeson's (and Du Bois's) passport as the result of a class-action suit, he published his autobiography, *Here I Stand.*

Although in later years he became a broken man who never regained his career or his stature as an artist, at that time his conviction in his beliefs–and in the wrongdoings of his own country–made Robeson, the defender of human rights, a powerful symbol of courage and defiance, and a race man. "To achieve the right of full citizenship which is our just demand," Robeson wrote, "we must ever speak and act like free men. When we criticize the treatment of Negroes in America and tell our fellow

citizens at home and the people abroad what is wrong with our country, each of us can say with Frederick Douglass: 'In doing this, I shall feel myself discharging the duty of a true patriot; for he is a lover of his country who rebukes and does not excuse its sins.'"[16]

The government's draconian response to Robeson's determination to fight against racism showed that, in taking the case against American anti-black racism to the international community, the actor and activist had struck a nerve. The United States government was not eager to see the nation's racial problems paraded before the world, compromising its image as a beacon of freedom and providing ammunition to its enemies, precisely as competition with the Soviet Union for allies among emerging Third World nations of color was growing keener. As the Cold War heated up through the '50s, civil rights leaders would remember that lesson. The threat of damage to the United States' international reputation would provide them with a powerful lever as they pressed a reluctant federal government to protect black people and defend civil rights at home.

<hr/>

THE YEARS THAT FOLLOWED WORLD WAR II SAW IMPORTANT SOCIAL AND CULTURAL CHANGES FOR AFRICAN AMERICANS, as black athletes and entertainers overcame long-standing barriers and entered the mainstream. When Jackie Robinson (1919–1972) donned the uniform of the Brooklyn Dodgers in 1947, he was only the most visible of a

<hr/>

[16] Paul Robeson, *Here I Stand* (Boston: Beacon Press, 1958), 73.

whole generation of popular figures who offered new role models and positive images of black people. Much of black America celebrated the glamorous wedding of Harlem Congressman Adam Clayton Powell, Jr., and singer Hazel Scott (1920–1981), thanks to splendid press coverage. Lena Horne (1917–2010), a favorite pinup of black soldiers during the war, became an even greater postwar heartthrob and Hollywood star. The celebrity of these new black icons and many, many more, as well as the successes of the growing civil rights movement and the NAACP's legal strategy, was promoted and sustained by the black press, with a particular push from a young publisher in Chicago.

John H. Johnson (1918–2005), the grandson of slaves, was just 27 years old when he first published *Ebony* magazine at the end of the war in 1945. Aimed at the emerging black middle class, the glossy magazine pledged in its debut issue "to mirror the happier side of Negro life—the positive, everyday achievements from Harlem to Hollywood."[17]

While Johnson's celebration of black achievement in a magazine was fresh, the black press had obviously existed long before *Ebony* came along. African Americans had been disseminating ideas through their own newspapers and magazines ever since the *Freedom's Journal* newspaper began publishing in 1827 to commemorate the abolition of slavery in the state of New York. But Johnson had identified, through a dazzling combination of intuition and business acumen, a desperate need in the black community for aspirational images of itself. The mainstream press printed little if any positive coverage of African Americans, and the southern press subscribed to a nefarious

"unwritten policy that prohibited the picture of a black person from appearing in any news publication unless it was in connection to a crime."[18]

Johnson's motivation in publishing *Ebony* was high-minded and commercial at the same time. In his memoir, *Succeeding Against the Odds*, he wrote that his goal for the magazine was to serve as "a medium to refuel the people, and to recharge their batteries . . . a medium to make Blacks believe in themselves, in their skin color, in their noses, in their lips, so they could hang on and fight for another day . . . a medium—bright, sparkling, readable—that would let Black Americans know that they were part of a great heritage."[19] But in launching this novel publication, he claimed with some amusement that he "wasn't trying to make history. I was trying to make money."[20]

For the first 20 years of its existence, *Ebony* covered fashion and celebrities, always with an eye on black success stories, whether they were found in the world of entertainment or sports or in the general population. One of its most widely read features was "Speaking of People," which many readers thought of as "Another Negro First!" The column documented strides that black people were making in integrating business and government positions, and the stories about these people inspired a generation of younger black students to aspire as well. In the '50s, in keeping with the changing times, *Ebony* began to publish articles of a more

---

[17] Tuck, *We Ain't What We Ought to Be*, 230.

[18] Walter C. Daniel, *Black Journals of the United States* (London: Greenwood Press, 1982), 159.

[19] John H. Johnson, *Succeeding Against the Odds* (New York: Warner Books, 1989), 157.

[20] Johnson, *Succeeding Against the Odds*, 156.

political nature, and always celebrated the work and achievements of the Reverend Dr. Martin Luther King, Jr. *Ebony*'s sister publication, the weekly newsmagazine *Jet*, also documented developments in the movement, most famously featuring the mutilated corpse of Emmett Till (a teenager who was lynched for ostensibly whistling at a white woman) on the cover of its September 15, 1955, edition. *Ebony* became the biggest-selling black magazine in America and remained that way for decades.

❦❦❦

IN THE POSTWAR YEARS, IT WASN'T JUST WHAT BLACK PEOPLE WERE READING THAT WAS NEW; IT WAS WHAT THEY WERE LISTENING TO AS WELL. And in 1949, that was WDIA. With "one of the white salesmen [at the station saying] that WDIA stands for 'We Done Integrated Already,'" according to the DJ Ford Nelson, WDIA was far ahead of its time, or maybe more accurately a hopeful sign of things to come.[21] Prior to WDIA, black-format radio stations simply did not exist. In 1948, two white station owners, Bert Ferguson and John R. Pepper, made what turned out to be a very shrewd business decision: They put a DJ named Nat D. on the air "and billed him as the Mid-South's first Negro disc jockey."[22] Was the owners' motive to aid

integration, to speed along a process that some believed was inevitable but that many hoped would never happen? Not necessarily, Nat D. Williams (1907–1983) wrote in a column from November 23, 1948, not long after WDIA decided on its format. "'They are businessmen,' he said. 'They don't necessarily love Negroes. They make that clear. But they do love progress and they are willing to pay the price to make progress. One of the most neglected markets in the Mid-South is the Negro market. And that's true because so many white businessmen take the Negro for granted.'"[23]

To appeal to the large and growing black population in Memphis, this meant providing something they had never heard before on the air: a steady stream of black music; black voices, not just singing, but delivering news and advertising; black programming. In short, "WDIA was a celebration of firsts: the first radio station in the country with a format designed exclusively for a black audience; the first station south of the Mason-Dixon line to air a publicly recognized black disc jockey; . . . the first Memphis station to gross a million dollars a year; the first in the country to present an open forum to discuss black problems; and, most important, the first to win the hearts and minds of the black community in Memphis and in the Mid-South with its extraordinary public service. For most blacks living within broadcast range, WDIA was 'their' station."[24]

With station owners everywhere hoping to capitalize on the success of WDIA, black-oriented radio stations began to crop up in almost every major urban center in the United

---

[21] Louis Cantor, *Wheelin' on Beale: How WDIA-Memphis Became the Nation's First All-Black Radio Station and Created the Sound That Changed America* (New York: Pharos Books, 1992), 173.

[22] Margaret McKee and Fred Chisenhall. *Beale, Black & Blue: Life and Music on Black America's Main Street* (Baton Rouge: Louisiana State University Press, 1981), 93.

[23] McKee and Chisenhall, *Beale, Black & Blue*, 93.

[24] Louis Cantor, *Wheelin' on Beale*, 1.

> "[WDIA] had to appeal to black audiences and at the same time not offend white audiences."

States. And unlike concert venues or night-clubs, radio waves couldn't be segregated; any listener of any race could tune in to whatever station they wanted in the privacy of their own home. According to the Birmingham DJ Shelley Stewart, "Music really started break-ing down the barriers long before politics in America began to deal with it."[25]

And the effect was noticed by self-declared white racists. George Lincoln Rockwell—self-appointed head of the American Nazi Party—told Alex Haley (1921–1992) in a *Playboy* interview in April 1966:

> Our white kids are being perverted, like Pavlov's dogs, by conditioned-reflex train-ing. For instance, every time a white kid is getting a piece of ass, the car radio is blar-ing nigger bebop. Under such powerful stimuli, it's not long before a kid begins unconsciously to connect these savage sounds with intense pleasure and thus transfers his natural pleasurable reactions in sex to an unnatural love of the chaotic and animalistic nigger music, which destroys a love of order and real beauty among our kids. This is how you niggers corrupt our white kids—without even laying a dirty hand on them. Not that you wouldn't like to.[26]

It was a contest that Rockwell had lost, even by the time he was interviewed by Haley. Simply put, integration was first heard by the postwar generation on the radio.

Yet in some ways WDIA was essentially apolitical, at least in terms of what it broadcast. None of the managers were black, and, in fact, only one-third of the on-air personalities were African American (one of whom was the future blues legend B. B. King).[27] These announcers, though, heeded the policy typical of white-run black stations of the period: they avoided con-troversy by staying away from music or talk that might be considered radical or inflamma-tory in any way, unlike John Johnson's editorial policies for *Jet* and *Ebony*. Nat D. Williams put it bluntly: "[WDIA] had to appeal to black au-diences and at the same time not offend white audiences."[28] But from the start, the very fact of WDIA's existence was an act of subtle subver-siveness. And as time went on, WDIA began to take a more open stance on politics, producing programming that called attention to issues of desegregation and the struggle for civil rights. "Many people in Memphis thought these pro-grams were helping race relations. African Americans in particular felt that WDIA had 'increased the white community's understand-ing of Negro problems, because so many white people listen too.'"[29]

[25] Tuck, *We Ain't What We Ought to Be*, 245–46.

[26] George Lincoln Rockwell, interview by Alex Haley, *Playboy*, April 1966, http://archive.org/stream/1966PlayboyInterview/MicrosoftWord-Document1#page/n0/mode/2up.

[27] Cantor, *Wheelin' on Beale*, 13.

[28] Cantor, *Wheelin' on Beale*, 51.

[29] Michael T. Bertrand, *Race, Rock, and Elvis* (Urbana: University of Illinois Press, 2000), 170.

WLAC was another such station. Broadcast from Tennessee across the South, by the 1950s, the station featured R & B programs at night, along with advertising aimed at black listeners, from hair pomade and blackstrap laxatives to baby chicks. The DJs exposed listeners to black music that they could get by mail order through Randy's Record Shop in Gallatin, Tennessee. Although the black audience knew that the DJs at WLAC were actually middle-aged white men who spoke in simulated African American dialect, they listened anyway, all across the country. The announcers' skin color was irrelevant and, on the radio, invisible; these DJs played the records that their audience wanted to hear, helping to give artists like Sam Cooke, Chuck Berry, Fats Domino, and Little Richard ever-wider exposure. These radio stations made integration and equality for blacks seem closer at hand than it actually was. But they integrated the musical tastes—and eventually the attitudes— of young white Americans in ways that the resistance to the Supreme Court's 1954 *Brown v. Board of Education* decision sought to restrict and contain. In other words, radio became one aspect of the emerging civil rights movement, although this was an inadvertent outcome of a commercial impulse. After all, the owners of these radio stations were primarily motivated to make money.

WDIA and especially WLAC also served to achieve another function: their music united the tastes of African American listeners in the North and the South, creating a common canon of music that these young people consumed. In this way, radio performed a cultural function within the race similar to the draft in World War II, which brought the children of migrants in the Great Migration into close proximity with the children of the older, settled northern black communities in large quartermaster camps of the segregated armed forces such as the Army's Camp Lee, in Petersburg, Virginia. In other words, the military's segregation policies during World War II served to "integrate" the black community fragmented by the Great Migration.

In 1954, music took a backseat to the headlines for the moment as radio listeners, both black and white, heard remarkable news from a press conference on the steps of the United States Supreme Court. In a landmark decision, the court ruled that segregated public schools violated the Constitution, holding that "in the field of public education, the doctrine of 'separate but equal' has no place. Separate is inherently unequal." When he heard the news, an astonished W. E. B. Du Bois reportedly said, "I have seen the impossible happen."[30] And indeed he had, except that this decision was the culmination of a long, well-planned, seemingly snail-like pace of assault through the legal system.

African Americans celebrated *Brown v. Board* as a "Second Emancipation." The unanimous Supreme Court decision represented the crowning triumph of the NAACP's patient legal strategy against state-sponsored segregation. It was the culmination of decades of litigating and strategizing by Charles Hamilton Houston, "the man who killed Jim Crow," and his team of black lawyers, among them Robert Carter and Thurgood Marshall, who would go on to be the first African American justice on the nation's highest court. The sole tragedy of the timing of the decision was that Houston

---

[30] David Levering Lewis, *W. E. B. Du Bois, 1919–1963: The Fight for Equality and the American Century* (New York: Macmillan, 2001), 557.

Little Rock, Arkansas, riot, September 6, 1957. Photograph. Bettmann, Corbis UK Ltd. Black student Elizabeth Eckford attempts to integrate Little Rock Central High School and is jeered at by angry whites as National Guardsmen look on. This is, perhaps, the iconic image of the school integration movement sparked by the Supreme Court's 1954 *Brown v. Board of Education* decision.

had died in 1950, four years before the seeds of reform that his legal strategy had planted could bear full fruit.

The Supreme Court's directive to desegregate "with all deliberate speed" went unheeded in many school systems across the South. In some places, like Piedmont, West Virginia, schools desegregated quickly and without incident the year after *Brown*. But elsewhere, desegregation would be a long and painful process. In Farmville, Virginia, for example, local authorities elected to keep the public schools closed for five years rather than integrate.

New Orleans was another segregationist holdout. A full six years after the *Brown* decision, a brave six-year-old, immortalized in newsreel footage and the Norman Rockwell painting *The Problem We All Live With* (which today hangs in the White House), became the first black student to integrate her elementary school in New Orleans. Ruby Bridges (b. 1954) became an icon of the innocence of the African American community's historic demands for full citizenship rights and the implacable, irrational nature of the racist opposition to those demands when she entered the William Frantz Elementary School flanked by federal marshals, dispatched to shield her from the seething mob of white adults hurling hateful epithets at her. International audiences who saw the images of the little black girl surrounded by armed soldiers broadcast on television reacted with outrage.

It wasn't just local school boards resisting enforcement of the law, but institutions of higher learning as well. The renowned broadcast journalist and writer Charlayne Hunter-Gault (b. 1942) was one of the first two black students to attend the University of Georgia in 1961, along with Hamilton Holmes (1941–1995). Vernon Jordan (b. 1935), the future president of the National Urban League and adviser to President Bill Clinton, was one of the lawyers who fought her case. He found a crucial bit of evidence about the academic qualifications of white students who had been admitted to the university, which his legal team, under the direction of Constance Baker Motley (1921–2005), used to win their the right to enroll.

The successful effort to end segregation in public education resulted from the NAACP's patient strategy of challenging segregationist laws in the courts. In the aftermath of the *Brown* decision, activists focused more intently on direct action to challenge Jim Crow, notably in Montgomery, Alabama, where segregated transportation remained in force.

Rosa Parks (1913–2005), a seamstress and secretary for the local NAACP branch, was among a group of local leaders looking for a way to challenge segregation on the city's buses. While the *Morgan v. Virginia* decision had desegregated buses traveling from state to state, it did nothing for the many African Americans commuting to work, day in and day out, in cities like Montgomery. The activists had considered several young women who had been harassed by white bus drivers as possible test cases, but none of them were ideal. One woman, Mary Louise Smith, was arrested just a month and a half before Rosa Parks. Shortly after Smith's arrest, her father was smeared as a drunk; while the 18-year-old maid insisted it was a vicious rumor, the damage had been done to her reputation. Even earlier that year, in March 1955, a 15-year-old named Claudette Colvin (b. 1939) was dragged kicking and screaming from an Alabama bus when she refused to give up her seat. Colvin was considered, quite unfairly, to be something of a wild card, though—pregnant at 15 and desperately poor—and hence not useful to the struggle as a role model for a people and a political movement still very much in the grip of the so-called politics of respectability.[31] Another example of injustice would have to be found to serve as the icon of the movement.

Rosa Parks fit the bill. A 42-year-old married woman with a proper, conservative appearance, she was, as her biographer Joyce

---

[31] Paul Hendrickson, "The Ladies Before Rosa: They Too Wouldn't Give Up Their Seats," *Washington Post*, April 12, 1998, http://search.proquest.com.ezproxy.cul .columbia.edu/docview/408359650/13A371C21997411072 A/1?accountid=10226.

Rosa Parks, Montgomery, Alabama, 1955. Photograph. Press Association Images.
Recorded as a "negro seamstress," Rosa Parks is fingerprinted by Deputy Sheriff D. H.
Lackey after her arrest for refusing to give up her seat for a white person.

Hanson put it, "beyond reproach to be a test case." Although perhaps she appeared meek, Parks was an unapologetic activist, a member of the Alabama Voters' League in addition to the NAACP. Despite her membership in the NAACP, she was not working under orders that day, as has been implied by many. "I spontaneously made that decision without any

leadership," she said ten years after the event, at a tribute dinner. "You can't be told what to do. You have to be motivated. You have to feel that you will not be pushed around."[32] In later years, Parks said that her decision to refuse that day

---

[32] Joyce A. Hanson, *Rosa Parks: A Biography* (Santa Barbara, CA: ABC-CLIO, 2011), 91.

was also motivated by the horrific lynching of 14-year-old Emmett Till in Money, Mississippi, on August 28, 1955, and the acquittal of his two white murderers just under a month later. For the alleged crime of speaking disrespect-fully (by their description) to a white woman, Emmett Till had his skull crushed in and an eye gouged out, his mutilated body thrown into the Tallahatchie River by his abductors, Roy Bryant and J. W. Milam, who boasted of their crime to a journalist after an all-white jury found them not guilty. "I thought about Emmett Till," Rosa Parks said, "and I could not go back."[33]

Inspired deeply by the teachings of Ella Baker and the educator and activist Septima Clark (1898–1987), Parks quietly but adamantly refused to relinquish her seat to a white man one day, knowing full well that she might be arrested. As Parks became an icon of quiet re-sistance, it was the resolve and resourceful-ness of grassroots people–maids, workers, and housewives–that sustained a boycott of the city buses that lasted 381 days. For more than a year, Montgomery's African American workers walked to work, carpooled, and endured shared inconvenience. With 75 percent of the ridership of Montgomery's buses black, the economic threat to the city was serious.[34] But the protest–both Parks's individual one and the massive one that followed–posed an even graver threat to the city's social order. Montgomery's adherence to Jim Crow laws was harsh, even by the standards of the Deep South, and to have it upended was a humiliation to the city. Finally, the Supreme Court upheld a lower-court ruling declaring Montgomery's segregated bus system unconsti-tutional. Ella Baker's organizing principle–that "authentic" leadership had to be built from the bottom up–had achieved its aims.

While the Montgomery bus boycott dem-onstrated the success of Baker's grassroots orga-nizing strategy, it also heralded the emergence of a new, young leader with a growing national profile who would bring widespread atten-tion to the freedom struggle. The Reverend Dr. Martin Luther King, Jr. (1929–1968), an eloquent and staunch advocate of nonviolent protest, had been chosen as the boycott's leader. Dr. King's presence on national television gave him unprecedented exposure and marked the critical role that this new medium would play in shaping the course of the movement.

Television could bring the ugly reality of segregation right into people's homes, and it offered civil rights activists engaged in the do-mestic battle for hearts and minds a powerful new tool. The rise of television, in fact, hap-pened concurrently with the beginning of the civil rights movement. Years later, one of the era's most celebrated activists, Congressman John Lewis (b. 1940), reflected on the impor-tance of the media to the movement's success. "If it hadn't been for the media–the print me-dia and television–the civil rights movement would have been like a bird without wings, a choir without a song."[35]

Buoyed by the success in Montgomery, Ella Baker and others pushed for more direct

---

[33] "A Pivotal Moment in the Civil Rights Movement: The Murder of Emmett Till," *Facing History and Ourselves*, 2013, http://www.facinghistory.org/resources/units/pivotal-moment-civil-rights-moveme.

[34] Cheryl F. Phibbs, *The Montgomery Bus Boycott: A History and Reference Guide* (Santa Barbara, CA: Greenwood, 2009), 59.

[35] Gene Roberts and Hank Klibanoff, *The Race Beat: The Press, the Civil Rights Struggle, and the Awakening of a Nation* (New York: Alfred A. Knopf, 2006), 407.

action. Over the years, Baker had continued her work with the NAACP, although she resigned from her national post as director of branches in 1946. For a time her focus turned more local, and while living in Harlem in 1952, she was elected president of the New York City NAACP, the first woman to hold this position. "Her new post," wrote her biographer Barbara Ransby, "provided her with the latitude and authority to orchestrate some of the kinds of political campaigns she had long envisioned."[36]

Baker was in her late 50s, and she had grown disillusioned with the cautious approach of the leaders of her generation, most notably Martin Luther King, Jr. She became frustrated with the hierarchical setup of the preeminent civil rights organizations; and legal strategies and speeches, she believed, were not advancing the movement quickly or dramatically enough. It would be young college students, committed to nonviolence and willing to risk everything—including the disapproval of their more cautious parents—who would pick up where the Montgomery bus boycott had left off. These were the children of a generation that did not speak up. John Lewis said his own parents, sharecroppers in Pike County, Alabama, didn't have time to fight for what was "right" or "wrong"; their struggle to survive on a daily basis was a daunting enough prospect.[37]

As early as 1943, there had been sit-ins. What started as relatively isolated events in cities like Chicago, St. Louis, and Baltimore showed the first signs of being a movement by the late '50s, when students began to stage sit-ins in southern cities.[38] No one took much notice until February 1, 1960, when four African American students—Joseph McNeil (b. 1942), Franklin McCain (b. 1941), Ezell Blair, Jr. (b. 1941), and David Richmond (1941–1990)—sat down at a segregated Woolworth's lunch counter in Greensboro, North Carolina. They were refused service, but they remained. For days the protest grew; each day more students and their supporters poured into Woolworth's. And so did their opponents. Pelted with food and lighted cigarette butts and humiliating racial slurs, the African American students responded nonviolently. Northern white students began to join their cause as well. The sit-in movement spread to cities throughout the South. It would be the end of July before Woolworth's finally crumbled to pressure and desegregated its lunch counters.

Baker was inspired by this powerful act of civil disobedience, and she encouraged young people to form their own organizations rather than be drawn into the older, more established ones trying to recruit them, such as the NAACP, CORE, and the SCLC (Southern Christian Leadership Conference), of which Baker herself was a cofounder. She did not want to see the quietly rebellious energy of the sit-ins quashed, for she felt that it was this sort of act that would draw the most withering attention to the injustice of segregation, and which held the most potential to effect change. It was young people, with their "brazen fighting spirit," who became the movement's foot soldiers under Baker's guidance.[39]

[36] Ransby, *Ella Baker*, 147–48.

[37] John Lewis, interview by Henry Louis Gates, Jr., October 25, 2012.

[38] Henry Hampton and Steve Fayer, *Voices of Freedom: An Oral History of the Civil Rights Movement from the 1950s Through the 1980s* (New York: Bantam, 1991), 53.

[39] Ransby, *Ella Baker*, 244.

In an attempt to harness the momentum of the sit-in movement, Baker organized a meeting of student activists from around the country at her alma mater, Shaw University in North Carolina, over Easter weekend, 1960. Diane Nash (b. 1938) attended this event, where a new organization, the Student Nonviolent Coordinating Committee (SNCC), was born. Nash was an instant Baker acolyte. "No one was more impressed by Baker's message and the compelling image that she projected than Diane Nash," wrote Baker's biographer.[40]

As a native of Chicago, Nash admitted to feeling "naïve" when she first came face to face with segregation in the South as a student at Fisk University in Tennessee, the alma mater of W. E. B. Du Bois. "The first time she encountered segregation, really encountered it, was when she attended the Tennessee State Fair soon after arriving. There she saw the 'white' and 'colored' signs on the restroom doors. When she asked about it, the other students shrugged and told her that that was just the way the world worked."[41] That indignity, coupled with the inspiration of what other students were doing around the country, had led Nash to become a leader of the Nashville Student Movement in 1959. She and her fellow students, John Lewis among them, began staging sit-ins and other direct actions that aroused sympathy in the North and vitriol in the South. In fact, the first stage of Nashville's movement began just 12 days after the Greensboro sit-in, on February 13, 1960, and ended three months later when Nashville became the first southern city to desegregate its lunch counters, more than two months ahead of Woolworth's corporate decision.

Even as boycotts and sit-ins challenged the racist status quo, many African Americans were unsatisfied with the pace of progress. Sit-ins were direct, democratic, effective—and illegal. Students who participated in them were objects of violence and scorn. While it was undeniable that they entered the civil rights battle at tremendous risk to themselves, for some it was not enough. Many young African Americans turned to leaders who rejected nonviolent resistance entirely, including advocates of armed self-defense—like Robert F. Williams (1925–1996) and the Deacons of Defense—or radical voices like Detroit's fiery Reverend Albert Cleage, Jr. (1911–2000).

But no one channeled the currents of black anger and frustration with more power and eloquence than Malcolm X (1925–1965) of the Nation of Islam. The sensationalist documentary *The Hate That Hate Produced* introduced Malcolm to a national audience. "You cannot find one black man—I don't care who he is," Malcolm said to the young news correspondent Mike Wallace, "who has not been personally damaged in some way by the devilish acts of the collective white man."[42]

Unlike other prominent black activists at the time, Malcolm X scorned integration. He expressed a deep anger that simmered in many African Americans, but which they dared not display openly. Malcolm's radical message resonated in the urban ghettos of the North and on the West Coast. But it also angered people,

[40] Ransby, *Ella Baker*, 246.

[41] Andrew B. Lewis, *The Shadows of Youth: The Remarkable Journey of the Civil Rights Generation* (New York: Hill and Wang, 2009), 49–50.

[42] Malcolm X, interview by Mike Wallace, *The Hate That Hate Produced*, *News Beat*, WNTA-TV (CBS), July 13–17, 1959. Interview footage is available at http://archive.org/details/PBSTheHateThatHateProduced.

black and white, who believed that he offered no constructive plan for reshaping society and who feared that his vocalized militancy would scare away potential white allies.

Malcolm's radicalism may not have been universally embraced, but it was emblematic of the diversity of opinions among African Americans about how best to achieve racial justice and equality. He voiced the widespread impatience with the scope and pace of change that extended well beyond the radical margins of black opinion. By 1963, when *Ebony* marked the centennial of the Emancipation Proclamation, even the resolutely upbeat magazine reflected this frustration in its editorial: "In this 100th year of de jure freedom, today's Negro is not too impressed with how far he has come from bondage."[43]

A mood of protest swept the country, igniting what the media called the "Negro Revolt of 1963." That year's "epidemic of militant action" —so described by the radical Detroit minister the Reverend Albert Cleage—culminated in two massive demonstrations, which showed that African Americans in both the North and South were not going to give up until they achieved true equality.[44]

The first took place in Detroit on June 23, 1963, when an estimated 200,000 people gathered for the Walk for Freedom. Less than two weeks prior, on June 12, Medgar Evers (1925–1963), a civil rights activist and Mississippi's first NAACP field secretary, was assassinated in his own driveway by a white segregationist, Byron De La Beckwith. (It would be 31 years before a jury would convict him of first-degree murder.) Evers's death loomed large over the march, and demonstrators of all leanings carried signs memorializing him.[45]

Twenty years after the wartime riot that had broken out in Belle Isle, advocates of nonviolence and integration marched in the Detroit streets side by side with champions of black nationalism, self-defense, and revolution in an extraordinary display of solidarity across ideological differences. The radical activist Grace Lee Boggs (b. 1915), who for many years aligned herself with Malcolm X, was one of the organizers of the march; Judge Damon Keith, who was in Martin Luther King, Jr.'s camp, had a seat on the podium during King's closing address. Boggs and Keith occupied very different positions in the civil rights movement, but the participation of each was emblematic of the march's goal of unity within the black community. Money raised by organizers went to the SCLC, to be used for continuing civil rights organizing in the South. The NAACP, initially reluctant, endorsed the march, as did the AFL-CIO and local Democratic Party affiliates. Detroit claimed at least partial ownership of the march, with Mayor Jerry Cavanagh putting forth his city, which had so often seethed with racism and brutality, as one that was home to progress in race relations. The Reverend Cleage, one of the march's organizers, said in a speech that day, "Negroes are discriminated

---

[43] "Outgrowing the Ghetto Mind," *Ebony* 18, no. 10 (August 1963): 98.

[44] Peniel E. Joseph, *Waiting 'Til the Midnight Hour: A Narrative History of Black Power in America* (New York: Henry Holt and Co., 2006), 84.

[45] Joseph, *Waiting 'Til the Midnight Hour*, 82.

FACING PAGE: Malcolm X, by Ed Ford. *New York World Telegram & Sun*, 1964. Photograph. Library of Congress.

against on every hand, right here in Detroit.... We must FIGHT and FIGHT and FIGHT."[46]

Cleage expected little to nothing from white America. What he wanted from the march was black solidarity. He had first come to prominence in Detroit in 1961, when he began to publish the *Illustrated News*, a paper that promoted black self-defense and stood in sharp contrast in tone to Detroit's other three black weeklies. He raged against police brutality and workplace and educational inequality, and was no supporter of integration. A forceful presence in his native Detroit, Cleage garnered widespread attention across the nation with his Black Christian Nationalist Movement, formed in 1967.

Even in religion, Cleage railed, blacks were dominated by whites. This had to end. "For him there was no better example of the enduring myth of black inferiority than biblical images," wrote the historian Peniel Joseph. "White supremacy was so powerful that even the religious figures blacks looked to for eternal salvation were white."[47] On Easter 1967, Cleage unveiled his Black Madonna, an 18-foot-tall painting depicting a black Mary and Jesus that would give Cleage's Central Congregational Church its new name, the Shrine of the Black Madonna. For Cleage, this was the culmination of years of adherence to a philosophy that was considered too dangerous by the more moderate leaders of the civil rights movement.

On that day in 1963, though, powerful voices from all corners of the civil rights arena were heard. The march ended with a rousing speech by King, in which he implored African Americans to wait no longer for equality, although in far less inflammatory terms than Cleage. "Gradualism is little more than escapism and do-nothingism, which ends up in stand-stillism," Dr. King said, addressing those who were still arguing for a gradual approach. "We want all of our rights, and we want them here, and we want them now." Yes, demands needed to be made and heard, but, King reminded the audience, nonviolence was still key: "Black supremacy is as dangerous as white supremacy."[48] While followers of Martin and Malcolm might march side by side, on this point of nonviolence they remained divided.

At the end of the day, King won over even more people to the cause, including one of the city's most apolitical African American businesspeople: the founder of Motown Records, Berry Gordy (b. 1929). Gordy touted his company as "The Sound of Young America," and Gordy's Young America was in no way political. Motown artists like Smokey Robinson and Diana Ross and the Supremes crossed over to white audiences and defined the sound of an era. Martin Luther King, Jr.'s, message—that segregation hurt both black and white Americans—was right in line with Gordy's crossover music strategy. In his autobiography, *To Be Loved*, Gordy wrote, "I saw Motown much like the world Dr. King was fighting for, with people of different races and religions, working together harmoniously for a common

---

[46] Joseph, *Waiting 'Til the Midnight Hour*, 83.

[47] Joseph, *Waiting 'Til the Midnight Hour*, 55.

[48] "We Want Freedom Now, King Tells Negro Rally: 125,000 Take Part in Massive Detroit Demonstration Marking Riot Anniversary," *Los Angeles Times*, June 24, 1963.

FACING PAGE: Martin Luther King, Jr., in the Washington Temple Church, Brooklyn, by O. Fernandez. *New York World Telegram & Sun,* 1962. Photograph. Library of Congress.

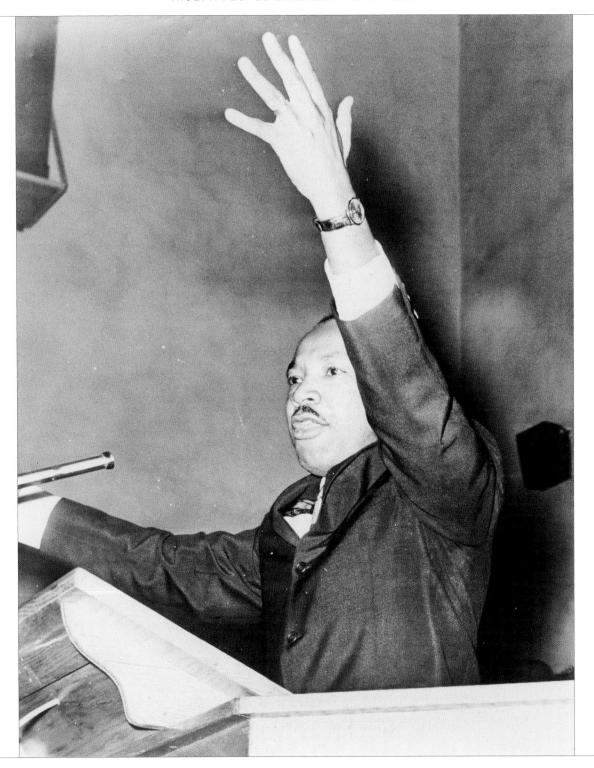

goal."[49] Gordy released a commemorative LP of King's Detroit speech, titled *The Great March to Freedom*, to coincide with King's landmark appearance at the March on Washington later that summer.

In August 1963, 250,000 people gathered in the nation's capital for the March on Washington for Jobs and Freedom, overshadowing the Walk for Freedom in the public's conscience. It was here that King delivered his famous "I Have a Dream" speech, his message ringing out for all to hear: "Now is the time to make real the promises of democracy. Now is the time to rise from the dark and desolate valley of segregation to the sunlit path of racial justice. Now is the time to lift our nation from the quick sands of racial injustice to the solid rock of brotherhood. Now is the time to make justice a reality for all of God's children."[50]

While a quarter of a million participated, millions more witnessed the March on Washington on television. The grassroots organizers of the civil rights movement were being helped tremendously by the broadcasting of these events on television. In *The New York Times*, the television critic Jack Gould wrote: "The medium of television is proving an indispensable force in the Negro's pursuit of human rights. . . . The gentle entrance and exit of so much petitioning humanity was an editorial in movement. Its eloquence could not be the same in only frozen word or stilled picture."[51] The March on Washington inspired solidarity demonstrations all over the world– from James Baldwin's symbolic walk to the American Embassy in Paris before the event, to marches that day in capitals from Oslo to Cairo. In Ghana, marchers carried signs that said, "America, Africa is watching you."[52]

In a strange twist of fate, one person who wasn't watching was W. E. B. Du Bois. The pioneer in the campaign to bring the shame of American race relations before the world died in Ghana on the night before the March on Washington, effectively passing the mantle to King.

THE IMPACT OF THESE DEMONSTRATIONS WAS FELT IN EVERY ECHELON OF AMERICAN SOCIETY. The passage of the landmark Civil Rights Acts of 1964 and 1965 soon thereafter, which outlawed discrimination in public accommodations on the basis of race, religion, ethnicity, and gender, represented the culmination of decades of activism for integration and racial equality. Even the Harlem congressman Adam Clayton Powell, Jr., who was no fan of King and who used all kinds of threats to discourage King from protests he felt would embarrass him or hinder his efforts in Congress, showed great leadership in seeing that this legislation was passed.

Despite all the protests and marches and passage of the Civil Rights Acts, in 1965 most African Americans were still barred from

[49] Craig Hansen Werner, *A Change Is Gonna Come: Music, Race, and the Soul of America* (Ann Arbor: University of Michigan Press, 2006), 27.

[50] Martin Luther King, Jr., "I Have a Dream," *A Testament of Hope: The Essential Writings and Speeches of Martin Luther King, Jr.*, ed. James M. Washington (New York: HarperCollins, 1990), 218.

[51] Roberts and Klibanoff, *The Race Beat*, 348.

[52] Mary L. Dudziak, *Cold War Civil Rights: Race and the Image of American Democracy* (Princeton: Princeton University Press, 2011), 192.

voting in the nation's southern states. John Lewis and other student activists took the campaign for voting rights to Selma, Alabama, where African Americans made up the majority of the population, but accounted for a mere 1 percent of registered voters. That year, Lewis, as the leader of SNCC, planned a march from Selma to the state capitol building in Montgomery to call attention to black voting rights and register voters in Alabama. As a young man, Lewis had been drawn to the movement after hearing Martin Luther King, Jr., on the radio, and had been deeply touched when King sponsored him to come visit him in Atlanta.

Lewis, himself a native of Alabama, and local ministers invited their idol, King, to join the Selma campaign. But when 600 demonstrators met at Brown Chapel Church on March 7 to begin their protest march, King was not among them. Undeterred, Lewis led the protesters from the church. When they made it to the Edmund Pettus Bridge, they were met by armed state troopers sent by Alabama's governor, George Wallace. Also waiting at the river's edge that day were television cameras, documenting the events as they unfolded.

Police told the protesters to turn back, but they knelt and prayed instead. At that moment, with the whole world watching, the sheriff took to his bullhorn and ordered police to advance, unleashing a full-on assault on peaceful, praying demonstrators. "I remember how vivid the sounds were as the troopers rushed toward us," Lewis recalled, "the clunk of the troopers' heavy boots, the whoops of rebel yells from the white onlookers, the clip-clop of horses' hooves hitting the hard asphalt of the highway, the voice of a woman shouting, 'Get 'em! Get the niggers!'"[53]

Television networks cut into regularly scheduled programming to broadcast the brutal incident, which became known as "Bloody Sunday." It was the first time that this form of "We interrupt this broadcast" had been used for an unfolding news event involving black people.

People watched Bloody Sunday, and they couldn't look away. The deplorable images they saw spurred a remarkable number of viewers to respond. A surge of public support for the civil rights movement swept the country—and the world. Spontaneous and uncoordinated demonstrations coalesced into a national day of protest, with crowds gathering in support of the Selma marchers and voting rights everywhere, from Albuquerque to Milwaukee to Boston. But the White House was the true target.

On March 14, exactly one week after the events in Selma, a group that grew to 15,000 held a civil rights rally in Lafayette Park, across Pennsylvania Avenue from the White House. *The New York Times* reported that an African American woman from Mississippi addressed the excited crowd, saying, "It's a shame that all of us had to gather here today because of the hate in America."[54] In the days following the atrocities in Selma, protesters and picketers marched outside the fence around the White House, and there was even a sit-in inside, in the East Wing. While news of Selma and the ensuing reaction to it dominated the news for days, an embarrassed administration took aggressive steps to keep the story of the sit-in out of the news, and few people at the time knew about it.

---

53 John Lewis, with Michael D'Orso, *Walking with the Wind* (New York: Simon and Schuster, 1998), 340.

54 Nan Robertson, "In the Capital, Sermons on Courage in Selma; President Hears Strife Called the Nation's Heartbreak," *New York Times*, March 15, 1965.

John Lewis at the Edmund Pettus Bridge, Selma, Alabama; March 7, 1965. Photograph. Bettmann/ CORBIS, Corbis UK Ltd. SNCC leader John Lewis is shown being beaten by an Alabama state trooper during the famed Selma-to-Montgomery march in support of black voting rights.

President Lyndon Baines Johnson, of course, knew about it. While he did not meet with the sit-in demonstrators, he openly expressed his support for protesters across the nation. "The real hero of this struggle," he said, "is the American Negro. His actions and protests, his courage to risk safety and even to risk his life, have awakened the conscience of this nation. His demonstrations have been designed to call attention to injustice, designed to provoke change, designed to stir reform."[55] And stir reform they did. Less than six months after Selma, with the strong backing of President Johnson, Congress passed the Voting Rights Act, effectively putting an end to the discriminatory practices that kept black citizens from voting. Literacy tests, poll taxes, and harassment would no longer be permitted at the polls. The act took immediate effect, and the number of black voters increased dramatically. The results were seen in the next election cycle, as the number of black elected officials across the country grew from 300 in 1965 to 1,125 in 1969.

[55] "President's Park/Citizens Soapbox: A History of Protest at the White House," WhiteHouseHistory.org, http://www.whitehousehistory.org/whha_tours/citizens_soapbox/protest_04-civilrights.html.

James Meredith, by Marion S. Trikosko, October 1, 1962. Photograph. Library of Congress.
Meredith is shown with U.S. marshals and special Justice Department agent John Doar
(on Meredith's left) on their way to integrate the University of Mississippi.

DURING THE EARLY 1960S, THE COM-
PETING VIEWS ABOUT HOW BEST TO
ACHIEVE RACIAL JUSTICE SEEMED
roughly in balance within the African
American community, with nonviolent resis-
tance as the yin to the Black Nationalists' yang.
Now, by the middle of a wrenching decade,
the prevailing sentiment among the younger
generation was shifting. Indeed, the titles alone
of a series of books by black authors from this
period reveal the increasingly adamant politics
of what would become the Black Power era:
Nigger, by Dick Gregory (1964); *Manchild in the
Promised Land*, by Claude Brown (1965); *Black
Power: The Politics of Liberation in America*, by
Stokely Carmichael and Charles V. Hamilton
(1967); *Soul on Ice*, by Eldridge Cleaver (1968);
*Look Out Whitey! Black Power is Gon' Get Your
Mama!*, by Julius Lester (1968); *Die Nigger Die!*
by H. Rap Brown (1969); *Seize the Time*, by
Bobby Seale (1970); *Picking Up the Gun*, by Earl
Anthony (1970); *Revolutionary Suicide*, by Huey
P. Newton (1973); and *Dig the Nigger Up–Let's
Kill Him Again*, by Robert E. Chinn (1976).[56]
Young people were tired of waiting patiently
for justice, and after Bloody Sunday in 1965, it
became clear that nonviolence could easily be
met with brutality. The young people's rest-
lessness came into full view during what would

---

[56] We would like to thank Professor Lawrence D. Bobo
for directing us to several of these titles.

be considered "the last great march of the civil rights movement"–the March Against Fear, where the concept of Black Power was first articulated for a public audience.

In response to continuing violence at the polls after the passage of the Voting Rights Act, James Meredith (b. 1933)–known for integrating the University of Mississippi in 1962, just a few months after Charlayne Hunter and Hamilton Holmes had successfully integrated the University of Georgia–organized a personal crusade he called the March Against Fear. On June 5, 1966, he set out to walk from Memphis to Jackson, Mississippi, more than 200 miles away, accompanied by just a few other marchers. But on the second day, as he crossed the border from Tennessee into Mississippi, Meredith was shot by a white segregationist and severely wounded. Jack Thornell's photo of Meredith's buckshot-riddled body writhing in pain won the Pulitzer Prize for photography in 1967. While Meredith was hospitalized, Dr. King and other established civil rights leaders vowed to finish what he had started. So they began marching from Hernando, Mississippi, where Meredith was shot, to the Jackson County Courthouse, registering voters along the way.

Despite the commitment of movement leaders to nonviolence, the marchers were joined by the Deacons for Defense, an armed group of African American men (including many veterans of the Korean War) who argued that armed "self-defense was justified" to protect against white violence. Ten days after Meredith was shot, the Deacons stood guard at a nighttime rally in Greenwood, Mississippi, as Stokely Carmichael (1941–1998), a student leader of SNCC, took the stage to speak about white resistance to black voting and about the hypocrisy of an America that allowed its citizens to fight for democracy overseas yet denied it to them at home. "Black people have to take charge," Carmichael said. "Every courthouse in Mississippi should be burned down tomorrow.... Black citizens ought to demand Black Power.... We want Black Power!" The phrase turned into a call from Carmichael, "What do you want?" with the response from the marchers, "Black Power!" "What do you want?" "Black Power!"[57]

Along the march route later, with King on his right, a reporter turned to Stokely Carmichael and asked, "Mr. Carmichael, are you as committed to the nonviolent approach as Dr. King is?" to which he replied, to Dr. King's horror, "No, I am not. I never have [been] . . ."[58] The rhetoric had changed from nonviolence to Black Power, and the mainstream media seized upon it. Not only was there an apparent shift in thinking within the movement, but evidence of dissension as well. The ideological splits that had characterized the African American community since the 18th century, really, had manifested themselves in public through a medium that reached almost every home in the United States. The genie was out of the bottle.

The march persisted with opponents sharing one goal in mind, advocating different means of reaching it, yet still marching together. One thing was for sure: the foes of the movement did not distinguish their targets

---

[57] Aram Goudsouzian, *Down to the Crossroads: Civil Rights, Black Power, and the Meredith March Against Fear* (New York: Farrar, Straus and Giroux, forthcoming), 16.

[58] *Eyes on the Prize: America's Civil Rights Movement, 1954-1985,* "The Time Has Come (1964-1966)," first broadcast 1987 by PBS. Produced, directed, and written by James A. DeVinney and Madison Davis Lacy, Jr. Transcript. http://www.pbs.org/wgbh/amex/eyesontheprize/about/pt.html.

Stokely Carmichael and Martin Luther King, Jr., by Lynn Pelham, June 9, 1966. Photograph. Time & Life Pictures/Getty Images. Carmichael, to King's left and speaking to the sheriff, King, and others assembled to complete the March Against Fear in James Meredith's honor. Three days earlier, Meredith had been gunned down in an attempted assassination during his one-man march across Mississippi.

between the ideological camps within the movement. On June 23, local police attacked hundreds of marchers outside Canton, Mississippi, as they set up their tents for the night on the grounds of a black school. Without warning, police sprayed tear gas into the crowd, upping the abuse by pummeling the scattering people with rifle butts and jackboots. Martin Luther King and Stokely Carmichael were part of the crowd. "While our black brothers are fighting in Vietnam," Carmichael said later, "we're getting gassed for trying to vote in Canton, Mississippi."[59]

When the riot was over, the field resembled a war zone. Dr. Alvin Poussaint (b. 1934), a psychiatrist and a representative of the Medical Committee for Human Rights, set up a makeshift clinic and desperately tried to attend to the wounds and trauma created by the indiscriminate violence of the police. The march ended three days later, on June 26, with a rally 15,000 strong outside the state capitol building in Jackson. There, Poussaint addressed the brutalized crowd and incited them to overthrow the vicious system of segregation. "For many years we have been singing 'We Shall Overcome,'" Poussaint said. "A new day is here, brothers, and we should begin to think, act, and feel that 'we shall overthrow.' 'We shall overthrow' the

[59] Peniel E. Joseph, *Dark Days, Bright Nights: From Black Power to Barack Obama* (New York: Basic Civitas Books, 2010), 120.

vicious system of segregation, discrimination, and white supremacy. Deep in my heart," he concluded, "I do believe that, nonviolently, 'we shall overthrow.'"[60] Some scholars consider the March Against Fear the last freedom march and the first Black Power march.

Less than two years later in Memphis, the same city where the March Against Fear began, Martin Luther King, Jr., the father of the nonviolent civil rights movement, was killed by an assassin's bullet to the neck. He stood on the second-floor balcony of the Lorraine Motel—one of the few southern hotels that provided African American travelers overnight accommodations—preparing to speak before a march that was to be staged on behalf of the city's striking black sanitation workers. He had delivered his final, prescient address, "I've Been to the Mountaintop," at the Bishop Charles J. Mason Temple in Memphis the day before. The collective mourning that followed his death at age 39 soon gave way to great anxiety and despair. Rioting swept the nation as African Americans poured into the streets to vent their frustrations in cities like Boston, Chicago, Washington, D.C., and Detroit—again.

A generation had passed since the battle over housing and jobs at the start of World War II. But after Dr. King's assassination, rioting returned to the Motor City. Once again, the National Guard and federal troops had to be called in to quell the unrest. Throughout the era, Detroit had been America's canary in the coal mine when it came to race relations—a harbinger of things to come. As far as black Detroiters were concerned, there was unfinished business in the struggle for equality and justice, and an increasing frustration with the slow pace of change.

There was unfinished business for the president, too. In the wake of the assassination, President Johnson urged Americans to "reject the blind violence that has struck Dr. King, who lived by nonviolence."[61] Exactly one week after Dr. King's death, on April 11, Johnson signed into law the Civil Rights Act of 1968, known as the Fair Housing Act. The spontaneous outpouring of rage throughout the nation following Martin Luther King's assassination was a sign of both the black community's understandable frustration with the persistence of institutional racism as well as a new shared, bold assertiveness. Many African Americans mourning the standard-bearer of nonviolent resistance now voiced their support for Black Power. In retrospect, the death of Martin Luther King, Jr., would mark the death of the modern civil rights movement, if we take *Brown v. Board* in 1954 and the Montgomery bus boycott in 1955 as its arbitrary starting points. "Freedom now" was the catchphrase of black America. The postwar decades brought about huge changes in the lives of African Americans and unprecedented progress in the fight for equality and justice. But the era also exposed new fissures between blacks and whites, and quite profoundly, within the African American community itself.

---

[60] Jon M. Spencer, *Protest & Praise: Sacred Music of Black Religion* (Minneapolis: Fortress Press, 1990), 96.

[61] "President's Plea: On TV, He Deplores 'Brutal' Murder of Negro Leader," *New York Times*, April 5, 1968, https://ezproxy.library.nyu.edu/login?url=http://search.proquest.com/docview/118178748?accoun tid=12768.

FROM BLACK POWER TO THE WHITE HOUSE

1968–2013

THE COMBINATION OF EVENTS THAT THE COUNTRY CELEBRATED ON JANUARY 21, 2013, WOULD HAVE BEEN UTTERLY UNIMAGINABLE to virtually any of the historical figures whose lives and times we have been chronicling between the early 16th century and early 21st century: the second inauguration of the first black president, on the very day the country celebrated the first and only national holiday dedicated to the achievements of an African American hero.

Even the day's honoree, Dr. King himself, who famously said, "The arc of the moral universe is long, it bends toward justice," would have been astonished by both events.[1] But Dr. King would have been even more amazed, perhaps, both by the racialized class divide within the country, and the class divide *within* the African American community itself. And that is the other side of the story of the last four decades in African American history, the story that has unfolded since that terrible day in April 1968 when Dr. King was so brutally assassinated. It is both dire and depressing, especially since most of the pivotal figures in African American history would have reasonably assumed that for a black man to have been elected president, and for a fallen martyr to be honored with a national holiday each year, then surely a genuine revolution in race relations would have occurred in the United States.

But consider the following statistics:

1. In 2007, 71.6 percent of all births to non-Hispanic black mothers were to mothers who were unmarried (for whites, that figure is 27.8 percent; for Hispanics, it is 51.3 percent).[2]

2. Nearly half of all black children who begin kindergarten do not graduate from high school.[3]

3. Black unemployment is double that for whites—it was 16.3 percent in August 2010.[4]

4. At the end of 2007, 1 in 11 African American adults, or 9.2 percent, were under some form of criminal justice supervision. (That figure was 1 in 31 for all Americans, by comparison.)[5]

5. As of early 2008, 1 in 15 black men were in jail or prison; for those between 20 and 34, the rate, incredibly, was 1 in 9.[6]

We like to believe that statistics never tell the full story, but the story the preceding statistics tell is distressing and difficult to digest. How are today's African Americans faring compared to African Americans in the last year of Martin Luther King's life, 1968? According to the Harvard sociologist Lawrence Bobo:

> The percentage of blacks living far below the poverty line (50 percent or lower) has essentially remained constant since 1968 at 15 percent, even though the overall black poverty rate fell from 40 percent in 1968 to 30 percent in 2012. At the other extreme, the percentage of blacks in the comfortably middle-class category (incomes at least five times the poverty level) quadrupled, rising from a negligible

---

[1] Martin Luther King, Jr., "Love, Law, and Civil Disobedience," in *A Testament of Hope: The Essential Writings and Speeches of Martin Luther King, Jr.*, ed. James M. Washington, (New York: HarperCollins, 1990), 52. This is one of many instances in which Dr. King used this phrase.

[2] Joyce A. Martin, et al., National Center for Health Statistics, "Births: Final Data for 2007," *National Vital Statistics Reports* 58, no. 24, August 9, 2010; Table 15, 76.

[3] Michael Lomax, "Education Is the 21st-Century Liberator," *The Root*, January 16, 2013, http://www.theroot.com/views/education-21st-century-liberator.

[4] U.S. Bureau of Labor Statistics.

[5] Pew Center on the States, *One in 31: The Long Reach of American Corrections* (Washington, D.C.: The Pew Charitable Trusts, March 2009), 5.

[6] Pew Center on the States, *One in 100: Behind Bars in America 2008* (Washington, D.C.: The Pew Charitable Trusts, February 2008), 3, 7.

3 percent in 1968 to 13 percent in 2012. Overall, the black middle class grew from roughly one in four blacks in 1968 (27 percent) to almost half of all blacks in 2012 (47 percent). About half of this growth in the size of the middle class occurred between 1968 and 1978. The remaining growth is spread more evenly over the next three decades. It is worth noting that these changes leave blacks today more than twice as likely as whites to be in extreme poverty, at the low end, and half as likely as whites to be in the comfortable middle class at the high end (having reached the level of representation in this category in 2012 that whites had attained more than four decades earlier in 1968).[7]

These numbers show that the black middle class has seen growth over these last 40-some years, but poverty continues its assault on African Americans. Why do so many people in America's black underclass remain mired in poverty, trapped in segregated neighborhoods, schools, and communities? Why are so many African American men languishing in the penal system, either incarcerated, on probation, or marginalized for life as convicted felons? In 2012, black men were more likely to go to prison than to graduate with a four-year college degree.[8] How did we end up with such

deep socioeconomic contradictions within the African American community? Answering that question is the challenge of the historian exploring this most recent period in African American history.

✦✦✦

AS THE 1960S DREW TO A CLOSE, WITH THE IMPLEMENTATION OF THE NATION'S FIRST AFFIRMATIVE ACTION PROGRAMS and President Richard M. Nixon's promise of policies that would enable the development of what he boldly called "black capitalism," many working- and middle-class black people outside of the radical political groups were cautiously optimistic that true equality and self-determination were at last on the horizon. Stokely Carmichael's 1966 call for Black Power fit with the mood of the times both at home and abroad, resonating with the antiwar movement in the United States and the revolutionary rhetoric of the newly independent, postcolonial nations of Africa and Asia. But the riots in 1967 and 1968 in Chicago, Detroit, Los Angeles, and many other cities after Dr. King's assassination had shown that there were still deep structural problems to resolve in America, including residential segregation and unequal employment opportunities.

Indeed, affirmative action programs over the next 40 years would lead to an unprecedented level of integration of heretofore historically white educational, cultural, social, political, and financial institutions, inarguably the greatest social revolution in the history of the United States, certainly since the all-too-brief period of Reconstruction. In fact, the percentage of black people in the upper middle class

---

[7] Lawrence Bobo, e-mail message to the authors, January 30, 2013.

[8] Becky Pettit, *Invisible Men: Mass Incarceration and the Myth of Black Progress* (New York: Russell Sage Foundation, 2012), 18; see also Sam Roberts, "How Prisoners Make Us Look Good," *The New York Times Sunday Review*, October 27, 2012, http://www.nytimes.com/2012/10/28/sunday-review/how-prisoners-make-data-look-good.html?_r=0.

would quadruple during this period. Yet in spite of these many strides, the backlash started almost immediately: Federal and state programs meant to facilitate social and economic progress were dismantled before achieving their goals, leaving the poorest African Americans vulnerable to damaging forces. As traditional sources of economic mobility, such as the movement from unskilled to skilled labor in our nation's factories, evaporated, African Americans found themselves battling unemployment and underemployment; decaying, underfunded school systems segregated because of patterns of residential segregation; a drug epidemic of crack cocaine (and draconian laws punishing offenders, adversely affecting the male–female ratio); and obesity and poor health care. With the loss of job opportunities came the loss of hope for a wide swath of the African American community, precisely as another segment of that community was achieving its greatest economic and social mobility in history.

This is a country with both a black president and a black underclass still struggling with pernicious poverty, inadequate education, and an epidemic of incarceration. In this chapter, we examine what it means to be African American today and how the African American community has evolved over the last four decades.

◆◆◆

THE WANING DAYS OF THE CIVIL RIGHTS MOVEMENT, FOLLOWING James Meredith's 1966 March Against Fear at which, ironically, Stokely Carmichael's Black Power movement was born, witnessed an unprecedented amount of militant political activity by two warring schools of young political radicals frustrated by the pace of change and Dr. King's nonviolent protest tactics: the Black Panther Party and a loose and shifting coalition of black cultural nationalist groups.

On May 2, 1967, the Black Panther Party for Self-Defense became for many young people either the logical extension of the fading civil rights movement or a most colorful sign of its complete demise, depending on their point of view. Marching in formation around the Sacramento, California, courthouse, the Black Panthers—bearing arms and sporting black leather jackets, berets, and sunglasses—captured the imagination of a younger generation while striking fear in the old establishment, both white and black. Modeling themselves after Third World revolutionaries like Frantz Fanon, Amílcar Cabral, and Che Guevara, the Black Panthers attracted fervent admirers at home and abroad with their promise of revolution, while creating chaos and confusion in the ranks of the older civil rights leadership. They also attracted the attention of J. Edgar Hoover and the FBI.

Not quite a year later, on April 6, 1968, two days after Martin Luther King, Jr.'s assassination, several carloads of Black Panthers, including the Minister of Information Eldridge Cleaver (1935–1998), got into a 90-minute shootout with the Oakland police. A 17-year-old Panther, Bobby Hutton (1950–1968), was killed, and Cleaver went to jail. A few days later, *Ramparts* magazine published Cleaver's essay "The Death of Martin Luther King: Requiem for Nonviolence," in which he reflected on King's assassination and proclaimed the end of his dream of nonviolent change. "The violent phase of the black liberation struggle is here, and it will spread,"

Cleaver wrote. "From that shot, from that blood, America will be painted red."[9]

In June 1968, Cleaver was released and freed of all charges. But by then, he and his wife, the Black Panther Party's glamorous National Communications Secretary Kathleen Neal Cleaver (b. 1945), had become global icons of "radical chic," spreading the Panthers' message, "Power to the people!" Years later, Eldridge Cleaver would admit, from the secret hideout in Paris where he and Kathleen Cleaver holed up after the incident, that the shootout had been no accident; the Panthers had deliberately sought a confrontation with the police in one of the party's apparently routine "search and destroy" missions. That any bona fide political organization would even consider this sort of tactic is unbelievable today. But such were the times, such the heated rhetoric, such the urgency of "the revolution" that the Panthers and lots of left-wing groups thought was just around the corner.

The BPP had been founded in 1966 by Bobby Seale (b. 1936) and Huey Newton (b. 1942), who were soon joined by Cleaver, a writer and ex-convict who had served time in prison for rape, drugs, and assault. This was a new phase of the civil rights movement. No longer was there the focus, as there had been just a decade before, on making the public face of the movement a person who would appear "beyond reproach" or nonviolent, as with Rosa Parks or Dr. King himself. The Panthers—who began by embracing a black nationalist ideology but soon became Marxist-Leninist—were,

Eldridge Cleaver, by Marion S. Trikosko, October 18, 1968. Photograph. Library of Congress. At the time of this photograph, Cleaver served as minister of information for the Black Panther Party and addressed students outside at American University.

in a sense, the self-described "children of Malcolm X," but identified themselves with the cathartic effects of violent revolution as outlined by Frantz Fanon and as practiced by Che Guevara, Fidel Castro, and Mao Zedong.

They claimed to represent the voice and interests of the "black lumpenproletariat"—the underclass that was emerging in the inner cities as factory jobs disappeared and as major metropolitan areas became increasingly

---

9   Eldridge Cleaver, "The Death of Martin Luther King: Requiem for Nonviolence," *Post-Prison Writings and Speeches*, ed. Robert Scheer (New York: Random House, 1969), 75.

segregated, and their social-outreach programs focused upon the needs of the poor in their midst. In addition to armed self-defense against police harassment and brutality, the BPP provided community services like free breakfast programs for schoolchildren and medical clinics for needy residents in black underclass neighborhoods. If the NAACP, the Urban League, and the SCLC had sought to define the middle ground in African American politics, the Panthers easily and colorfully dominated its left wing.

The Panthers projected an idealized image of black manhood, styling themselves after the rebellious "field Negro" of Malcolm X's famous dichotomy between the loyal "house Negro" and his rebellious, "lower class" cousin who labored from sunup to sundown in the fields. Older civil rights organizations like the venerable NAACP the Panthers derided as servile house Negroes. "The house Negroes," Malcolm had said in 1963, "...would give their life to save the master's house. If the master's house caught on fire, the house Negro would fight harder to put the blaze out than the master would. . . . [B]ut that field Negro . . . When the house caught on fire, he didn't try to put it out; that field Negro prayed for a wind, for a breeze. . . . I'm a field Negro. The masses are the field Negro."[10] The NAACP had certainly lost its good standing with many African Americans over the course of the decade: Its approval rating among black people plummeted between 1963 and 1969, in part because of King's assassination, but also because passage of neither the

Civil Rights Act of 1964 nor the Voting Rights Act of 1965 had satisfied their expectations of dramatic, immediate change.

The message and the methods of the traditional civil rights organizations suddenly seemed out of step with the desires of the younger segment of the African American population. Soon, local chapters of the BPP sprang up across the country, from Oakland to Boston. It wasn't necessarily that black people were flocking to join the Black Panther Party; rather, the Panthers seemed to be serving a larger symbolic or psychological need as political or revolutionary gadflies, symbols of bravery and manhood, defiant irritants and excitants, whose sheer presence seemed to goad, prod, and spur. They were costumed in direct opposition to the buttoned-down, nonviolent respectability that had characterized the civil rights movement in the decade between the Montgomery bus boycott of 1955 and the passage of the Voting Rights Act in 1965. In many ways, the Panthers were the civil rights establishment's worst nightmare. And they occupied that role with alacrity.

The Panthers' call for Black Power was one among many heard across the country. The self-defense impulse of the Deacons for Defense was gaining traction. Within the black church, the Reverend Albert Cleage's radical "theology of Black Power," which he had been preaching for many years from his well-attended church in Detroit, was being listened to by older Christians. In 1969, a coalition of black churchmen even tried to elect Cleage president of the 50 million–member National Council of Churches. And African American women, chafing under the sexism

---

[10] Malcolm X, "Message to the Grass Roots," in *The Portable Malcolm X Reader*, eds. Manning Marable and Garrett Felber (New York: Penguin Books, 2013), 267–68.

of both the old civil rights organizations and the radical groups such as the Panthers, and inspired yet also frustrated by the mainstream white women's movement, joined together in new groups like the National Black Feminist Organization (NBFO) and the Third World Women's Alliance.

To the astonishment of many older and younger black male political leaders, the 1973 Statement of Purpose of the NBFO expressed the need of black women to confront head-on the double bind of racism and sexism. "Because we live in a patriarchy," the proclamation stated, "we have allowed a premium to be put on black male suffering. No one of us would minimize the pain or hardship or the cruel and inhumane treatment experienced by the black man. But history, past or present, rarely deals with the malicious abuse put upon the black woman. . . . We have been called 'matriarchs' by white racists and black nationalists; we have virtually no positive self-images to validate our existence." Fighting off the demeaning stereotypes through which they were portrayed, their statement continued, as "grinning Beulahs, castrating Sapphires, and pancake-box Jemimas," black women "must, together, as a people, work to eliminate racism, from without the black community, which is trying to destroy us as an entire people; but we must remember that sexism is destroying and crippling us from within."[11] Women needed to be part of the "vanguard," as Panther rhetoric liked to put it, and not be relegated outside of it.

---

[11] Miriam Schneir, *Feminism in Our Time: The Essential Writings, World War II to the Present* (New York: Vintage, 1994), 173–74.

◇◇◇

IF THE PANTHERS SEEMED TO HAVE SOLE POSSESSION OR DOMINANCE OF THE SOCIALIST LEFT IN ALL OF THIS POLITICAL FERMENT, another group was emerging at the same time that claimed dominance of the cultural nationalist pole of the radical black political spectrum. It, too, had its beginnings in the mid-1960s, just as the Black Panthers did. Both movements, in a sense, arose within the aftermath of despair that ensued following the assassination of Malcolm X in Harlem in February 1965, which in turn occurred just as the civil rights movement was reaching its zenith of power and effectiveness in the legislative realm with the passage of crucially important legislation by a Congress prodded by the zealous President Lyndon Baines Johnson, who clearly saw part of his historical legacy as dismantling de jure segregation, something his enormously popular predecessor, John F. Kennedy, had been unable to do.

After Malcolm X's tragic and brazen assassination, Maulana Karenga (born Ron Everett in 1941), an African studies doctoral student at UCLA, started an organization known as US (as in "us versus them"). Karenga preached the idea of racial salvation through cultural nationalism, celebrating both a mythic and historical African past, urging fluency in Swahili and the adoption of Swahili names, abandoning both the blues and the Christian religion (just as the Panthers advocated) and wearing traditional African clothes. His organization's most enduring cultural contribution would come in 1966, with the creation of the festival Kwanzaa, a holiday tradition that Karenga himself invented to celebrate "African" community and cultural values, both ancient and contemporary.

US, however, did not take a purely cultural approach. Karenga's highest-profile convert, LeRoi Jones (b. 1934), the former Beat poet and playwright and the founder in 1965 of the influential Black Arts Movement, raised the organization's recognition dramatically and helped spread its message nationally and internationally. Karenga renamed Jones Imamu Amiri Baraka, and Baraka established his own headquarters in Newark, New Jersey. The organization engaged in interventions within the political system (Baraka campaigned tirelessly and effectively for the election of Kenneth Gibson as Newark's first black mayor) and boasted its own paramilitary unit, the Simba Washiku ("Young Lions"). Together, Karenga and Baraka also mounted a campaign through the arts and philosophy both to redress the psychological and cultural effects of slavery and Jim Crow segregation and to underscore the weaknesses they perceived in the Marxist-Leninist approach of the Black Panthers.

But the Black Panthers scoffed at what they saw as the cultural nationalists' romantic, idealized vision of Africa and black nationalism. Huey Newton famously accused US and Karenga of purveying "'pork chop' nationalism," sneering that only bourgeois black people could afford to indulge in the wearing of dashikis and taking Swahili classes—frivolous luxuries in times that, the BPP said, called for armed self-defense and materialist analysis of the causes of black oppression and poverty.[12]

---

[12] Dean E. Robinson, *Black Nationalism in American Politics and Thought* (New York: Cambridge University Press, 2001), 67.

To some in a younger generation, the emergence of multiple and even contradictory models of black militancy was colorful, exhilarating, and inspiring. And in the heady years of revolution that defined the aftermath of the assassination of Dr. King, the fine points of ideology that distinguished the Panthers from US were often lost on the casual observer. Besides, for many people who would never join either faction, the groups' militant stances against entrenched white racism and for radical social and economic change were what galvanized support and enthusiasm, rather than their various "Ten Point Programs" (the Panthers'), or "*Nguzo Saba*" or "Seven Principles" (Karenga's). To some extent, this was "revolution as theatre," as theatrical critic Robert Brustein called it, or "radical chic," as the novelist Tom Wolfe derisively labeled it.

In August 1968, R & B legend James Brown (1933–2006) released the song "Say It Loud—I'm Black and I'm Proud," which captured that spirit of assertion and change, becoming an instant, massive hit and the highlight of Brown's concerts, evolving into a call-and-response between him and his audience. It is quite telling that followers of both the Panthers and US found common ground through the song—and through the Afro hairstyle—suggesting the strong black nationalist foundations that both groups shared, despite their divergent views of the compatibility of capitalism with fundamental black progress.

A new aesthetic, the idea that "black is beautiful," began to permeate the American cultural mainstream through art, music, and fashion. Because of the nature of the marketplace, radical chic quickly became co-opted by advertisers and manufacturers, both black and white, eager to cash in on a new trend. "The

James Brown and the Famous Flames, circa 1964. Photograph. Michael Ochs Archives, Getty Images. Brown appeared at Harlem's Apollo Theatre.

most visible signifier of soul was undoubtedly the Afro," said historian Robin Kelley. "What passed as 'authentic' ghetto culture was as much a product of market forces and the commercial appropriation of urban styles as experience and individual creativity."[13]

---

[13] Robin D. G. Kelley, *Yo' Mama's Disfunktional!: Fighting the Culture Wars in Urban America* (Boston: Beacon Press, 1998), 26.

Perhaps the most lasting impact of the black culture wars of the late '60s between the Panthers and the cultural nationalists was not mass membership for either group (the actual number of card-carrying members was quite small, in fact), but an acceptance of a radicalized political-cultural identity and the general embrace of and pride in black history and the arts and culture among the working classes and the educated middle classes. The important black

"The fact that the U.S. really got its first vicarious look at our culture [on *Soul Train*] was amazing. But the true stroke of genius, in my opinion, was how Don managed to show us how important we were, which was not an easy task."

sociologist E. Franklin Frazier (1894–1962) had lambasted an absence of this pride among the latter group in his classic critique, *The Black Bourgeoisie*, in 1957. But by the late '60s and early '70s, even middle-class black people were sporting modified Afros, peppering their discourse with words like *brother* and *sister*, and demonstrating a fluency in and comfort with all sorts of manifestations of black culture that previous generations might have not been as willing to declare, at least publicly. Even Berry Gordy's Motown was releasing more radical and politically conscious music, such as Marvin Gaye's (1939–1984) astonishingly popular and brilliant album, *What's Going On?* A cultural revolution, if not a violent political upheaval as Huey Newton and Bobby Seale envisioned when they started the Panthers, was most certainly going on, and black culture and thought were driving it.

When Don Cornelius (1936–2012) started the television program *Soul Train* in 1971, he introduced black culture to a mainstream national audience on a scale like never before. Viewers at home were entranced by the music and dances, the dancers' clothing and hairstyles, and even the house-made advertising for sponsors such as Johnson Products, an African American beauty company famous for hair products like Afro Sheen, the product of choice for those sporting Afros. By the mid-1970s, the show had entered

some 100 markets. The DJ and drummer for the band the Roots, Questlove, born Ahmir Thompson in 1971, essentially grew up with the show, and he said that it had a dramatic impact on him as well as on the African American community as a whole. "The fact that the U.S. really got its first vicarious look at our culture [on *Soul Train*] was amazing," he said. "But the true stroke of genius, in my opinion, was how Don managed to show us how important we were, which was not an easy task."[14]

Soul Train was part of the changing landscape of American culture. Black people were not only seen on *Soul Train*; while they were not exactly the norm on TV, black actors and actresses had become highly visible. The fervent rise of radical black politics, in an example of unintended consequences, was pushing mainstream media to expand its appeal to a broader and more diverse audience. And those signs of cultural integration also fostered the image of a corporate structure that was sensitive, flexible, and responsive. Some members of the radical left would point to these developments in retrospect as elements of the co-opting of their movement for fundamental, dramatic, revolutionary change.

[14] "Brand New Bag: Questlove on Don Cornelius," *Okayplayer* (February 1, 2012), http://www.okayplayer.com/news/brand-new-bag-questlove-on-don-cornlius.html.

Cultural integration was happening in Hollywood as well, at least for a spell. In 1971, the filmmaker Melvin Van Peebles (b. 1932) made *Sweet Sweetback's Baadasssss Song* for a half-million dollars. Black audiences, hungry for images of an African American "sticking it to the man," turned out in droves, and it grossed $10 million, a phenomenal ratio of cost to profit. Huey Newton called it "the first truly revolutionary Black film."[15] Out of *Sweetback*'s success a new genre, aimed at a previously untapped audience, was born: "blaxploitation." The NAACP and similar groups chastised the filmmakers for trafficking in racial stereotypes. The NAACP, however, didn't speak for the nation's taste in popular culture, and blaxploitation thrived.

All black art forms grew in popularity and significance. They have continued to grow throughout this historical period, to the extent that cultural forms such as rap and hip-hop, with their strong black-culture bases, have become the cultural expressions of choice for the last 30 years for America's youth culture, whether black or white, Asian or Latino. With their increased visibility and acceptance in almost all aspects of the culture industry—with the important exception of ownership of the means of production, as the Panthers, quoting Marx, liked to say—African Americans in the crucial years of transition following Dr. King's assassination and the end of the civil rights movement were "making black culture the template for the nation's cultural identity."[16]

---

[15] Ed Guerrero, *Framing Blackness: The African American Image in Film* (Philadelphia: Temple University Press, 1993), 87.

[16] Thomas C. Holt, *Children of Fire: A History of African Americans* (New York: Hill and Wang, 2010), 344.

⬥⬥⬥

THIS TREND WAS NOT LIMITED TO THE POPULAR DOMAIN. AS WE HAVE SEEN, ONE OF THE MOST DRAMATIC, AND PERHAPS IRONIC, aspects of the transition period following the collapse of the civil rights movement after Dr. King's death and the rise and fall of radical black politics—a fall abetted by the repressive tactics of the FBI, it must be said—was the curious manner in which black history and culture entered the broader American cultural mainstream. And nowhere has this proven to be more important than in the academy, with the field of African American studies. Black studies departments were created in universities across the country starting in 1968, attesting to the growing belief that African American history and culture deserved recognition and respect, but most immediately as a response to student demands and political pressure.

But as black culture, both high and low, transformed the public culture of the United States, repressive forces were at work. By the winter of 1968, the FBI's infamous director, J. Edgar Hoover, had declared the Black Panthers "the greatest threat to the internal security of the country" and systematically set out to destroy them through a secret program of intelligence gathering, propaganda, and disinformation tactics: COINTELPRO. This program went straight for the broader black radical political movement's Achilles' heel: the ideological disputes between its different organizations. And in January 1969, the simmering rivalry between the Panthers and US, until then essentially a war of words, took a violent turn.

When members of both groups attended a meeting to decide on the direction of UCLA's new Afro-American Studies Program, a shootout ensued that left two Panthers dead and sent several members of US to jail or into exile. The politics within black culture—and it is a tradition of internecine wars of words—turned suddenly and utterly deadly, in a way that Frederick Douglass and Martin R. Delany or W. E. B. Du Bois and Booker T. Washington never could have imagined. In their day, anti-black racists killed black people; black people did not kill each other, at least not over political differences. Nor had race-based name-calling—the "outing" of an opponent as an "Uncle Tom" or a supposed "race traitor"—ever become as viciously expressed in public, in the mainstream media, at any point in African American history as it did in this garrulous interregnum between the demise of the civil rights movement and the creation of its next manifestation, which in retrospect seems to have been primarily electoral.

❯❯❯

THE DECADE FOLLOWING MALCOLM X'S DEATH WAS A PERIOD OF NOISY AND RHETORICALLY VIOLENT TRANSITION between two large and not easily defined sets of forces. On the one hand, the clearly articulated and popularly supported agendas of the civil rights movement, which through its various and sometimes competing faces nevertheless pursued a set of related strategies designed to dismantle the Jim Crow past, proved to be devastatingly effective in realizing its goals. On the other hand, perhaps because it was difficult to imagine that the legislative agenda set in motion by Charles Hamilton Houston ever would be as fully realized as it was by 1965, no one organization seemed to have articulated an analysis that foresaw the *period after civil rights*—the period in which economic relations would prove to be more obviously determining factors in the condition and treatment, the fate and fortunes, of the larger black community than solely race-based forms of oppression, such as the status of black people before the law.

To be sure, economic relationships had been fundamental to the condition of black people since slavery, which itself is a racialized economic relationship par excellence. But color prejudice, xenophobia, and other manifestations of anti-black racism, as we have seen throughout this book, had functioned to convince many activists that the problems afflicting the African American community historically were rooted in ethnic tension or racial prejudice rather than in structural, economic relationships. But once de jure segregation had been effectively dismantled through the battle plan designed by Charles Hamilton Houston and engineered by Thurgood Marshall, the status of the larger segment of black people in America had not been magically transformed. In fact, to some observers who had naïvely expected that the accumulated problems of American race relations would be solved through these legal procedures, it seemed that social conditions for the lower classes on the economic ladder had somehow become worse since the movement ended. In other words, the movement won its stated goals, but then had to stop and ask itself, *Now what?*

While the Panthers had sought to provide one answer to this question, and the various black cultural nationalist groups another, it is important to remember that these debates unfolded at the level of the radical elite. Average

African Americans did not flock to join either the Black Panther Party or SNCC or US. Rather, black people—enabled by the passage of the Voting Rights Act of 1965—began to register and vote, and they did so overwhelmingly for the Democratic Party, especially after Lyndon Johnson's trouncing of Barry Goldwater in the 1964 presidential election. Johnson's unprecedented success in marshaling civil rights legislation through the Congress and his appointment of many black people to prominent positions in government, especially Thurgood Marshall's elevation as an associate justice of the Supreme Court, surely enabled him to shore up the "black vote."

In retrospect, perhaps the most telling legacy of the radical political battles in the waning years of the '60s would be in the subsequent involvement of an extraordinary number of black women and men in electoral politics, including many figures who had been actively involved in both civil rights and the more radical groups that sought to discredit the tactics of the civil rights movement, including three of Dr. King's lieutenants, Jesse Jackson, Sr. (b. 1941), who would mount the first plausible black presidential bid in 1984, following the symbolic candidacy of Congresswoman Shirley Chisholm (1924–2005) from New York in 1972; Andrew Young (b. 1932), who in 1972 would become, along with Barbara Jordan (1936–1996), the first black congressional representative elected from the South since 1898, and then in 1977 the first black U.S. ambassador to the United Nations; and Congressman John Lewis from Atlanta, elected in 1987. Also making their way into electoral politics were Marion Barry (b. 1936), elected twice as the mayor of the District of Columbia, first in 1979 and then again in 1995; Eleanor Holmes

Norton (b. 1937), elected in 1991 as a nonvoting delegate from the nation's capital as well; and the former Black Panther Bobby Rush (b. 1946), elected to Congress in 1993 to represent his district in Chicago.

And, in a classically American phenomenon, several leaders of the radical groups from the '60s would, over the following decades, be named to tenured professorships at prominent universities, including US organizers Maulana Karenga and Amiri Baraka and the former Panthers Kathleen Cleaver, Angela Davis (b. 1944), perhaps the principal icon of "the Revolution" in the late '60s and early '70s, and Julian Bond (b. 1940), who served 20 years in both chambers of the Georgia Legislature before becoming chairman of the board of the NAACP and a professor at various universities. Bob Moses (b. 1935), the brilliant and charismatic head of SNCC and the architect (with Ella Baker) of its grassroots Freedom Summers and massive southern voter registration drives, would attempt to reform the educational opportunities afforded poor black youth through his boldly innovative Algebra Project. In other words, many of the younger activists from both left-wing and centrist black political organizations in the '60s would over the next several decades turn to electoral politics and the academy in a continuing attempt to effect the social change not completed by the passage of civil rights laws.

But what of the simultaneous collapse of opportunity for such a wide swath of the lower working classes? This paradox prevails in the black community today and is a source of challenge and discord. Despite troubling evidence of destructive conflict within the radical movement at the time, a younger generation of African Americans saw a wealth of new avenues open to them, an unprecedented number of opportunities created by affirmative action programs. For example, the class of 1966 at Yale University graduated only six black students. Three years later, in 1969–the same year that the violent conflagration between the Panthers and US erupted on the campus of UCLA–96 African Americans entered the university as first-year students. Among them were Ben Carson (b. 1951), today the chief of pediatric neurosurgery at the Johns Hopkins University; Kurt Schmoke (b. 1949), elected the first black mayor of Baltimore in 1987; Sheila Jackson Lee (b. 1950), serving in Congress from Texas's 18th Congressional District since 1995; and Anthony Davis (b. 1951), the opera and jazz composer and professor, as well as a legion of doctors, lawyers, investment bankers, and venture capitalists.

Yale and its sister research universities were ahead of the curve, but the effort to diversify institutions of higher education and workplaces soon became a national phenomenon, suggesting that the integration of elite American educational and political and financial institutions at their highest levels became the principal form that the politics of integration assumed after the end of the civil rights movement. By 1972, the Equal Employment Opportunity Commission (EEOC) would develop guidelines for affirmative action that promised talented individuals a chance to make their mark on our world and become part of the emerging black middle class. Many of the students taking part in this wave of integration came from working-class families, and an education at an elite, historically white institution was their first step up the socioeconomic ladder.

Although gaining access to elite schools was a groundbreaking achievement, these pioneers often saw themselves as continuing the civil rights revolution, albeit in a different form. They refused to be obsequious or overly grateful for the opportunity they had earned, and black students felt entitled to demand the respect that had been denied their elders for far too long. At Yale, for example, a massive strike shut down the school in mid-April 1970, a protest organized in solidarity with the Black Panther trial taking place in New Haven at the time. It was a thrilling moment, even though Yale's president, Kingman Brewster–the mastermind behind the school's early diversity initiative–would subsequently lose his job when he expressed doubt that a black revolutionary could get a fair trial in America.

The integration of elite and heretofore largely white educational, cultural, and political organizations and institutions through affirmative action and the simultaneous collapse of factory jobs in the cities (the traditional method of achieving upward class mobility throughout the 20th century) would lead to the *intraracial* class divide described at the beginning of this chapter, and which the sociologist William Julius Wilson (b. 1935) would define in his seminal studies, *The Declining Significance of Race: Blacks and Changing American Institutions*, published in 1978; and *The Truly Disadvantaged: The Inner City, the Underclass, and Public Policy*, published in 1987. Only a relatively small proportion of the black community could take advantage of these expanded opportunities. While the lucky few were fighting for Black Power on elite college campuses, a great number of less fortunate young African Americans were overseas, battling the Vietcong.

"Black communities marched into the 1970s," Kelley said, "with at least some hope that black political power would bring a brighter day."

⬥⬥⬥

IN 1968, WHEN MAJOR COLIN POWELL (B. 1937) RETURNED FOR HIS SECOND TOUR OF DUTY IN VIETNAM, there were a half million American troops there. Where once African Americans had fought for the right to serve in an integrated military from the Civil War through World War II, now they were overrepresented in the nation's armed forces. African Americans made up about 11 percent of the United States population in 1967; estimates for the number of black troops in Vietnam were anywhere from 12 to 16 percent, and even higher in combat units. Unable to escape the draft as easily as middle-class white youth, and with fewer employment options, young African American men were more likely than their white counterparts to serve in this increasingly unpopular war. This trend would continue in the years ahead: The percentage of blacks in the armed forces would rise as high as 33 percent in 1979.[17]

While the African American presence in the military bespoke a lag in job opportunities for working-class black people, impressive gains in electoral politics, as we have seen, continued to buoy hopes for the future. In his book *Yo' Mama's Disfunktional!*, Robin Kelley reported numbers that could only be encouraging: In 1969, 994 black men and 131 black women

held public office; by 1975, the number of black elected officials had grown, incredibly, to 2,973 men and 530 women. The Congressional Black Caucus was founded in 1971 with a dozen members; by 2012, that number had nearly quadrupled. The presence of black people in the halls of power, which had previously been a whites-only domain in practice even if not in theory, bolstered the community tremendously. "Black communities marched into the 1970s," Kelley said, "with at least some hope that black political power would bring a brighter day."[18]

The African American mayor of Gary, Indiana, Richard Hatcher (b. 1933), who had won office in the majority-black city in 1967, hosted the first National Black Political Convention in 1972. In a sign that these were transitional times, every major civil rights and Black Power group attended, except for the NAACP. Although deep and often bitter political and ideological differences threatened to stall the proceedings, the 8,000 attendees from all 50 states joined in the chant, "It's nation time!" Strangely, though, the convention failed to endorse New York Congresswoman Shirley Chisholm's historic 1972 candidacy as the first African American woman to seek the Democratic presidential nomination.

Amiri Baraka, who as we have seen gained prominence during the mid-1960s as the founder of the Black Arts Movement and then at the end of the decade as the co-leader of the

[17] Robin D. G. Kelley, *Into the Fire: African Americans since 1970* (New York: Oxford University Press, 1996), 48.

[18] Kelley, *Yo' Mama's Disfunktional!*, 6.

major black cultural nationalist organization, brought unity to the diverse group by drafting a document that all could get behind. The Gary Declaration stated: "The American system does not work for the masses of our people, and it cannot be made to work without radical, fundamental changes.... The challenge is thrown to us here in Gary. It is the challenge to consolidate and organize our own Black role as the vanguard in the struggle for a new society."[19] The declaration's policy recommendations—urban renewal, quality education, welfare rights, and economic opportunity—could very well have been written by Dr. King and his associates just four years before, and proved to mainstream observers that Black Power had "come of age," as *The Washington Post* reported.[20] It was the first step of a national black political agenda.

As in Gary and Cleveland before it (where Carl Stokes was elected as the city's first black mayor in 1967), the era's greatest political gains were made at the level of cities, just as America's cities were becoming predominantly black. By 1977—just nine years after the death of Martin Luther King—more than 200 cities, among them New Orleans, Philadelphia, Newark, and Washington, D.C., had elected black mayors, two of whom would become prominent on

the national political scene: Maynard Jackson (1938–2003) in Atlanta and Tom Bradley (1917–1998) in Los Angeles, both elected in 1973.

Yet even as these mayors took office, America's cities were changing, a process accelerated by the national recession that hit in the 1970s. Jobs either moved out to the suburbs or out of the country completely, and white people and their tax revenue went along with them. Black people remained clustered in inner cities. The funk visionary George Clinton (b. 1941) coined a new term to describe the phenomenon in the Parliament song "Chocolate City," an ode to the growing black population in the nation's capital. By 1970, there were "chocolate cities" across the country: Washington, D.C., and Atlanta were more than 50 percent black; Detroit and New York more than 40 percent; and Philadelphia and Cleveland, more than a third.

———— ✕✕✕ ————

THIS TRANSFORMATION WAS TAKING PLACE AS THE RADICAL BLACK POWER MOVEMENT CONFRONTED SETBACKS that came from both without and within. By 1971, Maulana Karenga and the Black Panthers Huey P. Newton, H. Rap Brown (b. 1943), and Bobby Seale were all in jail, while Stokely Carmichael and Eldridge and Kathleen Cleaver were living abroad or in exile. The FBI's spying and disinformation campaign had done irreparable damage to the movement by inciting conflicts between revolutionaries of different ideologies, classes, and genders, effectively undermining

[19] Amiri Baraka, "The Gary Declaration: Black Politics at the Crossroads," National Black Political Convention, 1972, *BlackPast.org: Remembered and Reclaimed*, http://www.blackpast.org/?q=primary/gary-declaration-national-black-political-convention-1972.

[20] "Black Power Comes of Age," *Washington Post*, June 29, 1972.

FACING PAGE: General Colin Powell, Arlington, Virginia; January 23, 1991. Photograph. Jean Louis Atlan/Sygma, Corbis UK Ltd.

"You can't change a house from outside. You have to be inside the house. . . . I'm trying to sell us *in*. I'm trying to put pressure on the government not to forget about us."

any chance they might ever have had of gaining widespread grassroots membership, although their symbolic significance as advocates for black rights and full social, political, and economic equality cannot be underestimated.

And now some of the standard-bearers of black pride had begun to lose the people's trust. James Brown had already disappointed fans by performing his Black Power anthem at Richard Nixon's first inauguration, but when black America's "Soul Brother No. 1" enthusiastically endorsed Nixon for a second term in 1972, Brown earned a new nickname: "Nixon's clown." In his autobiography, he explained how he defended his motives to his jeering audience: "'You can't change a house from outside. You have to be inside the house. . . . I'm trying to sell us *in*. I'm trying to put pressure on the government not to forget about us.'"[21] Moreover, the white "silent majority" who elected Nixon was ready to stop making concessions to African Americans, becoming nervous about protecting their own economic interests as the economy began to stall and the country's coffers shrink. The times were a-changing, and not in the positive ways that Bob Dylan's song—which became a virtual anthem of the broad movement for social change in the '60s—had predicted. It was a time of retrenchment. Lyndon Baines Johnson's "Great Society" social programs now came under siege.

The post–civil rights era's optimism and African American unity began to be splintered by growing political and class differences and new social problems. Private-sector affirmative action initiatives and government programs created just a few years earlier were ended or stripped down before they'd been given a chance to work, and affirmative action programs began to be challenged in the courts. While a small black middle class continued to make impressive progress, the urban poor found it increasingly difficult to break out of ghettos that grew more entrenched, hopeless, and dangerous in the face of a national recession and new social ills like crack cocaine and AIDS.

The electoral gains of black people were not mirrored in their economic status. In fact, historian Robin Kelley has concluded that "one of the most striking features of the 1970s was the widening income gap between blacks and whites." From the beginning of the decade to the end, African Americans would suffer a major setback in income as compared to whites. The figures Kelley reported in his book *Into the Fire* are discouraging, to say the least. In 1970, African Americans were earning 71 cents for every dollar made by whites; by 1979, their earning power was barely over half that of whites, with African Americans now pulling in only 58 cents on the dollar.[22] Advancement was supposed to mean moving forward, so why were blacks backsliding?

---

[21] James Brown and Bruce Tucker, *James Brown: The Godfather of Soul* (New York: Thunder Mouth's Press, 1986, 1997), 232.

[22] Kelley, *Into the Fire*, 48.

THE 1950S AND '60S HAD SEEN THE GREATEST GROWTH OF THE BLACK MIDDLE CLASS IN HISTORY, but the American economy was changing. The disappearance of heavy industry, the decline of trade unions, and the departure of remaining American industry to foreign shores disproportionately affected black workers who were just starting to get ahead. By 1978, more than 30 percent of black families lived below the poverty line, compared with less than 9 percent of white families. One reason for this unequal impact was a simple, disappointing truth: The racial barriers of the past had never been completely erased.[23]

Almost two decades after the *Brown v. Board of Education* decision mandated racial integration, many of the nation's public schools were still segregated in practice. In September 1974, the federal district judge W. Arthur Garrity, Jr., implemented a plan to desegregate Boston's "racially imbalanced" public schools. Thousands of students were bused to schools outside their neighborhoods, and racial violence exploded. But this time, the anti-busing activists, who were fighting to keep black children out of predominantly white schools, mainly in an Irish working-class enclave of the city, portrayed themselves as the victims and garnered a surprising amount of support from other white communities throughout the country. Racial integration was fine, as long as it was residential, by neighborhood. And neighborhoods had become increasingly segregated racially since the mid-1960s.

Boston turned into as potent a symbol of white racism as Selma or Little Rock. The busing situation and the violence with which it was met exposed the hypocrisy of the city that a century earlier was the cradle of abolitionism and antislavery sympathy. While Boston might be able to boast a history of antislavery politics, this did not mean the city's residents 100 years later would be welcoming to African Americans in their neighborhoods and schools. White opponents to desegregation attacked the buses bringing black children into their neighborhoods with rocks, bottles, and racist graffiti. The schools became battlegrounds, with untold instances of arrests, injuries, and abuse.

Boston was the iconic case, but resistance to school desegregation was fierce across the country. In many cities, whites simply deserted the public schools to avoid desegregation, moving to the suburbs or paying for private education. By 1980, white students made up only 4 percent of public school enrollment in Washington, D.C.; 8 percent in Atlanta; and 9 percent in Newark.[24] Twenty-five years after the *Brown* decision, the goal of school integration seemed more elusive than ever.

Despite compelling evidence that racial disparities persisted in education and employment, affirmative action policies also sparked a fierce white backlash. In 1978, the Supreme Court ruled in the *Regents of the University of California v. Bakke* case that the use of racial quotas—setting aside a specific number of slots for a racial group—was unconstitutional. The court declared that the University of California's efforts to increase diversity in its medical school amounted to "reverse

---

[23] Kelley, *Into the Fire*, 48.

[24] Kelley, *Into the Fire*, 65.

discrimination." Disgruntled whites, resorting to legal tactics rather than fire hoses, again portrayed themselves as the victims, as they had done in the Boston public schools, unfairly deprived of rights and opportunity.

While those who had benefited from affirmative action programs continued their upward climb, those who hadn't were being left further behind. And it was no longer only the gap between black and white that was alarming; that gap that we have been tracing in this chapter between the black elite and the black poor was widening dramatically as well. Disparity among blacks was nothing new; we need only recall the concepts of the Talented Tenth and the New Negro—or, more to the point, the Old Negro—to realize this. But in the face of what were supposed to be the legacies of the civil rights movement and President Johnson's War on Poverty—increased opportunities and equality for black people across the board—this trend was expressing itself in new and distressing ways. While William Julius Wilson's *The Declining Significance of Race* described the improving conditions of the black middle class in relation to the decline of the black underclass in 1978, the situation only has continued to deteriorate and the black class gap widen over the past three decades. By 1980, the economic disparities between African Americans were as great as the differences between black and white Americans. Class divisions undermined the political unity that last manifested itself in the great March on Washington in 1963.

Ironically, as this class divide was opening, the African American experience continued to gain in symbolic stature: Black History Month was established in 1976, expanding on the effort of the historian Carter G. Woodson (1875–1950) 50 years earlier to devote national attention to black accomplishment through the creation of Negro History Week in 1926. Alex Haley's television miniseries *Roots* recorded an unprecedented number of viewers in 1977 by dramatizing America's history of slavery, once whitewashed out of national memory. One way to understand the extraordinary popularity of *Roots* was as a collective healing ritual just nine years after the murder of Dr. King. The audience for *Roots* reflected a combination of the legacy of the civil rights movement and nostalgia for its interracial coalition politics on the one hand, and the thrust of black nationalist identity politics, especially the identification of African Americans with Africa through a socially constructed, ostensibly "Pan-African" identity on the other. Alex Haley's great achievement was to bring together these two strands, two strands that traditionally, as we have seen, were diametrically opposed. This was something of a miracle, and the program's exceptional viewership reflects this extraordinary confluence of opposing forces. The result was the largest black and white audience ever to watch a television program about black history, before or since. Today, *Roots* remains the third most popular television series in American history.

◆◆◆

AS THE 1970S CAME TO AN END, POPULAR INTEREST IN AFRICAN AMERICANS MAY HAVE BEEN ON THE RISE, but that didn't benefit the population at large. Once Ronald Reagan was elected president, the black underclass was essentially sidelined by policies that at best ignored them and at worst dismantled the progress that had been made in the community. As the New Right took hold, plans for urban renewal (with side effects like the demolition of some poor neighborhoods and the gentrification of others) and practices such as "redlining" (denying services, loans, or jobs to residents of certain areas) helped to lock the black underclass into inner cities decimated by cutbacks in federal aid. A national recession spurred joblessness to its highest levels since the Great Depression. Black unemployment topped 20 percent and was even higher among African American youth, leaving "ghetto" residents vulnerable to the onslaught of urban blight, gang warfare, crime, and drugs.

The War on Poverty waged by the Johnson administration had been lost, replaced by President Reagan's new, unfairly enforced War on Drugs. Yet despite these difficulties—or perhaps because of them—a new African American cultural movement emerged that would have a massive global influence: hip-hop. The situation was growing dire and deadly, yet in the Bronx, an embattled "Chocolate City" if ever there was one, young people were planting the seeds of a new cultural movement that would change the face of black America yet again. DJs, rappers, and graffiti artists playing to their neighborhoods would soon reach an audience much vaster than any of them could have reasonably anticipated.

Afrika Bambaataa (b. 1957), the son of Jamaican and Barbadian immigrants, grew up in the Bronx River Projects with Black Nationalist and Black Muslim relatives. In 1971, as a result of a court mandate to desegregate, Bambaataa and other black students were bused to a previously all-white Bronx high

school. The story played out for Bambaataa as it did for so many African Americans. He got caught up in the extreme racial tensions in the school, becoming a warlord for a local gang. Fortunately, though, the teenager freed himself from the cycle of violence he'd become a part of and began honing his skills as a DJ. In 1975, after winning a trip to Africa—quite a prize for an essay contest—Bambaataa returned to the Bronx and founded the Zulu Nation, what has since become a veritable (and some would say venerable) institution.

The Zulu Nation was about not just music but also a "way of life." Its Seven Infinity Lessons prescribed rules and philosophies for its members, echoing the Nation of Islam and US in language and style, but with one very significant difference: Bambaataa was a proponent of integration, if not in the traditional sense (which America had come to see as being court-ordered), then in a spiritual one. Part Martin Luther King and part Malcolm X, Bambaataa, in his own innovative way, was helping to integrate the racially divided Bronx.

His music reflected that commitment to unity. In 1981, his first single, the appropriately named "Planet Rock," commingled the music of spaghetti westerns, the German electronic band Kraftwerk, and the Nigerian performer Fela Kuti over his own beats and scratches. Bambaataa's mixing of black and white music in one record led to the musical and cultural coming together of the until-then divergent populations of the Bronx and lower Manhattan—black street kids and white punks from the art scene. Hip-hop historian Jeff Chang called Bambaataa "the generative figure, the Promethean firestarter of the hip-hop generation. . . . The iron doors of segregation

Grandmaster Flash, DJ Kool Herc, Afrika Bambaataa, and Chuck D at Columbia University's Rap Summit, November 1993. Photograph. Kevin Mazuir/WireImage, Getty Images.

that the previous generation had started to unlock were battered down by the pioneers of the hip-hop generation. Soon hip-hop was not merely all-city; it was global—Planet Rock."[25]

As hip-hop was hungrily devoured by black and white listeners, it also became a platform for African American artists to give voice to the social conditions afflicting the inner cities. Bambaataa's Bronx compatriots,

Grandmaster Flash & the Furious Five, put out a record in 1982 that exemplified that potential. It was called "The Message," and it became an anthem for a generation, graphically describing the dreadful buildings where so many black youth were living in an urban wasteland, buildings that might provide four walls for the residents but offered no shelter to speak of.

Some hip-hop artists embraced the mission of conveying political messages through music. Melle Mel (b. 1961) exhorted voters to support the Reverend Jesse Jackson, Sr., in

[25] Jeff Chang, *Can't Stop Won't Stop: A History of the Hip-Hop Generation* (New York: St. Martin's Press, 2005), 92.

his 1984 bid for the Democratic presidential nomination in the single "Jesse." Bambaataa, Kurtis Blow (b. 1959), and DJ Kool Herc (b. 1955) joined the international effort to end apartheid in South Africa. MC Lyte (b. 1970) provided a woman's perspective (a woefully underrepresented point of view at that time, and still is to a large extent today) about drug addiction, domestic violence, and the frightening new HIV epidemic. And at a time when civil rights gains had stalled, Chuck D (b. 1960) and Public Enemy evoked the spirit of black nationalism on their album *Fear of a Black Planet*, in songs like "Power to the People."

Hip-hop had catapulted a purely African American art form to the fore, and it quickly evolved into a political and economic force with which to be reckoned. But two generations earlier, the Harlem Renaissance visionaries, and one generation before, the participants in the Black Arts Movement, had also idealistically hoped that their production of black art and popular culture would lead to African American advancement throughout society, the former in a sort of artistic or cultural version of trickle-down economics, the latter in terms of a genuine psychological revolution. But neither had happened—at least not in the ways that the creators of those movements had hoped. Could hip-hop succeed in this idealistic goal where the Harlem Renaissance and the Black Arts Movement had failed?

After all, hip-hop had never been just about politics. As it became more popular, its growing multiracial audience responded enthusiastically to its other aspects, especially the bragging, signifying, and macho posturing that glorified violence, misogyny, and materialism. Mainstream celebrities like Bill Cosby (b. 1937) and conservatives like Thomas Sowell (b. 1930) complained that hip-hop perpetuated old racial stereotypes, which might thrill white listeners but offered lamentable role models to black youth. The cultural critic Kevin Powell worried that hip-hop was turning into "a cultural safari for white people," especially for those more comfortable with images of black gangbangers than of black engineers or administrators.[26] Did hip-hop's popularity speed the emergence of two distinct black Americas or simply reflect it—or could hip-hop be the symbolic bridge between the classes within the black community?

❊❊❊

THE GREATEST IRONY WAS THAT YOUNG BLACK MEN FROM THE UNDERCLASS WERE FINALLY JOINING the pantheon of national cultural icons at the very moment that their brothers and sisters were being incarcerated in ever greater numbers thanks to a new urban problem: crack cocaine.

On the eve of crack's arrival, the decline in employment opportunities for young black men had already led to an increase of street crime like muggings and robberies. Cheap, available, and highly addictive, crack cocaine offered a new opportunity to get rich quickly, albeit at the expense of those whose lives would be ruined by their new habit. Violence increased as gangs and dealers battled over control of markets. Once again, many feared the black community was destroying itself from within.

---

[26] Stephen Tuck, *We Ain't What We Ought to Be: The Black Freedom Struggle from Emancipation to Obama* (Cambridge: Harvard University Press, 2010), 374.

Crack appeared just as the black middle class was itself fleeing to the suburbs, depriving inner cities of the moderating influence of people working "normal" jobs, as William Julius Wilson points out. By the late 1980s, low-income black neighborhoods like the Bronx and South Central Los Angeles had become virtual war zones, in which the police employed military-style tactics like helicopters, high-tech surveillance systems, SWAT teams, and even tanks to patrol and control. But selling crack was simply the best economic option for many young men in poverty—even though the consequences of getting arrested could be much more serious for them than for white drug dealers. While both black and white people were using and selling crack, black street dealers were much more likely to be arrested and much more likely to be convicted if charged. The racial disparity in drug-law enforcement and the very different penalties for crack versus powder cocaine laid the foundation for a new phenomenon: mass incarceration of African American men, the basis of a new racial caste system, which the legal scholar Michelle Alexander named "the new Jim Crow."

Sadly, the story of a young man named Reynolds Wintersmith (b. 1977) is not an isolated case, but it is a representative one. Wintersmith received a life sentence for conspiracy to sell crack in 1994, although he was just a teenager at the time of his first and only conviction. Wintersmith grew up with drug-addled parents—his mother died of a heroin overdose when he was 11—and he was raised by a grandmother who made and sold drugs out of their home. He started selling crack for a gang in Rockford, Illinois, when he was 16, unaware that new laws made the punishment for this crime a mandatory life sentence, and judges were given no discretion in imposing it. The judge who sentenced Wintersmith expressed regret: "You were 17 years old when you got involved in this thing. . . . Usually a life sentence is imposed in state courts when somebody has been killed or severely hurt, or you've got a recidivist; that is, a defendant who's been convicted time and again. . . . This is your first conviction, and here you face life imprisonment. . . . It gives me pause to think that that was the intent of Congress, to put somebody away for the rest of their life."[27] Wintersmith has spent his entire adult life in prison. Now in his mid-30s, he has been recommended for a federal pardon, but at the moment he continues to sit in jail for selling drugs as a teenager, his only offense. He had the misfortune to break a law that many believe is too harsh and that is enforced against black men more frequently than white.

Although the civil rights movement had vanquished the old Jim Crow years before, African Americans still received unfair treatment in the nation's criminal courts. Black defendants received harsher sentences; black jurors were less likely to be chosen to hear their cases. The list goes on. New sentencing laws increased the national incarceration rate across the board, but the percentage of black inmates, as we saw in those distressing statistics listed at the beginning of this chapter, also skyrocketed.

Once individuals served their time, they faced a huge list of collateral civil consequences that had an even larger impact on their lives and future. In many ways, facing freedom was

---

[27] "Faces of FAMM: Reynolds Wintersmith," *FAMM: Sentences That Fit, Justice That Works*, http://www.famm.org/facesofFAMM/FederalProfiles/ReynoldsWintersmith.aspx.

as difficult as facing jail time. The list of rights denied to felons was long, and the consequences so delimiting that the end of a sentence hardly guaranteed a new beginning. Convicted felons, for example, were not allowed to receive food stamps and were ineligible for public housing, which could make day-to-day survival on the outside a harrowing prospect. Educational opportunities—certainly a way up and out—were essentially nil; a convicted felon could not receive federal financial aid for school. For many people, especially the poor, the military—like a college education—offered the promise of both professional and financial stability; for convicted felons, enlisting in the military was forbidden. Ironically enough, also lost was the right to vote and to serve on a jury, rights that African Americans had fought so hard to secure after Reconstruction and again during the civil rights movement.

Civil rights lawyers tried to fight what they recognized as a gross imbalance in sentencing laws and other race-based inequities throughout the justice system. In 1978, Warren McCleskey, an African American man in Fulton County, Georgia, was tried and convicted on two counts of armed robbery and one count of murder. His victim: the white police officer responding to the robbery call. McCleskey was sentenced to death. In 1987, the case *McCleskey v. Kemp*, in which the NAACP Legal Defense and Educational Fund (LDP) argued that the application of the death penalty in Georgia was tied to race and thus unconstitutional, made it all the way to the Supreme Court. But the court ruled that racial disparities within our criminal justice system were "inevitable" and thus did not count as discrimination.[28] According to the American Constitution Society:

> Because of *McCleskey*, there is no remedy for—and, indeed, no constitutional problem with—the fact that Blacks are disproportionately stopped, searched, arrested, held on bail, charged with serious crimes (including death-eligible offenses), denied plea bargains, convicted, and sentenced to prison or execution. There is no constitutional basis for challenging the fact that one in three African American males will enter state or federal prison at some point in his lifetime; and that although African Americans make up only 12 percent of the U. S. population, they amount to 44 percent of sentenced inmates—the largest group behind bars.[29]

The NYU professor and civil rights lawyer Anthony Amsterdam, who worked on the *McCleskey* case, has called the verdict "the *Dred Scott* decision of our times."[30]

As the War on Drugs turned into a war on young African American men, anger seethed in inner cities across the country. By the late 1980s, gangsta rap dominated the hip-hop scene, with lyrics that glorified guns,

---

[28] *McCleskey v. Kemp* (1987), http://www
.law.cornell.edu/supct/html/historics/
USSC_CR_0481_0279_ZO.html.

[29] Christina Swarns and Eva Paterson, "Twenty-Five Years Later, *McCleskey* Decision Still Fosters Racism by Ignoring It," *ACSblog* (*American Constitution Society*), http://www.acslaw.org/acsblog/25-years-later-mccleskey-decision-still-fosters-racism-by-ignoring-it.

[30] Adam Liptak, "New Look at Death Sentences and Race," *New York Times*, April 29, 2008, http://www
.nytimes.com/2008/04/29/us/29bar.html.

money, and violence. But the gangsta rappers weren't creating social problems, as some critics charged; they merely reflected existing economic conditions and social tensions, particularly racial profiling and police harassment. Perhaps no group did this more vocally, and more controversially, than the Los Angeles rappers N.W.A. in their 1988 song "Fuck tha Police."

❖❖❖

IN 1991, ONE OF THE COUNTLESS MUNDANE CONFRONTATIONS BETWEEN A YOUNG BLACK MAN and the Los Angeles police became the match that would ignite a massive social explosion with deep national implications. On March 3, 1991, the black motorist Rodney King (1965–2012) was pulled over for evading a traffic stop. It seemed routine enough. But the four LAPD officers on the scene pulled him from his car and kicked him in the head, used a Taser on him, and beat him with batons as he writhed in pain on the ground. King ended up with a broken cheekbone, nine skull fractures, a shattered eye socket, a broken ankle, and 20 stitches in his face. A white man who lived nearby, George Holliday, recorded the brutal beating with a home video camera. Once he sold the videotape to a local television station, there was no containing it. The story went national, and then international. As shocking as the images were to the mainstream media and the nation, neither the L.A. hip-hop community nor ordinary residents were surprised by what they saw—police brutality this severe was nothing new to them. The rapper Ice Cube (b. 1969) remarked on Rodney King's treatment at the hands of the LAPD: "It's been happening to us for years. It's just that we didn't have a camcorder every time it happened."[31] Just as innovations like the cotton gin and television had shaped the course of African American history, now the technological advance of inexpensive, readily available home video cameras revolutionized national awareness of the reality of police brutality against young black men.

Across the country, and especially in Los Angeles, people waited to see how justice would be served. When an all-white jury acquitted all four LAPD officers on April 29, 1992, the city erupted in an outpouring of rage that became the most devastating urban uprising in the history of the United States. More than 5,000 buildings burned from West Los Angeles and Watts to Long Beach and Santa Monica, amassing around $785 million in property damage. There were 2,300 people injured, and at least 55 were killed.

Los Angeles's African American mayor, Tom Bradley, a son of sharecroppers who had been elected to office almost 20 years earlier, was powerless to stop the violence. Many black Los Angeles residents felt that Bradley had broken too many promises to their community, leaving South Central Los Angeles mired in poverty, gang violence, and crack while catering to downtown developers. Ultimately, having an African American mayor had not been enough to save black Los Angeles, and Bradley's timid calls for peace were ignored. He left office the following year.

---

[31] Robin D. G. Kelley, "Kickin' Reality, Kickin' Ballistics: Gangsta Rap and Postindustrial Los Angeles," *Droppin' Science: Critical Perspectives on Rap Music and Hip Hop Culture*, ed. William Eric Perkins (Philadelphia: Temple University Press, 1996), 118.

The rapper Ice Cube (b. 1969) remarked on Rodney King's treatment at the hands of the LAPD: "It's been happening to us for years. It's just that we didn't have a camcorder every time it happened."

Once again thanks to television, images of the L.A. riots were seared into the national consciousness. Just as the savage beating of Rodney King by white police officers had shocked and sickened the nation, now audiences were witness to another episode of horrific abuse: that of a white truck driver named Reginald Denny, pulled from his truck by a group of young black men who beat him until he was unconscious. That race relations were broken was evident night after night on news programs. Or were they? An image that few people saw was the courageous rescue of Denny by four black neighbors who came out of their homes and drove the injured man to the hospital.

When the flames died down, African Americans faced a dilemma: How could they move toward racial equality when, after the sacrifices of the civil rights movement and the demands for Black Power, black people could still be vulnerable to mistreatment and injustice or driven to the senseless violence of Denny's attackers? While some African American intellectuals and cultural icons (including the popular and influential talk show host Oprah Winfrey) tried to initiate a national debate on race in America, others looked inward to their own community.

In 1995, the Nation of Islam leader Louis Farrakhan (b. 1933) summoned African American men to convene in the nation's capital for what he declared would be a "Million Man March." Farrakhan and his co-organizer, Ben Chavis (b. 1948), called on black men to reaffirm their commitment to family values and "personal responsibility" instead of dependence on government handouts. Yet neither self-help efforts like the Million Man March nor the efforts of the black elite could provide a solution for the "truly disadvantaged" black underclass defined by William Julius Wilson.

⬥⬥⬥

THE CARDS SEEMED STACKED AGAINST THE BLACK UNDERCLASS ALREADY, but a natural disaster in August 2005 cast a harsh light on the glaring economic inequalities that seemed to have become permanently entrenched in 21st-century America. Before Hurricane Katrina, New Orleans was a predominantly African American city, with more than a quarter of its population living in poverty. As the hurricane approached, the city's black mayor, Ray Nagin (b. 1956), issued an evacuation order, but many of the city's residents, who lacked transportation or any way out, had no choice but to ride out the storm in their homes. Katrina actually bypassed New Orleans, aside from several hours of fierce wind and rain. But a few hours later, the levees broke, and lake waters flooded the city. Those who had remained in New Orleans—who were disproportionately black and poor—waited agonizing days for relief and rescue without power, food, clean water, or government assistance.

The news footage of mostly black people—living and dead, displaced and devastated—reminded the nation that the African American underclass was worse off than ever, from the many black residents who had no car to use to flee, to the thousands of people turned away at gunpoint when they tried crossing to white suburbs on foot. Stories about poor black people being sheltered in dirty and demeaning conditions in the New Orleans Superdome made many Americans question what exactly the government was doing to help.

And if the images that were played and replayed on people's television screens weren't shocking enough, the callousness of some in power—or those close to it—was jaw-dropping. Upon touring the Houston Astrodome, where many New Orleanians had been evacuated for shelter, the former first lady and current president's mother, Barbara Bush, said, "So many of the people in the arena here were underprivileged anyway, so this is working very well for them."[32] Her son, President George W. Bush, did not visit New Orleans for a full 17 days after the flood. By the time two and a half weeks had passed, however, President Bush did seem to have absorbed the damning message of Katrina, commenting that the disaster exposed "deep, persistent poverty" with "roots in a history of racial discrimination, which cut off generations from the opportunities of America."[33]

The disaster also exposed a shocking disparity between how black and white Americans saw their nation. The political scientist Melissa Harris-Perry conducted research for the Katrina Disaster Study and discovered that "while most white Americans saw the hurricane's aftermath as tragic, they understood it primarily as a natural disaster followed by technical and bureaucratic failures. Most black Americans saw it as a racial disaster. . . . The lack of coordinated response was itself an indication that black people did not matter to the government."[34] Of African Americans surveyed for the study, 66 percent believed that the response to the disaster would have been faster if the victims had been white, whereas 77 percent of white Americans believed that race made no difference.[35]

This shared understanding united an incredibly diverse range of African Americans. Congressman John Lewis was one of the first to point out that race was a critical factor in both the depiction of Katrina's victims and the government's response to the disaster. And on September 2, 2005, while speaking at a benefit concert for the victims of the hurricane, the hip-hop artist Kanye West (b. 1977) went off script to address the president's behavior directly: "I hate the way they portray us in the media. You see a black family, it says, 'They're looting.' You see a white family, it says, 'They're looking for food.' And you know, it's been five days [waiting for federal help] because most of

[32] "Barbara Bush Calls Evacuees Better Off," *New York Times*, September 7, 2005, http://www .nytimes.com/2005/09/07/nationalnationalspecial/ 07barbara.html.

[33] Tuck, *We Ain't What We Ought to Be*, 409.

[34] Melissa V. Harris-Perry, *Sister Citizen: Shame, Stereotypes, and Black Women in America* (New Haven: Yale University Press, 2011), 138–39.

[35] Harris-Perry, *Sister Citizen*, 11.

the people are black," he said spontaneously. "George Bush doesn't care about black people."[36]

And indeed, as rebuilding efforts got under way, African Americans, who had once made up 67 percent of the city's population, began to feel that they were not welcome to return to their hometown.[37] Public housing projects that had suffered little or no flood damage were torn down, the struggling public school system was shuttered for good, and labor contracts to rebuild the city were given to out-of-town companies rather than to local residents desperate for work. Some white New Orleanians promoted measures to ensure a new, "smaller" (which many understood to mean "less black") New Orleans. In 2006, the city's population dropped temporarily to only 46 percent black, which may well have been a factor in the election of New Orleans's first white mayor since the 1970s.[38]

Katrina was a tipping point. The deep inequalities exposed by the storm and the federal response to the disaster made it all too plain: The government really *didn't* seem concerned enough about black people—or poor black people, to be more precise. Given America's traditional stated values of equal opportunity for all, yet its fraught history of race relations, was anything better even possible?

[36] "Rapper Blasts Bush Over Katrina," *CBSNews.com*, 2009, http://www.cbsnews.com/2100-500487_162-814636.html.

[37] Madison Gray, "The Press, Race and Katrina," *Time*, August 30, 2006, http://www.time.com/time/nation/article/0,8599,1471224,00.html.

[38] Adam Nossiter, "New Orleans Population Is Reduced Nearly 60%," *New York Times*, October 7, 2006, http://www.nytimes.com/2006/10/07/us/07population.html?_r=0.

YES, IT WAS. JUST THREE YEARS AFTER HURRICANE KATRINA, THE ELECTION OF BARACK OBAMA (B. 1961) AMAZED AFRICAN AMERICANS AND THE WORLD. Many older people had never imagined that they would live to see a black president in the White House. Some people wondered, for a delirious moment, whether the United States had finally moved beyond race and its codependent, racism.

Barack Obama entered the public consciousness a year before Hurricane Katrina, at the 2004 Democratic National Convention, when the little-known state senator from Illinois stood up to give the keynote speech. Then running for the U.S. Senate, he described his unusual trajectory into politics as the son of a Kenyan exchange student and a white woman from Kansas: "I stand here knowing that my story is part of the larger American story," he said, "and that in no other country on earth is my story even possible."[39]

Obama had lost his first race for U.S. Congress against the former Black Panther Party member Bobby Rush (b. 1946), but he did win a seat in the U.S. Senate in fall 2004, becoming the only African American in that body and only the third popularly elected black senator in U.S. history, after Edward Brooke (b. 1919) of Massachusetts and Carol Moseley Braun (b. 1947) of Illinois. But he had greater ambitions. When he declared his intention to seek the Democratic presidential

[39] Barack Obama, Keynote speech, Democratic National Convention, July 27, 2004, *Washington Post*, http://www.washingtonpost.com/wp-dyn/articles/A19751-2004Jul27.html.

nomination in 2008, many Americans of all backgrounds were stunned by his audacity. Aside from the largely symbolic campaigns of Shirley Chisholm in 1972, Jesse Jackson, Sr., in 1984, and the Reverend Al Sharpton (b. 1954) in 2004, this was the first time that an African American had been taken seriously as a candidate for a major party. But even many within his own party said that America still was not ready.

African Americans were initially divided over whether or not to support Obama's candidacy. Some survivors of the civil rights generation, including John Lewis, endorsed Obama's opponent, Hillary Clinton. Some African Americans, scarred by the painful loss of Dr. King, Malcolm X, and others, feared that a too-prominent black leader would be at risk of assassination by white racists. Others, cynical after years of perceived betrayals by earlier black politicians, felt that Obama's blackness alone was not enough to earn their support. There were others still who did not believe that enough whites would ever vote for a black man and were loath to "waste" their own votes on a candidate who couldn't win. Despite these initial doubts, Obama's campaign took off first with the younger generation, which responded with unprecedented fervor—and new tools and strategies. Another technological advance changed the course of African American history: Internet fund-raising and social media.

As Obama's campaign built grassroots momentum, some black leaders began to re-evaluate his candidacy. In February 2008, Congressman John Lewis announced that he was changing his endorsement from Hillary Clinton to Barack Obama. "Something is

happening in America," he said, "and people are prepared and ready to make that great leap."[40]

As Obama was carried on a wave of what seemed like unstoppable momentum, his candidacy suffered a sudden setback. In March 2008, ABC News drew attention to Obama's pastor, the Reverend Jeremiah Wright (b. 1941), a man of Emmett Till's generation. In some of his sermons, the fiery pastor expressed anger about the nation's long history of enslaving and mistreating people of color, from Native Americans to contemporary black communities. Soon, video clips of Wright declaiming, "God damn America, for treating our citizens as less than human!" were all over television and the Internet.[41] Media outlets scrambled to learn more about Wright and told stories about radical politics and associations with alleged domestic terrorists of the '60s. Would the specter of black rage and radicalism frighten white voters away from Obama?

Obama responded quickly and decisively with what has come to be known as his "race speech." While acknowledging that Wright's words could be considered offensive, he also refused to whitewash the history of racial inequality in the United States. "The anger is real; it is powerful," he said. "And to simply wish it away, to condemn it without

---

[40] Jeff Zeleny and Patrick Healy, "Black Leader, a Clinton Ally, Tilts to Obama," *New York Times*, February 15, 2008, http://www.nytimes.com/2008/02/15/us/politics/15clinton.html?pagewanted=all&_r=0.

[41] A link to the video and full transcript of the Reverend Wright's speech are available at the *Dallas Morning News'* "Texas Faith" blog, http://religionblog.dallasnews.com/2008/03/listen-and-read-to-the-whole-g.html/.

understanding its roots, only serves to widen the chasm of misunderstanding that exists between the races." He compared the anger that Wright voiced to the white anger that flared in response to busing and affirmative action, and called on Americans to envision a country no longer "irrevocably bound to a tragic past."[42]

That speech was a turning point. Obama managed to reassure many white and black Americans both that he understood their points of view, and the painful history of race relations that had left residues of hurt, anger, and bitterness. Obama went on to win the Democratic nomination, and then the general election, becoming the first black president of the United States.

African Americans and whites alike were astounded by this historic event. The international and American media began to debate whether America had finally moved beyond its difficult past and become a "postracial" nation. Despite these optimistic musings, the fact remained that Obama had been only the third popularly elected black U. S. senator in our history, and when he left for the White House, not a single African American remained in the Senate. Obama himself cautioned reporters not to see his election as proof that America's "race problem" had been solved overnight. After all, even though 95 percent of African American voters chose Obama, he had won only 43 percent of the white vote.

The numbers were proof that at the polls, African Americans were almost unanimous in their support for Obama. During his first term,

though, there were countless reminders of the obstacles still facing African Americans, as well as the real progress that had been made. For the black elite, it was the best of times. Before the 2008 economic crash, those at the top—whoever they were and whatever their skin color—got richer while the poor got poorer. This was just as true for the highest level of African American hedge-fund managers, business executives, and entrepreneurs as it was for rich and powerful whites.

So, while money afforded African Americans at the top some measure of color blindness from whites, there was no "trickle down" for blacks at the bottom of the economic ladder. A look inside urban city schools across the country might make it impossible to believe that almost six decades have gone by since the Supreme Court passed *Brown v. Board of Education*. The residents of poor, predominantly black neighborhoods like Roxbury in Boston, one of the communities where the "Battle of Boston" raged in 1974, have few options but the city's worst schools. What remains of affirmative action continues to draw critics and court cases, and recent victories for affirmative action, such as in Michigan, no longer have the same equalizing effect they once had, when affirmative action initially functioned as a class elevator. Today, it often tends to perpetuate the class status of middle-class African Americans through their children.

The specter of racial profiling, which Harvard Law professor and legal theorist Charles Ogletree called "the presumption of guilt" based on skin color, continued to haunt America. On February 26, 2012, an unarmed teenager, Trayvon Martin, was shot dead by a vigilante neighbor in Florida. Was the fear of

---

[42] The full transcript of Barack Obama's "race speech" is available at *The New York Times*, March 18, 2008, http://www.nytimes.com/2008/03/18/us/politics/18text-obama.html?pagewanted=all.

Inauguration of President Barack Obama, with Michelle Obama and Vice President Joe Biden, by Carol M. Highsmith, January 24, 2009. Photograph. Library of Congress.

black men still as deep-rooted as it had been in the days of Jim Crow?

Dishearteningly, the racial caste system developed in the 1980s and '90s still obtains throughout our society, perhaps most obviously in the nation's prisons. Civil rights advocate and scholar Michelle Alexander questioned how far America has come in more than a century. "Today," she said, "a criminal freed from prison has scarcely more rights, and arguably less respect, than a freed slave or a black person living 'free' in Mississippi during the height of Jim Crow."[43] And indeed, reminders of Jim Crow are everywhere. The Jim Crow

---

[43] Michelle Alexander, *The New Jim Crow: Mass Incarceration in the Age of Colorblindness* (New York: The New Press, 2010), 138.

Museum in Michigan is full of shockingly racist Obama paraphernalia, all created and distributed since 2008.

Many African Americans continued to question how this could go on with a black man occupying the Oval Office. Scholars such as Cornel West and journalists and activists such as Tavis Smiley pointedly questioned whether the president was doing enough to solve the structural problems afflicting poor black people. Was he taking their loyalty for granted? Others asked whether the election of this mixed-race son of an African exchange student was just another example of how black immigrants were leaving native-born African Americans behind.

There was no question that Obama saw himself as black: He identified himself as such in the 2010 census, even though he could have checked off multiple races. But with his international background, could he truly understand what it meant to be African American? And Obama's efforts to work with his intractable opponents in Congress revealed that a significant slice of white America—colored deep red down the wide center of the country on the electoral map—feared black people and resented their success just as much as ever.

Obama's reelection in 2012 offered a new perspective on these questions: A significant majority of Americans still saw their black president as the best person to lead the nation, even in the midst of an economic crisis. Although racism and racial disparities in incarceration rates and poverty remain pressing issues, the face America shows the world—and itself—has changed forever with the election, and reelection, of the nation's first black president.

✕✕✕

THE QUESTIONS RAISED ABOUT BARACK OBAMA'S "BLACKNESS" QUOTIENT REMINDED THE NATION HOW MUCH MORE DIVERSE black America had become since the passage of the Immigration and Nationality Act of 1965. That law had marked a radical break from past policies, opening the United States to immigration from Africa and Asia, which had previously been excluded. It also removed the national-origins quota system that had been in place since the 1920s. As a result, African Americans are no longer the nation's largest minority group, with blacks accounting for only 13.1 percent of the population, compared to the 16.7 percent who identify as Hispanic or Latino.[44] The 1965 law also changed the demographics of the African American population, as 3.4 million new black immigrants arrived from Africa and the Caribbean, about eight times as many people of African descent as came here during the entire transatlantic slave trade.

Newly arrived black immigrants have often succeeded here in ways that have eluded African Americans for generations. Nigerian Americans, for example, enjoy an average educational level that exceeds any other minority ethnic group, including Asian Americans. At Harvard and other Ivy League schools, the children of recent black immigrants outnumber African Americans in the undergraduate student body. Some native-born black African Americans flat-out resent it when African and Caribbean immigrants move up the ladder to

---

[44] United States Census Bureau, January 10, 2013, http://quickfacts.census.gov/qfd/states/00000.html.

economic success more rapidly than they do. Is it easier for black immigrants to succeed here because they arrive on these shores free of the legacy of America's painful racial history? And how long does that so-called immigrant mentality persist? At what point do immigrants or their descendants become simply black Americans?

A major motivation drawing immigrants here is the promise of better economic opportunity and political and religious freedom. And even though black people around the world are well aware of our history of slavery and Jim Crow, it is a fact of history to them and not of personal heritage, and nothing symbolizes America's promise better than the world-famous African American icons of politics, music, sports, and the arts. Murals of Tupac Shakur (1971–1996), Muhammad Ali (b. 1942), and Malcolm X and posters of African leaders posed next to Barack Obama cover the walls of the public spaces of Dakar, Senegal; Accra, Ghana; Luanda, Angola; Johannesburg, South Africa; Freetown, Sierra Leone; and Lagos, Nigeria. West African rappers echo and re-interpret American culture in their own music and performances. African American culture and the long struggle for freedom and civil rights have come to represent a global ideal; and hip-hop, a cultural form forged by dis-enfranchised African Americans of the most entrenched underclass in uniquely American cities, has become an indisputable global force.

Over its three-decade history, hip-hop has evolved through various phases, at times stressing the entertainment element far more than its political thrust. At its most effective and most strident, hip-hop music continued the tradition of political protest that characterized the younger generation of black radicals in the '60s, to some extent. And in some ways, early rap lyrics seemed to be an extension of the form of literary naturalism practiced by the great writer Richard Wright.

❖❖❖

SO AT THE DAWNING OF THE 21ST CEN-TURY, WHAT OF THE BATTLE BETWEEN THE BLACK CULTURAL NATIONALISTS of the US organization and the latter phase of SNCC, among other organizations, as opposed to the Marxist-Leninist platform of the Black Panther Party, which led to the deadly shootout on the campus of UCLA in January 1969, the sad episode in the history of African Americans we encountered at the beginning of this chapter? Since the fall of the Berlin Wall in 1989, if not well before, there has not been a serious mass political movement advocating either the violent overthrow of the capitalist system or a socialist revolution within the African American community. While that may change if the conditions haunting the chronically poor are not addressed, this does not appear likely.

At the same time, no major black cultural nationalist political movements are vying for the attention and support of the African American people, either. The "Back to Africa" movements that have been such a colorful part of the story of the African American people for 200 years, starting with Paul Cuffee's successful attempt to transport a handful of former slaves to the British colony of Sierra Leone in 1815 and ranging through Marcus Garvey's Universal Negro Improvement Association of the early 20th century to the strident nationalism of

Malcolm X during the Nation of Islam phase of his political evolution in the '50s and early '60s, have largely grown silent over the past two decades. Why? The answer to that question is quite complex, but one reason, we think, certainly stems from the fact that Africans themselves are "voting with their feet," as it were, and migrating willingly to the United States in the largest numbers this country has seen since the forced migration of their own ancestors and ours during the long and dreadful history of slavery.

But the other reason for this is even more fascinating: It is fair to say that black cultural nationalism has "gone mainstream." There was the creation of African American studies departments, which at several colleges and universities have become top-ranked research programs and even Ph.D.-granting programs that attract a wide cross section of the student bodies at historically white institutions of higher learning. Long gone is the violence that characterized the birth of black studies on the campus of UCLA, replaced today by the sort of healthy debates over the interpretation of historical events that represent the best of academic inquiry. Each January we have the annual national observance of the King national holiday, which serves as the entrée to Black History Month, which virtually every elementary, middle, and high school, and college and university observe in their own meaningful ways, and which the United States Postal Service celebrates as well, with its Black Heritage series of stamps, usually issued in February. Kwanzaa stands alongside Christmas and Hanukkah as a staple of the American December holiday season, and of many public school curricula.

Black musical culture (jazz, the blues, rhythm and blues, soul music, and most certainly hip-hop) has without a doubt become the lingua franca of American popular culture, along with speech patterns and phrases and "black" dance forms (a process set in motion and effected by Don Cornelius's syndicated television program, *Soul Train*). There is a long roster of print, radio, and broadcast journalists who have distinguished themselves in every form of media. There has been thorough integration of the most popular American team sports—even country-club sports like golf (with Tiger Woods [b. 1975]). And of course the canon of American literature and history (along with other disciplines such as sociology and even the curriculum of law schools) has been thoroughly integrated as a result of both the black studies movement and the so-called canon wars of the multicultural movement of the '80s and '90s. All these things, and many more, attest to the mainstreaming of African American history and culture, and their embrace not just by African Americans, but by Americans.

❊❊❊

IN THE AFOREMENTIONED FIELDS THERE HAS BEEN TREMENDOUS PROGRESS, but in surveying the landscape of recent African American history, it must be noted that this most recent period can be—perhaps *should* be—characterized as the era of great achievement for African American women. In virtually every field of endeavor, women have risen, starting appropriately enough with the election of Shirley Chisholm in November 1968 as the first black woman ever to serve in the House of Representatives. Four years later, Chisholm,

as we have described, would also mount the very first campaign for the presidency, in the same year that Barbara Jordan would become the first black woman from the South to win election to Congress. In 1977, Patricia Harris (1924–1985) was confirmed as President Jimmy Carter's secretary of housing and urban development, the first African American woman appointed to a Cabinet post. Two years later, Hazel Johnson (1927–2011) became the first African American woman promoted to the rank of general in the United States Army, while in 1998 Lillian E. Fishburne (b. 1949) would become the first African American woman promoted to the rank of rear admiral in the U.S. Navy. While she wasn't breaking any barriers for women, as Chisholm, Jordan, Harris, Johnson, and Fishburne did, Vanessa Williams (b. 1963) achieved another sort of first in 1984: She was crowned Miss America, the first African American to win this title.

One year later, in 1985, Oprah Winfrey (b. 1954) launched *The Oprah Winfrey Show*, which would dominate daytime television for the next quarter of a century, broadcast in more than 100 countries and garnering a legion of Emmy Awards and fiercely dedicated fans. According to Forbes, Winfrey is currently the only African American billionaire. In 1989, the Reverend Barbara Harris (b. 1930) was elected the first female bishop of the Episcopal Church; more than a decade would pass before the Reverend Vashti Murphy McKenzie (b. 1947) became the first female bishop of the African Methodist Episcopal Church, in 2000. In 1991, Sharon Pratt Kelly (b. 1944) won election as mayor of Washington, D.C., the first

Oprah Winfrey, Los Angeles, August 19, 1986. Photograph. Associated Press, Association Images.

African American woman to do so in any large U.S. city; and in 1992, Carol Moseley Braun was elected to the Senate. To this day, she remains the only African American woman ever to hold that seat. Just a year later, the astronaut Dr. Mae Jemison (b. 1956) became the first African

FACING PAGE: Shirley Chisholm, by Thomas J. O'Halloran, January 25, 1972. Photograph. Library of Congress.

Condoleezza Rice with President George W. Bush, Crawford, Texas, August 16, 2008. Photograph. Saul Leob/AFP, Getty Images.

American woman in space on the crew of the space shuttle *Endeavour*.

There is no field in this period, it seems, that women haven't dominated. In 2002, Serena Williams (b. 1981) won the first of five ladies' singles titles at Wimbledon, and she and her sister Venus (b. 1980) won the ladies' doubles. That same year, Halle Berry (b. 1966) became the first African American woman to win an Oscar for Best Actress. In 2005, Condoleezza Rice (b. 1954) succeeded Colin Powell as the United States secretary of state (two African American secretaries of state back to back!). Four years later, Susan Rice (b. 1964)—no relation—was confirmed as the United States ambassador to the United Nations, like Condoleezza Rice, the first African American female to hold that position. But perhaps the most symbolic event of all in this long (and partial) list of honors accorded to African American women was the awarding in 1999 of the Congressional Gold Medal to Rosa Parks, and the issuing in 2013 of a United States postage stamp in her honor.

Toni Morrison, Paris, November 8, 2006. Photograph. Francois Guillot/AFP, Getty Images.

While African American female accomplishments in electoral politics, entertainment, and sports would be quite impressive, it would be in the production of literature that African American women would fundamentally redefine the canon. Indeed, some scholars characterize the last four decades as "Woman's Era" in the African American literary tradition, echoing the title of a periodical published earlier in the history of black feminism. The period commenced with the publication in 1969 of Maya Angelou's (b. 1928) classic autobiography, *I Know Why the Caged Bird Sings*, which became an instant bestseller and has remained extraordinarily popular over these last four decades. The next year saw the publication of the stunningly brilliant debut novels of Toni Morrison (b. 1931) and Alice Walker (b. 1944), *The Bluest Eye* and *The Third Life of Grange Copeland* respectively, as well as the authoritative anthology *The Black Woman*, edited by Toni Cade Bambara (1939–1995). Octavia Butler (1947–2006) joined the chorus a year later with the publication of her boldly experimental science fiction neo-slave narrative *Kindred*. Morrison's publication of *Sula* in 1973–the same year in which the National Black Feminist Organization was founded– signaled that a major new talent was evolving. A year later, Morrison, who was working as an editor at Random House, published Angela Davis's *Autobiography*, followed in 1975 by Gayl Jones's (b. 1949) searching novel about slavery and rape, *Corregidora*.

In many ways, 1975 was a hallmark year in the history of black women's writing, not only because *Corregidora* broke new formal ground in the ways in which black women narrate fictional versions of their history, but also because the first formal dramatic critique of black male chauvinism and misogyny took Broadway by storm under the curious title *For Colored Girls Who Have Considered Suicide When the Rainbow Is Enuf*, by Ntozake Shange (b. 1948). In 1979, Michele Wallace (b. 1952), in what has been thought of as a sort of companion piece to Shange's play, published a probing critique of the history of black sexism and misogyny, *Black Macho and the Myth of the Superwoman*, which generated a firestorm of angry reaction from many black male writers and critics, including a special issue of *The Black Scholar* magazine. But a subject that had long been treated as a taboo–intraracial sexism, especially in the civil rights movement and the Black Power era–had been opened to debate and would continue to be debated throughout the remainder of the century and beyond.

In one of the most important contributions to African American canon formation, Alice Walker redefined the concept of African American women's literary ancestry by tracing her line of formal descent from Zora Neale Hurston in two essays published in *Ms.* magazine, the seminal "In Search of Our Mothers' Gardens" in 1974, and "In Search of Zora Neale Hurston" in 1975. Walker would go on in 1983 to win both the Pulitzer Prize and the National Book Award for her strikingly original novel *The Color Purple*, which was a formal signifying riff upon Hurston's novel, *Their Eyes Were Watching God* (1937), which Walker and Hurston's biographer, Robert Hemenway, resurrected from obscurity. *Their Eyes* would become one of the most widely taught novels in American, African American, and women's literature classes over the course of the rest of the century, as would novels by Morrison and Walker herself. Even Spike Lee's (b. 1957) first major film, *She's Gotta Have It*, which won the Best New Director Award at the Cannes Film Festival in 1986, reflected the force of the black women's literary and artistic movement, just as Julie Dash's (b. 1962) *Daughters of the Dust*– the first nationally released feature film by an African American woman–would as well.

But 1993 stands as the banner year in the history of black women's writing. On January 20, Maya Angelou gave an affecting reading of her poem "On the Pulse of the Morning" at the inauguration of President William Jefferson Clinton; poet Rita Dove (b. 1952) became the first African American woman and the youngest ever United States poet laureate; and on October 7, Toni Morrison became the first African American to win the Nobel Prize in Literature. Nine years later, Suzan-Lori Parks (b. 1963) would become the first African American woman to win the Pulitzer Prize for Drama, for *Topdog/Underdog*.

This era of black women's writing, characterized by a remarkable degree of both creativity

Spike Lee, 1994. Photograph. Fotos International/Getty Images.

and productivity, amounted to a literary renaissance, one with perhaps more lasting implications than even the Harlem Renaissance of the '20s. It was capped, most recently, by Elizabeth Alexander's (b. 1962) reading of her superb poem "Praise Song for the Day," at the first inauguration of President Barack Obama.

✦✦✦

AT THIS POINT IN OUR HISTORY, IT IS DIFFICULT TO IMAGINE EVEN THE MOST CONSERVATIVE AFRICAN AMERICAN'S home without some black cultural artifacts on display and some form of black music on its sound system. These are radical changes since 1968, the beginning of the time period of this chapter. And Barack Obama's election most certainly would have been impossible had not the African American community voted overwhelmingly in his favor in both of his presidential contests, a reflection of what we might think of as a black cultural nationalist identification at its most fundamental level. These might not have been the forms of the *naturalization* or *Americanization* of African American culture on the minds of the Black Power and Black Arts advocates of the '60s and '70s, but the "blackening" or the *Africanization* of American culture is certainly a triumph that the founders of these movements can claim, if indeed they would not find these forms of broad acceptance a form of co-optation.

While no one could argue that we still have a very long way to go in terms of the full recognition of African American history and culture, it would be difficult to argue that American society has not made dramatic progress in this direction since the assassination of the Reverend Dr. Martin Luther King, Jr. And of course the election—and maybe more important, the reelection—of a black president speaks volumes about the growth of (lowercase) black power.

Yet there remain deep social and economic inequalities that still need to be resolved, that divide black Americans from white, and black middle-class Americans from their working-class brothers and sisters. Perhaps building the bridge that will reach across those divides is the ultimate challenge of the next chapter in the history of the African American people.

BIBLIOGRAPHY

1946-7-28-ABC Lear Radio Show. http://archive.org/details/1946RadioNews.

Adams, John. *Diary*. http://www.masshist.org/digitaladams/aea/cfm/doc.cfm?id=D24.

Akyeampong, Emmanuel K., and Henry Louis Gates, Jr., eds. *Dictionary of African Biography*. 6 vols. New York: Oxford University Press, 2012.

Allmendinger, David F., and William Scarborough. "The Days Ruffin Died." *Virginia Magazine of History and Biography* 97 (1997): 75–96.

Anderson, Jervis. *A. Philip Randolph: A Biographical Portrait*. Berkeley: University of California Press, 1973.

Anderson, William J. *Life and Narrative of William J. Anderson, Twenty-four Years a Slave; Sold Eight Times! In Jail Sixty Times!! Whipped Three Hundred Times!!! or The Dark Deeds of American Slavery Revealed* . . . Chicago: Daily Tribune Book and Job Printing Office, 1857.

Andrews, William L. *To Tell a Free Story: The First Century of Afro-American Autobiography, 1760–1865*. Urbana: University of Illinois Press, 1986.

Aptheker, Herbert. *American Negro Slave Revolts*. New York: International Publishers, 1969.

——, ed. *A Documentary History of the Negro People in the United States from Colonial Times Through the Civil War*. New York: Citadel Press, 1962.

Arsenault, Raymond. *Freedom Riders: 1961 and the Struggle for Racial Justice*. New York: Oxford University Press, 2006.

Ayers, Edward. "Anti-Slavery Sentiment Emerges in Pre-Revolutionary America." http://www.historyisfun.org/antislavery-sentiment.htm.

Bailey, Ronald. "The Other Side of Slavery: Black Labor, Cotton, and Textile Industrialization in Great Britain and the United States." *Agricultural History* 68 (Spring 1994): 35–50.

Bailyn, Bernard. *The Ideological Origins of the American Revolution*. Cambridge: Belknap Press of Harvard University Press, 1967.

Ball, Edward. *Slaves in the Family*. New York: Farrar, Straus and Giroux, 1998.

"Banneker" to Thomas Hamilton, January 22, 1860. New York *Weekly Anglo-African*, January 28, 1860.

Baraka, Amiri. "The Gary Declaration: Black Politics at the Crossroads," National Black Political Convention, 1972. In *BlackPast.org: Remembered and Reclaimed*.

"Barbara Bush Calls Evacuees Better Off." *New York Times*. September 7, 2005.

Bellefontaine, Edgar J. "Chief Justice William Cushing: Stalwart Federalist and Reluctant Abolitionist, The Massachusetts Years, 1772–1789." *Supreme Judicial Court Historical Society Annual Report* 20–23 (1993).

Beltrán, Gonzalo Aguirre. *Tribal Origins of Slaves in Mexico*. Washington, D.C.: 1946?.

Bennett, Herman L. *Africans in Colonial Mexico: Absolutism, Christianity, and Afro-Creole Consciousness, 1570–1640*. Bloomington: University of Indiana Press, 2003.

Bentley, Eric, ed. *Thirty Years of Treason: Excerpts from Hearings Before the House Committee on Un-American Activities, 1938–1968*. New York: Viking Press, 1971.

Berlin, Ira. *Many Thousands Gone: The First Two Centuries of Slavery in North America*. Cambridge: Belknap Press of Harvard University Press, 1998.

——. *Slaves Without Masters: The Free Negro in the Antebellum South*. New York: Oxford University Press, 1974.

——, and Leslie M. Harris, eds. *Slavery in New York*. New York: The New Press and the New-York Historical Society, 2005.

Bertrand, Michael T. *Race, Rock, and Elvis.* Urbana: University of Illinois Press, 2000.

Bindman, David. "The Black Presence in British Art: Sixteenth and Seventeenth Centuries." In *The Image of the Black in Western Art: From the Age of Discovery to the Age of Abolition,* edited by David Bindman and Henry Louis Gates, Jr., III, 1, 235–70. Cambridge: Belknap Press of Harvard University Press, 2010.

Biographical Directory of the United States Congress, 1774–Present. http://bioguide.congress.gov/biosearch/biosearch.asp.

Birzer, Dedra McDonald. "Esteban." In *African American National Biography,* edited by Henry Louis Gates, Jr., and Evelyn Brooks Higginbotham, 3:197–9. New York: Oxford University Press, 2008.

"Black-American Representatives and Senators by Congress, 1870–Present." *History, Art & Archives: United States House of Representatives.*

"Black Power Comes of Age." *Washington Post.* June 29, 1972.

Blanck, Emily. "Seventeen Eighty-Three: The Turning Point in the Law of Slavery and Freedom in Massachusetts." *New England Quarterly* 75 (March 2002): 24–51.

Blight, David W. *Frederick Douglass's Civil War: Keeping Faith in Jubilee.* Baton Rouge: Louisiana State University Press, 1989.

——. *A Slave No More: Two Men Who Escaped to Freedom, Including Their Own Narratives of Emancipation.* Orlando, FL: Harcourt, Inc., 2007.

Bluett, Thomas. *Some Memoirs of the Life of Job, the Son of Solomon, the High Priest of Boonda in Africa . . .* London: Richard Ford, 1734.

Branch, Taylor. *At Canaan's Edge: America in the King Years, 1965–68.* New York: Simon and Schuster, 2006.

——. *Parting the Waters: America in the King Years, 1954–63.* New York: Simon and Schuster, 1988.

——. *Pillar of Fire: America in the King Years, 1963–65.* New York: Simon and Schuster, 1998.

"Brand New Bag: Questlove on Don Cornelius." *Okayplayer,* February 1, 2012.

Brasseaux, Carl A., and Glenn R. Conrad, eds. *The Road to Louisiana: The Saint-Domingue Refugees, 1792–1809.* Lafayette, LA: Center for Louisiana Studies, University of Southwestern Louisiana, 1992.

Breen, T. H., and Stephen Innes. *"Myne Owne Ground": Race and Freedom on Virginia's Eastern Shore, 1640–1676.* New York: Oxford University Press, 1980, 2005.

Brown, Christopher Leslie. *Moral Capital: Foundations of British Abolitionism.* Chapel Hill: University of North Carolina Press, 2006.

Brown, James, and Bruce Tucker. *James Brown: The Godfather of Soul.* New York: Thunder Mouth's Press, 1986, 1997.

Brown, John. *Slave Life in Georgia: A Narrative of the Life, Sufferings, and Escape of John Brown, A Fugitive Slave, Now in England.* London: British and Foreign Anti-Slavery Society, 1855.

Brundage, W. Fitzhugh. "Beyoncé, Bert Williams, and the History of Blackface in America." In *UNC Press Blog,* March 2, 2011.

——. *Lynching in the New South: Georgia and Virginia, 1880–1930.* Urbana: University of Illinois Press, 1993.

Bullock, Steven C. "The Revolutionary Transformation of American Freemasonry, 1752–1792." *William and Mary Quarterly,* 3d ser., 47 (July 1990): 349–69.

Bundles, A'Lelia. *On Her Own Ground: The Life and Times of Madam C. J. Walker.* New York: Scribner, 2002.

——. "Walker, Madam C. J." *AANB Online,* African American Studies Center, Oxford University Press.

Butler, Benjamin F. *Autobiography and Personal Reminiscences: Butler's Book, A Review of His Legal, Political, and Military Career.* Boston: A. M. Thayer, 1892.

Cabeza de Vaca, Álvar Núñez. *The Journey of Álvar Núñez Cabeza de Vaca (1842).* http://www.pbs.org/weta/thewest/resources/archives/one/cabeza.htm.

Cantor, Louis. *Wheelin' on Beale: How WDIA-Memphis Became the Nation's First All-Black Radio Station and Created the Sound That Changed America.* New York: Pharos Books, 1992.

Carson, Clayborne. *In Struggle: SNCC and the Black Awakening of the 1960s.* Cambridge: Harvard University Press, 1981.

Center for Digital Research in the Humanities, University of Nebraska–Lincoln. *Louisiana Railway Accommodations Act. Railroads and the Making of America.* http://railroads.unl.edu/documents/view_document.php?id=rail.gen.0060.

Chang, Jeff. *Can't Stop Won't Stop: A History of the Hip-Hop Generation.* New York: St. Martin's Press, 2005.

Christian, Charles M. *Black Saga: The African American Experience, A Chronology.* New York: Civitas, 1999.

Clavin, Matthew J. *Toussaint Louverture and the American Civil War: The Promise and Peril of a Second Haitian Revolution.* Philadelphia: University of Pennsylvania Press, 2010.

Cleaver, Eldridge. "The Death of Martin Luther King: Requiem for Nonviolence." In *Post-Prison Writings and Speeches,* edited by Robert Scheer, 73–79. New York: Random House, 1969.

Coleman, Trevor W. *Crusader for Justice: Federal Judge Damon J. Keith.* Detroit: Wayne State University Press, forthcoming.

Conforti, Joseph. "The Invention of the Great Awakening, 1795–1844." *Early American Literature* 26:2 (1991): 99–118.

Coombs, John C. "Beyond the 'Origins Debate': Rethinking the Rise of Virginia Slavery." In *Early Modern Virginia: Reconsidering the Old Dominion,* edited by Douglas Bradburn and John C. Coombs, 239–278. Charlottesville: University of Virginia Press, 2011.

Cornish, Dudley Taylor. *The Sable Arm: Negro Troops in the Union Army, 1861–1865.* New York: W. W. Norton, 1966.

Craft, William, and Ellen Craft. *Running a Thousand Miles for Freedom: The Escape of William and Ellen Craft from Slavery,* edited by R. J. M. Blackett. Baton Rouge: Louisiana State University Press, 1999.

Current, Richard N. *Those Terrible Carpetbaggers: A Reinterpretation.* New York: Oxford University Press, 1988.

Curry, Leonard P. *The Free Black in Urban America, 1800–1850: The Shadow of the Dream.* Chicago: University of Chicago Press, 1981.

Curtin, Philip D. *The Rise and Fall of the Plantation Complex: Essays in Atlantic History.* New York: Cambridge University Press, 1998.

Daniel, Walter C. *Black Journals of the United States.* London: Greenwood Press, 1982.

Davis, David Brion. *Inhuman Bondage: The Rise and Fall of Slavery in the New World.* New York: Oxford University Press, 2006.

——. *The Problem of Slavery in Western Culture.* Ithaca, NY: Cornell University Press, 1966.

Douglass, Frederick. "What Shall Be Done with the Slaves If Emancipated?" *Douglass' Monthly,* January 1862.

Drescher, Seymour. *Abolition: A History of Slavery and Antislavery.* Cambridge: Cambridge University Press, 2009.

Drew, Charles R. Charles R. Drew to Jacob Billikopf, April 15, 1944. In The Charles R. Drew Papers. *Profiles in Science: National Library of Medicine.*

Drumgoold, Kate. *A Slave Girl's Story.* Brooklyn: np., 1898.

Duberman, Martin B. *Paul Robeson.* New York: Alfred A. Knopf, 1988.

Du Bois, W. E. B. *Black Reconstruction in America, 1860–1880.* Cleveland, OH: Meridian Books, 1962.

———. "Close Ranks" editorial. In *W. E. B. Du Bois: A Reader*, edited by David Levering Lewis, 697. New York: Henry Holt and Company, 1995.

———. "Intermarriage" editorial. *The Crisis* 5, no. 4 (February 1913).

———. "The Prize Fighter" editorial. *The Crisis* 8, no. 4 (August 1914).

Dudziak, Mary L. *Cold War Civil Rights: Race and the Image of American Democracy*. Princeton: Princeton University Press, 2011.

Dunmore. *Proclamation of Earl of Dunmore*. http://www.pbs.org/wgbh/aia/part2/2h42t.html.

Dyson, Michael Eric. *Come Hell or High Water: Hurricane Katrina and the Color of Disaster*. New York: Basic Civitas, 2006.

Egerton, Douglas R. *Death or Liberty: African Americans and Revolutionary America*. New York: Oxford University Press, 2009.

———. *Gabriel's Rebellion: The Virginia Slave Conspiracies of 1800 & 1802*. Chapel Hill: University of North Carolina Press, 1993.

———. *He Shall Go Out Free: The Lives of Denmark Vesey*. Rev. ed. Lanham, MD: Rowman & Littlefield, 2004.

Elliott, Mark E. *Color-Blind Justice: Albion Tourgée and the Quest for Racial Equality from the Civil War to* Plessy v. Ferguson. New York: Oxford University Press, 2006.

———. "Race, Color Blindness, and the Democratic Public: Albion W. Tourgée's Radical Principles in *Plessy v. Ferguson*." *Journal of Southern History* 67 (May 2001): 287–330.

Eltis, David, and David Richardson, eds. *Atlas of the Transatlantic Slave Trade*. New Haven: Yale University Press, 2010.

———. Trans-Atlantic Slave Trade Database. http://www.slavevoyages.org/tast/database/search.faces.

Eyes on the Prize: America's Civil Rights Movement, 1954–1985. "The Time Has Come (1964–1966)," first broadcast 1987 by PBS. Produced, directed, and written by James A. DeVinney and Madison Davis Lacy, Jr. Transcript. http://www.pbs.org/wgbh/amex/eyesontheprize/about/pt.html.

"Faces of FAMM: Reynolds Wintersmith." *FAMM: Sentences That Fit, Justice That Works*.

Fairclough, Adam. *A Class of Their Own: Black Teachers in the Segregated South*. Cambridge: Belknap Press of Harvard University Press, 2007.

Faust, Drew Gilpin, ed. *The Ideology of Slavery: Proslavery Thought in the Antebellum South, 1830–1860*. Baton Rouge: Louisiana State University Press, 1981.

Finkenbine, Roy E., ed. *Sources of the African-American Past: Primary Sources in American History*. New York: Longman, 1997.

Floyd-Wilson, Mary. "Moors, Race, and the Study of English Renaissance Literature: A Brief Retrospective." *Literature Compass* 3 (2006): 1044–52.

Foner, Eric. *Freedom's Lawmakers: A Directory of Black Officeholders During Reconstruction*. Baton Rouge: Louisiana State University Press, 1996.

———. *Reconstruction: America's Unfinished Revolution, 1863–1877*. New York: Harper & Row, 1988.

Forbes, Robert Pierce. *The Missouri Compromise and Its Aftermath: Slavery and the Meaning of America*. Chapel Hill: University of North Carolina Press, 2007.

Franklin, John Hope, and Loren Schweninger. *Runaway Slaves: Rebels on the Plantation*. New York: Oxford University Press, 1999.

Freedmen and Southern Society Project. http://www.history.umd.edu/Freedmen/sf015.htm.

Freeman, Rhoda. "The Free Negro in New York City in the Era Before the Civil War." Ph.D. diss., Columbia University, 1966.

French, Scot. *The Rebellious Slave: Nat Turner in American Memory*. Boston: Houghton Mifflin, 2004.

Frey, Sylvia R. "Between Slavery and Freedom: Virginia Blacks in the American Revolution." *Journal of Southern History* 49 (August 1983): 375–98.

——. *Water from the Rock: Black Resistance in a Revolutionary Age.* Princeton: Princeton University Press, 1991.

Gaines, Jane M. *Fire and Desire: Mixed-Race Movies in the Silent Era.* Chicago: University of Chicago Press, 2001.

Garnet, Henry Highland. *Memorial Discourse.* Philadelphia: Joseph M. Wilson, 1865.

Garrity, John A., and Mark C. Carnes, eds. *American National Biography.* 24 vols. New York: Oxford University Press, 1999.

Garrow, David J. *Bearing the Cross: Martin Luther King, Jr., and the Southern Christian Leadership Conference.* New York: Vintage, 1988.

Gates, Henry Louis, Jr. "100 Amazing Facts about the Negro." *100 Amazing Facts About the Negro. The Root,* October 15, 2012.

——. "The 1st Black Man to See the Baby Jesus." *100 Amazing Facts about the Negro. The Root,* December 24, 2012.

——. "George Washington's Runaway Slave, Harry." *100 Amazing Facts about the Negro. The Root,* December 10, 2012.

——. "How Many Slaves Landed in the US?" *100 Amazing Facts about the Negro. The Root,* October 15, 2012.

——. "North America's 1st Black President?" *100 Amazing Facts about the Negro. The Root,* November 5, 2012.

——. "North America's 1st Black Town?" *100 Amazing Facts about the Negro. The Root,* December 3, 2012.

——. "Tarantino 'Unchained,' Part 1: 'Django' Trilogy." *100 Amazing Facts about the Negro. The Root,* December 23, 2012.

——. "Tarantino 'Unchained,' Part 2: On the N-Word." *100 Amazing Facts about the Negro. The Root,* December 25, 2012.

——. "Tarantino 'Unchained,' Part 3: White Saviors." *100 Amazing Facts about the Negro. The Root,* December 25, 2012.

——. "3 Women 'Red Tails' Left Out.'" *The Root,* January 25, 2012.

——. "The Truth Behind '40 Acres and a Mule.'" *100 Amazing Facts about the Negro. The Root,* January 7, 2013.

——. "W. E. B. Du Bois' Talented Tenth in Pictures," *The Root.com,* December 2, 2010.

——. "What Was America's 1st Black Town?" *100 Amazing Facts about the Negro. The Root,* December 31, 2012.

——. "Which Slave Wrote His Way Out of Slavery?'" *100 Amazing Facts about the Negro. The Root,* November 26, 2012.

——. "Who Led the 1st Back-to-Africa Effort?" *100 Amazing Facts about the Negro. The Root,* December 17, 2012.

——. "Who Was the 1st Black to Explore the West?" *100 Amazing Facts about the Negro. The Root,* November 19, 2012.

——. "Who Was Africa's 1st Ambassador to Europe?" *100 Amazing Facts about the Negro. The Root,* November 12, 2012.

——. "Who Was the First African American?'" *100 Amazing Facts about the Negro. The Root,* October 22, 2012.

——. "Who Was the First Black Saint?" *100 Amazing Facts about the Negro. The Root,* October 29, 2012.

——. *Life Upon These Shores: Looking at African American History, 1513–2008.* New York: Alfred A. Knopf, 2011.

——. *The Trials of Phillis Wheatley: America's First Black Poet and Her Encounters with the Founding Fathers.* New York: Basic Civitas Books, 2003.

——, and Evelyn Brooks Higginbotham, eds. *African American National Biography.* 8 vols. New York: Oxford University Press, 2008.

——, and Gene Andrew Jarrett, eds. *The New Negro: Readings on Race, Representations, and African American Culture, 1892–1938*. Princeton: Princeton University Press, 2007.

——, and Donald Yacovone, eds. *Lincoln on Race and Slavery*. Princeton: Princeton University Press, 2009.

Giddings, Paula J. *Ida: A Sword Among Lions: Ida B. Wells and the Campaign Against Lynching*. New York: Amistad Press/Harper Collins, 2008.

Gilbert, Alan. *Black Patriots and Loyalists: Fighting for Emancipation in the War for Independence*. Chicago: University of Chicago Press, 2012.

Gilchrist, Brenda J. "Detroit's 1943 Race Riot, 50 Years Ago Today, Still Seems Too Near." *Detroit Free Press*. June 20, 1993.

Girard, Philippe R. *The Slaves Who Defeated Napoleon: Toussaint Louverture and the Haitian War of Independence, 1801–1804*. Tuscaloosa: University of Alabama Press, 2011.

Glatthaar, Joseph T. *Forged in Battle: The Civil War Alliance of Black Soldiers and White Officers*. New York: Free Press, 1990.

Goodwin, Robert. *Crossing the Continent, 1527–1540: The Story of the First African-American Explorer of the American South*. New York: HarperCollins, 2008.

Gordon-Reed, Annette. *The Hemingses of Monticello: An American Family*. New York: W. W. Norton, 2008.

Goudsouzian, Aram. *Down to the Crossroads: Civil Rights, Black Power, and the Meredith March Against Fear*. New York: Farrar, Straus and Giroux, forthcoming.

Gould, Eliga H. "Entangled Histories, Entangled Worlds: The English-Speaking Atlantic as a Spanish Periphery." *American Historical Review* 112 (2007): 766–86.

Grant, Colin. *Negro with a Hat: The Rise and Fall of Marcus Garvey*. New York: Oxford University Press, 2008.

Grant, Douglas. *The Fortunate Slave: An Illustration of African Slavery in the Early Eighteenth Century*. London: Oxford University Press, 1968.

Grant, Joanne. *Ella Baker: Freedom Bound*. New York: Wiley, 1998.

Gray, Christopher. "Streetscapes/Blumstein's Department Store; How a Black Boycott Opened the Employment Door." *New York Times*. November 20, 1994.

Gray, Madison. "The Press, Race and Katrina." *Time*. August 30, 2006.

Gray, Thomas R. ed. *The Confessions of Nat Turner*. Baltimore: Thomas R. Gray, 1831.

Green, Victor Hugo. *The Negro Motorist Green Book: An International Travel Guide, 1949 ed*. New York: Victor H. Green & Co., Publishers, 1949.

Gregory, James N. *The Southern Diaspora: How the Great Migrations of Black and White Southerners Transformed America*. Chapel Hill: University of North Carolina Press, 2005.

Grossman, James R. *Land of Hope: Chicago, Southerners, and the Great Migration*. Chicago: University of Chicago Press, 1989.

Guelzo, Allen C. *Lincoln's Emancipation Proclamation: The End of Slavery in America*. New York: Simon and Schuster, 2004.

Guerrero, Ed. *Framing Blackness: The African American Image in Film*. Philadelphia: Temple University Press, 1993.

Gutiérrez, Ramón A. *When Jesus Came, the Corn Mothers Went Away: Marriage, Sexuality, and Power in New Mexico, 1500–1846*. Stanford, CA: Stanford University Press, 1991.

Gutman, Herbert G. *The Black Family in Slavery and Freedom, 1750–1925*. New York: Vintage Books, 1977.

Habib, Imtiaz. *Black Lives in the English Archives, 1500–1677*. Burlington, VT: Ashgate, 2008.

Hahn, Steven. *A Nation Under Our Feet: Black Political Struggles in the Rural South from Slavery to the Great Migration.* Cambridge: Harvard University Press, 2003.

Hall, Prince. *A Charge Delivered to the African Lodge, June 24, 1797, at Menotomy, Mass.* Boston: Benjamin Edes, 1797.

Hamilton, Kenneth Marvin. "The Origins and Early Promotion of Nicodemus: A Pre-Exodus, All-Black Town." *Kansas History* 5 (1982): 220–42.

Hamilton, Neil A. "Garvey, Marcus." In *American Social Leaders and Activists, American Biographies,* 157–60. New York: Facts on File, 2002.

Hampton, Henry, and Steve Fayer. *Voices of Freedom: An Oral History of the Civil Rights Movement from the 1950s Through the 1980s.* New York: Bantam, 1991.

Hancock, David. *Citizens of the World: London Merchants and the Integration of the British Atlantic Community, 1735–1785.* Cambridge: Cambridge University Press, 1995.

Handlin, Oscar, and Mary F. Handlin. "Origins of the Southern Labor System." *William and Mary Quarterly,* 3d ser., 7, no. 2 (April 1950): 199–222.

Hanson, Joyce A. *Rosa Parks: A Biography.* Santa Barbara, CA: ABC-CLIO, 2011.

Harlan, Louis R. *Booker T. Washington.* 2 vols. New York: Oxford University Press, 1972–1983.

Harold, Claudrena N. *The Rise and Fall of the Garvey Movement in the Urban South, 1918–1942.* New York: Routledge, 2007.

Harris, Robert L., Jr. "Charleston's Free Afro-American Elite: The Brown Fellowship Society and the Humane Brotherhood." *South Carolina Historical Magazine,* 82 (October 1981): 289–310.

Harris, William H. *Keeping the Faith: A. Philip Randolph, Milton P. Webster, and the Brotherhood of Sleeping Car Porters, 1925–37.* Urbana: University of Illinois Press, 1991.

Harris-Perry, Melissa V. *Sister Citizen: Shame, Stereotypes, and Black Women in America.* New Haven: Yale University Press, 2011.

Haygood, Wil. *King of the Cats: The Life and Times of Adam Clayton Powell, Jr.* Boston: Houghton Mifflin, 1993.

Hendrickson, Paul. "The Ladies Before Rosa: They Too Wouldn't Give Up Their Seats." *Washington Post,* April 12, 1998.

Henri, Florette. *Black Migration: Movement North, 1900–1920.* Garden City, NY: Anchor Press, 1975.

Hermann, Janet Sharp. *The Pursuit of a Dream.* New York: Oxford University Press, 1981.

Heywood, Linda M., and John K. Thornton. *Central Africans, Atlantic Creoles, and the Foundation of the Americas, 1585–1660.* Cambridge: Cambridge University Press, 2007.

Higginbotham, Evelyn Brooks. *Righteous Discontent: The Women's Movement in the Black Baptist Church, 1880–1920.* Cambridge: Harvard University Press, 1993.

Hinks, Peter P. *To Awaken My Afflicted Brethren: David Walker and the Problem of Antebellum Slave Resistance.* University Park: Pennsylvania State University Press, 1997.

——, and Stephen Kantrowitz, eds. *All Men Free and Brethren: Essays on the History of African American Freemasonry.* Ithaca, NY: Cornell University Press, 2013.

Hodges, Graham Russell. *Root & Branch: African Americans in New York and East Jersey, 1613–1863.* Chapel Hill: University of North Carolina Press, 1999.

Hoffer, Peter Charles. *Cry Liberty: The Great Stono River Slave Rebellion of 1739.* New York: Oxford University Press, 2010.

Holt, Thomas C. *Children of Fire: A History of African Americans.* New York: Hill and Wang, 2010.

Horton, James O., and Lois E. Horton. *Hard Road to Freedom: The Story of African America.*

New Brunswick, NJ: Rutgers University Press, 2002.

——. *In Hope of Liberty: Culture, Community and Protest among Northern Free Blacks, 1700–1860.* New York: Oxford University Press, 1996.

Huggins, Nathan I. *Harlem Renaissance.* New York: Oxford University Press, 1978, 2007.

Hughes, Langston. *The Big Sea: An Autobiography.* New York, Macmillan, 1993.

Jackson, Kenneth T. *The Ku Klux Klan in the City, 1915–1930.* New York: Oxford University Press, 1967.

Johnson, Charles S. "The New Frontage on American Life." In *The New Negro,* edited by Alain Locke, 278–98. New York: Atheneum, 1992.

Johnson, John H. *Succeeding Against the Odds.* New York: Warner Books, 1989.

Johnson, Michael, and James L. Roark. *Black Masters: A Free Family of Color in the Old South.* New York: Oxford University Press, 1984.

Johnson, Samuel. *Taxation No Tyranny: An Answer to the Resolution and Address of the American Congress.* London: Printed for T. Cadell, 1775.

Johnson, Walter. *Soul by Soul: Life Inside the Antebellum Slave Market.* Cambridge: Harvard University Press, 1999.

Jonas, Gilbert. *Freedom's Sword: The NAACP and the Struggle Against Racism in America, 1909–1969.* New York: Routledge, 2005.

Jones, Eldred. *The Elizabethan Image of Africa.* Charlottesville: University Press of Virginia for the Folger Shakespeare Library, 1971.

Joseph, Peniel E. *Dark Days, Bright Nights: From Black Power to Barack Obama.* New York: Basic Civitas Books, 2010.

——. *Waiting 'Til the Midnight Hour: A Narrative History of Black Power in America.* New York: Henry Holt and Company, 2006.

Joyner, Charles. *Down by the Riverside: A South Carolina Slave Community.* Urbana: University of Illinois Press, 1984.

Kelley, Robin D. G. *Into the Fire: African Americans since 1970.* New York: Oxford University Press, 1996.

——. "Kickin' Reality, Kickin' Ballistics: Gangsta Rap and Postindustrial Los Angeles." In *Droppin' Science: Critical Perspectives on Rap Music and Hip Hop Culture,* edited by William Eric Perkins, 117–58. Philadelphia: Temple University Press, 1996.

——. *Race Rebels: Culture, Politics, and the Black Working Class.* New York: Free Press, 1996.

——. *Yo' Mama's Disfunktional!: Fighting the Culture Wars in Urban America.* Boston: Beacon Press, 1998.

King, Martin Luther, Jr. "I Have a Dream." In *A Testament of Hope: The Essential Writings and Speeches of Martin Luther King, Jr.,* edited by James M. Washington, 217–20. New York: HarperCollins, 1990.

——. "Love, Law, and Civil Disobedience." In *A Testament of Hope: The Essential Writings and Speeches of Martin Luther King, Jr.,* edited by James M. Washington, 43–53. New York: HarperCollins, 1990.

Klein, Herbert S., and Ben Vinson III. *African Slavery in Latin America and the Caribbean.* New York: Oxford University Press, 2007.

Knight, Michael T. "Recognizing 233 Years of Black Marines." Marine Corps Base Camp Pendleton. *Marines: The Official Website of the United States Marine Corps.*

Landers, Jane. *Atlantic Creoles in the Age of Revolutions.* Cambridge: Harvard University Press, 2010.

——. *Black Society in Spanish Florida.* Urbana: University of Illinois Press, 1999.

——. "Juan Garrido." In *African American National Biography,* edited by Henry Louis Gates, Jr., and Evelyn Brooks Higginbotham. 8 vols. 3:456–57. New York: Oxford University Press, 2008.

Law, Robin. *The Slave Coast of West Africa, 1550–1750: The Impact of the Atlantic Slave Trade on an African Society*. New York: Oxford University Press, 1991.

Lee, Chana Kai. *For Freedom's Sake: The Life of Fannie Lou Hamer*. Urbana: University of Illinois Press, 1999.

Leffall, LaSalle D., Jr. Interview by Jason Gart. In The Charles Drew Papers, *Profiles in Science: National Library of Medicine*. November 19, 2012.

Lepore, Jill. *New York Burning: Liberty, Slavery, and Conspiracy in Eighteenth-Century Manhattan*. New York: Alfred A. Knopf, 2005.

Lewis, Andrew B. *The Shadows of Youth: The Remarkable Journey of the Civil Rights Generation*. New York: Hill and Wang, 2009.

Lewis, David Levering. *W. E. B. Du Bois: Biography of a Race, 1868–1919*. New York: Henry Holt and Company, 1993.

——. *W. E. B. Du Bois, 1919–1963: The Fight for Equality and the American Century*. New York: Macmillan, 2001.

——. *When Harlem Was in Vogue*. New York: Penguin, 1981, 1997.

Lewis, John. *Walking with the Wind*. In collaboration with Michael D'Orso. New York: Simon and Schuster, 1998.

Linebaugh, Peter, and Marcus Rediker. *The Many-headed Hydra: Sailors, Slaves, Commoners, and the Hidden History of the Revolutionary Atlantic*. Boston: Beacon Press, 2000.

Liptak, Adam. "New Look at Death Sentences and Race." *New York Times*. April 29, 2008.

Littlefield, Daniel F., Jr. *The Chickasaw Freedmen: A People Without a Country*. Westport, CT: Greenwood Press, 1980.

Litwack, Leon F. *Been in the Storm So Long: The Aftermath of Slavery*. New York: Alfred A. Knopf, 1979.

——. *How Free Is Free?: The Long Death of Jim Crow*. Cambridge: Harvard University Press, 2009.

——. *North of Slavery: The Negro in the Free States, 1790–1860*. Chicago: University of Chicago Press, 1961.

——. *Trouble in Mind: Black Southerners in the Age of Jim Crow*. New York: Alfred A. Knopf, 1998.

Logan, Rayford W. *The Betrayal of the Negro: From Rutherford Hayes to Woodrow Wilson*. New York: Da Capo Press, 1965, 1997.

Lomax, Michael. "Education Is the 21st-Century Liberator." *The Root*. January 16, 2013.

Love, Spencie. *One Blood: The Death and Resurrection of Charles R. Drew*. Chapel Hill: University of North Carolina Press, 1996.

Lovejoy, Paul E. *Slavery, Commerce, and Production in the Sokoto Caliphate of West Africa*. Trenton, NJ: Africa World Press, 2005.

——. *Transformations in Slavery: A History of Slavery in Africa*. New York: Cambridge University Press, 2000.

Malcom X. *The Hate That Hate Produced, News Beat*. Interview by Mike Wallace. WNTA-TV (CBS), July 13–17, 1959.

——. "Message to the Grass Roots." In *The Portable Malcolm X Reader*, edited by Manning Marable and Garrett Felber, 265-73. New York: Penguin Books, 2013.

Marks, Carole. *Farewell, We're Good and Gone: The Great Black Migration*. Bloomington: Indiana University Press, 1989.

Martin, Joyce A., et al. National Center for Health Statistics. "Births: Final Data for 2007." *National Vital Statistics Reports* 58, no. 24 (August 9, 2010): Table 15, 76.

Massachusetts Constitution. http://www.nhinet.org/ccs/docs/ma-1780.htm.

Matthews, Victoria Earle. "The Value of Race Literature." In *The New Negro: Readings on Race, Representation, and African American Culture, 1892–1938*, edited by Henry Louis Gates, Jr., and Gene Andrew Jarrett, 287–296. Princeton: Princeton University, 2007.

Matthewson, Tim. "Jefferson and Haiti." *Journal of Southern History* 61 (May 1995): 209–48.

McFeely, William S. *Frederick Douglass*. New York: W. W. Norton, 1991.

McIlwaine, H. R., ed. *Minutes of the Council and General Court of Colonial Virginia*. Richmond: Virginia State Library, 1979.

McKee, Margaret, and Fred Chisenhall. *Beale, Black & Blue: Life and Music on Black America's Main Street*. Baton Rouge: Louisiana State University Press, 1981.

McMurray, Linda O. *To Keep the Waters Troubled: The Life of Ida B. Wells*. New York: Oxford University Press, 1998.

McNeil, Genna Rae. *Groundwork: Charles Hamilton Houston and the Struggle for Civil Rights*. Philadelphia: University of Pennsylvania Press, 1983.

McPherson, James M. *The Abolitionist Legacy: From Reconstruction to the NAACP*. Princeton: Princeton University Press, 1975, 1995.

Medley, Keith Weldon. *We as Freemen: Plessy v. Ferguson*. Gretna, LA: Pelican Publishing, 2003.

Meier, August. *Negro Thought in America, 1880–1915: Racial Ideologies in the Age of Booker T. Washington*. Ann Arbor: University of Michigan Press, 1963.

Melish, Joanne Pope. *Disowning Slavery: Gradual Emancipation and "Race" in New England, 1780–1860*. Ithaca, NY: Cornell University Press, 1998.

Miller, Edward A., Jr. *Gullah Statesman: Robert Smalls from Slavery to Congress, 1839–1915*. Columbia: University of South Carolina Press, 1994.

Miller, Floyd J. *The Search for a Black Nationality: Black Emigration and Colonization, 1787–1863*. Urbana: University of Illinois Press, 1975.

Mohr, Clarence L. *On the Threshold of Freedom: Masters and Slaves in Civil War Georgia*. Baton Rouge: Louisiana State University Press, 1986, 2001.

Morehouse, Henry Lyman. "The Talented Tenth." *The American Missionary* 50, no. 6 (June 1896); Project Gutenberg, November 21, 2006.

Morgan, Edmund S. *American Slavery, American Freedom: The Ordeal of Colonial Virginia*. New York: W. W. Norton, 1975.

———. "Slavery and Freedom: The American Paradox." *Journal of American History* 59 (June 1972): 5–29.

Morgan, Marcyliena H. *The Real Hiphop: Battling for Knowledge, Power, and Respect in the LA Underground*. Durham, NC: Duke University Press, 2009.

Morgan, Philip D. *Slave Counterpoint: Black Culture in the Eighteenth-Century Chesapeake and Lowcountry*. Chapel Hill: University of North Carolina Press, 1998.

———, and Andrew Jackson O'Shaughnessy. "Arming Slaves in the American Revolution." In *Arming Slaves: From Classical Times to the Modern Age*, edited by Christopher Leslie Brown and Philip D. Morgan. New Haven: Yale University Press, 2006.

Morris, Thomas D. *Southern Slavery and the Law, 1619–1860*. Chapel Hill: University of North Carolina Press, 1996.

Moses, Wilson J. *The Golden Age of Black Nationalism, 1850–1925*. New York: Oxford University Press, 1978, 1988.

Nash, Gary B. *The Forgotten Fifth: African Americans in the Age of the Revolution*. Cambridge: Harvard University Press, 2006.

———. "Introduction." In *The Negro in the American Revolution*, by Benjamin Quarles, xiii–xxvi. Chapel Hill: University of North Carolina Press, 1966.

Nell, William C. *The Colored Patriots of the American Revolution*. Boston: Robert F. Wallcut, 1855.

Newitt, Malyn. *A History of Portuguese Overseas Expansion, 1400–1668*. New York: Routledge, 2005.

——, ed. *The Portuguese in West Africa, 1415–1670: A Documentary History*. Cambridge: Cambridge University Press, 2010.

Newman, Richard S. *Freedom's Prophet: Bishop Richard Allen, the AME Church, and the Black Founding Fathers*. New York: New York University Press, 2008.

New York Times. "President's Plea: On TV, He Deplores 'Brutal' Murder of Negro Leader." April 5, 1968.

Northup, Solomon. *Twelve Years a Slave: Narrative of Solomon Northup, A Citizen of New-York, Kidnapped in Washington City in 1841*. Auburn, NY: Derby and Miller; London: Sampson Low, Son & Co., 1853.

Nossiter, Adam. "New Orleans Population Is Reduced Nearly 60%." *New York Times*. October 7, 2006.

Oates, Stephen B. *The Fires of Jubilee: Nat Turner's Fierce Rebellion*. New York: Harper & Row, 1975.

Obama, Barack. Keynote speech, Democratic National Convention, transcript. *Washington Post*. July 27, 2004.

O'Brien, William. "Did the Jennison Case Outlaw Slavery in Massachusetts?" *William and Mary Quarterly*, 3d ser., 17 (April 1960): 223–41.

"Outgrowing the Ghetto Mind." *Ebony*. 18, 10 (August 1963): 98.

Ovington, Mary White. *Black and White Sat Down Together: The Reminiscences of an NAACP Founder*. New York: Feminist Press at the City University of New York, 1995.

Paine, Thomas. "Justice and Humanity" and "To Americans," *Pennsylvania Journal and the Weekly Advertiser*, March 8, 1775.

Pearson, Hugh. *The Shadow of the Panther: Huey Newton and the Price of Black Power in America*. Reading, MA: Addison-Wesley, 1994.

Pease, William, and Jane H. Pease. *The Web of Progress: Private Values and Public Styles in Boston and Charleston, 1828–1843*. Athens: University of Georgia Press, 1991.

Perdue, Theda. *Slavery and the Evolution of Cherokee Society, 1540–1866*. Knoxville: University of Tennessee Press, 1979.

Perman, Michael. *Struggle for Mastery: Disfranchisement in the South, 1888–1908*. Chapel Hill: University of North Carolina Press, 2001.

Perry, Bruce. *Malcolm: The Life of a Man Who Changed Black America*. Barrytown, NY: Station Hill Press, 1991.

Pettit, Becky. *Invisible Men: Mass Incarceration and the Myth of Black Progress*. New York: Russell Sage Foundation, 2012.

Pew Center on the States. *One in 31: The Long Reach of American Corrections*. Washington, D.C.: The Pew Charitable Trusts, March 2009.

——. *One in 100: Behind Bars in America 2008*. Washington, D.C.: The Pew Charitable Trusts, February 2008.

Pezuela y Lobo, Jacobo de la. *Historia de la isla de Cuba*. Madrid: Carlos Bailly-Bailliere, 1868.

Phibbs, Cheryl F. *The Montgomery Bus Boycott: A History and Reference Guide*. Santa Barbara, CA: Greenwood, 2009.

Phillips, Wendell. "Toussaint l'Ouverture." In *Selections from the Works of Wendell Phillips*, edited by A. D. Hall, 121–58. Boston: H. M. Caldwell Co., 1902.

Pilgrim, David. "The Garbage Man: Why I Collect Racist Objects." In *Jim Crow Museum of Racist Memorabilia*, February 2005.

"A Pivotal Moment in the Civil Rights Movement: The Murder of Emmett Till." In *Facing History and Ourselves*, 2013.

"Poverty in the United States." *National Poverty Center, University of Michigan Gerald R. Ford School of Public Policy.* http://www.npc.umich.edu/poverty/.

Powell, Colin. "Foreword" to *Hope & Glory: Essays on the Legacy of the 54th Massachusetts Regiment*, edited by Martin H. Blatt, Thomas J. Brown, and Donald Yacovone. Amherst: University of Massachusetts Press, 2011.

"President's Park/Citizens Soapbox: A History of Protest at the White House." WhiteHouseHistory.org.

Price, George R., and James Brewer Stewart, eds. *To Heal the Scourge of Prejudice: The Life and Writings of Hosea Easton.* Amherst: University of Massachusetts Press, 1999.

Putz, Andrew. "Skullduggery," *Indianapolis Monthly* (October 2003): 128–31, 224–27.

Pybus, Cassandra. *Epic Journeys of Freedom: Runaway Slaves of the American Revolution and Their Global Quest for Liberty.* Boston: Beacon Press, 2006.

Quarles, Benjamin. *The Negro in the American Revolution.* Chapel Hill: University of North Carolina Press, 1961, 1996.

Quintal, George, Jr., comp. *Patriots of Color: A Peculiar Beauty and Merit.* Boston: Boston National Historical Park, 2004.

Rabinowitz, Howard N. *Race Relations in the Urban South.* Athens: University of Georgia Press, 1978, 1996.

Raboteau, Albert J. *Canaan Land: A Religious History of African Americans.* New York: Oxford University Press, 2001.

——. *A Fire in the Bones: Reflections on African-American Religious History.* Boston: Beacon Press, 1995.

Rampersad, Arnold. *The Life of Langston Hughes.* New York: Oxford University Press, 2002.

Ramsey, William L. "'Something Cloudy in Their Looks': The Origins of the Yamasee War." *Journal of American History* 90 (June 2003): 44–75.

Ransby, Barbara. *Ella Baker and the Black Freedom Movement: A Radical Democratic Vision.* Chapel Hill: University of North Carolina Press, 2003.

"Rapper Blasts Bush Over Katrina." *CBSNews.com.* 2009.

Rasmussen, Daniel. *American Uprising: The Untold Story of America's Largest Slave Revolt.* New York: HarperCollins, 2011.

Reidy, Joseph. *From Slavery to Agrarian Capitalism in the Cotton Plantation South: Central Georgia, 1800–1880.* Chapel Hill: University of North Carolina Press, 1992.

Reinhardt, Mark. *Who Speaks for Margaret Garner?* Minneapolis: University of Minnesota Press, 2010.

Restall, Matthew. "Black Conquistadors: Armed Africans in Early Spanish America." *The Americas* 57 (October 2000): 171–205.

Reynolds, David S. *John Brown Abolitionist: The Man Who Killed Slavery, Sparked Civil War, and Seeded Civil Rights.* New York: Alfred A. Knopf, 2005.

Richardson, Joe M. *Christian Reconstruction: The American Missionary Association and Southern Blacks, 1861–1890.* Athens: University of Georgia Press, 1986.

Richardson, Marilyn, ed. *Maria W. Stewart, America's First Black Woman Political Writer: Essays and Speeches.* Bloomington: Indiana University Press, 1987.

Ripley, C. Peter, et al., eds. *The Black Abolitionist Papers, The United States, 1830–1865.* 3 vols. Chapel Hill: University of North Carolina Press, 1991–1992.

Roberts, Gene, and Hank Klibanoff. *The Race Beat: The Press, the Civil Rights Struggle, and the Awakening of a Nation.* New York: Alfred A. Knopf, 2006.

Roberts, Sam. "How Prisoners Make Us Look Good." *New York Times Sunday Review*, October 27, 2012.

Robertson, Nan. "In the Capital, Sermons on Courage in Selma; President Hears Strife Called the Nation's Heartbreak." *New York Times*, March 15, 1965.

Robeson, Paul. *Here I Stand*. Boston: Beacon Press, 1958.

Robinson, Dean E. *Black Nationalism in American Politics and Thought*. New York: Cambridge University Press, 2001.

Rockwell, George Lincoln. Interview by Alex Haley. *Playboy*. April 1966.

Rodriguez, Junius P. "Always 'En Garde': The Effects of Slave Insurrection upon the Louisiana Mentality, 1811–1815." *Louisiana History*, 33 (Autumn 1992): 399–416.

Rolinson, Mary G. *Grassroots Garveyism: The Universal Negro Improvement Association in the Rural South, 1920–1927*. Chapel Hill: University of North Carolina Press, 2007.

Rose, Willy Lee. *Rehearsal for Reconstruction: The Port Royal Experiment*. New York: Random House, 1964.

Runstedtler, Theresa. *Jack Johnson, Rebel Sojourner: Boxing in the Shadow of the Global Color Line*. Berkeley: University of California Press, 2012.

Sam and W[illia]m Vernon to Capt. Caleb Godfrey. November 8, 1755. http://www.choices.edu/resources/documents/SlaveVoyage.pdf

Schama, Simon. *Rough Crossings: Britain, the Slaves, and the American Revolution*. New York: HarperCollins, 2006.

Schneir, Miriam. *Feminism in Our Time: The Essential Writings, World War II to the Present*. New York: Vintage, 1994.

Schweninger, Loren. "Black-Owned Businesses in the South, 1790–1880." *Business History Review* 63 (1989): 22–60.

——. "Property-Owning Free African-American Women in the South, 1800–1870." *Journal of Women's History* 1 (1990): 13–44.

——. "A Vanishing Breed: Black Farm Owners in the South, 1651–1982." *Agricultural History* 63 (1989): 41–60.

Seraile, William. *Fire in His Heart: Bishop Benjamin Tucker Tanner and the A.M.E. Church*. Knoxville: University of Tennessee Press, 1998.

Sernett, Milton C. *Bound for the Promised Land: African American Religion and the Great Migration*. Durham, NC: Duke University Press, 1997.

Sesay, Chernoh M., Jr. "Freemasons of Color: Prince Hall, Revolutionary Black Boston, and the Origins of Black Freemasonry, 1770–1807." Ph.D. diss., Northwestern University, 2006.

——. "Prince Hall." In *African American National Biography*, edited by Henry Louis Gates, Jr., and Evelyn Brooks Higginbotham, 4:22–24. New York: Oxford University Press, 2008.

Shugerman, Jed Handelsman. "The Louisiana Purchase and South Carolina's Reopening of the Slave Trade in 1803." *Journal of the Early Republic* 22 (Summer 2002): 263–90.

Sibthorpe, A. B. C. *The History of Sierra Leone*. New York: Humanities Press, 1971.

Skocpol, Theda, Ariane Liazos, and Marshall Ganz, eds. *What a Mighty Power We Can Be: African American Fraternal Groups and the Struggle for Racial Equality*. Princeton: Princeton University Press, 2006.

Smalls, Robert. "Election Methods in the South." *North American Review* 151 (November 1890): 593–600.

Sobel, Mechal. *The World They Made Together: Black and White Values in Eighteenth-Century Virginia*. Princeton: Princeton University Press, 1987.

Spencer, Jon M. *Protest & Praise: Sacred Music of Black Religion*. Minneapolis: Fortress Press, 1990.

Spingarn, Adena. "When 'Uncle Tom' Became an Insult." *The Root.* May 17, 2010.

Spivey, Donald. *Schooling for the New Slavery: Black Industrial Education, 1868–1915.* Westport, CT: Greenwood Press, 1978.

Stewart, James Brewer. "Modernizing 'Difference': The Political Meanings of Color in the Free States, 1776–1840." *Journal of the Early Republic* 19 (Winter 1999): 691–712.

Still, William. *The Underground Railroad.* Philadelphia: Porter & Coates, 1872.

Sugrue, Thomas J. *Sweet Land of Liberty: The Forgotten Struggle for Civil Rights in the North.* New York: Random House, 2008.

Sullivan, Patricia. *Days of Hope: Race and Democracy in the New Deal Era.* Chapel Hill: University of North Carolina Press, 1996.

——. *Lift Every Voice: The NAACP and the Making of the Civil Rights Movement.* New York: The New Press, 2009.

Swarns, Christina, and Eva Paterson. "Twenty-Five Years Later, *McCleskey* Decision Still Fosters Racism by Ignoring It." *ACSblog* (*American Constitution Society*).

Sweet, James H. "African Identity and Slave Resistance in the Portuguese Atlantic." In *The Atlantic World and Virginia, 1550–1624*, edited by Peter Mancall, 228–50. Chapel Hill: University of North Carolina Press, 2007.

Tadman, Michael. *Speculators and Slaves: Masters, Traders, and Slaves in the Old South.* Madison: University of Wisconsin Press, 1996.

Thomas, Lamont D. *Rise to Be a People: A Biography of Paul Cuffee.* Urbana: University of Illinois Press, 1986.

Thornbrough, Emma Lou. *T. Thomas Fortune: Militant Journalist.* Chicago: University of Chicago Press, 1972.

Thornton, John K. *Africa and Africans in the Making of the Atlantic World, 1400–1800.* New York: Cambridge University Press, 1998.

——. "The African Experience of the '20. And Odd Negroes' Arriving in Virginia in 1619." *William and Mary Quarterly*, 3d ser., 55 (1998): 421–34.

——. "Cannibals, Witches, and Slave Traders in the Atlantic World." *William and Mary Quarterly*, 3d ser., 60, no. 2 (April 2003): 273–94.

——. *The Kongolese Saint Anthony: Dona Beatriz Kimpa Vita and the Antonian Movement, 1684–1706.* Cambridge: Cambridge University Press, 1998.

——. "Legitimacy and Political Power: Queen Njinga, 1624–1663." *Journal of African History* 32 (1991): 25–40.

Trelease, Allen W. *White Terror: The Ku Klux Klan Conspiracy and Southern Reconstruction.* Westport, CT: Greenwood Press, 1971, 1979.

Trotter, Joe William, Jr., ed. *The Great Migration in Historical Perspective.* Bloomington: Indiana University Press, 1991.

Trudeau, Noah Andre. *Like Men of War: Black Troops in the Civil War, 1862–1865.* Boston: Little, Brown & Co., 1998.

Tuck, Stephen. *We Ain't What We Ought to Be: The Black Freedom Struggle from Emancipation to Obama.* Cambridge: Harvard University Press, 2010.

The Tuscarora War. http://www.nchistoricsites .org/bath/tuscarora.htm.

Tushnet, Mark V. *The NAACP's Legal Strategy Against Segregated Education, 1925–1950.* Chapel Hill: University of North Carolina Press, 1987, 2004.

Tuttle, William M. *Race Riot: Chicago in the Red Summer of 1919.* Urbana: University of Illinois Press, 1970, 1996.

1830 Census. Washington: Printed by Duff Green, 1832.

USCT Casualties of USCT Units at the Battle of New Market Heights. http://www.nps .gov/rich/historyculture/casualties.htm.

Van Deburg, William L. *New Day in Babylon: The Black Power Movement and American Culture, 1965–1975.* Chicago: University of Chicago Press, 1992.

Vaughan, Alden T. "A Sense of Their Own Power: Black Virginians, 1619–1989." *Virginia Magazine of History and Biography* 97 (July 1989): 311–54.

Vorenberg, Michael. *Final Freedom: The Civil War, the Abolition of Slavery, and the Thirteenth Amendment.* New York: Cambridge University Press, 2001.

Wade, Wyn Craig. *The Fiery Cross: The Ku Klux Klan in America.* New York: Oxford University Press, 1998.

Walker, David. *Appeal, in Four Articles . . .* Boston: D. Walker, 1830.

Washington, Booker T. *Up from Slavery.* 1901. Repr. New York: Tribeca Books, 2012.

Washington, George. Papers. http://gwpapers .virginia.edu/documents.

Washington (Penn.) *Reporter.* June 19, 1862.

"We Want Freedom Now, King Tells Negro Rally: 125,000 Take Part in Massive Detroit Demonstration Marking Riot Anniversary." *Los Angeles Times.* June 24, 1963.

Weisenburger, Steven. *Modern Medea: A Family Story of Slavery and Child-Murder from the Old South.* New York: Hill and Wang, 1998.

Wells, Ida B. *Crusade for Justice: The Autobiography of Ida B. Wells,* edited by Alfreda M. Duster. Chicago: University of Chicago Press, 1970.

Werner, Craig Hansen. *A Change Is Gonna Come: Music, Race, and the Soul of America.* Ann Arbor: University of Michigan Press, 2006.

"The Western Migration." *In Motion: The African-American Migration Experience.* http://www.inmotionaame.org/print.cfm;jsessionid=f83 02383641353079584716?migration=6&bhcp=1.

Wiencek, Henry. *An Imperfect God: George Washington, His Slaves, and the Creation of America.* New York: Farrar, Straus and Giroux, 2003.

Wilson, William Julius. *More Than Just Race: Being Black and Poor in the Inner City.* New York: W. W. Norton, 2009.

Winch, Julie. *A Gentleman of Color: The Life of James Forten.* New York: Oxford University Press, 2002.

———. *Philadelphia's Black Elite: Activism, Accommodation, and the Struggle for Autonomy, 1787–1848.* Philadelphia: Temple University Press, 1988.

Wood, Peter H. *Black Majority: Negroes in Colonial South Carolina from 1670 Through the Stono Rebellion.* New York: W. W. Norton, 1974.

———. *Strange New Land: Africans in Colonial America.* New York: Oxford University Press, 2003.

Woodson, Carter G., ed. *Free Negro Owners of Slaves in the United States in 1830.* Washington, D.C.: Association for the Study of Negro Life and History, 1924.

Woodward, C. Vann. *The Strange Career of Jim Crow.* New York: Oxford University Press, 2002.

Wright, Jeremiah. "God Damn America" speech. *Dallas Morning News.* "Texas Faith" blog.

Yacovone, Donald, ed. *Freedom's Journey: African American Voices of the Civil War.* Chicago: Lawrence Hill Books, 2004.

———. *Samuel Joseph May and the Dilemmas of the Liberal Persuasion, 1797–1871.* Philadelphia: Temple University Press, 1991.

———. *A Voice of Thunder: The Civil War Letters of George E. Stephens.* Urbana: University of Illinois Press, 1997.

Zeleny, Jeff, and Patrick Healy. "Black Leader, a Clinton Ally, Tilts to Obama." *New York Times.* February 15, 2008.

Zilversmit, Arthur. "Quok Walker, Mumbet, and the Abolition of Slavery in Massachusetts." *William and Mary Quarterly,* 3d. ser., 25 (October 1968): 617–24.

INDEX

ACKNOWLEDGMENTS

Without the support and sponsorship of the following people, *The African Americans* could never have been produced: Glenn H. Hutchins, who was the first person to express support for this project even when it was a vague idea, and the Hutchins Family Foundation; Patricia Harrison, Vinnie Curren, Jennifer Lawson, John Prizer, and Joseph Tovares at the Corporation for Public Broadcasting; Paula Kerger, Michael Jones, Beth Hoppe, John Wilson, and Shawn Halford at PBS; Ingrid Saunders Jones at The Coca-Cola Company; Dr. Georgette Bennett and Dr. Leonard Polonsky in memory of Rabbi Marc H. Tanenbaum; Howard and Abby Milstein Foundation, in partnership with HooverMilstein and Emigrant Bank; Richard Gilder; Richard Plepler, CEO of HBO; Ben Carson and Gail Christopher and Alice Warner-Mehlhorn at the W. K. Kellogg Foundation; Virgis Colbert, Michele Barlow, Andrew Plepler, Pam Seagle, and Meredith Verdone at Bank of America; Jennifer Feldman and Rob Jackson at McDonald's; Darren Walker at the Ford Foundation; and Jim Leach, Karen Mittelman, and Jeff Hardwick at the National Endowment for the Humanities. We are deeply appreciative of the support each of these individuals and organizations has given us.

We would like to thank the following people for their assistance with the research for this book and the PBS documentary series: Nicole Bozorgmir, Rebecca Brillhart, Johni Cerny, Brittany Clemons, Sheldon Cheek, William M. Ferraro, Samantha Gowda, Hazel Gurland-Pooler, Rachel Hawatneh, Marial Iglesias Utset, Paul Kaplan, Alistair McKay, Talleah Bridges McMahon, Stephen Robinson, Paul Taylor, and Leah Williams.

The expertise of our board of scholarly advisers was invaluable, including William Andrews, Mia Bay, Ira Berlin, David Bindman, David Blight, Vincent Brown, Lonnie Bunch, Clayborne Carson, Laurent Dubois, Brent Edwards, David Eltis, Eric Foner, Glenda Gilmore, Annette Gordon-Reed, Steven Hahn, Evelynn Hammonds, Linda M. Heywood, Evelyn Brooks Higginbotham, Darlene Clark Hine, Thomas Holt, Gerald Horne, Walter Johnson, Peniel E. Joseph, Robin D. G. Kelley, Jane Landers, Jill Lepore, Thomas Mellins, Ingrid Monson, Philip Morgan, Susan O'Donovan, Eva Sheppard Wolf, John Stauffer, Thomas Sugrue, Patricia A. Sullivan, James H. Sweet, John K. Thornton, and Stephen Tuck.

Others who shared their time and knowledge with us, for which we are deeply grateful, are Malachi "Shine de God Son" Abdul, Michael Allen, Edward Ball, Abu Bangara, Gralen Banks, Mark Bauerlein, W. Kamau Bell, Daina Ramey Berry, Michael Bertrand, Ambrose Boani, Lawrence Douglass Bobo, Donald Bogle, Jerome Bridges, Ruby Bridges, Vincent Brown, Jennifer M. Bryant, A'Lelia Bundles, Rochelle Bush, Sue Cane, Kathleen Cleaver, Anthony Cohen, Tyrone Davis, Steven Deyle, Angela Dillard, Roland Doucette, Martin Duberman, Douglas Egerton, Phoebe Ferguson, David C. Forbes, Donna Ford, Dennis Frye, Paula Giddings, Thavolia Glymph, Adam Goodheart, Ben Goold, Aram

Goudsouzian, Derek Hankerson, Kenneth Hodges, Vanessa Holden, Charlayne Hunter-Gault, Darryl Johnson, Kennedy Johnson, Hari Jones, Damon Keith, Sean Kelley, Kate Clifford Larson, John Lewis, Paul Lovejoy, Lansana "Barmmy Boy" Mansaray, Mimi Miller, Willie Minor, Philip Misevich, Marcyliena Morgan, Diane Nash, Cassandra Newby-Alexander, Richard Newman, Trevor O'Brien, Joseph Opala, Christopher Parker, Gene Peters, Eulah Peterson, David Pilgrim, Clementa Pinckney, Keith Plessy, Thomalind Martin Polite & Antawn Polite, Alvin Poussaint, Colin Powell, Bernard Powers, Cassandra Pybus, Dan Rather, Noah Reeves, Jane Root, Emrys "Fisher" Savage, Kurt Schmoke, Rebecca J. Scott, Kissinor Sengu, Isatu Smith, Ada Summers, Paul Sylvester, Nikki Taylor, Ahmir "Questlove" Thompson, Michael Twitty, Mark Kelly Tyler, Darrell White, Kaye Wise Whitehead, Heather Andrea Williams, and William Julius Wilson; Joanna Mountain, Anne Wojcicki, and Ashley Gould of 23 and Me; Bennett Greenspan of FamilyTreeDNA; and Dr. Rick Kittles of AfricanAncestry.

We'd especially like to thank Julie Wolf for her brilliantly expert copyediting of the various drafts of this manuscript, and Abby Wolf for her superb command of every aspect of the intellectual life of the Du Bois Institute. Marial Iglesias Utset graciously and generously read and fact-checked the final manuscript, and our debt to her is enormous. Amy Gosdanian coolly and calmly coordinated every aspect of the demanding shooting and writing schedule of the Institute's director. We were helped tremendously by Steven Niven and Tom Wolejko, who always stepped in when needed. We'd like to thank the agents who represented this project, Bennett Ashley, Paul Lucas, and Tina Bennett.

Finally, Henry Louis Gates, Jr., would like to thank his co-executive producers, Dyllan McGee and Peter Kunhardt, with whom he developed this project; Rachel Dretzin, series senior producer; Asako Gladjo, senior story producer; Phil Bertelsen, Sabin Streeter, and Jamila Wignot, producers; and Graham Smith, director of photography. Also invaluable to this project were Julie Anderson, Jane Buckwalter, Caroline Croen, Harry Forbes, Dan Greenberg, Lisa Mantone, David Raphael, Stephen Segaller, Harvey Seslowsky, Neal Shapiro, and Kellie Specter at Channel 13 in New York.

ABOUT THE AUTHORS

HENRY LOUIS GATES, JR., is the Alphonse Fletcher University Professor and director of the Hutchins Center for African and African American Research at Harvard University. He is the author of 16 books, including *Life Upon These Shores: Looking at African American History, 1513–2008*, and *Tradition and the Black Atlantic*, and has made 12 documentaries, including *Finding Your Roots*, *Black in Latin America*, and *Looking for Lincoln*. He is also the editor-in-chief of *The Root*, a daily online magazine. He is the recipient of 51 honorary degrees and numerous awards. In 1981, he was a member of the first class awarded "genius grants" by the MacArthur Foundation, and in 1998, he became the first African American scholar to be awarded the National Humanities Medal. He was named to *Time's* "25 Most Influential Americans" list in 1997, to *Ebony's* "Power 150" list in 2009, and to *Ebony's* "Power 100" list in 2010 and 2012. *The Henry Louis Gates, Jr., Reader*, a collection of Professor Gates's essays, was published in 2012.

DONALD YACOVONE, the manager of research and program development at the Hutchins Center's W. E. B. Du Bois Institute at Harvard University, earned his Ph.D. from the Claremont Graduate School and has taught at Pitzer College, the University of Arizona, and Millersville University of Pennsylvania. He was an editor at the Black Abolitionist Papers project before becoming the senior associate editor at the Massachusetts Historical Society, where he founded and edited *The Massachusetts Historical Review* and organized many public history programs in the Boston area. An expert in Victorian manhood, the antislavery movement, and the 54th Massachusetts Regiment, he has published six books, including *Samuel Joseph May and the Dilemmas of the Liberal Persuasion*; *A Voice of Thunder: The Civil War Letters of George E. Stephens*; and most recently, *Lincoln on Race and Slavery*, with Henry Louis Gates, Jr.

SMILEYBOOKS

TITLES OF RELATED INTEREST

AMERICA I AM BLACK FACTS: The Timelines of African American History, 1601–2008, by Quintard Taylor

AMERICA I AM JOURNAL: The African American Imprint, edited by Clarence Reynolds and Smiley Books

AMERICA I AM LEGENDS: Rare Moments and Inspiring Words, edited by Smiley Books, Foreword by Tavis Smiley

BRAINWASHED: Challenging the Myth of Black Inferiority, by Tom Burrell

BROTHER WEST: Living and Loving Out Loud, by Cornel West with David Ritz

HOPE ON A TIGHTROPE: Words and Wisdom, by Cornel West

THE RICH AND THE REST OF US: A Poverty Manifesto, by Tavis Smiley and Cornel West

TAPPING THE POWER WITHIN: A Path to Self-Empowerment for Women, by Iyanla Vanzant

PLEASE VISIT THE DISTRIBUTOR OF **SMILEYBOOKS**:

HAY HOUSE USA: www.hayhouse.com®
HAY HOUSE AUSTRALIA: www.hayhouse.com.au
HAY HOUSE UK: www.hayhouse.co.uk
HAY HOUSE SOUTH AFRICA: www.hayhouse.co.za
HAY HOUSE INDIA: www.hayhouse.co.in